VISUAL QUICKSTART GUIDE

PRO TOOLS 7

FOR MACINTOSH AND WINDOWS

Steven Roback

Peachpit Press

Pro Tools 7 for Macintosh and Windows: Visual QuickStart Guide
Steven Roback

Peachpit Press
1249 Eighth Street
Berkeley, CA 94710
510/524-2178
800/283-9444
510/524-2221 (fax)

Find us on the World Wide Web at: www.peachpit.com
To report errors, please send a note to: errata@peachpit.com

Peachpit Press is a division of Pearson Education.

Editor: Matt Purcell
Production Editor: Andrei Pasternak
Development Editor: Anne Marie Walker
Tech Editor: Tom Dambly
Compositor: Christi Payne
Indexer: Karin Arrigoni
Cover design: Peachpit Press

ISBN 0-321-34898-2

9 8 7 6 5 4 3 2 1

Printed and bound in the United States of America

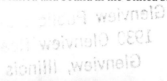

Dedication

To Mom and Dad

For your immense kindness, love, and belief in me, I am grateful beyond words, and truly lucky.

Acknowledgments

It's impossible for me to express the depth of gratitude I have for the people who helped me complete this book. Again, I extend my thanks to those who worked on the first and second books in this series, *Pro Tools 5: Visual QuickStart Guide* and *Pro Tools 6: Visual QuickStart Guide*—Missy Roback, Rebecca Gulick, and Claudia Curcio.

For this third and final book that I will be authoring in this series, I want to thank Nancy Davis, above all, for believing in me and Becky Morgan, for her unending patience and professionalism.

Anne Marie Walker deserves credit for a great editing job and her professional attitude as well. Tom Dambly must be credited with rescuing me at the eleventh hour with his outstanding authorship of the MIDI and Video chapters, and for applying his comprehensive knowledge of Pro Tools as tech editor of this publication. I must thank Matt Purcell, who did an outstanding job getting me to deliver when all the odds were against it...Matt, thanks for putting up with me.

Finally, I wish to thank Stephanie Beaurain, who helped me see what I could not and stayed long enough to help me make the right choices. "Ous est vous, mon petit wasso. Quand je voler avec tous, je vous vivre."

Good luck, Pro Tools users; I look forward to hearing your genius in the future.

Signing off, Steven Roback

TABLE OF CONTENTS

TABLE OF CONTENTS

TABLE OF CONTENTS

INTRODUCTION

Pro Tools is a computer-based audio recording system that runs on Macintosh and Windows operating systems. Pro Tools HD systems are considered the de facto standard for hard-disk audio recording in professional studios worldwide. Digidesign now offers a range of increasingly popular Pro Tools LE systems, which are designed for use in home studios and project studios.

Pro Tools' popularity is due, in part, to its successful migration of a traditional recording studio environment to the computer realm. Pro Tools is well regarded for its technical stability and the functional aesthetic of its user interface. It's also famous for its powerful recording, editing, mixing, automation, and real-time DSP effects.

What is Pro Tools LE?

Pro Tools LE is the software that comes with several of Digidesign's hard-disk audio recording systems, including Digi 002, Digi 002 Rack, Mbox, Mbox 2, and Mbox 2 Pro. These systems are designed primarily for use in home recording studios and project studios. Pro Tools LE hardware systems are compact and portable, yet contain many outstanding hardware features, including built-in audio mic preamps and S/PDIF and Optical digital I/O. Pro Tools LE software is nearly identical to its higher-end Pro Tools HD software counterpart. The main difference is how each version of Pro Tools handles DSP (digital signal processing): Pro Tools HD systems include PCI cards with built-in DSP processing chips; Pro Tools LE systems rely entirely on the host computer's CPU for all DSP-processing tasks. Because Pro Tools LE systems are host-based, the number of tracks and plug-ins you can use simultaneously depends on your computer's CPU power. Generally speaking, faster computers perform better.

Sessions created with Pro Tools LE are compatible with Pro Tools HD systems. This means that you can record tracks using a modest Pro Tools LE system, and then, when you're ready, take them to a studio and mix them on a Pro Tools HD system. Because Pro Tools LE software is so similar to the HD version, upgrading to the higher-end system has almost no learning curve.

Who should use this book?

This book is for musicians, engineers, producers, composers, soundtrack creators, film and video producers, music supervisors, broadcasters, Webcasters, students, audiophiles, MP3 addicts, iTunes lovers, vicarious listeners, and anyone else who wants a simple, clear, and complete explanation of how to use Pro Tools digital audio software. While this book focuses on Pro Tools 7 LE, the majority of software features discussed herein apply to all Pro Tools systems, including legacy systems running Pro Tools 5 or 6 LE, Pro Tools HD, and Pro Tools M-Powered equipment. (For more information on Pro Tools HD and M-Powered systems, see www.digidesign.com.)

What's in this book?

This book contains comprehensive, step-by-step instructions on most aspects of Pro Tools 7 LE, including hardware setup, recording and playback, editing, mixing, effects plug-ins, automation, file management, MIDI, and CPU performance. We've also included recording-related sidebars to inspire you and help you make better-sounding recordings.

Structured like a recording session, this book includes the following sections:

Part I: Getting Started with Pro Tools LE. This section covers setting up your Pro Tools LE system. You'll also learn the basics of Pro Tools software and the layout of the Mix and Edit windows.

Part II: Recording in Pro Tools. This section teaches you how to record and play back audio in Pro Tools. You'll learn how to create new sessions and how to work with tracks.

Part III: Audio File Management. This section introduces you to Pro Tools' file management features. You'll learn basic functions, such as locating, importing, exporting, and backing up your audio files. You'll also learn how to use DigiBase, Pro Tools' comprehensive file-management utility.

Part IV: Editing Audio. This section shows you how to edit audio in Pro Tools. You'll learn how to select and move audio regions, and how to save time using edit playlists. You'll also learn a few advanced features such as creating fades and crossfades, and repairing waveforms.

Part V: Mixing Audio. This section covers mixing audio in Pro Tools. You'll learn about stereo imaging and audio signal flow, as well as how to add effects using real-time DSP plug-ins. You'll also learn how to automate a mix and how to bounce a final mix down to disk.

Part VI: MIDI Sequencing. This section introduces Pro Tools' MIDI sequencing features. You'll learn how to record, edit, and play back MIDI in Pro Tools.

Part VII: Getting the Most from Pro Tools. This section provides an overview of using Pro Tools to work with sound in digital video. It also suggests ways to maximize Pro Tools LE's performance. You'll learn how to set memory buffers and memory-intensive functions to achieve the best results during recording, editing, and mixing, and you'll see how making tracks and other items inactive can free up valuable CPU power. You'll also learn how to use DSP plug-ins efficiently, and how to squeeze extra space out of your hard drive.

Appendixes and Glossary. Appendix A shows you how to connect Digi 002, Digi 002 Rack, Mbox, Mbox 2, and Mbox 2 Pro hardware to your studio. Appendix B presents complete descriptions of all Pro Tools 7.3 preferences. A glossary provides a list of Pro Tools–specific and general recording terms.

About the sidebars

We've included a few sidebars to help you understand some important recording concepts. In creating these sidebars, we tried to present simple topics that we wish we had at our fingertips when we first started recording. Some of these topics include mic placement, gain staging, and monitoring a mix.

How to use this book

If you're new to Pro Tools, use this book as a visually oriented instructional manual to step you through each phase of the recording process. If you're already familiar with Pro Tools, use this book as a visual reference guide to quickly refresh your memory. Either way, there's lots of Pro Tools information within.

What's new in Pro Tools 7 LE?

Pro Tools 7 LE is a more efficient version of Pro Tools and includes simplified menus, time and CPU conserving editing, automation and MIDI features, support for multiprocessor computers, and better RTAS plug-in performance.

Pro Tools 7 LE software is compatible with the following Pro Tools hardware systems: Digi 002, Digi 002 Rack, Mbox, Mbox 2, and Mbox 2 Pro. For more information on Pro Tools 7 compatibility issues, see Digidesign's Web site at *www.digidesign.com*.

Pro Tools 7 LE software includes the following new features:

System configuration and capabilities:

◆ Up to 160 channels of hardware I/O

◆ Increased sends and busses

◆ 999 Markers/Memory Locations per session

Sessions and compatibility:

◆ New session file format (".ptf")

◆ Support for long file names

◆ Removal of +6 dB option for new sessions

◆ All sessions are Mac/PC compatible

◆ Recommended BWAV dialog

◆ Cross-platform and language session compatibility

◆ Traditional Chinese localization

General Performance Enhancements:

◆ Faster session opening on Windows XP

◆ Improved editing speed

◆ Improved window redraw on Windows XP

Pro Tools menus and windows:

◆ Improved and expanded menus

◆ Tooltips

◆ Consolidated Regions list with improved search tools

◆ Shortcuts and new tools for Mix and Edit window views

◆ Resizable I/O Setup and Disk Allocation windows

DigiBase changes and additions:

◆ Support for standard MIDI files

◆ Bar|Beat display of duration (length) for tick-based audio and MIDI files

◆ New Tempo column

◆ Support for Avid video files (OMF and MXF only)

◆ Improved window interaction for Windows XP

Track features:

◆ Instrument tracks

◆ Software and hardware instruments

◆ Unrestricted MIDI and audio routing

◆ Multichannel surround formats

◆ Increased sends per track to 10

◆ Ability to move and copy sends

◆ Increased busses on Pro Tools LE and M-Powered to 32

◆ New Duplicate Tracks dialog and options

◆ Color coding improvements

Audio and MIDI composition:

◆ Region groups

◆ Region looping:

◆ Audio and MIDI regions

◆ Groups across multiple tracks

◆ Nested groups

◆ Fades and crossfades across grouped regions

◆ Support for audio and MIDI regions

◆ Support for region groups

◆ Drag and drop import of audio, REX, ACID, and MIDI

◆ Drag and drop audio files to plug-ins

DigiBase:

◆ DigiBase Support for drag and drop of REX, ACID, region groups, and standard MIDI

File management:

◆ Ability to preview files from Windows Explorer or the Finder

◆ Link Track and Edit Selection

Zooming enhancements:

◆ Improved Zoom Toggle for streamlined MIDI and audio editing

◆ Continuous zoom with Zoom tool

◆ Marquee Zoom both vertical and horizontal zoom on MIDI tracks

◆ Independent vertical track zoom

◆ Automatic "Show All Notes" scaling for vertical zoom of MIDI regions

Additions to Strip Silence:

◆ New Extract function (extract silence)

◆ New Separate function

Additions to Separate Regions:

◆ New Separate on Grid command

◆ New Separate at Transients command

◆ Improvements to Replace Regions

New MIDI features:

◆ Real-Time MIDI Properties

◆ Sample-based (tempo-independent) MIDI

◆ MIDI region previewing in the Regions list

◆ Selection of note ranges from onscreen mini-keyboard

◆ New preference for "Default Thru Follows Track Selection"

◆ New Select/Split Notes window

◆ New Grid/Groove Quantize window

◆ Groove Quantize support for Input Quantize

◆ New Remove Duplicate Notes command

◆ Legato and Overlap additions

◆ Transpose Window enhancements

◆ New Import MIDI to Timeline options

DSP plug-in enhancements:

◆ Multiple RTAS processors

RTAS performance enhancements:

◆ Increased RTAS buffer size

◆ Increased flexibility with RTAS and TDM plug-ins

◆ RTAS processing plug-ins on auxiliary inputs and master faders

◆ Voice usage for RTAS plug-ins on auxiliary inputs and master faders

◆ HTDM conversion to RTAS

◆ RTAS plug-ins support for changes to track width (mono/stereo)

◆ Side-chain processing support for RTAS plug-ins

◆ Addition of easy page tables

◆ Significantly decreased load times

◆ Improved TDM plug-in load priorities to minimize DSP shuffling

◆ RMS and Peak calibration modes for SignalGenerator, Gain, and Normalize plug-ins

◆ Time Adjuster RTAS version

◆ Trim plug-in +12 dB Update

◆ EQ III Band-Pass mode

◆ Synchronic updates

◆ Additional Bomb Factory support

◆ Special Edit commands for automation

◆ New shortcuts to enable plug-in parameters

Avid interoperability enhancements:

◆ Support for AAF Embedded media

◆ MediaStation compatibility on
Macintosh OS X 10.4

For more information on the new features in
Pro Tools 7 LE, see Digidesign's Web site at
www.digidesign.com.

Additional information

For additional information on Pro Tools LE
or Pro Tools HD, see Digidesign's Web site at
www.digidesign.com. The site offers a wealth
of information on all Pro Tools-related topics, including downloadable software updates
and product manuals, product support, and
upgrade plans. Also, refer to the *Pro Tools
Reference Guide* that comes with the product.

A (Very) Brief History of Multi-Track Recording

Thomas Edison invented the world's first recording and playback machine in 1877. But it wasn't until the 1930s, when renowned guitarist and electronics innovator Les Paul began overlaying multiple guitar tracks on acetate discs that multi-track recording was born.

Les Paul: Recording Pioneer

Paul's contributions to the development of multi-track recording cannot be overstated. In 1949, he adapted a rare Magnetophone tape machine to create sound-on-sound recording—better known as overdubbing. Along the way, Paul literally invented most of the audio gear used in recording studios today, including equalizers, delays, reverbs, and many other audio effects processing devices.

Paul's experimentation with close-up miking techniques also left a lasting impact on vocal production. In 1951 he produced two widely acclaimed, million-selling songs, *How High the Moon* and *Mockin' Bird Hill*, which featured beautifully layered overdubs of his wife, vocalist Mary Ford.

The Beatles: A Multi-Track Revolution

By the 1960s, four-track tape machines were available, but it wasn't until producer George Martin and The Beatles began churning out four- and eight-track masterworks like *Rubber Soul*, *Revolver*, *Sgt. Pepper's Lonely Hearts Club Band*, and *Abbey Road* that the true creative potential of multi-track recording became widely apparent.

Between 1966 and 1970, The Beatles applied all of their energy to studio recording and in the process wrote the book on pop music recording. Things that today sound like ordinary elements of pop music—feedback, multiple vocal and guitar overdubs, backwards instruments, tape delays (flange), exotic instruments (sitar)—were used for the first time by Martin and The Beatles as they explored the limits of multi-track recording.

Eno and the Wizard

By the 1970s and '80s, recording on 16-and 24-track tape machines had become the professional standard. Musicians and producers such as Todd Rundgren and Brian Eno quickly took advantage of the expanded track count. Rundgren's 1973 album *Wizard/A True Star* showed the potential of multi-track recording in the hands of an artist with great musical inventiveness. The album features a stirring mix of electric guitars, pianos, organs, synthesizers, vocals, and percussion, strung together with surprising crossfades and creatively applied effects.

continues on next page

A (Very) Brief History of Multi-Track Recording *(continued)*

Inspired by ambient pioneer John Cage, Brian Eno took multi-track into the realm of chaos theory. Eno used random analog tape loops to create unpredictable ambient soundscapes. His use of randomness to generate sonic atmospherics—best exemplified in his 1975 album *Another Green World* and his *Ambient* series—shows how random sound combinations can create a striking sense of place. Eno's evocative multi-track production has inspired a generation of musicians and producers across many genres of music, from rock and psychedelia to hip-hop and trance.

Today, recording on 24-track analog tape is still considered an excellent, if expensive, way to record.

Digital Audio: Bringing the Studio Home

Recording audio to a computer hard disk is now commonplace in professional studios. Perhaps the most important innovation of hard-disk recording is the ability to edit audio using a graphic interface. Computer editing has given musicians, engineers, and producers new freedom to move, shape, and rearrange sounds in virtually unlimited combinations.

Advances in digital recording have also led to an explosion in the number of home-based recording studios (often called *project studios*). Now anyone with a home computer can take advantage of the once prohibitively expensive features of recording studios, including effects processing and mix automation.

Part I: Getting Started with Pro Tools LE

SETTING UP YOUR PRO TOOLS LE SYSTEM

1

This chapter introduces you to Digidesign's Pro Tools 7 LE hardware systems, including Digi 002, Digi 002 Rack, Mbox 2 Pro, Mbox 2, and Mbox. It describes each system's hardware specs, as well as basic hard drive and memory requirements.

This chapter also touches on the capabilities of Pro Tools 7 LE software, including the number of recording and playback channels the software supports for each system.

Pro Tools 7 M-Powered software is also available for Digidesign-qualified M-Audio devices. Pro Tools 7 M-Powered software contains nearly all the same basic features as Pro Tools 7 LE and HD software. Thus, while M-Audio hardware is beyond the scope of this book, users of Pro Tools 7 M-Powered software will find the following chapters indispensable.

For more information on Pro Tools M-Audio devices, see the Digidesign Web site at www.digidesign.com.

Understanding Pro Tools LE Hardware Systems

Pro Tools LE is the software component of Digidesign's rapidly expanding line of entry- to mid-level hard-disk recording systems. Pro Tools LE systems are economical and easy to set up, making them ideal for home and project studios. Unlike Digidesign's pro-level HD systems (which include PCI or PCIe cards equipped with their own processing chips), Pro Tools LE systems use the host computer's CPU for all processing tasks. As a result, the number of tracks available during a Pro Tools LE session depends on the host computer's processing speed.

Each Pro Tools LE hardware system offers a unique audio interface with different I/O (input and output) options. All Pro Tools LE hardware systems require Pro Tools LE software. Pro Tools LE hardware systems supported by Pro Tools LE 7 software include the following:

Digi 002: Digi 002 is a FireWire-based Pro Tools LE system with its own mixing-board-like control surface. The system features four built-in mic preamps, eight channels of analog I/O, eight channels of ADAT optical I/O, and two channels of S/PDIF digital I/O. Digi 002 supports sample rates up to 96 kHz.

Digi 002 Rack: Digi 002 Rack is a rack-mountable version of Digi 002 without the control surface. The unit's compact, FireWire-based design makes it suitable for live situations or small project studios. Like the original, the Digi 002 Rack has four built-in mic preamps, eight channels of analog I/O, eight channels of ADAT optical I/O, and two channels of S/PDIF digital I/O, and supports sample rates up to 96 kHz.

Mbox 2 Pro: Mbox 2 Pro is a highly portable, FireWire-based digital audio and MIDI interface that supports sample rates up to 96kHz. It includes two built-in mic preamps (XLR-1/4-inch TRS combo jacks) and two DI inputs (1/4-inch TRS), six analog outputs, two channels of S/PDIF digital I/O, one MIDI In and one MIDI Out port., and Word Clock I/O.

Mbox 2: Mbox 2 is a USB-based two-channel digital audio and MIDI interface that supports sample rates up to 48kHz. It includes two built-in mic preamps, two channels of analog I/O, two channels of S/PDIF digital I/O, and one MIDI In and one MIDI Out port. Each analog input includes separate jacks for mic (3-pin XLR), line (1/4-inch TRS), and DI (1/4-inch TS) cables.

Mbox: Mbox is a two-channel digital audio interface for USB computers. It includes two built-in mic preamps, two channels of analog I/O, and two channels of S/PDIF digital I/O. Mbox also includes two analog line inserts for outboard effects processing.

Pro Tools LE legacy systems: Pro Tools 7 does not support Digi 001 and Audiomedia III. For detailed information on these Pro Tools LE legacy systems, see the *Pro Tools 6 for Macintosh and Windows Visual QuickStart Guide* or the Digidesign Web site at www.digidesign.com.

Table 1.1 shows the capabilities of each Pro Tools LE system.

PRO TOOLS LE HARDWARE SYSTEMS

Table 1.1

Pro Tools LE 7 Systems Features

SYSTEM	ANALOG I/O	DIGITAL I/O	MICPREAMPS	LINE INPUTS	CONNECTION	RESOLUTION
Mbox 2	2/2	2(S/PDIF)	2	2	USB	24-bit/48kHz
Mbox 2 Pro	4/6	2(S/PDIF)	2	2	FireWire	24-bit/96kHz
Digi 002 and Digi 002 rack	8/8	8(ADAT)/2(S/PDIF)	4	4	FireWire	24-bit/96kHz

System Requirements

Recording digital audio requires lots of processing power. Because Pro Tools LE systems rely on the host computer's CPU for all processing tasks, you'll want the fastest computer possible. The faster your computer, the more tracks of audio you can record and the more real-time effects you can add to a mix.

The following system requirements are provided *only* as example of the equipment neeeded to run an efficient Pro Tools LE hardware system. For current detailed information on system requirements and computer compatibility, see *www.digidesign.com*.

Running Pro Tools LE 7 Systems on Mac OS X 10.4.2

On Macintosh computers, all Pro Tools LE 7 systems require Mac OS X 10.4.2 Tiger. Thus, to run a Pro Tools 7 system, you'll need a qualified Macintosh computer running Mac OS 10.4.2, as described here.

To run Digi 002 or Digi 002 Rack with Pro Tools LE 7 on Mac OS X 10.4.2:

You need one of the following:

- Apple Power Mac G5 (dual-processor models: 1.8 GHz, 2.0 GHz, 2.3 GHz, 2.5 GHz, 2.7 GHz; single-processor models: 1.6 GHz, 1.8 GHz)

- Apple Power Mac G4 (dual-processor models: 1.0 GHz, 1.25 GHz, 1.42 GHz; single-processor models: 1.0 GHz, 1.25 GHz)

- Apple PowerBook G4 (1.0 GHz, 1.25 GHz, 1.33 GHz, 1.5 GHz, 1.67 GHz)

- iMac G5 LCD flat screen (1.6 GHz 17-inch LCD, 1.8 GHz 17- and 20-inch LCD, 2.0 GHz 17- and 20-inch LCD)

- iMac G4 LCD flat screen (1.0 GHz 15- and 17-inch LCD, 1.25 GHz 17- and 20-inch LCD)

- iBook G4 (1.0 GHz 12- and 14-inch LCD, 1.2 GHz 12- and 14-inch LCD, 1.33 GHz 12- and 14-inch LCD, 1.42 GHz 14-inch LCD)

- Mac mini (1.25 GHz, 1.42 GHz)

Plus the following:

- Pro Tools LE 7
- Mac OS X 10.4.2
- 512 MB RAM minimum (more recommended)
- Color monitor (1024x768 minimum)
- Apple QuickTime 7
- Qualified IDE/ATA, SATA, SCSI with HBA (host bus adapter) card, or FireWire disk drive(s) (recommended)

To run Mbox, Mbox 2 or Mbox 2 Pro with Pro Tools LE 7 on Mac OS X 10.4.2:

You need one of the following:

- Apple Power Mac G5 (dual-processor models: 1.8 GHz, 2 GHz, 2.3 GHz, 2.5 GHz, 2.7 GHz; dual-core processor models: 2 GHz, 2.3GHz; single-processor models: 1.6 GHz, 1.8 GHz)

- Apple Power Mac G4 (dual-processor models: 1.0 GHz, 1.25 GHz, 1.42 GHz; single-processor models: 1.0 GHz, 1.25 GHz)

- Apple PowerBook G4 (1.0 GHz, 1.25 GHz, 1.33 GHz, 1.5 GHz, 1.67 GHz)

- iMac G5 LCD flat screen (1.6 GHz 17-inch LCD, 1.8 GHz 17- and 20-inch LCD, 2.0 GHz 17- and 20-inch LCD, 1.9 GHz 17-inch LCD, 2.1 GHz 20-inch LCD)

- iMac G4 LCD flat screen (1.0 GHz 15- and 17-inch LCD, 1.25 GHz 17- and 20-inch LCD)

- iBook G4 (1.0 GHz 12- and 14-inch LCD, 1.2 GHz 12- and 14-inch LCD, 1.33 GHz 12- and 14-inch LCD, 1.42 GHz 14-inch LCD)

- Mac mini (1.25 GHz, 1.42 GHz)

Plus the following:

- Pro Tools LE 7

- Mac OS X 10.4.2

- 512 MB RAM minimum (more recommended)

- Color monitor (1024x768 minimum); 17-inch or larger recommended

- Apple QuickTime 7.0

- Qualified ATA/IDE, SATA, SCSI with HBA (host bus adapter) card, or FireWire disk drive(s) (recommended)

- One available built-in USB port (powered USB port required; passive USB hub will not function properly)

For additional information on compatible Macintosh computers, see Digidesign's Web site at www.digidesign.com.

Running Pro Tools LE 7 Systems on Windows XP

Pro Tools LE 7 systems run on Windows XP Professional and Home Edition (with Service Pack 2 required). Pro Tools LE 7 does not support Windows 98, Me, 2000, NT, 95, or 3.1.

To run Digi 002 or Digi 002 Rack with Pro Tools LE 7 on Windows XP:

You need one of the following:

- Intel Pentium 4 or Xeon (2.4 GHz or faster)

- AMD Athlon 64 or 64 FX

- AMD Athlon XP (2000+)

Plus the following:

- Windows XP Professional or Home Edition (Service Pack 2 required)

- Pro Tools LE 7 for Windows XP

- 512 MB RAM (more recommended)

- Color monitor (1024x768 minimum); 17-inch or larger recommended

- Apple QuickTime 6.5 (or later)

- 1394 (FireWire) controller/interface

- Qualified ATA/IDE, SATA, SCSI with HBA (host bus adapter) card, or FireWire disk drive

SYSTEM REQUIREMENTS

Memory and Disk Matters

Recording multiple tracks of 24-bit digital audio can devour hard drive space. For instance, a mono audio track recorded at 24-bit resolution and a 44.1 kHz sample rate consumes 7.5 MB of hard drive space per minute; the same track recorded at 16-bit, 44.1 kHz consumes 5 MB per minute. **Table 1.2** shows how quickly your disk can fill up with audio files.

If you're strapped for disk space, consider recording at 16-bit resolution. Otherwise, acquire additional hard drives for your system.

Up to Speed

Make sure you use the fastest drive possible. A slow hard drive will limit the number of tracks you can record and the quality of audio playback. When selecting a hard drive, be sure it meets the following requirements for Pro Tools LE systems:

◆ ATA/IDE, SATA, SCSI, or FireWire drive

◆ 7,200-rpm drive spin speed

◆ 10-ms seek time (minimum average)

For optimal track count, consider using two drives when recording at high sample rates (88.2 kHz or 96 kHz).

Managing Hard Drive Space

It's important to efficiently manage your hard drive space. You don't want to run out of space in the middle of a session, or worse, in the midst of recording a live track.

Pro Tools' Disk Space window can help you manage your hard drive space. When you complete a session, use the Compact function to keep your audio files lean. For more on compacting files, see Chapter 8, "File Management Basics."

The RAM Rule

Having adequate RAM helps ensure a smooth running system. Make sure you have the minimum amounts recommended—and consider adding more. Remember, you can never have too much RAM.

Table 1.2

Hard Drive Space Requirements

# OF TRACKS, LENGTH	16-BIT/44.1 KHz	16-BIT/48 KHz	24-BIT/44.1 KHz	24-BIT/48 KHz	24-BIT/96 KHz
1 track (mono), 1 minute	5 MB	5.5 MB	7.5 MB	8.2 MB	17.2 MB
2 tracks (stereo), 5 minutes	50 MB	55 MB	75 MB	83 MB	172 MB
24 tracks, 1 minute	120 MB	132 MB	180 MB	198 MB	412.8 MB
24 tracks, 5 minutes	600 MB	662 MB	900 MB	991 MB	2064 MB
24 tracks, 60 minutes	7 GB	7.8 GB	10.5 GB	11.6 GB	24.2 GB
32 tracks, 5 minutes	800 MB	883 MB	1.2 GB	1.3 GB	2.8 GB
32 tracks, 60 minutes	9.4 GB	10.8 GB	14 GB	15.4 GB	31 GB

To run Mbox, Mbox 2, or Mbox 2 Pro with Pro Tools LE 7 on Windows XP:

You need one of the following:

◆ Intel Pentium 4 or Xeon (2.4 GHz or faster)

◆ AMD Athlon 64 or 64 FX

◆ AMD Athlon XP (2000+)

Plus the following:

◆ Windows XP Professional or Home Edition (Service Pack 2 required)

◆ Pro Tools LE 7 for Windows XP

◆ 512 MB RAM (more recommended)

◆ Color monitor (1024x768 minimum); 17-inch or larger recommended

◆ Apple QuickTime 6.5 (or later)

◆ 1394 (FireWire) controller/interface

◆ Qualified ATA/IDE, SATA, SCSI with HBA (host bus adapter) card, or FireWire disk drive

◆ One available built-in USB port (powered USB port required; passive USB hub will not function properly)

For additional information on requirements for running Pro Tools LE 7 on Windows XP, see Digidesign's Web site at www.digidesign.com.

Connecting System Hardware

Before you can begin recording, you must properly connect your Pro Tools LE system to your computer.

To connect Digi 002, Digi 002 Rack, or Mbox 2 Pro:

1. Connect the FireWire cable that came with your system to either of the two FireWire ports on the back panel of the unit.

2. Do one of the following, depending on your system configuration:

▲ Connect the other end of the FireWire cable to an available FireWire port on your computer.

▲ Connect the other end of the FireWire cable to an available FireWire port on a FireWire hard drive connected to your computer.

To connect Mbox or Mbox 2:

◆ Connect a USB cable to the USB port on the Mbox or Mbox 2 to any available built-in USB port on your Macintosh or Windows XP computer. Mbox and Mbox 2 require a powered USB port to operate. Mbox and Mbox 2 will not function properly if connected to a passive USB hub. For more information on installing system hardware, see the *Getting Started* guide that came with your system.

For instructions on connecting your studio to your Pro Tools LE system, see Appendix A, "Connecting Your Studio."

Installing Pro Tools LE 7 Software

Now that you've connected your Pro Tools LE hardware, you're ready to install your Pro Tools LE software.

If you're a Macintosh user, insert the Pro Tools LE 7 installation CD and double-click the Install Pro Tools LE 7 icon. Follow the onscreen instructions.

If you're a Windows user, insert the Pro Tools LE 7 installation CD, open the Installer folder, and double-click the Setup program.

For detailed instructions on installing and configuring Pro Tools LE 7 on a Macintosh or Windows computer, see the *Getting Started* guide that came with your system.

SOFTWARE BASICS

Now that you've connected your Pro Tools 7 LE hardware, you're no doubt itching to lay down some tracks. But first, you'll need to familiarize yourself with some Pro Tools 7 software basics and configure your system.

This chapter introduces you to the key elements of a Pro Tools 7 *session*, including session files audio files, tracks, waveforms, regions, playlists, channels, and I/O setup

You'll also learn how to configure your Pro Tools 7 LE hardware and allocate your computer's CPU resources for optimal performance.

Understanding Sessions

A Pro Tools session is the virtual workspace in which you record audio. Think of it as a recording studio inside your computer: It contains all the elements you need to record, edit, process, mix, master, manage, and store audio recordings.

Before you begin recording in Pro Tools 7, it's a good idea to acquaint yourself with the following basic elements of a Pro Tools session.

What is a Session file?

When you start a new Pro Tools project, you create a new *session file*. A session file is the "control center" of a Pro Tools session: it maps and directs all the elements in a session, including audio files, MIDI data, edits and mix information (**Figure 2.1**).

Keep in mind that a session file is not an audio file (a session file contains no audio data). Rather, a session file is linked to audio files recorded into a session; and it contains data that tells Pro Tools how to manipulate these linked audio files.

You can edit a session and save it as a new session file. This lets you save multiple versions of a project, and easily back up your editing and mixing work. A session file is stored in a Session Folder.

Figure 2.1 A Pro Tools 7 LE session file (.ptf) icon.

Figure 2.2 Audio file icons.

Figure 2.3 An Audio Files folder inside a Session folder.

About Session file format (.ptf) in Pro Tools 7

Session files in Pro Tools 7 have a new file format: *ptf (Pro Tools File)*. Each session file name must end with the three-letter (.ptf) extension to be recognized properly. .ptf session files created in Pro Tools 7 are not compatible with earlier versions of Pro Tools software.

For more information on Pro Tools sessions, see *Chapter 4: Starting a New Session*.

What is an audio file?

When you record audio into a Pro Tools session, it's saved on your hard disk as an *audio file* (**Figure 2.2**). Audio files are stored in the Audio Files folder within the Session folder (**Figure 2.3**).

Audio files are listed in the Regions list and are displayed as waveforms on separate tracks within the Pro Tools Edit window (**Figure 2.4**).

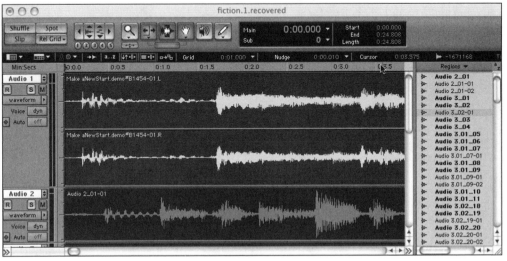

Figure 2.4 Audio files are represented by waveforms. The Regions list (right side of Edit window) shows session audio files.

What is a MIDI file?

MIDI (Musical Instrument Digital Interface) is a data protocol that lets digital audio devices (such as keyboards, synthesizers, sound modules, samplers, sequencers, and computers) communicate with each other. MIDI is most often used to record and play parts performed on a keyboard to trigger sounds on a synthesizer.

When you record MIDI tracks in Pro Tools, your performance is stored in the Pro Tools session file. You can later play back the MIDI tracks and duplicate your performance exactly. You can also export MIDI tracks as Standard MIDI Format (SMF) files.

For more information on MIDI in Pro Tools 7, see *Part VI: MIDI Sequencing.*

What are tracks?

A Pro Tools *track* is where audio, MIDI, and automation data is recorded, displayed and edited. Tracks also let you route audio in and out (input and output) of your system from external audio sources; and tracks let you route audio to and from other tracks (internal busses).

Pro Tools 7 gives you five types of tracks: audio tracks, MIDI tracks, Instrument tracks, Auxiliary Inputs, and Master Faders.

UNDERSTANDING SESSIONS

When you record audio into a session, it's displayed as a waveform on an *audio track* in the Edit window (**Figure 2.5**). Audio tracks in Pro Tools LE can be mono or stereo. (Pro Tools HD systems also support multi-channel, surround-sound formats.)

Similarly, when you record MIDI into Pro Tools, the MIDI data is displayed on a *MIDI track* in the Edit window (**Figure 2.6**).

Instrument tracks integrate both MIDI and audio track capabilities into a single track (**Figure 2.7**). You can use Instrument tracks to record MIDI parts while monitoring a MIDI instrument's audio output, which simplifies the MIDI recording process.

Figure 2.5 An audio track in the Edit window.

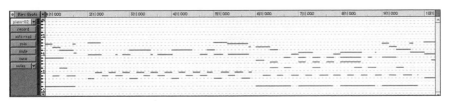

Figure 2.6 A MIDI track in the Edit window.

Figure 2.7 An Instrument track in the Mix window.

UNDERSTANDING SESSIONS

Auxiliary Input tracks are used for routing audio signals and for adding effects to other audio tracks (**Figure 2.8**). Auxiliary Inputs accept audio routed from internal busses and external audio sources.

Master Fader tracks route audio signals from (output) a session (**Figure 2.9**). Master faders let you adjust volume and pan, and add effects to audio output.

For more information on tracks, see *Chapter 5: Working with Tracks.*

Figure 2.8 An Auxiliary Input track in the Mix window.

Figure 2.9 A Master Fader track in the Mix window.

What are waveforms and regions?

Audio files are displayed as *waveforms* in the Pro Tools Edit window (**Figure 2.10**). A waveform is a graph of an audio signal's sound pressure level (in decibels) versus time.

A waveform's appearance will vary depending on the audio source. Drums, for instance, will have sharp peaks and valleys that represent the sudden attack and decay of a drum hit (**Figure 2.11**). Instruments with softer attacks and longer decays, such as keyboards or vocals, will generally have smoother waveform shapes (**Figure 2.12**).

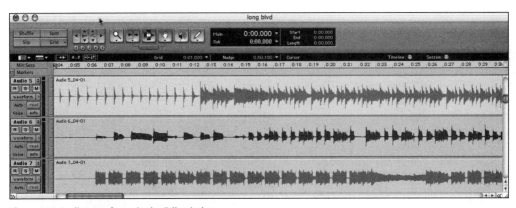

Figure 2.10 Audio waveforms in the Edit window.

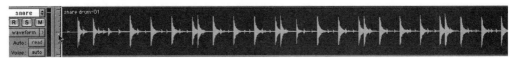

Figure 2.11 A waveform of a drum part. The sharp peaks and valleys indicate the fast attack and decay of a drum hit.

Figure 2.12 A waveform of a keyboard part. Its smooth shape indicates the slow attack and decay of a keyboard.

A region is a visual representation of audio file data (or MIDI data) stored on hard disc. Regions are displayed in tracks in the Edit window. They are also listed in the Edit window's Regions list.

A region can be any length—from an entire audio file to a single verse, hook, bar, or note. You can create new regions by selecting a segment of a larger region in a track (**Figure 2.13**). The selected region points to that segment of the original audio or MIDI data on your hard disk. 7Once you create a region you can easily copy, loop, and arrange them in playlists to create new song structures (**Figure 2.14**).

Audio regions are most frequently displayed in waveform view. Audio regions let you work freely with your recordings (play, edit, mix, process, automate) without fear of losing or damaging irreplaceable recordings.

For more information on waveforms and regions, see *Chapter 5: Working with Tracks and Part IV: Editing Audio.*

Whole file audio region

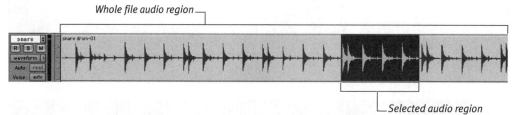

Selected audio region

Figure 2.13 A selected audio region. You can create smaller regions from larger ones.

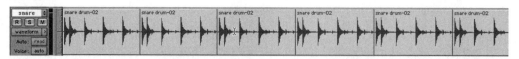

Figure 2.14 Use the Duplicate or Repeat command to copy an audio region multiple times and create a drum loop.

UNDERSTANDING SESSIONS

Audio 4_02.1.grp-01.rgrp

Figure 2.15 A Region Group file (.rgrp) icon.

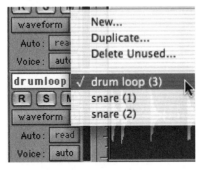

Figure 2.16 The Playlist Selector pop-up menu.

About Region Group file format (.rgrp) in Pro Tools 7

Pro Tools 7 also introduces a new Region Group file format: (.rgrp) (**Figure 2.15**). Region Group files store references to selected portions of audio or MIDI files. This lets you quickly import and export audio and MIDI tracks constructed from multiple source audio or MIDI files.

For more information on Region Group files, see the *Pro Tools Reference Guide*.

What is a playlist?

A *playlist* is a group of regions arranged on a single audio or MIDI track. You can create several different playlists on a given track and use the Playlist Selector pop-up menu to choose which one to play (**Figure 2.16**). You can then easily switch between them on the fly during a mix.

A playlist can include a single region or multiple regions. It can include the same sound, such as regions from a vocal or guitar part, or different sounds, such as individual sound effects.

✔ Tip

- By using multiple playlists and switching between them, you can try alternate arrangements of material on a single track, instead of using up an additional track.

For more information on playlists, see *Chapter 7: Recording and Playing Back Audio* and *Part IV: Editing Audio*.

UNDERSTANDING SESSIONS

What is a channel?

The term *channel* has two separate but related meanings in Pro Tools. The first refers to the actual physical inputs and outputs of the Pro Tools system. For example, the Digi 002 and Digi 002 Rack both have 18 channels each of input and output (I/O). (See *Chapter 1: Setting Up Your Pro Tools LE System.*)

A channel also refers to a mixer strip in the Pro Tools Mix window, which is called a *channel strip* (**Figure 2.17**). Channel strips let you control the mix functions of a track, such as level, mute, pan, and sends. Channel strips will vary slightly depending on whether the track is an audio track, MIDI track, auxiliary input, or master fader.

For more information on channels, see *Chapter 3: The Mix and Edit Windows.*

Figure 2.17 An audio channel strip in the Mix window.

What is an I/O Setup?

The way that audio is routed in, out, and through a recording system is called a *signal path*. In Pro Tools you can create many different configurations of signal paths. Each configuration is called an I/O Setup.

The I/O Setup dialog box (**Figure 2.18**) lets you create I/O Setups. You can assign track inputs and outputs, inserts, and internal busses for routing to internal plug-ins or external hardware effects.

You can also export and import I/O Setup configurations as I/O Settings files. This lets you save your favorite I/O Setups and reuse them in future sessions.

✔ Tip

■ Pro Tools LE includes default I/O Setups, so you can quickly begin recording. For more information on I/O Setup, see *Chapter 4: Starting a New Session*.

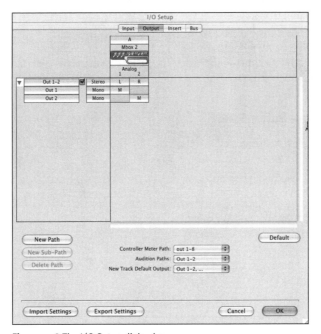

Figure 2.18 The I/O Setup dialog box.

Configuring Your Pro Tools 7 LE System

When you first launch Pro Tools LE, you'll need to allocate your host computer's CPU resources, and select Pro Tools LE hardware settings from within the program.

For information on launching Pro Tools LE, see the *Getting Started Guide* that comes with your Pro Tools LE system.

Allocating CPU resources

Pro Tools LE systems use the host computer's CPU to process all audio recording, playback, mixing, and effects processing. The program provides the following adjustable parameters, which let you allocate your CPU's resources for optimal performance of these tasks.

Hardware Buffer Size

The Hardware Buffer Size (H/W Buffer Size) determines the amount of hardware cache used for host processing tasks, including audio and MIDI track playback, mix automation, and RTAS plug-in processing. Higher buffer sizes allow for more audio processing and RTAS effects. Lower buffers decrease monitoring latency.

To set the Hardware Buffer Size:

1. Choose Setup > Playback Engine (**Figure 2.19**).

   The Playback Engine dialog box appears (**Figure 2.20**).

2. From the H/W Buffer Size pop-up menu, select the audio buffer size (in samples) (**Figure 2.21**).

3. Click OK.

Figure 2.19
Choose Playback Engine from the Setup menu.

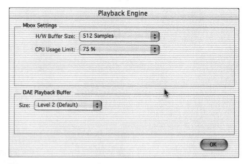

Figure 2.20 The Playback Engine dialog box.

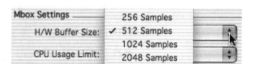

Figure 2.21 Select an audio buffer size for host processing tasks from the H/W Buffer Size pop-up menu.

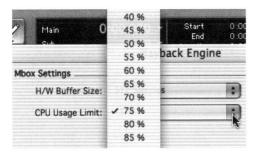

Figure 2.22 Select a percentage of CPU resources to allocate to host-processing tasks.

CPU Usage Limit

The CPU Usage Limit controls the percentage of CPU resources allocated to Pro Tools host processing tasks. Higher CPU Usage Limit settings reserve more processing power for Pro Tools and are useful for playing back large sessions or adding more RTAS effects.

To set the CPU Usage Limit:

1. Choose Setup > Playback Engine.

   The Playback Engine dialog box appears.

2. From the CPU Usage Limit pop-up menu, select the percentage of CPU processing you want to allocate to Pro Tools (**Figure 2.22**).

3. Click OK.

DAE Playback Buffer Size

Digidesign Audio Engine (DAE) is Digidesign's real-time operating system for digital recording systems. Running in the background and directing traffic between Pro Tools and the computer's CPU, DAE provides much of the digital recording, effects processing, mix automation, and MIDI functionality of Pro Tools.

The DAE Playback Buffer Size determines the amount of memory allocated within DAE to manage disk buffers. Smaller buffer sizes can improve playback and recording initiation speed, but performance can become unreliable on slower hard drives. Large buffer sizes will let you make more edits but may cause time lags to occur before playback or recording begins.

To set the DAE Playback Buffer Size

1. Choose Setup > Playback Engine.
   The Playback Engine Dialog Box appears.

2. From the DAE Playback Buffer pop-up menu, select a playback buffer size (**Figure 2.23**).

3. Click OK.

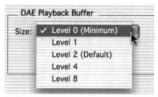

Figure 2.23 Select a playback buffer size from the DAE Buffer Size pop-up menu.

Configuring system hardware

The Hardware Setup dialog box in the Setup menu lets you select your system's default sample rate, clock source, and input format. (Input format options vary somewhat, depending on which Pro Tools LE hardware system you are using.)

Figure 2.24 Choose Hardware from the Setup menu.

Default Sample Rate

The Hardware Setup dialog box displays the current session's sample rate. You cannot change the sample rate of an open session. The default sample rate setting is available in the Hardware Setup dialog box only when no session is open (after the Pro Tools application has been launched). The Default Sample Rate setting determines the selected sample rate when you open the New Session dialog box.

You can change this sample rate when you create a new session.

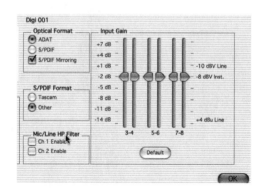

Figure 2.25 The Hardware Setup Dialog box.

To change the default Sample Rate:

1. Close the current session. If necessary, launch Pro Tools LE from the application icon. Make sure no session is open.

2. Choose Setup > Hardware (**Figure 2.24**).
   The Hardware Setup Dialog box appears (**Figure 2.25**).

3. From the Sample Rate pop-up menu, select a sample rate (**Figure 2.26**).

4. Click OK.

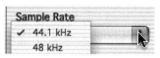

Figure 2.26 Choose the desired sample rate in the Mbox Hardware Setup dialog box.

Figure 2.27 Select the desired clock source in the Clock Source pop-up menu. Use Internal when recording analog signal into Pro Tools.

Figure 2.28 The Digi 002 and Digi 002 Rack Hardware Setup dialog box lets you set ADAT optical, Optical SPDIF, and SPDIF/RCA digital input formats.

Clock Source

The Hardware Setup dialog box lets you select a Clock Source for your system. When recording analog signal directly into Pro Tools, you'll generally want to use Internal as the clock source.

When recording digital signal into Pro Tools from an external digital device, you'll generally want use the external digital device as the clock source.

All Pro Tools LE hardware systems accept SPDIF/RCA external digital devices as the clock source. Additionally, Digi 002 and Digi 002 Rack accept ADAT Optical (or "Lightpipe") and Optical S/PDIF external digital devices as the clock source.

To select the Clock Source:

1. Choose Setup > Hardware.

   The Hardware Setup dialog box appears.

2. From the Clock Source pop-up menu, select the desired clock source (**Figure 2.27**).

3. Click OK.

Input Formats

The Hardware Setup dialog box lets you select the audio input format for your system. The input format options available in the Hardware Setup dialog box differ, depending on the Pro Tools LE system.

When recording from a digital source into Pro Tools, it is necessary to select the appropriate digital input format. The Digi 002 and Digi 002 Rack Hardware Setup dialog box lets you select ADAT optical, Optical SPDIF, and SPDIF/RCA (**Figure 2.28**). Selecting an input format is only necessary when connecting a digital input to these systems.

CONFIGURING YOUR PRO TOOLS 7 LE SYSTEM

25

If you're an Mbox user, you'll need to choose between analog or digital input formats. The Mbox Hardware Setup dialog box lets you set Input Channels 1–2 to Analog or SPDIF/RCA digital format.

To set the Input Format:

1. Choose Setup > Hardware.

   The Hardware Setup dialog box appears.

2. When recording from a digital source, select the desired digital input format (Digi 002, Digi 002 Rack).

   or

   In the Channel 1–2 Input box, select either analog or SPDIF/RCA digital format (Mbox) (**Figure 2.29**).

3. Click OK.

For more information on Input Formats, see the *Getting Started Guide* that came with your Pro Tools LE system.

Figure 2.29 When using Mbox or Mbox 2, set Channel 1–2 inputs to either Analog or SPDIF/RCA digital input formats.

Compatible Audio File Formats

Pro Tools LE lets you record audio in these file formats:

◆ Macintosh: SDII (48kHz maximum sample rate), WAV, and AIFF

◆ Windows: WAV and AIFF (SDII not supported on Windows XP)

Pro Tools LE also lets you import and export audio in these formats:

◆ Macintosh: SDII, SDI, WAV, MP3, and Sound Resource (AIFL)

◆ Windows: SDII, SDI, WAV, AIFF, MP3, and WMA (Windows Media)

For more information on audio files, see Chapter 4: Starting a New Session and Part III: Audio File Management.

Pro Tools File Types

Pro Tools generates several file types, which you can quickly import and export between sessions. The file types include:

◆ **Session file (.ptf):** This file stores all session information including audio files, MIDI data, edits, and mix information.

◆ **Audio file:** Audio recorded into a session is stored as an audio file. You can import and export audio in a number of file formats (see the *Compatible Audio File Formats* sidebar).

◆ **MIDI file:** This file stores MIDI data recorded on MIDI tracks in a Pro Tools session.

◆ **Region Group file (.rgrp):** You can save Region Group information in these files and import them into other sessions.

◆ **I/O Settings file:** You can import and export I/O configurations as I/O Settings files for use in future sessions.

◆ **Fade file:** Fades and crossfades for a session are saved as Fade files. They are stored in the Fade Files folder inside the Session folder.

◆ **Plug-in Settings files:** You can save the current settings of any RTAS plug-in and apply them to future uses of that plug-in.

CONFIGURING YOUR PRO TOOLS 7 LE SYSTEM

THE MIX AND EDIT WINDOWS

3

Most of the action in Pro Tools takes place in two main windows: the Mix window and the Edit window. Learning the layout and features of these windows will help you master Pro Tools' recording and editing features.

This chapter will introduce you to the main features of the Mix window, including channel strips, track controls, sends, inserts, and inputs and outputs. And you'll learn how to adjust the display of the Mix window to get the most from limited screen space. You'll learn the layout of the Edit window, too. I'll point out important editing features such as Zoom buttons, Edit modes, Edit tools, and the Regions list. The latter is an invaluable tool for managing your audio files and MIDI data.

The Mix Window

If you're familiar with an analog mixing board, you'll recognize the Pro Tools Mix window (**Figure 3.1**). It looks just like a hard-wired mixer, but it's more flexible.

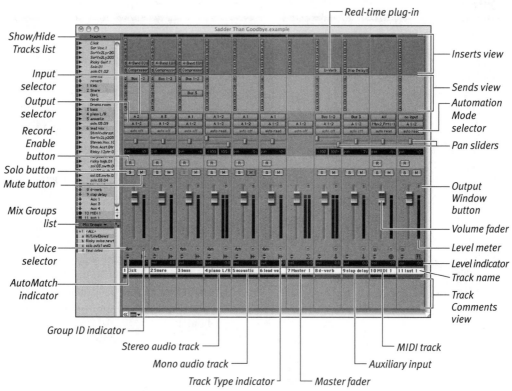

Figure 3.1 The Pro Tools Mix window.

To open the Mix Window

1. Select Window > Mix, or Command-Equal (=) (Macintosh) or Control-Equal (=) (Windows).

   The Mix Window appears.

Each track in a Pro Tools session is displayed in the Mix window as a *channel strip* (**Figure 3.2**). Channel strips include track controls for inputs and outputs, volume,

mute, solo, automation, and record-enable. Channel strips also include sections for sends, inserts, MIDI instrument controls, comments, and track color.

There are five types of channel strips: audio tracks, MIDI tracks, auxiliary inputs, instrument tracks, and master faders (**Figure 3.3**). All channel strips except MIDI tracks can be mono or stereo (**Figure 3.4**).

Audio track channel strip | Auxiliary input channel strip | Master fader channel strip | MIDI track channel strip | Instrument track channel strip

Figure 3.2 An audio track channel strip in the Mix window.

Figure 3.3 Channel strips. Each track type (audio, auxiliary input, master fader, MIDI, and Instrument) has a slightly different channel strip.

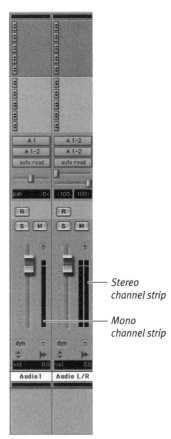

Stereo channel strip

Mono channel strip

Figure 3.4 Mono and stereo audio track channel strips.

THE MIX WINDOW

Audio track channel strips

Audio track channel strips (**Figure 3.5**) provide controls for audio volume, pan, solo, mute, record-enable, and automation. They also let you route channel inputs and outputs, sends, and inserts.

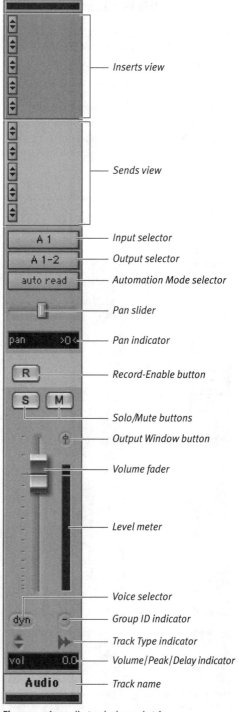

Inserts view

Sends view

Input selector

Output selector

Automation Mode selector

Pan slider

Pan indicator

Record-Enable button

Solo/Mute buttons

Output Window button

Volume fader

Level meter

Voice selector

Group ID indicator

Track Type indicator

Volume/Peak/Delay indicator

Track name

Figure 3.5 An audio track channel strip.

The Mix Window

Figure 3.6 Select Track > New.

To create an audio track channel strip:

1. Select Track > New, or Shift-Command-N (Macintosh) or Shift-Control-N (Windows) (**Figure 3.6**).

   The New Tracks dialog box appears (**Figure 3.7**).

2. Select Mono or Stereo from the pop-up menu (**Figure 3.8**).

3. Select Audio Track from the pop-up menu (**Figure 3.9**).

4. Enter the number of tracks and click Create.

Figure 3.7 The New Tracks dialog box.

Figure 3.8 Select Mono or Stereo from the pop-up menu.

Figure 3.9 Select Audio Track from the pop-up menu.

MIDI track channel strips

MIDI track channel strips (**Figure 3.10**) provide controls for volume, pan, solo, mute, and automation. You can also make MIDI patch assignments and MIDI channel assignments through this strip.

To create a MIDI track channel strip:

1. Select Track > New, or Shift-Command-N (Macintosh) or Shift-Control-N (Windows). The New Tracks dialog box appears.

2. Select MIDI Track from the pop-up menu (**Figure 3.11**).

3. Enter the number of tracks and click Create.

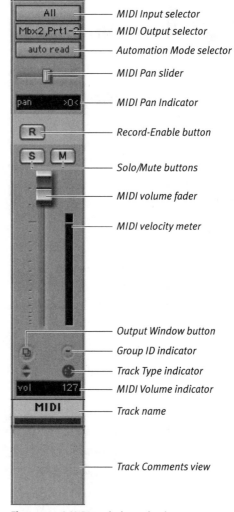

— MIDI Input selector
— MIDI Output selector
— Automation Mode selector
— MIDI Pan slider
— MIDI Pan Indicator
— Record-Enable button
— Solo/Mute buttons
— MIDI volume fader
— MIDI velocity meter
— Output Window button
— Group ID indicator
— Track Type indicator
— MIDI Volume indicator
— Track name
— Track Comments view

Figure 3.10 A MIDI track channel strip.

Figure 3.11 Select MIDI Track from the pop-up menu.

THE MIX WINDOW

Figure 3.12 An auxiliary input channel strip.

Auxiliary input channel strips

Auxiliary input channel strips (**Figure 3.12**) are similar to audio track channel strips, but they accept input only from internal bus or external hardware sources.

You can use an auxiliary input to create an *effects loop*, in which audio is routed to an auxiliary input, and an effect (such as EQ, compression, or reverb) is added. The *effects return* is then routed to the main mix. For more information on effects loops, see *Chapter 15: Adding Effects to a Mix*.

You can also use auxiliary inputs to create submixes. This lets you consolidate multiple tracks of audio onto one channel strip. For more information on submixes, see *Chapter 14: Mixing Basics*.

To create an auxiliary input channel strip:

1. Select Track > New, or Shift-Command-N (Macintosh) or Shift-Control-N (Windows).

   The New Tracks dialog box appears.

2. Select Mono or Stereo from the pop-up menu.

3. Select Auxiliary Input from the pop-up menu (**Figure 3.13**).

4. Enter the number of auxiliary inputs and click Create.

Figure 3.13 Select Auxiliary Input from the pop-up menu.

Instrument track channel strips

Instrument track channel strips (**Figure 3.14**) combine features of audio track channel strips and MIDI track channel strips.

You can use an instrument track to record MIDI data while monitoring the audio output of a triggered MIDI device. For more information on recording MIDI, see *Part VI: MIDI Sequencing*.

To create an instrument track channel strip:

1. Select Track > New, or Shift-Command-N (Macintosh) or Shift-Control-N (Windows).

    The New Tracks dialog box appears.

2. Select Mono or Stereo from the pop-up menu.

3. Select Instrument Track from the pop-up menu (**Figure 3.15**).

4. Enter the number of instrument tracks and click Create.

— *Post-fader insert*

Figure 3.14 An Instrument track channel strip.

Figure 3.15 Select Instrument Track from the pop-up menu.

Master fader channel strips

Master fader channel strips (**Figure 3.16**) let you control the output level of the main mix. You can also use them to control output levels for submixes, bus paths, sends, and inserts.

To create a master fader channel strip:

1. Select Track > New, or Shift-Command-N (Macintosh) or Shift-Control-N (Windows).

   The New Tracks dialog box appears.

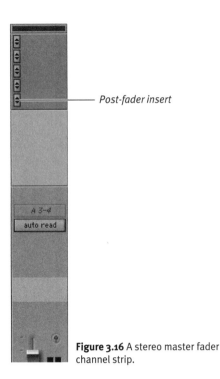

Figure 3.16 A stereo master fader channel strip.

— *Post-fader insert*

2. Select Mono or Stereo from the pop-up menu.

3. Select Master Fader from the pop-up menu (**Figure 3.17**).

4. Enter the number of master faders and click Create.

✔ Tips

■ The inserts section of a master fader is always post-fader. This means that the inserts occur in the signal path after the track's fader. (The inserts section of audio tracks and auxiliary inputs is always pre-fader.)

■ Post-fader inserts are convenient for adding an effect, such as an aural exciter or dither, to the main mix. But avoid the temptation to add compression or other dynamic effects to the main mix. Compression can make a mix sound boxy, and it can also remove audio information that a mastering engineer may want to more precisely sculpt using EQ and other effects. Compression can also change the overall level of a mix and create audible inconsistencies between mixes.

For more information about track types and creating new tracks, see *Chapter 5: Working with Tracks.*

Figure 3.17 Select Master Fader from the pop-up menu.

Viewing Channel Strips

The Mix window is dedicated primarily to the display of track channel strips. You can expand, contract, and narrow the view of channel strips according to your needs (**Figure 3.18**).

Pro Tools 7 introduces the convenient Mix Window View selector (lower-left corner of Mix Window), which lets you quickly adjust the display of channel strips (**Figure 3.19**)

A fully expanded channel strip displays:

◆ Track controls (always open)

◆ Sends (A–E) and (F–J)

◆ Inserts

◆ Track comments

◆ Track colors

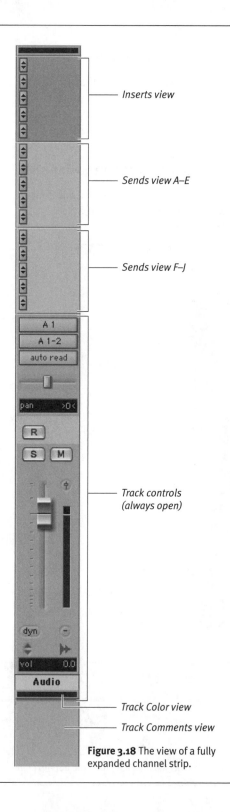

Inserts view

Sends view A–E

Sends view F–J

Track controls (always open)

Track Color view

Track Comments view

Figure 3.18 The view of a fully expanded channel strip.

Figure 3.19 The Mix Window View selector lets you quickly expand the view of channel strips in the Mix window.

Figure 3.20 Select View > Mix Window > All.

To view expanded channel strips:

◆ Select View > Mix Window > All (**Figure 3.20**).

 or

◆ Click the Mix Window View selector and select All (**Figure 3.21**).

To view narrow channel strips:

◆ Select View > Narrow Mix (**Figure 3.22**). The Mix window displays narrow channel strips (**Figure 3.23**).

Figure 3.21 The Mix Window View selector pop-up menu.

Figure 3.22 Select View > Narrow Mix.

Figure 3.23 The Narrow Mix window view.

THE MIX WINDOW

Track controls

Channel strips in the Mix window offer track controls for recording and playing back audio and MIDI tracks (**Figure 3.24**). Audio and MIDI track channel strips have the following track controls:

Input selectors: Input selectors let you route audio inputs or internal busses to an audio track or auxiliary input (**Figure 3.25**). Available inputs depend on your I/O Setup configuration.

Output selectors: Output selectors let you route audio to any available audio output or internal bus (**Figure 3.26**). Available outputs depend on your I/O Setup configuration.

Automation mode: The Automation mode selector lets you control how track automation is written and played back. You can choose from Auto Off, Auto Read, Auto Write, Auto Touch, and Auto Latch modes. For more information on automation modes, see *Chapter 16: Automating a Mix.*

Pan slider: The Pan slider controls the balance of a track between left and right output channels. Pan sliders appear on the channel strips of stereo tracks or mono tracks routed to a stereo output.

Pan indicator: The Pan indicator shows you the left and right output balance of a track. Pan values range from <100 (full left) to >100 (full right).

Record-Enable: The Record-Enable button puts audio and MIDI tracks into Record-Ready mode. Once a track is record-enabled, click the Record button, and then the Play button in the Transport window to start recording.

Solo: The Solo button mutes all tracks except the soloed track. This lets you monitor a track by itself. You can solo multiple tracks simultaneously.

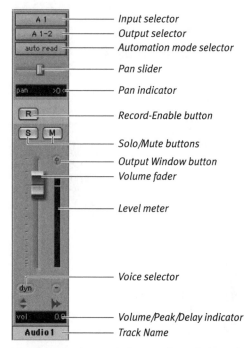

Figure 3.24 Track controls for an audio track channel strip in the Mix window.

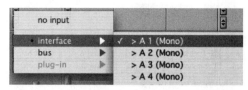

Figure 3.25 Input selectors let you route audio input.

Figure 3.26 Output selectors let you route audio output.

Mute: The Mute button silences a track. You can mute multiple tracks simultaneously.

Output Window button: The Output Window button opens a separate floating channel strip. Output windows provide controls for track output.

Volume fader: The Volume fader controls the monitor volume of a track in playback, as well as the monitor volume of a track in record.

Level meter: The Level meter displays an audio signal's volume level as it's recorded to the hard disk. It also displays a signal's volume level as it's played back from the hard disk.

The color of the Level meter light indicates the status of the audio signal: Green indicates nominal (safe) levels, yellow indicates pre-clipping, and red indicates clipping.

Voice selector: In Pro Tools 7 LE, the Voice selector lets you toggle between Dynamic voice selection and Off. When set to Dynamic voice selection, Pro Tools automatically assigns voices to a track. When set to Off, a track's voice assignment remains unchanged.

Volume/Peak/Delay indicator: The Volume/Peak/Delay indicator shows the current volume input level, the most recent peak playback level, and on Pro Tools HD systems, the delay time in samples incurred by a TDM plug-in on that channel. Command-click (Macintosh) or Control-click (Windows) the indicator to switch between level, peak, and delay.

Track Name: When you create a track with the New Track command, it's automatically given a track name.

THE MIX WINDOW

✔ Tips

- Use the Pro Tools Preferences window to adjust a Peak Hold setting for the Track Level meter. This will help you monitor input and output levels. Select Setup > Preferences (**Figure 3.27**), click the Display tab, and then choose from three Peak Hold settings: 3 Second, Infinite, or None (**Figure 3.28**).

- Pro Tools remembers both record and playback fader levels for each audio track. Linking these faders in the Pro Tools Preferences window will keep them from changing position when you record-enable a track. Select Setup > Preferences, click the Operation tab, and then select the Link Record And Play Faders check box (**Figure 3.29**).

- To rename a track, double-click the track name at the bottom of a channel strip. A dialog box appears (**Figure 3.30**). Enter the new track name and click OK.

Figure 3.27 Select Setup > Preferences.

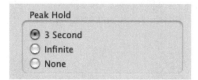

Figure 3.28 In the Preferences dialog box, click the Display tab, and then choose a Peak Hold option.

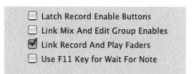

Figure 3.29 Select the Link Record And Play Faders check box in the Operation Preferences dialog box.

Figure 3.30 The Rename Track dialog box.

What Are Safe Modes?

You can put certain track controls into Safe mode. This disables the control and protects your work from inadvertent technical mishaps. Safe modes include:

Record Safe: Disables the Record-Enable button. To toggle Record Safe mode, Command-click (Macintosh) or Control-click (Windows) the Record-Enable button.

Solo Safe: Disables the Solo button. To toggle Solo Safe mode, Command-click (Macintosh) or Control-click (Windows) the Solo button.

Automation Safe: Suspends automation recording. You can toggle outputs, sends, and plug-ins into Automation Safe mode to prevent you from overwriting previously recorded automation (**Figure 3.31**).

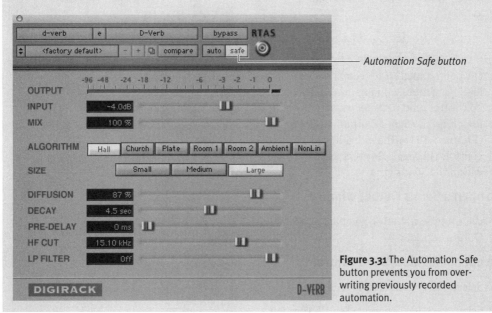

Automation Safe button

Figure 3.31 The Automation Safe button prevents you from overwriting previously recorded automation.

The Sends view

Sends let you route audio to internal busses or external outputs for effects processing or submixing. In Pro Tools 7, you can assign up to ten sends per audio track, auxiliary input, or instrument track. Sends are divided into two views: Sends A–E and Sends F–J (**Figure 3.32**).

To show the Sends A–E view or the Sends F–J view:

◆ Select View > Sends A–E or Sends F–J.

or

◆ Click the Mix Window View selector and select Sends A–E or Sends F–J.

Output parameters for sends include level, pan, mute, and pre- and post-fader. To control send parameters, you can use either the Sends Output window (**Figure 3.33**) or the individual send controls (**Figure 3.34**) that appear within the Sends view.

To open a Sends Output window:

◆ Click any Send button to open a Sends Output window.

To open individual send controls:

1. Select View > Sends A–E or Sends F–J.

2. Select an individual send (Send A through Send E) or (Send F through Send J) (**Figure 3.35**). Individual send controls appear in the Sends View section.

For more information on Sends, see *Chapter 15: Adding Effects to a Mix.*

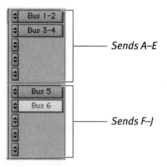

Figure 3.32 The Sends A–E view and the Sends F–J view.

Figure 3.33 A Sends Output window.

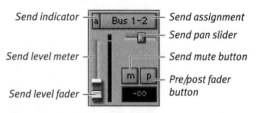

Figure 3.34 Individual send controls.

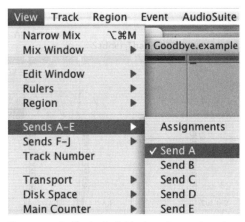

Figure 3.35 To display individual send controls, select View > Sends A–E *or* Sends F–J. Then select a send (Send A through Send E *or* Send F through Send J).

Figure 3.36 The Inserts view.

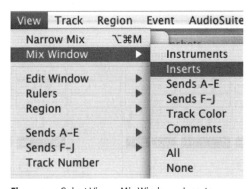

Figure 3.37 Select View > Mix Window > Inserts.

Figure 3.38 Click an assigned Insert button to show its Effects Plug-in window.

The Inserts view

Inserts let you add effects on individual channel strips. The Inserts view (**Figure 3.36**) lets you access five pre-fader inserts per audio track, auxiliary input, or instrument track You can assign internal software effects and external hardware effects to inserts.

To show the Inserts view:

◆ Select View > Mix Window > Inserts (**Figure 3.37**).

   or

◆ Click the Mix Window View selector and select Inserts.

   The Inserts view also gives you access to Effects Plug-in windows.

To show an Effects Plug-in window:

◆ Click an assigned Insert button (**Figure 3.38**). The assigned Effects Plug-in window opens (**Figure 3.39**).

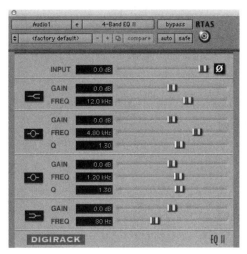

Figure 3.39 An open Effects Plug-in window (4-Band EQII).

THE MIX WINDOW

45

The Track Color view

In Pro Tools 7 you can color code your tracks using the Track Color view.

To show the Track Color view:

◆ Select View > Mix Window > Track Color (**Figure 3.40**).

or

◆ Click the Mix Window View selector and select Track Color.

For more information on color coding tracks, see *Chapter 5: Working with Tracks*

The Track Comments view

The Track Comments view shows any comments entered into the Track Name/Comments dialog box.

To show the Track Comments view:

◆ Select View > Mix Window > Comments (**Figure 3.41**).

or

◆ Click the Mix Window View selector and select Comments.

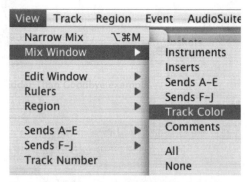

Figure 3.40 To show the Track Color view, select View > Mix Window > Track Color.

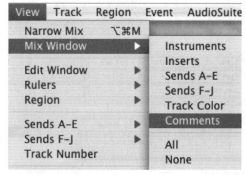

Figure 3.41 To show the Track Comments view, select View > Mix Window > Comments.

Figure 3.42 The Tracks list in the Mix window.

The Tracks list

The Tracks list (**Figure 3.42**) in the Mix window displays the names of all the tracks in the current session. You can show or hide a track by selecting or deselecting it, and you can rearrange tracks by dragging them up or down.

The Tracks pop-up menu at the top of the list gives you options for showing, hiding, and sorting tracks (**Figure 3.43**).

The Mix Groups list

The Mix Groups list (**Figure 3.44**) in the Mix window shows all the mix groups in a session. You can enable a group by highlighting its name in the list.

The Mix Groups pop-up menu at the top of the list lets you create new groups; display edit groups or mix groups; and suspend or delete groups (**Figure 3.45**).

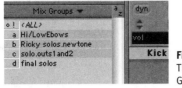

Figure 3.43 The Tracks list pop-up menu.

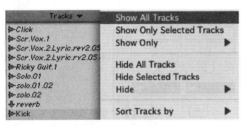

Figure 3.44 The Mix Groups list.

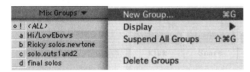

Figure 3.45 The Mix Groups pop-up menu.

THE MIX WINDOW

Viewing the Tracks list and the Mix Groups list

The Tracks list and the Mix Groups list are displayed at the left of the Mix window. You can open and close this section of the Mix window as needed to accommodate the display of track channel strips.

To open/close the Tracks list and the Mix Groups list:

◆ Click the double arrow at the bottom left of the Mix Window (**Figure 3.46**).

The Tracks list and the Mix Groups list appear at the left side of the Mix window (**Figure 3.47**).

✔ Tip

■ If a hidden track is part of a group, operations performed on the group will be performed on the hidden track as well. Disable groups with hidden tracks to avoid making unwanted changes. For information on enabling and disabling groups, see *Chapter 5: Working with Tracks*.

Figure 3.46 To open/close the Tracks list and the Mix Groups list, click the double arrow icon in the lower-left corner of the Mix window.

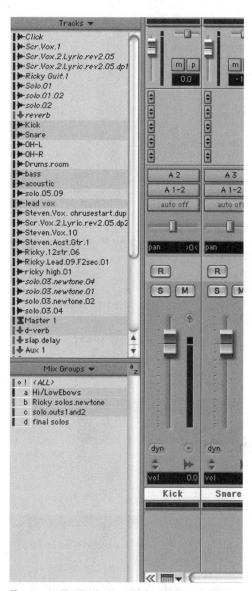

Figure 3.47 The Tracks list and the Mix Groups list in the Mix Window.

The Edit Window

The Edit window (**Figure 3.48**) gives you a visual read-out of audio, MIDI, and automation data against a timeline. It also offers tools for selecting, viewing, and arranging this recorded data. In addition, the Edit window features tools for managing audio files and MIDI files.

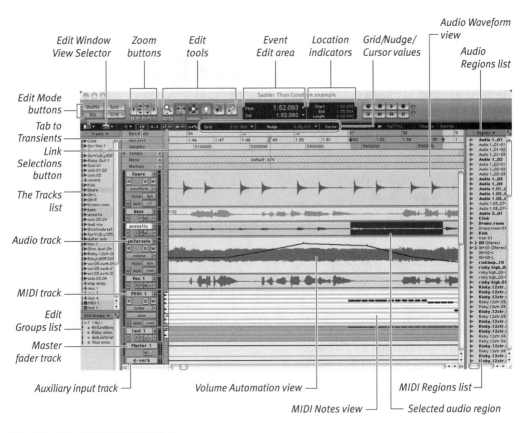

Figure 3.48 The Pro Tools Edit window.

THE EDIT WINDOW

To open the Edit window:

◆ Select Window > Edit, or Command-
Equal (=) (Macintosh) or Control-Equal
(=) (Windows).

The Edit Window appears.

Viewing the Edit window

The Edit window displays the same channel
strips as in the Mix window, with a few
additional features outlined below. You can
expand the Edit window to view the full
channel strips, but they are displayed horizontally, not vertically.

In Pro Tools 7, the Edit window includes an
Edit Window View selector, which lets you
quickly customize the view of channel strips.

To view expanded channel strips in the Edit window:

◆ Select View > Edit Window > All.

   or

◆ Click the Edit Window View selector and
select All (**Figure 3.49**).

The expanded channel strip view
appears (**Figure 3.50**).

For more information on channel strips,
see *The Mix Window* section earlier in
this chapter.

✔ Tips

■ Edit Window channel strips, unlike Mix
Window channel strips, include an I/O
(Input/Output) View, which shows track
input and output assignments. You can
hide the I/O View to conserve track
viewing space. To show or hide the I/O
View, select Display > Edit Window
Shows > I/O View.

■ To toggle between the Mix and Edit
windows, press Command-Equal (=)
(Macintosh) or Control-Equal (=)
(Windows).

Figure 3.49 To view a fully expanded channel strip in
the Edit window, click the Edit Window View selector
and select All.

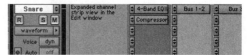

Figure 3.50 An expanded channel strip in the Edit
window.

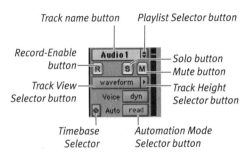

Figure 3.51 The Edit window track controls.

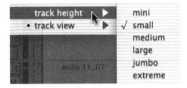

Figure 3.52 The Playlist selector.

Figure 3.53 The Track Height selector.

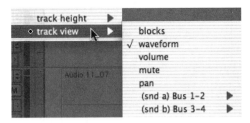

Figure 3.54 The Track View selector.

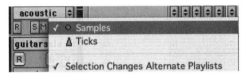

Figure 3.55 The Timebase selector.

Track controls

Most of the Edit window's track controls (**Figure 3.51**) are identical to those in the Mix window. For information on Record-Enable, Solo, Mute, Automation mode selector, and Track Name, see the *Track Controls* section earlier in this chapter.

In addition to the above track controls, the Edit window contains the following:

◆ **Playlist selector:** The Playlist selector lets you create and manage multiple *edit playlists* on each track (**Figure 3.52**).

An edit playlist is a snapshot of the current arrangement of regions on a track. Edit playlists gives you the flexibility to experiment with region editing ideas. For more information on playlists, see *Chapter 2: Software Basics,* and *Chapter 10: Editing Basics.*

◆ **Track Height selector:** The Track Height selector lets you adjust the vertical size of a track. You can select from mini, small, medium, large, jumbo, and extreme (**Figure 3.53**). You can also toggle back and forth between track height settings.

◆ **Track View selector:** Although you'll mainly use the Waveform view, the Track View selector lets you see a visual readout of other track information. On audio tracks you can select from blocks, volume, pan, mute, send level, send mute, and send pan (**Figure 3.54**).

◆ **Timebase selector:** The Timebase selector lets you switch individual tracks between tick-based timing and sample-based timing (**Figure 3.55**).

THE EDIT WINDOW

51

Edit modes

The Edit window's four Edit Mode buttons (**Figure 3.56**) let you choose how regions are moved in the window. You can select from the following modes:

◆ **Shuffle:** Shuffle mode automatically snaps a region to the end of another region. For instance, if you select an audio region and delete it, the region to the right snaps to the region on the left.

◆ **Spot:** Spot mode lets you move a selected region to an exact time location. When you move a selected region in Spot mode, the Spot dialog box opens (**Figure 3.57**). This lets you enter a new start time for the selected region.

◆ **Slip:** Slip mode lets you move regions freely in a track, with few limitations. In Slip mode you can overlap regions or separate regions with space (silence).

◆ **Grid:** Grid mode lets you snap selected regions to a user-defined time grid.

✔ Tip

■ To switch between edit modes, use the following function keys: F1 (Shuffle), F2 (Slip), F3 (Spot), F4 (Grid).

For more information on Edit modes, see *Chapter 10: Editing Basics.*

Figure 3.56 The Edit Mode buttons.

Figure 3.57 The Spot Mode dialog box. Move a selected region by entering a new start time.

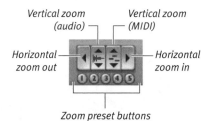

Figure 3.58 The Zoom buttons.

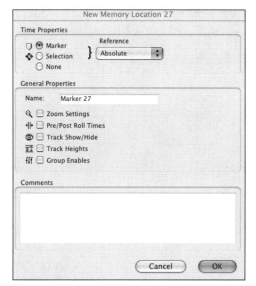

Figure 3.59 Memory Location dialog box. Press Enter on the numeric keypad to set a new memory location.

Zoom buttons

The Edit window's Zoom buttons (**Figure 3.58**) let you zoom quickly in and out of audio and MIDI tracks. Zoom buttons include:

◆ **Horizontal Zoom In/Out:** Zooms in and out horizontally on a track. Option-click (Macintosh) or Alt-click (Windows) either Horizontal Zoom button to restore the previous zoom level.

◆ **Vertical Zoom In/Out (audio):** Zooms in and out vertically on audio tracks. Option-click (Macintosh) or Alt-click (Windows) either Vertical Zoom button to restore the previous zoom level.

◆ **Vertical Zoom In/Out (MIDI):** Zooms in and out vertically on a MIDI track. Option-click (Macintosh) or Alt-click (Windows) either Vertical Zoom button to restore the previous zoom level.

◆ **Zoom Presets:** You can save up to five horizontal zoom presets. Command-click (Macintosh) or Control-click (Windows) any Zoom Preset button to save the current horizontal zoom value.

✔ Tip

■ You can save zoom settings in the Memory Location dialog box (**Figure 3.59**) when you enter a memory location. You'll find details for setting memory locations in *Chapter 10: Editing Basics.*

Edit tools

The Edit window's Edit tools (**Figure 3.60**) let you select, audition, view, and move regions. The tools include:

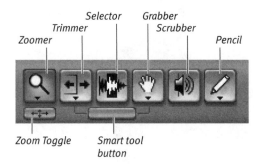

Figure 3.60 The Edit tools.

◆ **Zoomer:** The Zoomer tool lets you zoom in quickly on a track. To zoom in horizontally, click or drag the Zoomer tool. To zoom in horizontally and vertically, press Command (Macintosh) or Control (Windows) while dragging.

◆ **Zoom Toggle:** The Zoom Toggle lets you switch back and forth between the current zoom view and a predefined zoom view.

◆ **Standard Trimmer:** The Standard Trimmer tool lets you quickly expand or condense a region. To use it, click or drag near the start or end point of the region.

◆ **Time Trimmer:** The Time Trimmer tool lets you expand or compress a region by dragging its start or end points. The Time Trimmer uses the Time Compression/ Expansion AudioSuite plug-in to create a new file. For more information on AudioSuite plug-ins, see the *DigiRack Plug-Ins Guide.*

◆ **Selector:** The Selector tool lets you make a selection anywhere on a track by clicking and dragging. To adjust the length of a selection, Shift-click or Shift-drag with the Selector. To extend an edit selection to other tracks, Shift-click with the Selector in the desired tracks.

◆ **Time Grabber:** The Time Grabber tool lets you select and move regions anywhere within a track or between tracks by clicking and dragging. To move a region with the Time Grabber, select a region and drag it to a new location.

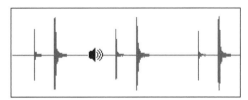

Figure 3.61 Run the Scrubber tool over an audio region to scrub audio.

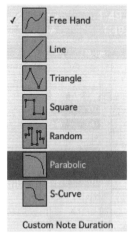

Custom Note Duration

Figure 3.62 The Pencil tool pop-up menu.

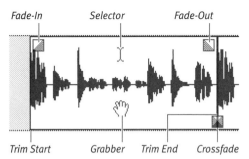

Figure 3.63 The Smart tool lets you use several Edit tools simultaneously.

Fade-In   Selector   Fade-Out

Trim Start   Grabber   Trim End   Crossfade

Figure 3.64 The Smart tool automatically changes between the Selector, Grabber, and Trimmer tools as you move your cursor over a region. You can also create fades with the tool.

◆ **Separation Grabber:** The Separation Grabber tool lets you separate and move a region within or between tracks. To separate regions, click a selected region with the Separation Grabber.

◆ **Scrubber:** The Scrubber tool lets you audition or *scrub* audio regions. Scrubbing—a term borrowed from analog recording—refers to running the tape manually back and forth over the playback head. Scrubbing is useful for locating edit points that might be difficult to find visually. To scrub a track, click and drag the Scrubber tool over an audio region (**Figure 3.61**).

◆ **Pencil:** The Pencil tool lets you insert MIDI notes, edit MIDI note velocities, draw automation and controller events, and repair audio waveforms at the sample level. Clicking the Pencil tool summons its pop-up menu (**Figure 3.62**), which lets you choose from seven Pencil shapes.

You can also use the Pencil tool as an eraser to delete notes, program changes, and sysex events. Press Option (Macintosh) or Alt (Windows) to change the Pencil tool to an Eraser.

◆ **Smart Tool:** The Smart tool (**Figure 3.63**) lets you use several Edit tools without having to switch between them. As you move the Smart tool within a region, it automatically changes between the Selector, Grabber, and Trimmer, and lets you create fades as well (**Figure 3.64**).

THE EDIT WINDOW

✔ Tips

- Use the Grabber pop-up menu (**Figure 3.65**) to choose between the Time Grabber, Separation Grabber, and Object Grabber. Clicking the Grabber tool summons the pop-up menu. The Time Grabber is the default Grabber tool.

- Use the Trimmer pop-up menu (**Figure 3.66**) to choose between the Standard Trimmer and the Time Trimmer. Clicking the Time Trimmer tool summons the pop-up menu. The Standard Trimmer is the default Trimmer tool.

- Use the following function keys to select and/or toggle Edit tools: F5 (Zoomer), F6 (Standard Trimmer), F7 (Selector), F8 (Time/Separation Grabber), F9 (Scrubber), F10 (Pencil), F6 and F7 simultaneously (Smart tool).

The Event Edit area

The Edit window's Event Edit area (**Figure 3.67**) displays the start point, end point, and length of a selected region or note. The selection indicators display a selection in minutes and seconds, bars and beats, or samples, depending on the current time format of the Main Time Scale (see *Location indicators* later in this chapter).

When you select a MIDI note, the right side of the Event Edit area displays MIDI note attributes such as pitch, attack velocity, and release velocity. You can change the value of a selection indicator or note attribute by entering a new value in its field.

✔ Tip

- Press slash (/) on the numeric keypad to select the start field and to navigate from field to field. Press Enter to accept a new value.

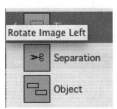

Figure 3.65 The Grabber tool pop-up menu.

Figure 3.66 The Trimmer pop-up menu.

Figure 3.67 The Event Edit area showing the start time, end time, and length of an audio region selection.

Main time scale

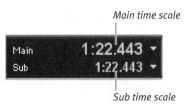

Sub time scale

Figure 3.68 Location indicators show the Main time scale and Sub time scale.

Figure 3.69 Click the Location indicator pop-up menu to change the Main and Sub time scale time formats (Bars:Beats, Min:Secs, or Samples).

Location indicators

The location indicators (**Figure 3.68**) display the current play position in both the Main time scale and Sub time scale.

The Main time scale is the primary time format of your session (see time formats, below). The Sub time scale is an additional timing reference that can be useful with synchronization. To change the time format of either scale, click the pop-up menu to the right of its field (**Figure 3.69**).

You can choose from these time formats:

◆ Bars:Beats

◆ Minutes:Seconds (Min:Secs)

◆ Samples

✔ Tip

■ Press Equal (=) on the numeric keypad to select the Main time scale in the location indicator. Press period (.) to navigate the indicator's time fields; press Enter to go to a new location.

Grid/Nudge values, Current Cursor display

The Edit window also provides fields for quickly entering Grid and Nudge values during editing. The Current Cursor display gives you information about the location of the cursor.

◆ **Grid value:** The Grid value field (**Figure 3.70**) lets you define the size of the grid used in Grid mode. You can define a Grid value that matches the time format currently used by the Main time scale, or select a different time format from the pop-up menu to the right of the field (**Figure 3.71**). For more information on using grids, see *Chapter 10: Editing Basics*.

◆ **Nudge value:** The Nudge value field lets you define the distance you can nudge a selected region with the plus and minus keys on the numeric keypad. Use the pop-up menu to the right of the field to select a nudge value. For more information on the Nudge feature, see *Chapter 10: Editing Basics*.

◆ **Cursor location:** The Cursor location field displays the location of the cursor in the same time format as the current Main time scale.

◆ **Cursor value:** The Cursor value field displays information about the cursor location based on the current track view. For instance, Volume view shows a dB value, Note view shows a MIDI note value, and Velocity view shows a velocity value.

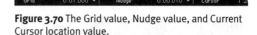

Figure 3.70 The Grid value, Nudge value, and Current Cursor location value.

Figure 3.71 Select a new Grid value or time format using the Grid value pop-up menu.

Figure 3.72 The Edit Groups list.

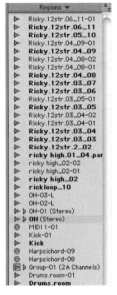

Figure 3.73 The Regions list.

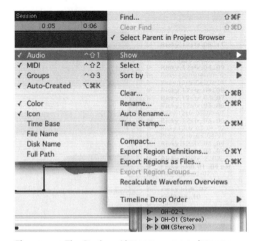

Figure 3.74 The Regions List pop-up menu lets you import, sort, compact, and delete audio files.

The Edit Groups list

Much like the Mix Groups list in the Mix window, the Edit Groups list (**Figure 3.72**) displays all the edit groups in a session. You can enable or disable a group by selecting its name in the Groups list. Highlighted groups are enabled.

To create a new group, or suspend or delete groups, use the Edit Groups pop-up menu at the top of the list. For more information on groups, see *Chapter 5: Working with Tracks*.

The Regions list

Audio regions, MIDI regions, and region groups appear in the Regions list (**Figure 3.73**). You can drag regions from the list onto any audio or MIDI track.

The Regions list has an indispensable pop-up menu (**Figure 3.74**), which lets you import, sort, compact, and delete audio files, MIDI regions, and region groups. For more information on handling audio files, see *Chapter 8: File Management Basics*.

Viewing the Regions list

The Regions list is displayed at the right side of the Edit window. You can open and close this section of the Edit window as needed to accommodate the display of tracks.

To open/close the Regions list:

◆ Click the double arrow at the bottom right of the Edit window.

The Regions list appears at the right side of the Edit window.

THE EDIT WINDOW

Displaying Transport controls in the Edit window

In Pro Tools 7, you have the option of displaying a scaled-down version of the Transport window at the top of the Edit window (**Figure 3.75**). This can save you the time it takes clicking back and forth between separate Edit and Transport windows, and thus can increase your editing efficiency.

To display Transport controls in the Edit window:

◆ Select View > Edit Window > Transport.

For more information on the Transport Window, see *Chapter 7: Recording and Playing Back Audio.*

Figure 3.75 To display transport controls in the Edit window, select View > Edit Window > Transport.

Part II: Recording in Pro Tools

STARTING A NEW SESSION

When you start a new project in Pro Tools, you start a new *session*. A Pro Tools session is analogous to a session in a real-world recording studio: It contains all the elements you need to record, edit, process, mix, master, and store audio recordings.

This chapter tells you how to start a new Pro Tools session from scratch. First, I'll show you how to create a new session and how to configure basic parameters such as sample rate, bit depth, audio file type, and I/O Setup.

Then we'll look more closely at I/O Setups. You'll learn how to define new signal paths and map channels, and how to save your I/O Setups to use in later sessions. I'll also cover how to create new session templates and discuss sharing sessions between Pro Tools LE and Pro Tools HD systems.

Creating a New Session

Each time you create a new session, Pro Tools places a new Session folder (**Figure 4.1**) on your hard drive. In Pro Tools 7 this folder contains a Session file (.ptf), a WaveCache.wfm file, an Audio Files folder, a Region Groups folder, and a Fade Files folder (**Figure 4.2**).

The session file contains data that maps the current configuration of your session, including your latest mix, edit, and automation settings. And it keeps track of all audio files attached to your session. All Pro Tools 7 session file names end with a .ptf (Pro Tools File) extension.

The WaveCache.wfm file stores all waveform display data for the session. Each time you open a session, Pro Tools 7 refers to this file and is thus able to quickly redraw the session's audio waveforms.

All audio files recorded or imported during a Pro Tools session are stored in the Audio Files folder; all region groups exported from a session are logged in the Region Groups folder; and all fades and crossfades created during a session are stored in the Fade Files folder. Audio files and other basic session elements are discussed in *Chapter 2: Software Basics*.

When you create a new session, the New Session dialog box appears (**Figure 4.3**). Here, you can name the session and set session file parameters, such as Audio File Type, Sample Rate, Bit Depth, and I/O Settings.

Figure 4.1 A Pro Tools Session folder.

Figure 4.2 The contents of a Pro Tools 7 Session folder: a Session file (.ptf), an Audio Files folder, a Fade Files Files folder, a Region Groups folder, and a WaveCache.wfm file.

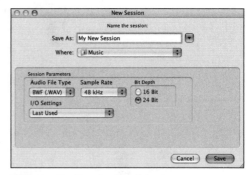

Figure 4.3 The New Session dialog box.

Figure 4.4 Choose File > New Session.

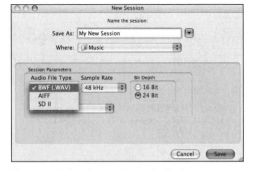

Figure 4.5 Select the session audio file format.

To create a new session:

1. Choose File > New Session (**Figure 4.4**).

2. Choose the destination hard drive for your session. (Make sure you're using a dedicated audio hard drive.)

3. Select the session audio file format (**Figure 4.5**).

   Sound Designer II (SDII) files are not supported on Windows systems or at sample rates above 48 kHz. For best cross-platform compatibility, set the file type to BWF (WAV).

4. Select a sample rate (44.1 kHz, 48 kHz, 88.2 kHz, or 96 kHz) and a bit depth (16- or 24-bit). (For more information see the sidebar, *What Are Sample Rate and Bit Depth?* later in this chapter.)

6. Select the I/O settings for the session.

7. Name the session and click Save.

Opening a session

Use the Open Session dialog box to open existing sessions. Pro Tools will automatically scan the session directory for the associated audio and fade files.

If the number of tracks in a session exceeds the maximum number of voices available on your system, those extra tracks are set to *voice off* when the session is opened.

To open an existing session:

1. Choose File > Open Session.

   The Open Session dialog box appears (**Figure 4.6**).

2. Select a session and click Open.

✔ Tip

■ Use the DigiBase Work7space browser to quickly locate and open a session file (**Figure 4.7**). Double-click the session file icon to open it. For more information on DigiBase see *Chapter 9: Managing Audio Files with DigiBase*.

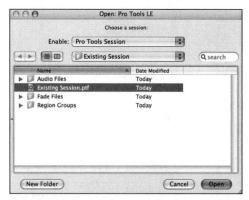

Figure 4.6 The Open Session dialog box.

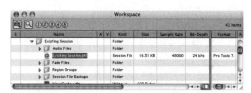

Figure 4.7 The DigiBase Workspace browser lets you quickly locate and open your Pro Tools session file.

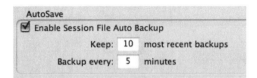

Figure 4.8 Enable AutoSave to protect your session files: Choose Setup > Preferences. Click the Operation tab. In the AutoSave panel click "Enable Session File Auto Backup."

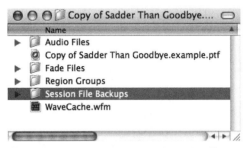

Figure 4.9 AutoSave stores automatic session file backups in the Session File Backups folder inside the Session folder.

Figure 4.10 Choose File > Revert to Saved.

Saving a session

The Save command saves the changes you make to a session, writing over the previously saved version of the session file. The Save command cannot be undone.

To save a session:

◆ Choose File > Save.

✔ Tips

■ Save your session frequently. You don't want to lose detailed mix, edit, or automation data because of a computer crash or inexplicable technical mishap.

■ To automatically back up your session files: Choose Setup > Preferences. Click the Operation tab. In the AutoSave section of the Operation panel click Enable Session File Auto Backup (**Figure 4.8**). Session file backups are stored in a Session File Backup folder, which is automatically added to the Session folder (**Figure 4.9**).

Reverting to a previously saved session

If you want to discard changes that you have made to a session file and subsequently saved, use the Revert to Saved command. Revert to Saved recalls the last saved version of a session.

To revert to the last saved version of a session:

◆ Choose File > Revert to Saved (**Figure 4.10**).

The Save As command

The Save As command lets you rename a copy of a session. It closes the current session and leaves the renamed copy open. The Save As command duplicates session files only—it does not duplicate audio or fade files.

To rename a session:

1. Choose File > Save As

   The Save Session As dialog box appears (**Figure 4.11**).

2. Enter a new name for your session

   Pro Tools 7 lets you name files with as many characters as your operating system supports.

3. Click Save.

   The renamed session document is saved in the Session folder along with the original session. Any new audio files that you record in the renamed session are stored in the same Audio Files folder created with the original session.

✔ Tip

- The Save As command is useful for developing sessions in successive stages: You save a session at any stage and continue working on a renamed copy.

The Save Copy In command

The Save Copy In command (**Figure 4.12**) lets you save a copy of the current session file, along with its audio files, fade files, plug-in settings files, and movie or video files. You can also designate a new session file format, audio file format, bit depth, sample rate, and +6 or +12 maximum fader gain for the session copy.

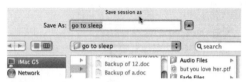

Figure 4.11 The Save As dialog box lets you rename a session file copy.

Figure 4.12 Choose File > Save Copy In.

Figure 4.13 The Save Copy In dialog box.

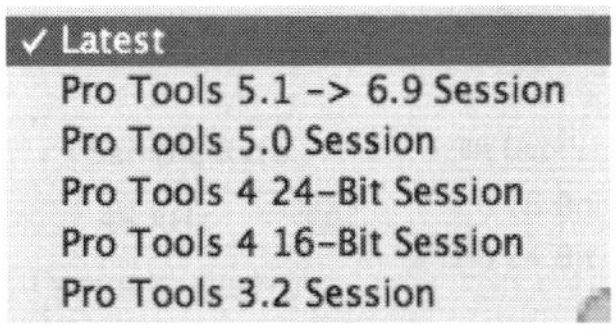

Figure 4.14
Select a session
format.

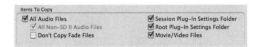

Figure 4.15 Select session parameters, including Audio File Type, Sample Rate, Bit Depth, and Fader Gain (when converting to Pro Tools 5.1-6.9 formats only) .

Figure 4.16 Select Items To Copy.

The Save Copy In command is useful for changing the sample rate or bit depth of a session. It's also useful for generating session files and audio files for use on a different Pro Tools system or operating system platform.

The Save Copy In command does not close the original session—the original session remains the open and active session.

To save a session copy in a new location:

1. Choose File > Save Copy In.

   The Save Copy In dialog box appears (**Figure 4.13**).

2. Choose a destination and type a name for the new session file.

3. Select the session format for the session copy (**Figure 4.14**). Select "Latest" to save the session copy in Pro Tools 7 format.

4. Select the session parameters (Audio File Type, Sample Rate, and Bit Depth,) for the session copy (**Figure 4.15**).

5. Select the Items To Copy to the new session (**Figure 4.16**).

6. Click Save to save the session in the new location.

✔ Tip

■ A Pro Tools session can use mixed audio file types. If your original session uses mixed file types, the Save Copy In command will not convert audio files unless you specify that they be converted. Sessions with mixed audio file types require more processing power and can thus reduce system performance.

continues on next page

CREATING A NEW SESSION

- If you are saving a session to an earlier (5.1–6.9) Pro Tools format, and want to create session and audio files that can be used in both the Macintosh or Windows version of Pro Tools, select Enforce Mac/PC Compatibility (Macintosh) or Enforce PC /Mac compatibility (Windows).

- If, when saving a session to an earlier Pro Tools format, you save a session with a +12 dB maximum fader gain as a session with a +6 dB maximum fader gain, any automation breakpoints over +6 dB will be lowered to +6 dB.

Closing a session

You can work on only one session at a time in Pro Tools. The Close Session command closes the current session, leaving the Pro Tools application open so you can create or open another session.

To close a session:

◆ Choose File > Close Session.

The current session closes, leaving the Pro Tools application open.

Quitting Pro Tools

Pro Tools will prompt you to save changes you've made to a session before it quits.

To quit a session on Mac OS:

◆ Choose Pro Tools > Quit Pro Tools

To quit a session on Windows:

◆ Choose File > Exit.

Creating an I/O Setup

A *signal path* refers to the way that audio is routed in, out, and through a Pro Tools session. A signal path can have many different configurations. For instance, you may want to bus audio to a DSP plug-in or output audio to an external hardware effect. This signal path configuration is called an I/O Setup. For more on I/O Setup, see *Chapter 2: Software Basics*.

Using the I/O Setup dialog box

The I/O Setup dialog box (**Figure 4.17**) lets you create I/O Setups. Use this checkerboard-like dialog box to define track inputs and outputs, inserts, and bus paths. You can save your definitions as I/O Settings files for use with later sessions. (See *Importing and Exporting I/O Settings Files* later in this chapter.)

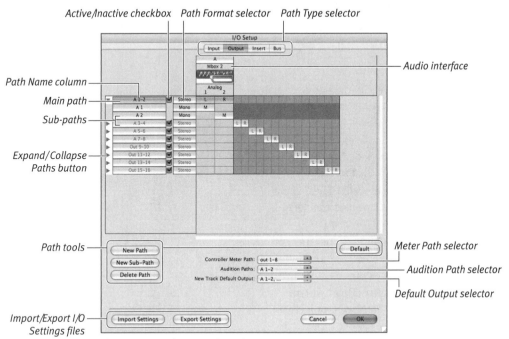

Figure 4.17 The I/O Setup dialog box.

CREATING AN I/O SETUP

To open the I/O Setup dialog box:

1. Make sure your audio interface is enabled and configured properly in the Hardware Setup dialog box.

2. Choose Setup > I/O (**Figure 4.18**).

The I/O Setup dialog box appears. Its parameter controls include the following:

Path Type tabs: The Path Type tabs let you choose a path type (input, output, insert, or bus).

Path/sub-paths arrows: The Path/sub-paths arrows let you expand the path name to display the sub-paths associated with a main path.

Path Name column: The Path Name column displays the current path name. Enter a new name in the field to rename a path.

Active/Inactive checkbox: The Active/Inactive button lets you turn a path on or off.

Path Format selector: The Path Format selector lets you choose a format (mono or stereo) for each path.

Channel grid: The Channel grid lets you map out paths between the I/O interface and channels in a session.

Path tools: Path tools let you customize paths. Path tools include New Path, New Sub-Path, Delete Path, and Default.

Default Output selector: The Default Output selector lets you set the default output assignments for new tracks.

Audition Path selector: The Audition Path selector lets you configure Audio Regions list previewing.

Meter Path selector (Pro Control only): The Meter Path selector lets you set the paths displayed across the Pro Control Output meters.

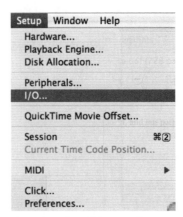

Figure 4.18 Choose Setup > I/O.

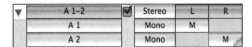

Figure 4.19 Main path stereo outputs and corresponding sub-path mono outputs.

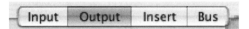

Figure 4.20 Click a path type tab (Input, Output, Insert, or Bus).

Figure 4.21 Choose a path format (Mono or Stereo).

Defining new paths

The I/O Setup dialog box lets you define main paths and sub-paths. *Main paths* are logical groupings of inputs, outputs, inserts, or busses, such as a stereo (two-channel) output. *Sub-paths* are signal paths within the main path. For example, a main path stereo output has two mono sub-paths (**Figure 4.19**).

You can define new main paths and sub-paths in the I/O Setup dialog box.

To create a new path:

1. Choose Setup > I/O.

2. Click a path type tab (Input, Output, Insert, or Bus) (**Figure 4.20**).

3. Click the New Path button, or press Command-N (Macintosh) or Control-N (Windows).

   or

   Select a main path and click the New Sub-Path button.

4. Double-click the Name field and enter a path name. (The path names appear globally in Pro Tools' track-routing selectors.)

5. Choose a format (Mono or Stereo) from the Path Format selector (**Figure 4.21**).

6. Configure other path types (Input, Output, Insert, or Bus).

7. Click OK.

✔ Tip

- You don't need to configure the I/O Setup before you begin recording—Pro Tools' default I/O Setups are adequate for most basic recording situations. As you expand your system, however, you'll likely want to experiment with new I/O Setups.

CREATING AN I/O SETUP

Mapping channels

Once you've defined a path, you can map it in the I/O Setup dialog box's channel grid (**Figure 4.22**). Channel mapping is subject to these limitations:

◆ No two main output paths, insert paths, or main bus paths can partially or completely overlap.

◆ A new output or bus path must be entirely independent of other paths, or it must be a sub-path completely contained within a main path.

◆ Output and insert paths can overlap, but they cannot be used at the same time.

To map channels:

1. Select a main path or sub-path (**Figure 4.23**).

2. In the row for the selected path, click in the grid column under the audio interface and channel (**Figure 4.24**).

Remapping channels

You can move individual assignments to different channels and redefine a path.

To remap channels in a path:

◆ Drag the channel to the new location in the grid (**Figure 4.25**).

Other channel assignments automatically move (shuffle) to accommodate the dragged channels.

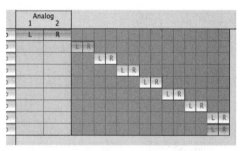

Figure 4.22 The I/O Setup dialog box's channel grid.

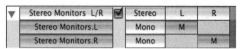

Figure 4.23 Select a main path or sub-path.

Figure 4.24 Map channels in the channel grid.

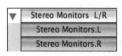

Figure 4.25 Remap a channel by dragging it to a new location in the grid.

Figure 4.26 Inactive paths are italicized.

Figure 4.27 Click the Active/Inactive button.

Making paths active or inactive

Paths can be active (on) or inactive (off). You can switch paths between these states on single tracks or session wide.

To toggle a track path assignment between active and inactive:

◆ In either the Mix or Edit window, Command-Control-click (Macintosh) or Control-Start-click (Windows) on a track Input, Output, Insert, or Send selector.

Inactive paths are italicized and grayed out in the track path selectors (**Figure 4.26**).

To toggle a global path assignment between active and inactive:

1. Choose Setup > I/O.

2. Select a path type tab (Input, Output, Insert, or Bus).

3. Click the Active/Inactive checkbox (**Figure 4.27**).

✔ Tip

■ Active paths use system resources. Make paths inactive whenever possible to conserve CPU power and improve system performance.

About I/O Settings files

When you start a session, you can choose from several I/O Setup configuration options:

- ◆ **Default I/O Setups:** These Pro Tools factory presets give you useful basic main path and sub-path definitions.

- ◆ **Custom Presets:** You can store and recall custom presets using the import and export features in the I/O Setup dialog box.

- ◆ **Last Used:** The most recent I/O Setup configuration is saved as a Last Used settings file (**Figure 4.28**).

Importing and exporting I/O Settings files

You can import and export I/O Setup configurations as I/O Settings files. This lets you save I/O Setups for reuse.

To export and save an I/O Setup configuration:

1. Click Export Settings in the I/O Setup dialog box (**Figure 4.29**).

2. Name and save the settings file (**Figure 4.30**).

Figure 4.28 The Last Used settings file.

Figure 4.29 Click Export Settings to save I/O Settings files.

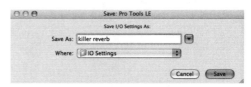

Figure 4.30 Name and save the settings file.

Figure 4.31 Click Import Settings to import a settings file.

To import an I/O Settings file:

1. Click Import Settings in the I/O Setup dialog box (**Figure 4.31**).

2. Select the desired settings file in the dialog box. Click OK.

3. You'll be asked if you want to delete the existing unused paths.

4. Select one of the following:

   Yes if you want to delete existing paths. This remaps the original session path definitions to your current audio interface.

   No if you don't want to delete existing paths. This adds session paths to the current I/O Setup.

Initializing I/O Setup

Before Pro Tools recognizes a new I/O Setup as valid, each path must have a name, a format (mono or stereo), and a valid channel mapping. See *Mapping Channels* earlier in this chapter for channel mapping requirements.

To set the current I/O Setup configuration:

◆ Click OK in the I/O Setup dialog box.

CREATING AN I/O SETUP

Creating Custom Session Templates

You can create a custom session template that retains all the parameters of a session, including mixer configurations, track setups, signal path routing, track views, and preference settings. This saves you the hassle of re-creating your studio setup each time you start a new session.

Creating Macintosh session templates

You can create a session template on the Macintosh by saving a session as a *stationery pad*. Once you do this, the session acts as a template that you can open and save just as you would a normal session.

To create a custom session template on Mac OS:

1. Configure your session parameters as desired.

2. Choose File > Save.

3. Name the session and click Save.

4. Close the session.

5. Locate the session file that you just saved.

6. Click once on the file to select it.

7. Choose File > Get Info.
   A File Information window appears.

8. Click the Stationery Pad check box to save the file as a template, and then close the window (**Figure 4.32**).

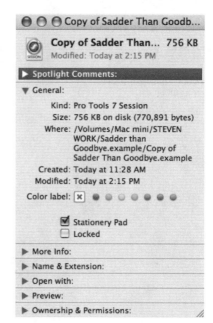

Figure 4.32 To save a file as a template, choose File > Get Info and click the Stationery Pad check box.

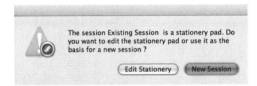

Figure 4.33 Choose whether to edit the session template or start a new session.

To open a custom session template on Mac OS:

◆ Double-click a session that was previously saved as a stationery pad.

   or

1. Select File > Open Session.

   The Open Session dialog box appears.

2. Select the session template file and click Open.

   You are prompted to either edit the session template or start a new session (**Figure 4.33**).

3. Choose Edit Stationery if you want to edit the session template.

   or

   Choose New Session.

   This creates a new Session folder containing a new session file (based on the template), with a new Audio Files folder and a new Fade Files folder.

Creating Windows session templates

You can create a Windows session template by making a session file a Read Only document.

To create a custom session template on Windows:

1. Configure the session parameters as desired.

2. Choose File > Save.

3. Name the session and click Save.

4. Close the session.

5. Locate the session file that you just saved.

6. Right-click the file and choose Properties.

7. Under Attributes, deselect Archive and select Read Only.

To open a custom session template on Windows:

◆ Double-click a session file that was previously saved as Read Only.

    or

1. Select File > Open Session.

    The Open Session dialog box appears.

2. Select the session template file and click Open.

    When you first save the session, Pro Tools asks you to rename it. Your original session template remains unchanged.

✔ Tip

■ To modify a session template in Windows, reopen its properties, deselect the Read Only option, and select the Archive option. Make your modifications, then reopen its properties and change it back to a Read Only file.

Figure 4.34 Use the Session Format pop-up menu to select the desired previous version of Pro Tools software.

Using Sessions Created in Pro Tools 7 with Earlier Versions of Pro Tools Software

Pro Tools 7 session files (.ptf) cannot be opened in earlier versions of Pro Tools software (Pro Tools 6.9.x or earlier). However, you can make a Pro Tools 7 session file (.ptf) compatible with previous versions of Pro Tools by using the Save Copy In command and choosing a destination session format. Sessions created in earlier versions of Pro Tools software can be opened in Pro Tools 7.

To make a Pro Tools 7 session file (.ptf) compatible with previous versions of Pro Tools software:

1. Select File > Save Copy In.

   The Save Copy In dialog box appears.

2. Click the Session Format pop-up menu and select the desired previous version of Pro Tools software (**Figure 4.34**).

3. Click Save

   A session copy is saved that is compatible with the selected previous version of Pro Tool software.

When saving a Pro Tools 7 session file (.ptf) to Pro Tools 5.1 –> 6.9 session file format, the following occurs:

◆ Fader Gain levels and automation breakpoints higher than +6 dB will be changed to +6 dB.

◆ Long names will be shortened to 31 characters.

◆ Instrument tracks will be split into separate Auxiliary Input and MIDI tracks.

◆ The following attributes will be dropped:
  ▲ Region groups
  ▲ Region loops
  ▲ Sample-based MIDI regions
  ▲ Sends F–J and any associated automation
  ▲ Marker/Memory Locations 201–999
  ▲ Busses 17–32 (Pro Tools LE and Pro Tools M-Powered)

When saving a Pro Tools 7 session file (.ptf) to Pro Tools 5.0 session file format, the following occurs:

◆ Long names will be shortened to 31 characters.

◆ Instrument tracks will be split into separate Auxiliary Input and MIDI tracks.

◆ The following attributes will be dropped:
  ▲ Region groups
  ▲ Region loops
  ▲ Sample-based MIDI regions
  ▲ Sample-based MIDI tracks
  ▲ Sends F–J and any associated automation
  ▲ Marker/Memory Locations 201–999
  ▲ Busses 17–32 (Pro Tools LE and Pro Tools M-Powered)
  ▲ Multi-mono plug-ins

▲ Multichannel tracks (Pro Tools HD only)

▲ Sends assigned to multichannel paths of subpaths of multichannel paths

◆ I/O settings will be rerouted as follows:

▲ Tracks assigned to "No Output" will be routed to busses 31 and 32

▲ Tracks/sends assigned to busses 33–64 will be routed to busses 31 and 32

▲ Tracks assigned to multichannel paths of sub-paths will be routed to busses 31 and 32

▲ Tracks/sends assigned to stereo paths referring to even/odd channels (such as 2–3) will be routed to busses 31 and 32

Sharing Sessions Between Pro Tools 7 HD and Pro Tools 7 LE and M-Powered

Sessions created on Pro Tools 7 HD systems will run on Pro Tools 7 LE and M-Powered systems. However, because LE systems have less processing capability than HD systems, the following limitations apply:

◆ All tracks beyond the first 32 tracks, including inactive tracks, are set to *voice off.*

◆ Any assignments to busses beyond 32 are made inactive.

◆ Any instrument tracks beyond 32 are made inactive.

◆ TDM plug-ins with RTAS equivalents are converted; those without equivalents are made inactive.

◆ Multichannel surround tracks are discarded.

◆ Any sends beyond A–E are removed.

◆ Unavailable input and output paths are made inactive.

What Are Sample Rate and Bit Depth?

Sample rate, measured in kilohertz (kHz), is the number of times per second that sound wave information is gathered, or *sampled*, during the digital audio recording process. In Pro Tools, you can record at sample rates of 44.1 kHz, 48 kHz, 88.2 kHz, and 96 kHz, depending on the system.

The sample rate used to record a sound determines the recording's frequency range and thus, its accuracy. For this reason, higher sample rates generally produce more accurate audio recordings. A basic rule of digital audio, the *Nyquest Theorem*, states that the sample rate must be twice the value of a sound's highest frequency for that sound to be accurately reproduced. For example, CD audio is sampled at 44.1 kHz, whereas the human hearing range extends to only 20 kHz. Having the sample rate at twice the highest frequency of human hearing ensures that all of a sound's *overtones* (high-frequency components of a sound) within the range of human hearing will be recorded. Recording at a sample rate of 48 kHz, 88.2 kHz, or 96 kHz ensures even greater accuracy.

Bit depth (also known as *bit resolution*) is the number of bits used to describe each individual sample taken during recording. For example, if you're recording at 24-bit resolution and a sample rate of 44.1 kHz, there will be 44,100 individual 24-bit representations of the sound recorded each second. That's a lot of data! Pro Tools let you record audio at both 16 and 24 bits.

Although higher sample rates and bit depths generally produce more accurate recordings, they also consume more disk space. In fact, 24-bit resolution requires 50 percent more hard disk space than 16-bit resolution.

If you're low on disk space, recording at 16-bit/44.1 kHz (CD audio) is a good option: It sounds good, it saves disk space, and it eliminates the need for any sample-rate or bit-depth conversion process, which can degrade digital audio. For more information on sample rate, bit depth, and file sizes, see Table 1.2 in *Chapter 1: Setting Up Your Pro Tools LE System.*

WORKING WITH TRACKS

A track is a designated space in a recording system that's assigned to carry a single audio signal. Tracks let you direct the flow of audio into your system, through DSP effects, and then back out to your ears and/or mix-down machine. Every audio or MIDI signal that comes into Pro Tools is routed to a track.

This chapter shows you how to work with tracks in Pro Tools. You'll learn the five basic track types—audio tracks, auxiliary inputs, master faders, MIDI tracks, and instrument tracks—and then we'll show you how to create them and assign inputs and outputs.

We'll also discuss some of Pro Tools' track-viewing features, such as adjusting track height and color-coding track waveforms, which can help you reduce monitor clutter and eye strain.

Finally, you'll learn how to create and work with groups of tracks in the Mix and Edit windows.

About Track Types

Pro Tools includes five types of tracks
(**Figure 5.1**):

Audio tracks: Audio tracks control
recorded or imported audio files.

Auxiliary inputs: Auxiliary inputs let you
add mono or stereo effects to bused signals.
They're also useful for submixes and other
audio-routing tasks.

Master faders: Master faders control the
level of a session's main outputs. They're also
useful for inserting effects on the main mix.

MIDI tracks: MIDI tracks store MIDI note,
instrument, and controller data.

Instrument tracks: Instrument tracks
combine audio track and MIDI track features. You can use them to monitor the
audio output of an internal (software) or
external (hardware) MIDI device (such as
a synthesizer or sound module).

Each track type has a corresponding channel strip, which appears in the Mix and Edit
windows. Tracks that handle audio (audio
tracks, auxiliary inputs, and master faders)
can be formatted for either mono (one
track) or stereo (two track).

Pro Tools also allows Movie tracks, which
display a picon (picture-icon) overview of
imported QuickTime movies (**Figure 5.2**).
The closer you zoom in on the track, the
more frames you see. Movie tracks appear
only in the Edit window.

For more information on track types and
channel strips, see *Chapter 3: The Mix and
Edit Windows.*

Figure 5.1 Pro Tools track types: audio, auxiliary
inputs, master faders, MIDI, and instrument.

Figure 5.2 A
movie track in
the Edit window.

ABOUT TRACK TYPES

Figure 5.3 Choose Track > New to launch the New Tracks dialog box.

Figure 5.4 Select a track type from the Track Type pop-up menu.

Figure 5.5 Select Mono or Stereo from the Track Format pop-up menu.

Creating New Tracks

The New Track command lets you create mono or stereo audio tracks, as well as MIDI tracks. (Pro Tools TDM systems also let you create multichannel tracks.)

To create a new track:

1. Choose Track > New *or* press Shift-Command-N (Macintosh) or Shift-Control-N (Windows) (**Figure 5.3**). The New Tracks dialog box appears.

2. Select a track type from the Track Type pop-up menu (**Figure 5.4**).

3. Select Mono or Stereo from the Track Format pop-up menu (**Figure 5.5**).

4. Enter the number of new tracks and click Create.

✔ Tip

■ If you want a new track to appear next to a specific track, click that track's name to select it. If you want a track to appear last in a session, make sure no track names are selected.

CREATING NEW TRACKS

Using the New Tracks Dialog Box to Create Multiple Track Types

The New Tracks dialog box in Pro Tools 7 lets you create multiple copies of each track type simultaneously. Thus, you can create a track layout for a session very quickly. For example, you could create 6 audio tracks, 3 auxiliary inputs, 2 MIDI tracks, and a stereo master fader (or any variation thereof) using a single New Track dialog box.

To create multiple track types simultaneously:

1. Choose Track > New *or* press Shift-Command-N (Macintosh) or Shift-Control-N (Windows).

   The New Tracks dialog box appears (**Figure 5.6**).

2. Select a track type, track format, and number of new tracks.

3. Click + to add additional track types.

   An additional new track selection bar appears (**Figure 5.7**).

4. Repeat step 2 for each additional track type you want to create (**Figure 5.8**).

5. Click Create.

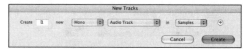

Figure 5.6 The New Tracks dialog box.

Figure 5.7 Click + to add additional track types in the New Tracks dialog box.

Figure 5.8 Multiple track types being created simultaneously in the New Tracks dialog box.

Figure 5.9 Default track names.

Figure 5.10 Double-click the track name to rename the track.

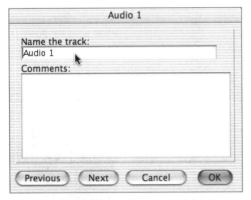

Figure 5.11 The Track Name/Comments dialog box.

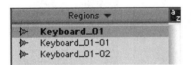

Figure 5.12 An audio file in the Regions list. The appended digits refer to the take number.

Figure 5.13 Audio regions in the Regions list. The second set of digits refers to the region number.

Naming Tracks

When you create new tracks, Pro Tools, by default, names them according to their track type, and then appends them with consecutive numbers. For example, if you create two new audio tracks, the default names will be Audio 1 and Audio 2 (**Figure 5.9**).

Pro Tools 7 lets you create track names of virtually unlimited length (determined by the maximum number of characters that your operating system allows). You can also add comments to any track.

To rename a track or add comments:

1. In the Mix or Edit window, double-click the track name (**Figure 5.10**).

   The Track Name/Comments dialog box appears.

2. Type a new track name (**Figure 5.11**).

3. Type comments for the track in the Comments text box.

4. Click the Previous or Next button to rename another displayed track.

5. When you're finished, click OK.

Understanding audio file and region names

Audio files and regions are named after the track on which they're recorded. For example, when you record audio on a track called Keyboard, the audio file written to disk will be called Keyboard_01. The appended digits refer to the *take number* (**Figure 5.12**). In addition, when you separate an audio file into regions, a region name appears in the Regions list with a second set of digits that refers to the *region number* (**Figure 5.13**).

When you record stereo tracks, the audio files and region names for the left and right channels are appended with .L and .R suffixes, respectively.

NAMING TRACKS

Assigning Audio Track Inputs and Outputs

After you've created a new audio track in Pro Tools, it's important to properly route audio in and out of the track. You can assign audio track inputs and outputs using either Mix or Edit window channel strips.

Audio tracks and auxiliary inputs let you assign audio input from audio interfaces and internal busses (**Figure 5.14**). In turn, you can assign outputs from audio tracks and auxiliary inputs to audio interfaces and internal busses (**Figure 5.15**).

When you create new tracks for a session, they're automatically assigned inputs in ascending order. For example, if you're using an Mbox 2 audio interface and you create two new mono audio tracks, they'll be assigned In 1 and In 2, respectively (**Figure 5.16**). Similarly, if you create two new stereo tracks, they'll be assigned consecutive stereo input pairs: In 1–2 and S/PDIF 3–4 (**Figure 5.17**).

Outputs are automatically assigned to the first output pair or according to the I/O Setup.

The inputs, outputs, and busses available to tracks are defined as *paths* in a session's I/O Setup. You can use a default I/O Setup or create your own in the I/O Setup dialog box. For instructions on creating a customized I/O Setup, see *Chapter 4: Starting a New Session.*

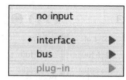

Figure 5.14 The Input selector pop-up menu lets you assign input from audio interface channels or internal busses.

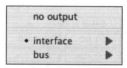

Figure 5.15 The Output selector pop-up menu lets you assign output to audio interface channels or internal busses.

Figure 5.16
New mono audio tracks with automatically assigned consecutive inputs: Mic/Line 1 and Mic/Line 2.

Figure 5.17
New stereo audio tracks with automatically assigned consecutive input pairs: In 1–2 and S/PDIF 3–4.

ASSIGNING AUDIO TRACK INPUTS AND OUTPUTS

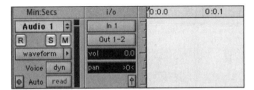

Figure 5.18 Inputs and outputs shown in the Edit window I/O view.

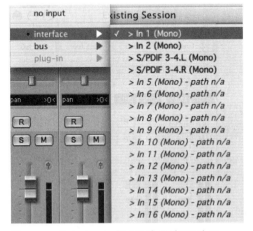

Figure 5.19 Select an audio interface channel or internal bus from the Input selector.

To assign an audio track input:

1. Display track inputs and outputs in the Edit window as follows (track inputs and outputs are always visible in audio track channel strips in the Mix window):

    Choose View > Edit Window > I/O.

    The Edit window I/O view appears (**Figure 5.18**).

2. In the Mix or Edit window, click the track Input selector, and choose from the available audio interface channels and busses (**Figure 5.19**).

    Select No Input to remove all the input assignments on that track.

To assign an audio track output:

1. Display track inputs and outputs in the Edit window as follows:

   View > Edit Window > I/O.

   Track inputs and outputs are always visible in audio track channel strips in the Mix window.

2. In the Mix or Edit window, click the track Output selector and choose from the available audio interface channels and busses (**Figure 5.20**).

   Select No Output to remove all the output assignments on that track. The playlist becomes dimmed on tracks with no output assignments.

✔ Tip

- Use the No Output option with care. Assigning an audio track, auxiliary input, or master fader to No Output erases pan and plug-in automation.

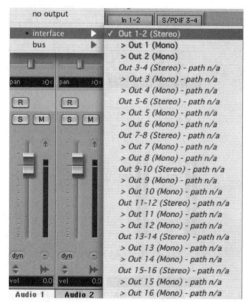

Figure 5.20 Select an audio interface channel or internal bus from the Output selector.

What Is a Bus?

Much as a city bus picks up people from many different stops and delivers them to a bus depot, an audio *bus* carries audio signals from many different tracks and delivers them to a single destination track.

Busses are used mainly to *send* audio signals from one or more audio tracks to a single auxiliary input, where a DSP effect is added. A bus lets you add the same effect to many different tracks simultaneously. For example, to add the same reverb to a vocal track and guitar track, you'd bus them to the same auxiliary input where both signals would be treated by the same reverb plug-in. (In this case, the bus would be called a *reverb send*.)

You can also use busses to create *submixes*. Submixes let you control multiple tracks of audio from a single track. For example, submixes can be useful for making headphone mixes for performers. They can also help simplify mixing tasks by bringing multiple groups of tracks—such as basic rhythm tracks, vocals, guitars, or strings—under the control of a single fader.

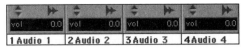

Figure 5.21 To enable track position numbering, choose View > Track Number.

Figure 5.22 Track position numbers appear next to each track name.

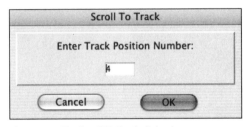

Figure 5.23 To navigate directly to a track position number, choose Track > Scroll To Track and enter the track position number.

Figure 5.24 The Scroll To Track dialog box.

Using Track Position Numbering

Pro Tools 7 assigns a track position number to each track according to its sequential position in the Mix and Edit window. When you change the position of a track, it is renumbered according to its new position.

To view track position numbers in the Mix and Edit window:

1. Choose View > Track Number (**Figure 5.21**).

   Track numbers appear next to each track name in the Mix and Edit windows (**Figure 5.22**).

Navigating by track position number

Using the Scroll To Track command in the Track menu, you can quickly navigate to any track by entering its track position number.

To navigate directly to a track position number:

1. Choose Track > Scroll To Track (**Figure 5.23**). Or Press Command-Option-F (Macintosh) or Control-Alt-F (Windows).

   The Scroll To Track dialog box appears (**Figure 5.24**).

2. In the Scroll To Track dialog box, enter the Track Position Number.

3. Click OK.

USING TRACK POSITION NUMBERING

Selecting Tracks

Selecting tracks is necessary to perform operations such as duplicating tracks, deleting tracks, showing and hiding specific tracks, and grouping tracks.

To select an individual track:

◆ Click the name of any track channel strip.

The track name becomes highlighted, indicating the track is selected (**Figure 5.25**).

To deselect an individual track:

◆ Command-click (Macintosh) or Control-click (Windows) on any highlighted track name.

The track name becomes unhighlighted, indicating the track is deselected.

To select all tracks:

◆ Option-click (Macintosh) or Alt-click (Windows) on any unhighlighted track name.

The track names of all channel strips become highlighted, indicating all tracks are selected.

Figure 5.25 Click a track name to select it. Highlighted track names indicate a track is selected.

Figure 5.26 To select noncontiguous tracks, Command-click (Macintosh) or Control-click (Windows) the desired track names.

Figure 5.27 To select a range of tracks, click the first track name in the range and Shift-click the last track name in the range. The selected range of tracks becomes highlighted.

To deselect all tracks:

◆ Option-click (Macintosh) or Alt-click (Windows) on any highlighted track name.

The track names of all channel strips become unhighlighted, indicating all tracks are deselected.

To select noncontiguous tracks:

◆ Command-click (Macintosh) or Control-click (Windows) the names of any track channel strips you want to select.

The selected noncontiguous tracks become highlighted (**Figure 5.26**).

To select a range of tracks:

1. Click the name of the first track in the range of tracks you want to select.

2. Shift-click the name of the last track in the range of tracks you want to select.

All tracks between the first track selected and the last track selected become highlighted, indicating the range of tracks selected (**Figure 5.27**).

SELECTING TRACKS

Duplicating Tracks

Pro Tools 7 introduces the Duplicate Tracks dialog box, which lets you create multiple copies of selected tracks along with selected track data. This lets you perform multiple edits on the copies of a track while maintaining easy access to your original track configuration.

The "Data to duplicate" options in the Duplicate Tracks dialog box lets you copy track data as follows:

◆ Active Playlists

◆ Alternate Playlists

◆ Automation

◆ Inserts

◆ Sends

◆ Group assignments

To duplicate a track in the Mix or Edit window:

1. Select the track(s) you want to duplicate in the Mix or Edit window.

2. Choose Track > Duplicate (**Figure 5.28**). Or press Option-Shift-D (Macintosh) or Alt-Shift-D (Windows).

   The Duplicate Tracks dialog box appears (**Figure 5.29**).

3. Select the "Data to duplicate" options as desired.

4. Select the "Insert after last selected track" option to place duplicate tracks adjacent to source tracks.

   or

   Deselect the "Insert after last selected track" option to place duplicate tracks after all visible tracks (at the far right of the Mix window and at the bottom of the Edit window) (**Figure 5.30**).

Figure 5.28 To duplicate a selected track, choose Track > Duplicate.

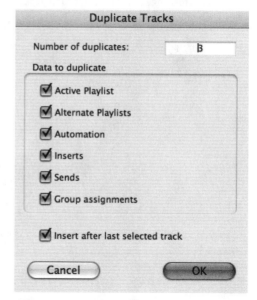

Figure 5.29 The Duplicate Tracks dialog box.

Figure 5.30 To place duplicate tracks adjacent to source tracks, select "Insert after last selected track" in the Duplicate Tracks dialog box.

Figure 5.31 To delete a track, choose Track > Delete.

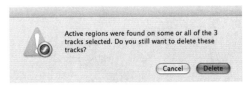

Figure 5.32 Pro Tools provides this warning before permanently deleting tracks.

Deleting Tracks

Deleting tracks from a session does not delete the audio files or MIDI data associated with that track from your hard drive—audio and MIDI regions are retained in the Regions list. However, deleting tracks does remove associated track playlists (assemblages of regions on a track).

To delete a track:

1. Select the track you want to delete by clicking the track name in the track channel strip. (For more information on selecting tracks, see the *Selecting Tracks* section earlier in this chapter).

2. Choose Track > Delete (**Figure 5.31**).

    A warning box appears asking you if you are sure you want to delete the selected tracks from the session (**Figure 5.32**).

3. Click Delete.

    The selected track is deleted from the session.

Viewing Tracks

Pro Tools gives you many different ways to view tracks in a session. These viewing options help you mix and edit more quickly and efficiently.

Using the Tracks list

The Tracks list (**Figure 5.33**), located in both the Edit and Mix windows, displays all the tracks in a session. You can show or hide a track by selecting or deselecting its name. A hidden track will continue to play normally as part of the session. Inactive tracks appear in italics in the Track list.

The Tracks list pop-up menu (**Figure 5.34**) gives you options for showing or hiding tracks. You can show/hide tracks according to track type, group, or name.

If a hidden track is a member of an active group, performing edits on other group members in the Edit window will not affect the hidden track. In the Mix window, however, performing operations other than record-enable on group members *will* affect the hidden track.

To hide a track:

◆ Click a highlighted track name in the Tracks list (**Figure 5.35**).

The selected track's channel strip disappears from the Mix and Edit windows.

To show a track:

◆ Click a track name that is not highlighted in the Tracks list.

The selected track's channel strip reappears in the Mix and Edit windows.

Figure 5.33 The Tracks list.

Figure 5.34 The Tracks list pop-up menu.

Figure 5.35 Click a highlighted track name to hide a track.

VIEWING TRACKS

Figure 5.36 Select a track type from the Tracks list pop-up menu.

To hide all tracks:

1. Click the Tracks list pop-up menu at the top of the Tracks list.

2. Choose Hide All Tracks.

To show all tracks:

1. Click the Tracks list pop-up menu at the top of the Tracks list.

2. Choose Show All Tracks.

To show tracks by track type:

1. Click the Tracks list pop-up menu at the top of the Tracks list.

2. Choose Show Only.

3. Select a track type (**Figure 5.36**).

To show noncontiguous tracks:

◆ Command-click (Macintosh) or Control-click (Windows) the name of the unhighlighted tracks that you want to show in the Tracks list.

 The selected noncontiguous tracks become visible in the Mix and Edit windows.

To hide noncontiguous tracks

◆ Command-click (Macintosh) or Control-click (Windows) the name of the highlighted tracks that you want to hide in the Tracks list.

 The selected noncontiguous tracks disappear in the Mix and Edit windows.

To show a range of tracks

1. Click the name of the first track in the range of tracks you want to show in the Tracks list.

2. Shift-click the name of the last track in the Tracks list that you want to show.

 All tracks between the first selected track and the last selected track are displayed.

VIEWING TRACKS

Adjusting the track size

Pro Tools provides several ways to adjust track sizes. In both the Mix and Edit windows, you can expand channel strips to display the Inserts, Sends, Input/Output, and Track Comments views. The Mix window also lets you choose between narrow and wide channel strip views. The Edit window gives you a wide range of preset track height views, including mini, small, medium, large, jumbo, and extreme.

For more information on viewing tracks in the Mix and Edit windows, see *Chapter 3: The Mix and Edit Windows*.

To view the narrow Mix window:

◆ Select View > Narrow Mix. Or press Option-Command-M (Macintosh) or Alt-Control-M (Windows).

The Narrow Mix window appears (**Figure 5.37**).

To change the track height view in the Edit window:

1. Click the Track Height Selector button.

   The Track Height pop-up menu appears.

2. Select a track height.

   or

1. Click in the ruler at the far left of any track's playlist.

   The Track Height pop-up menu appears (**Figure 5.38**).

2. Select a track height.

   or

1. Place the edit cursor in the track.

2. Press Control–Up Arrow key (Macintosh) or Start–Up Arrow key (Windows) to increase the track height. Press Control–Down Arrow key (Macintosh) or Start–Down Arrow key (Windows) to decrease the track height.

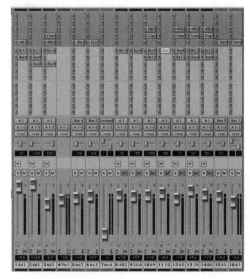

Figure 5.37 The Narrow Mix window.

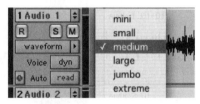

Figure 5.38 The Track Height pop-up menu.

Figure 5.39 The Zoom Toggle button beneath the Zoomer tool in the Edit window lets you switch back and forth between two customized views.

Zoom Toggling Views

The Zoom Toggle button lets you quickly switch between customized views in the Edit window (**Figure 5.39**). Zoom Toggle recalls the following viewing parameters: zoom level, track view, track height, and grid value.

To store a Zoom Toggle view:

1. Make an edit selection on one or more tracks in the Edit window.

2. Click the Zoom Toggle button beneath the Zoomer tool in the Edit window to enable zoom toggling.

   The Zoom Toggle button becomes blue, indicating that zoom toggle is enabled.

3. Select a Zoom Toggle view by selecting zoom level, track height, track view, and grid settings as desired.

4. Click the Zoom Toggle button to store your selected settings.

   The Zoom Toggle button becomes gray, indicating zoom toggle is not enabled.

To use Zoom Toggle:

1. Click the Zoom Toggle button or Press Control-E (Macintosh) or Start-E (Windows), or with Commands Focus enabled, press E.

   The selection is zoomed to the stored Zoom Toggle view.

2. Click the Zoom Toggle button again to return to the original Edit window view.

For more information on using zoom tools, adjusting track heights, and expanding channel strip views, see *Chapter 3: The Mix and Edit Windows* and *Chapter 10: Editing Basics*.

Using Continuous Zoom

Continuous zoom lets you zoom in and out on individual tracks or multiple tracks seamlessly. Continuous zoom makes it much easier to maintain your orientation as you search for appropriate edit locations.

Figure 5.40 The Zoomer tool in the Edit window.

To use continuous zoom on an individual track or a group of tracks:

1. Select the Zoomer tool (**Figure 5.40**).

2. Press and hold Control (Macintosh) or Start (Windows) and move the zoom tool as follows:

   ▲ Drag up to zoom in vertically.

   ▲ Drag down to zoom out vertically.

   ▲ Drag right to zoom in horizontally.

   ▲ Drag left to zoom out horizontally.

   By default, all tracks move together when zoomed horizontally. Tracks zoom in and out horizontally centered on the location where you click.

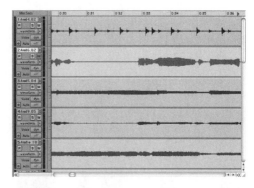

To zoom in and out vertically on all audio tracks with continuous zoom:

1. Select the Zoomer tool.

2. Press and hold Control-Shift (Macintosh) or Start-Shift (Windows) and drag the Zoomer tool up or down.

   All audio tracks zoom vertically in and out continuously (**Figure 5.41**).

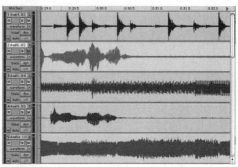

Figure 5.41 Continuous zoom lets you vertically zoom all tracks simultaneously.

For more information on using zoom tools, adjusting track heights, and expanding channel strip views, see *Chapter 3: The Mix and Edit Windows* and *Chapter 10: Editing Basics*.

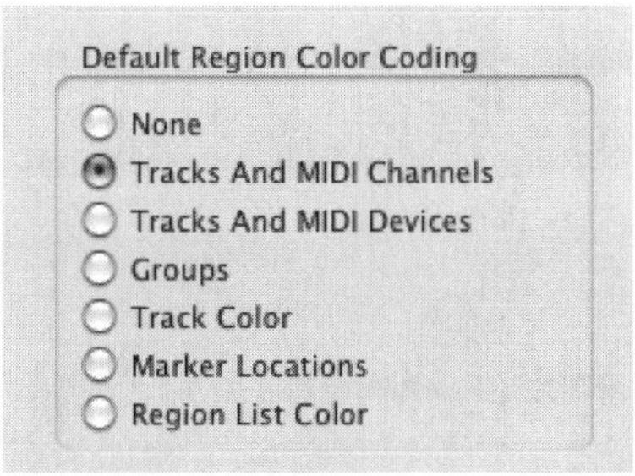

Default Region Color Coding

- ○ None
- ◉ Tracks And MIDI Channels
- ○ Tracks And MIDI Devices
- ○ Groups
- ○ Track Color
- ○ Marker Locations
- ○ Region List Color

Figure 5.42 The Edit Window Color Coding options in the Display Preferences window.

Color-coding Regions in Tracks

Color-coding is handy for differentiating regions in tracks in the Edit window. You can assign colors using the Region Color Coding options in the Display Preferences window (**Figure 5.42**). Select from these default color-coding options:

None: Turns off color assignments to regions.

Tracks and MIDI Channels: Assigns colors to regions according to the track number and MIDI channel assignment.

Tracks and MIDI Devices: Assigns colors to regions according to the track number and MIDI device type.

Groups: Assigns colors to regions according to the group ID of their tracks.

Track Color: Assigns colors to regions based on the track color assignment.

Marker Locations: Assigns a color to the marker location ruler between selected marker locations.

Region List Color: Assigns a color to each region in a track based on its color in the Region list.

COLOR-CODING REGIONS IN TRACKS

Using the Color Palette

The Color Palette lets you apply custom colors to tracks, regions, groups, and markers (**Figure 5.43**). The Color Palette includes the following options:

Figure 5.43 The Color palette.

◆ **Apply to Selected:** The Apply to Selected pop-up menu lets you select the item to which you will apply color. You can apply color to Tracks, Regions in Tracks, Regions in Region List, Markers, and Groups.

Figure 5.44 Click the Apply to Selected pop-up menu and select an item to add color.

◆ **Hold:** The Hold button lets you apply the same color to multiple items without reselecting it.

◆ **Default:** The Default button lets you reset a selected item to its default color settings.

◆ **None:** The None button removes all color from selected items. Waveform displays in the Edit window become black and white

To apply a color from the Color Palette:

1. Choose Window > Color Palette.
   The Color Palette appears.

2. Click the Apply to Selected pop-up menu and select the item you want to color-code (**Figure 5.44**).

3. Select a color from the palette.

For more information on color-coding tracks in Mix and Edit windows, see the *Pro Tools Reference Guide*.

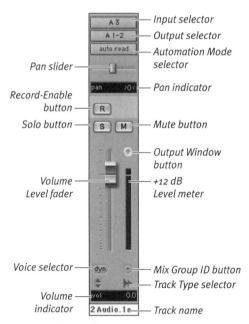

Input selector
Output selector
Automation Mode selector
Pan slider
Pan indicator
Record-Enable button
Solo button
Mute button
Output Window button
Volume Level fader
+12 dB Level meter
Voice selector
Mix Group ID button
Track Type selector
Volume indicator
Track name

Figure 5.45 The audio channel strip track controls.

Using Track Controls

Track controls on audio and MIDI channel strips let you control level, pan, mute, solo, record-enable, and automation (**Figure 5.45**). For more information on channel strips, see *Chapter 3: The Mix and Edit Windows*.

You can open an Output window (**Figure 5.46**) by clicking a channel strip's Output Window button (**Figure 5.47**). Output windows contain the same track controls as channel strips, but they are larger and can float independently over the Mix and Edit windows. This gives you quick access to track controls while you're mixing and editing. For more information on Output windows, see *Chapter 14: Mixing Basics*.

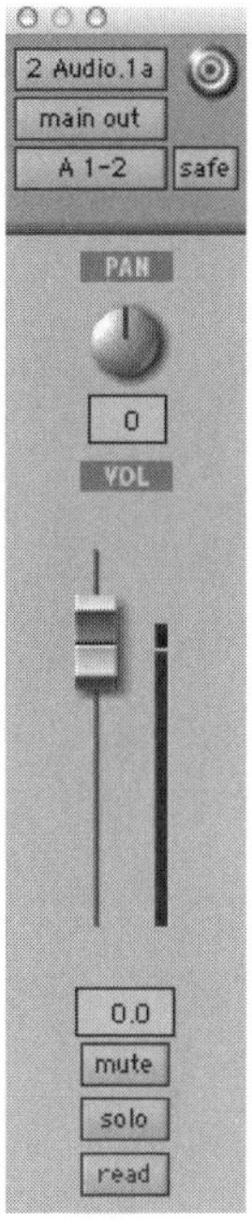

Output Window button

Figure 5.46 The audio channel strip Output window.

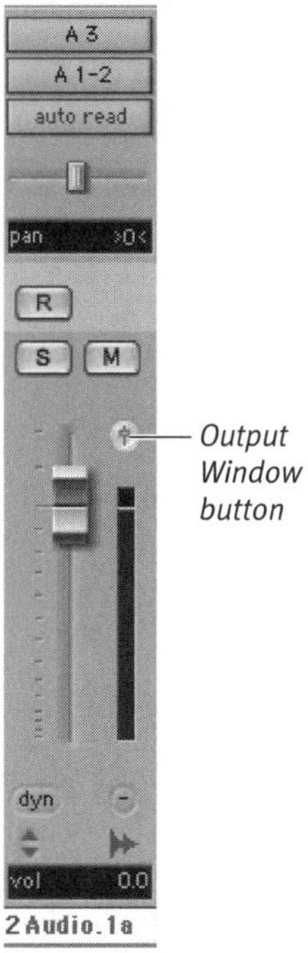

Figure 5.47 The Output Window button on the audio channel strip.

About +12 dB Volume Fader Gain in Pro Tools 7

In Pro Tools 7 all volume faders provide a maximum gain level of +12 dB (**Figure 5.48**). The +6 dB fader gain option available in earlier versions of Pro Tools has been removed from the New Session dialog box.

You can convert Pro Tools 7 sessions to earlier versions of Pro Tools containing the +6 dB fader gain option using the Save Copy In command.

Muting and soloing tracks

Mute and *Solo* turn tracks off and on. The Mute button silences a track. The Solo button mutes all tracks except the soloed track, so you can audition tracks separately during playback. You can mute and solo multiple tracks simultaneously.

To mute a track:

◆ Click the Mute button on a track (**Figure 5.49**).

The track is silenced.

To solo a track:

◆ Click the Solo button on the track.

The button is highlighted and all other tracks are muted (**Figure 5.50**).

When you solo more than one track, they're usually *latched,* which means each soloed track is added to the mix. But Pro Tools also lets you unlatch Solo buttons, so you can solo just one track at a time.

Figure 5.48 The +12 dB volume fader.

Figure 5.49 The Mute button.

Figure 5.50 The Solo button.

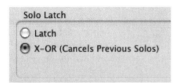

Figure 5.51 To unlatch Solo buttons: Select X-OR (Cancels Previous Solos) in the Solo Latch options of the Operations Preference window.

Figure 5.52 Sends A–E and Sends F–J.

To unlatch solo buttons:

1. Choose Setup > Preferences.

2. Click the Operation Window tab.

3. Select X-OR (Cancels Previous Solos) (**Figure 5.51**).

   When X-OR is enabled, pressing subsequent Solo buttons cancels previous solos.

4. Click Done.

For more information on mute, solo, volume level, pan, record-enable, automation, and other track controls, see *Chapter 3: The Mix and Edit Windows*.

About Sends in Pro Tools 7

Pro Tools 7 provides 10 sends per track, which are divided into two independently viewable groups: Sends A–E and Sends F–J (**Figure 5.52**).

Earlier versions of Pro Tools provide only five sends per track. When you convert a Pro Tools 7 session to an earlier version of Pro Tools, Sends F–J will be discarded, along with any automation data recorded for Sends F–J.

In addition, a Pro Tools HD 7 session opened on a Pro Tools 7 LE or M-Powered system will retain its first 32 busses per send; additional sends become inactive.

For more information on sends, see *Chapter 3: The Mix and Edit Windows* and *Chapter 14: Mixing Basics*.

Grouping Tracks

By grouping tracks, you can perform operations on multiple tracks simultaneously. For example, you can group tracks so that their faders move together and their relative volumes are maintained. Or, you can make edits across multiple tracks.

Pro Tools lets you create up to 26 groups. It also lets you create nested groups (subgroups within groups). Grouping affects the following track parameters:

* Track Timebase   * Send levels

* Volume levels   * Send mutes

* Solos   * Track view

* Mutes   * Track height

* Automation   * Editing functions
  modes

Grouping does not affect these parameters:

* Record-enable   * Output

* Panning   assignments

* Send panning   * Inserting
                          plug-ins

To create a group:

1. Shift-click the tracks that you want to include in the group (**Figure 5.53**).

2. Choose Track > Group or click the Group list pop-up menu and select New Group.

   The New Group dialog box appears (**Figure 5.54**).

3. Enter a name for the group and choose a Group ID (a letter from a to z) from the pop-up menu (**Figure 5.55**).

4. Choose a Group Type (Edit, Mix, or Edit and Mix).

5. Click OK.

   The new group is added to the Groups list.

Figure 5.53 Shift-click the track names to select the tracks you want in a group.

Figure 5.54 The New Group dialog box.

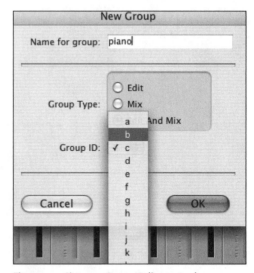

Figure 5.55 Choose a Group ID (from a to z).

GROUPING TRACKS

Figure 5.56 The Groups list.

Figure 5.57 A filled-in circle means all members of a group are currently selected.

Figure 5.58 A hollow circle means only some members of a group are currently selected.

Figure 5.59 A circle with a dot inside means all members of a group are currently selected, plus additional members outside of the group.

Figure 5.60 Enable a group by clicking its name in the Groups list.

Using the Groups list

The Groups list (**Figure 5.56**) lets you manage groups in a session. The list displays the name of each group, a group ID (a letter from a to z), and symbols that indicate the group's selection status in the Mix or Edit window. Here's what the symbols mean:

◆ A filled-in circle (**Figure 5.57**) indicates that all members of the group are currently selected.

◆ A hollow circle (**Figure 5.58**) indicates that only some members of the group are currently selected.

◆ A circle with a dot inside (**Figure 5.59**) indicates that all members of the group are currently selected, along with additional members outside of the group.

By default, every session has a group named All, which includes every track in the session. You cannot edit or delete the All group.

To enable a group:

◆ In the Groups list, click the name of the group that you want to enable. The group name is highlighted to indicate that it's enabled (**Figure 5.60**).

To disable a group:

◆ In the Groups list, click the name of the group that you want to disable.

To rename a group:

1. In the Groups list, double-click to the left of the group's name.
   The New Group dialog box appears.

2. Enter a new name for the group.

3. Click OK.
   The group is renamed in the Groups list.

GROUPING TRACKS

Using the Groups List pop-up menu

The Groups list pop-up menu lets you create new groups, display groups by type (Edit, Mix, or Edit and Mix), suspend groups, change group members, and delete groups.

To change the members of a group:

1. Shift-click the tracks that you want to keep in the group.

2. Choose New Group from the Group pop-up menu (**Figure 5.61**).

   The New Group dialog box appears.

3. In the New Group dialog box, select the group ID that you want to update.

4. Click OK.

   The new group definition overwrites the original one.

To delete a group:

1. In the Groups list, select the name of the group that you want to delete.

2. Choose Delete Selected Groups from the Group pop-up menu.

   Be careful: You can't undo this deletion.

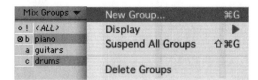

Figure 5.61 The Group pop-up menu.

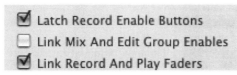

Figure 5.62 Deselect the Link Mix And Edit Group Enables check box.

— *Mix Group ID button*

Figure 5.63 The Mix Group ID button.

Figure 5.64 The Mix Group ID button shows the active Mix Group members.

Linking Mix and Edit groups

You can create three types of groups: Mix groups, Edit groups, and Mix and Edit groups. By default, a Mix and Edit Group's enable functions are linked. This means that when you enable a group in the Mix window, it's also enabled in the Edit window.

But you may not always want Mix and Edit Groups linked. For example, you may want to keep tracks grouped in the Mix window to maintain relative fader levels, but ungroup them in the Edit window so you can edit a single track. For this reason, Pro Tools lets you unlink groups.

To unlink Mix and Edit groups:

1. Choose Setup > Preferences.

2. Click the Operation tab.

3. Deselect the Link Mix And Edit Group Enables check box (**Figure 5.62**).

4. Click Done.

✔ Tip

■ Click a channel strip's Mix Group ID button (**Figure 5.63**) to view the active mix groups (**Figure 5.64**).

GROUPING TRACKS

About Track Priority and Voice Assignments

Although Pro Tools LE hardware systems are limited to a maximum of 32 simultaneous playback voices (depending on the system), a Pro Tools session can contain additional audio tracks beyond this fixed playback number. When a session contains more tracks than playback voices, Pro Tools assigns a playback priority for tracks according to their order in the Mix window, Edit window, or Track list.

Pro Tools 7 LE dynamically assigns voices to tracks (unlike HD systems, which let you assign specific voices to tracks). Pro Tools LE systems do, however, let you turn a track's voice selection off (**Figure 5.65**). This is useful if you wish to free up voices for use with other tracks.

For more information on track priority and voice assignments, see the *Pro Tools Reference Guide*.

To increase a track's playback priority:

◆ In the Edit window, drag the Track Name button to a higher position. Tracks in a higher position in the Edit window have higher playback priority than tracks in a lower position.

 or

◆ In the Mix window, drag the Track Name button to the left. Tracks to the left of the Mix window have higher playback priority than tracks to the right.

 or

◆ In the Track list, drag the track to a higher position. Tracks in a higher position on the list have higher playback priority than tracks in lower positions.

Figure 5.65 To turn off dynamic voice assignment, click the Voice selector.

Figure 5.66 Command-Control-click (Macintosh) or Control-Start-click (Windows) the Track Type Indicator to make a track inactive.

Making Tracks Inactive

Pro Tools lets you make Audio, Auxiliary Input, and Master Fader tracks inactive. Making a track inactive deactivates all plug-ins, sends, voices, and automation; consequently, the track uses no CPU power. If you're running low on processing power, making unused tracks inactive can help improve system performance.

To make a track inactive:

◆ Command-Control-click (Macintosh) or Control-Start-click (Windows) the Track Type Indicator in the Mix Window (**Figure 5.66**).

The track becomes inactive and appears grayed out.

GETTING READY TO RECORD

6

The instruments are plugged in, the microphones are turned on, and you're ready to record. Well, almost. There are just a few more critical steps to take before you press the Record button. This chapter will take you through them.

We'll start with a look at Pro Tools' record modes: Non-destructive, Destructive, Loop, and QuickPunch. You'll learn how to record-enable tracks, and how to set proper audio input and output levels.

Then we'll discuss how to monitor audio in Pro Tools. We'll cover monitor modes and show you some useful workarounds for minimizing monitoring latency.

We'll finish with a look at Pro Tools' features for allocating hard drives and generating a click track for your session.

Setting Record Modes

Pro Tools LE has four record modes; each provides a different method of recording audio to hard disk.

Non-destructive Record: This is the default record mode. When you record on a track with existing audio regions, the regions are protected and both old and new audio files remain on your hard drive. The files are available as regions from the Regions list.

In Non-destructive Record mode, you can select a record range within a track's playlist, or you can input a start and stop time in the Transport window.

Destructive Record: In this mode, recording over existing regions permanently replaces the original audio. Although this mode can help you save hard disk space, it's generally best to use Non-destructive Record mode, because it helps prevent you from accidentally erasing your recordings.

Loop Record: This mode lets you record multiple takes while the same section of audio repeats. It's helpful when you want to quickly record multiple takes of a part without losing spontaneity. Loop Record mode is non-destructive. For more information on Loop Recording, see *Chapter 7: Recording and Playing Back Audio.*

QuickPunch: This mode lets you punch in (initiate recording) and punch out (stop recording) on a record-enabled audio track at any time during playback. See *Chapter 7: Recording and Playing Back Audio.*

Figure 6.1 Choose a different record mode from the Options menu.

Figure 6.2 The Record button displays the current record mode: a blank circle for Non-destructive...

Figure 6.3 D for Destructive...

Figure 6.4 A loop symbol for Loop Record...

Figure 6.5 ...and P for QuickPunch mode.

Figure 6.6 The Link Selections button in the Edit window.

To set a record mode:

◆ Pro Tools is automatically set to Non-destructive Record mode. To enable Destructive Record, Loop Record, or QuickPunch mode, select the desired mode from the Options menu (**Figure 6.1**).

  or

◆ Control-click (Macintosh) or right-click (Windows) the Record button in the Transport window to cycle among the four modes. The Record button displays a blank circle for Non-destructive, D for Destructive, a loop symbol for Loop Record, and P for QuickPunch mode (**Figures 6.2** through **6.5**).

✔ Tip

■ If you want to set a record range by selecting within a track's playlist, you must first link the Edit and Timeline selections. To do this, click the Link Selections button in the Edit window (**Figure 6.6**). For more information on linking Edit and Timeline selections, see *Chapter 12: Working with Regions.*

Record-Enabling Tracks

Before you can record an audio or MIDI track, you must first *record-enable* it. This opens the track to audio or MIDI input. You can record-enable individual tracks or multiple tracks simultaneously. When you have record-enabled a track, you can then set appropriate audio input level and start recording.

To record-enable an audio or MIDI track:

◆ In either the Mix or Edit window, click the track's Record-Enable button (**Figure 6.7**).

To record-enable all audio or MIDI tracks:

◆ Option-click (Macintosh) or Alt-click (Windows) the Record-Enable button on any audio or MIDI track.

To record-enable all selected tracks:

◆ Shift-Option-click (Macintosh) or Shift-Alt-click (Windows) the Record-Enable button on any selected track.

✔ Tips

■ To select multiple tracks, Command-click (Macintosh) or Control-click (Windows) their track names.

■ Record-enabling a track that belongs to a group does not record-enable other tracks in the group. To record-enable all tracks in a group, click to the left of the group name in the Groups list. This selects the group. Then Shift-Option-click (Macintosh) or Shift-Alt-click (Windows) the Record-Enable button on a selected track.

Figure 6.7 Click a track's Record-Enable button to prepare for recording.

Figure 6.8 The Latch Record-Enable Buttons check box in the Operation Preferences window.

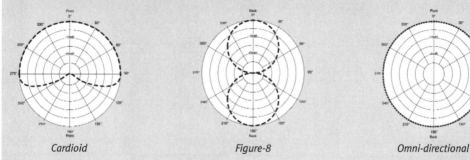

Figure 6.9 To put a track in Record Safe mode, Command-click (Macintosh) or Control-click (Windows) the track's Record-Enable button.

- If the Latch Record-Enable Buttons check box (**Figure 6.8**) in the Operation Preferences window is selected, you can record-enable multiple tracks simultaneously.

- If you want to record-enable only one track at a time, clear the Latch Record-Enable Buttons check box. Record-enabling a subsequent track will take a previously record-enabled track out of Record-Enable mode.

- Record Safe mode deactivates a track's Record-enable button. The Record-enable button must be on for recording to occur on a track. Thus, Record-Safe mode prevents any recoding on that track. To put a track in Record Safe mode, Command-click (Macintosh) or Control-click (Windows) a track's Record-Enable button (**Figure 6.9**). To put all tracks in Record Safe mode, Command-Option-click (Macintosh) or Control-Alt-click (Windows) the Record-Enable button on any track.

RECORD-ENABLING TRACKS

Microphone Polarity Patterns

A microphone's polarity pattern refers to the directions from which it picks up sound. The most common polarity patterns are as follows (**Figure 6.10**):

Cardioid (or directional): Cardioid mics pick up sound only from in front of them.

Figure-8 (or bi-directional): Figure-8 mics pick up sound from both the front and back.

Omni-directional: Omni-directional mics capture sounds from all directions.

Cardioid *Figure-8* *Omni-directional*

Figure 6.10 The three most common microphone polarity patterns are cardioid, figure-8, and omni-directional.

Microphone Types

Microphones have different sound properties and applications, depending on how they're constructed. The most common microphone types include:

Dynamic microphones: Dynamic mics (such as the Shure SM57 and SM58) can handle lots of volume, which makes them perfect for close-miking drums, amplifiers, and loud vocalists. They are also durable enough to survive most live settings. Dynamic mics tend to accentuate mid-range and can sometimes make tracks sound boxy. Still, they have many applications both live and in the studio. They are also the least expensive type of microphone.

Condenser microphones: Condenser mics are more sensitive and accurate than dynamic mics, and as a result, are used frequently in recording studios. Condenser mics come with either large or small diaphragms. Large diaphragm mics tend to pick up more low end frequencies and have less self-noise. Small diaphragm condensers generally have an even frequency response and are particularly good at capturing higher-end sound, such as violin.

A condenser mic requires a small amount of voltage to function (between 9 and 48 volts). Thus, you'll need to plug it into a mixer or preamp with *phantom power*—a low-level electric current sent from the mic preamp to the condenser mic. Condenser mics come with either tube or solid-state electronics. Tube condensers tend to sound warmer, whereas solid-state condensers tend to be more transparent (they have less sound coloration). Condenser mics cost more than dynamic mics, but you can find some good models at reasonable prices.

Ribbon microphones: Ribbon mics are expensive and fragile, but they can produce a unique silky tone—the result of a slight roll-off that tends to occur in the high end. Ribbon mics were popular from the 1930s to the 1960s, but were pretty much replaced in the studio by condenser mics. In recent years, however, many musicians and producers have returned to them to capture their vintage tone.

Microphone Placement Techniques

Microphone placement has a major influence on the sound of a recording. The mic's location in the room, its distance from the source, and the room's size, shape, and reflectivity all affect the sound going to disk. Before placing mics, consider the sound you want. For instance, do you want to capture the pure instrument sound alone, or do you want to capture a blend of instrument and room sound? Experiment with the following microphone placement techniques until you find a sound you like. You may be surprised to discover a sound you didn't know was there.

Close (or spot) miking: Close miking involves placing the mic anywhere from two inches to two feet away from the audio source. This technique is useful for picking up the pure sound of an audio source with little or no room sound. But keep your ears open and check your levels—you don't want the mic too close to the source. If you're getting too many transient peaks (or clipping), pull the mic back and turn it a bit off-axis.

Distant miking: Distant miking involves placing the mic anywhere from two to five feet from an audio source. This technique lets you capture a blend of the source audio and the room sound. Distant miking is often used along with close miking to add varying amounts of depth to the raw sound.

Ambient (or room) miking: In ambient miking, the mic is placed far enough away from the audio source that it picks up more of the room's reflected sound than the instrument's direct sound. You can place the mic either close to the source but in the opposite direction or across the room. Ambient miking is useful if you want to add spaciousness or a unique room sound to a track.

Stereo miking: Stereo miking involves using two mics to capture a stereo image of an audio source. The most common stereo miking approaches are:

- **X-Y (coincident) pairs:** X-Y pair miking involves placing two mics at right angles (along the x and y axes), with the diaphragms of each mic as close together as possible without touching.

- **Blumlein technique:** The Blumlein technique uses two figure-8 pattern microphones positioned at right angles, with their diaphragms as close together as possible. The two mics are mounted on separate stands, one above the other. Because figure-8 pattern mics pick up sound from both front and back, the Blumlein technique can help capture more realistic stereo images.

- **Spaced pairs:** Spaced pair miking involves placing mics at a distance from the source and a distance from each other. This technique is useful for recording band setups or any larger group of players. If not spaced properly, spaced pairs can have phase problems. To avoid this, use the 3:1 rule: Place mics three times farther apart than they are from the sound source.

- **Stereo microphones:** Stereo microphones include two separate diaphragms in one mic. They also have two channels outputs, which let you record each channel to its own track. Stereo mics are a good alternative if you don't want to worry about potential phasing problems.

Setting Audio Input Levels

The mic pre-amps built into the Digi 002 and Digi 002 Rack (Mic/Line 1–4), Mbox 2 and Mbox (Mic/Line 1–2) interfaces have gain knobs, which let you boost and cut audio input levels.

Digi 002 has 4 additional line-level inputs (analog inputs 5–8). These inputs cannot be adjusted inside Pro Tools. To get proper input levels for these inputs you need to adjust the level output at the audio source.

Set audio input levels to the loudest volume possible without *clipping* the signal. Ideally, a signal should top out in the yellow zone of a track's level meter. An audio signal that enters the red zone is too loud and should be reduced to prevent clipping and digital distortion.

At the same time, make sure the signal isn't too soft. If you have to boost it later, you may add unwanted noise to your track. For more information on clipping and distortion, see the *What is Clipping?* sidebar on this page.

To adjust the input level on the Digi 002 or Digi 002 Rack (Mic/Line inputs 1–4):

1. Connect an instrument or microphone to the input. (Apply phantom power to the mic by pressing the 48V switch on the Digi 002's back panel, if required.)

2. Create an audio track by choosing Track > New, or press Shift-Command-N (Macintosh) or Shift-Control-N (Windows).

3. Assign a track input (Mic/Line 1–4) using the Input selector.

What Is Clipping?

Clipping is digital distortion that occurs when you record a signal at levels that overload your system's inputs. When a signal clips, it distorts, and the peaks of its waveform are literally clipped off.

Unlike the snarling but warm overtones of analog distortion produced by certain pieces of vintage gear such as tube amps and electric guitars, digital distortion sounds like a high-pitched buzzer—it has artistic applications, but it's bothersome to most people's ears.

Ideally, input levels should be as high as possible in the yellow zone of the level meter—without clipping the red. But don't trash an irreplaceable take because of a few errant spikes. Pro Tools offers some headroom between the level at which the meter indicates clipping and the level at which clipping actually occurs. The bottom line: Always listen to your takes carefully and trust your ears.

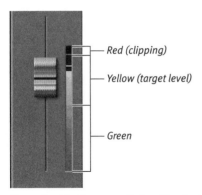

Red (clipping)

Yellow (target level)

Green

Figure 6.11 Ideally, your audio input levels should be in the yellow zone of the level meter.

4. Click the track's Record-Enable button.

Play the instrument or audio source at the same volume you'll play it at when you record.

5. Adjust the input gain for the channel using the gain knob on the Digi 002's front panel.

To adjust the input level on the Mbox 2 or Mbox (Mic/Line inputs 1–2):

1. Connect an instrument or microphone to the input. (Apply 48V phantom power to the mic, if required.)

2. Create an audio track by choosing Track > New.

3. Assign a track input (Mic/Line 1 or 2) using the Input selector.

4. Click the track's Record-Enable button.

Play the instrument or audio source at the same volume you'll play it at when you record.

5. Adjust the input gain for the channel using the gain knob on the front of the Mbox 2 or Mbox.

Increase or decrease the gain until you achieve the highest possible signal level without clipping (**Figure 6.11**). Ideally, the levels should top out in the yellow zone of the track's level meter.

For information on connecting external audio devices to your Pro Tools LE system, see *Appendix A: Connecting Your Studio.*

SETTING AUDIO INPUT LEVELS

Monitoring Audio

Pro Tools offers two modes for monitoring audio input while recording.

Auto Input Monitoring: This mode lets you monitor the playback of an existing track until a punch-in point is reached. At the punch-in point, the track is automatically record-enabled and monitoring switches to the audio input signal. When the punch-out point is reached, monitoring switches back to playback of the existing track. When this mode is enabled, the Record button in the Transport window is gray.

Input Only Monitoring: This mode monitors only the audio input of record-enabled tracks. When this mode is enabled, the Record button in the Transport window is green.

To enable Auto Input Monitoring:

◆ Choose Track > Auto Input Monitoring (**Figure 6.12**).

To enable Input Only Monitoring:

◆ Choose Track > Input Only Monitoring.

Linking Record and Playback faders

Pro Tools remembers both Record and Playback fader levels for each audio track, so you can set different fader levels for each function. Linking the faders in the Preferences window keeps them from unexpectedly changing positions when you record-enable a track.

To link Record and Playback faders:

1. Choose Setup > Preferences.

2. Click the Operation tab.

3. Select the Link Record And Play Faders check box (**Figure 6.13**).

Figure 6.12 To enable Auto Input Monitoring, choose Track > Auto Input Monitoring.

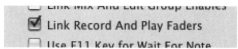

Figure 6.13 The Link Record And Play Faders check box in the Operation Preferences window.

✔ Tip

■ To toggle between Auto Input Monitoring mode and Input Only Monitoring mode, press Option-K (Macintosh) or Alt-K (Windows).

MONITORING AUDIO

Monitoring at Safe Levels

Hearing is priceless, and hearing loss is epidemic. Long-term exposure to loud sound can cause hearing loss and tinnitus (permanent ringing in the ears). So don't abuse your ears by sitting in front of cranked speakers for hours or by falling asleep with your headphones blasting. Keep the monitors in check and take lots of breaks in the studio.

You don't need to crank the monitors to hear a mix accurately. In fact, the more you crank them, the more distorted the sound becomes—and the quicker your ears fatigue. Although it *is* important to listen at a level loud enough to hear all the elements in the mix, it's just as important to evaluate your mixes at low levels. As the volume drops, key elements may begin to fade or become too loud.

The ideal level to monitor audio is around 80 dB. Anything over 85 dB is considered hazardous, and earplugs—not cheap drugstore models, but custom-molded *musician's earplugs*—are strongly recommended. (See **Table 6.1** for a list of common sounds and their decibel levels.)

Sounds May Damage Your Hearing If:

◆ The noise hurts your ears.

◆ It makes your ears ring.

◆ You're slightly deaf for several hours after being exposed to the noise.

◆ You have to shout over background noise to make yourself heard.

Did You Know?

◆ The longer you're exposed to a loud noise, the more damaging it may be.

◆ The closer you are to the source of intense noise, the more damaging it is.

◆ Stuffing cotton balls or wads of tissue paper into your ears is not adequate protection; it reduces noise by a mere 7 dB.

◆ Properly fitted musician's earplugs or ear muffs reduce noise by 15 to 30 dB.

Source: American Tinnitus Association

MONITORING AUDIO

Minimizing Monitoring Latency

The lag time between audio entering and leaving your recording system is known as *latency*. Pro Tools LE systems are susceptible to latency because of the heavy processing load placed on the host computer's CPU.

You may experience latency during recording as a delay between when an audio signal is recorded and when it's heard back in the monitors. Latency is, of course, disconcerting to performers, causing time problems, and in rare cases, insanity. Either way, it can mess up your session.

Fortunately, Pro Tools provides effective workarounds for latency. There's a direct relationship between latency time and the Pro Tools LE hardware buffer size: The larger the buffer size, the larger the latency (**Table 6.2**). While you may want a larger buffer size to handle extra tracks or additional plug-ins, if you want to minimize latency, you'll need to set a smaller buffer size.

Table 6.1

Decibel Levels of Common Sounds	
DECIBELS (DB)	**FAINT**
20	Ticking watch
30	Whisper, dripping faucet
40	Refrigerator
DECIBELS (DB)	**MODERATE**
0	Rainfall
60	Conversation
65	Washing machine
70	Restaurant
DECIBELS (DB)	**VERY LOUD**
80	Alarm clock
85	Busy street
90	Subway
105	Chain saw
110	Dance club
DECIBELS (DB)	**EXTREMELY LOUD**
120	Band practice, thunderclap
130	Jackhammer, rock concert
DECIBELS (DB)	**PAINFUL**
140	Gunshot, firecracker
150	Jet take-off

Source: American Tinnitus Association

Table 6.2

Hardware Buffer Size and Monitor Latency	
BUFFER SIZE	**LATENCY (MS) AT 44.1/48KHZ (SAMPLE RATE) (SAMPLES)**
128	-2.9/2.7 (use for recording drums and other time-critical instruments)
256	-5.8/5.3 (use for recording vocals and instruments with slower attacks)
512	11.6/10.7 (use when mixing with 24 tracks)
1024	-23.2/21.3 (use for final mix-down or with many plug-ins)

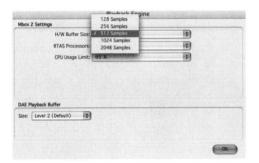

Figure 6.14 Set the hardware buffer size in the Playback Engine dialog box.

To set the hardware buffer size:

1. Choose Setup > Playback Engine.

2. Choose the number of samples for the hardware buffer from the Hardware Buffer Size pop-up menu (**Figure 6.14**).

3. Click OK.

Using low latency monitoring (Digi 002 and Digi 002 Rack only)

Reducing the hardware buffer size will minimize latency, but it won't eliminate it. For this reason, Digi 002 and Digi 002 Rack systems provide a low latency monitoring option. This lets you monitor audio at a latency of only 3.0 milliseconds, which is the time it takes for a signal to pass through your system's D/A (digital to analog) and A/D (analog to digital) converters.

When using low latency monitoring, the following limitations apply:

◆ You can record only on a track with inputs set to an audio interface (not a bus).

◆ You can monitor only tracks assigned to outputs 1–2.

◆ All plug-ins and sends assigned to record-enabled tracks (routed to outputs 1–2) are automatically bypassed.

◆ Record-enabled tracks will not register on master fader level meters.

◆ When using the Bounce To Disk command, only audio tracks are included— auxiliary inputs are ignored.

MINIMIZING MONITORING LATENCY

To use low latency monitoring:

1. Record-enable the audio track (or auxiliary input).

2. Assign each track to either output 1 or 2 using the Output selector.

3. Select Options > Low Latency Monitoring.

For more information on Low Latency Monitoring, see the *Pro Tools Reference Guide*.

About Zero Latency Monitoring (Mbox 2 and Mbox)

Mbox 2 and Mbox hardware interfaces include a Mix knob that lets you monitor your audio input signal without latency. The Mix knob lets you blend the analog audio input signal with the audio output signal leaving Pro Tools.

For more information on zero-latency monitoring see the *Getting Started with Mbox 2 or Mbox* Guide provided with your system.

MINIMIZING MONITORING LATENCY

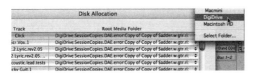

Figure 6.15 Assign a hard drive to each track by clicking the Root Media Folder column in the Disk Allocation dialog box.

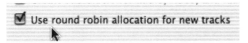

Figure 6.16 Select the Round Robin allocation check box to automatically distribute audio to multiple hard drives.

Allocating Hard Drives

To enhance system performance, Pro Tools lets you record audio tracks simultaneously to different hard drives. You can automatically distribute audio to drives using the Round Robin feature in the Disk Allocation dialog box.

To allocate audio hard drives:

1. Choose Setup > Disk Allocation.

2. In the Disk Allocation dialog box, assign a hard drive for each track by clicking in the Root Media Folder column and selecting a volume in the Disk Allocation pop-up menu (**Figure 6.15**).

   A new Session folder is created on each hard drive.

3. To automatically distribute new audio tracks among system hard drives, select the Use Round Robin Allocation for New Tracks check box (**Figure 6.16**).

4. To save new audio files to an existing folder (without creating another new Session folder), select the Custom Allocation Options check box, click the Change button, and choose the folder.

   To create subfolders in this folder, select the Create Subfolders for Audio, Video, and Fade Files check box.

5. Click OK.

ALLOCATING HARD DRIVES

✔ Tips

■ If you run out of space on an external hard drive, you can allocate recording to the system drive. Although Digidesign doesn't generally recommend doing this, it can be a lifesaver in an emergency. To allocate recording to the system drive, select the Round Robin Allocation option in the Disk Allocation dialog box and click OK. Next, open the Workspace browser and set the Volume Designator for your system volume to Record (**Figure 6.17**). This lets you record and play back audio from the volume.

■ For more information on Workspace volume designation, see *Chapter 9: Managing Audio Files with DigiBase* or the *Pro Tools Reference Guide*.

Figure 6.17 In the Workspace browser, set the Volume designator to Record if you want to record audio to your system volume.

Figure 6.18 Use the Open Ended Record Allocation option to limit a disk's audio recording.

Allocating Hard Drive Space

You can also allocate the amount of hard drive space used for recording on individual drives. By managing a drive's recording space, you can prevent it from slowing down as it fills up with audio files.

To allocate a portion of your hard drive for recording:

1. Choose Setup > Preferences.

2. Click the Operation tab.

3. In the Open Ended Record Allocation section, select the Limit To check box and enter a number of minutes to allocate (**Figure 6.18**).

4. Click Done.

ALLOCATING HARD DRIVE SPACE

Recording Audio with the Click Plug-in

No matter how musically proficient you are, recording to a *click track* is a good idea. A click track provides an absolute time reference, which can help you produce takes with a steadier feel. It can also help you keep your tracks properly aligned later on when you're overdubbing, editing, and mixing.

Pro Tools provides a MIDI-based Click plug-in (**Figure 6.19**), which generates an audio click track during a session. You can set the Click plug-in to a tempo and meter of your choice. Because the Click plug-in receives its tempo and meter data from the current session, if your session contains tempo and meter changes, the click will follow those changes accordingly. The Click plug-in lets you choose from several different preset click sounds.

To use the Click plug-in:

1. In the MIDI controls panel of the Transport Window, click the Metronome Click button to enable the Click option (**Figure 6.20**).

2. Create a mono auxiliary input and insert the click plug-in.

3. From the Click plug-in settings pop-up menu, select a click sound preset (**Figure 6.21**).

4. Choose Setup > Click.

   or

   Double-click the Metronome Click button or Countoff button in the Transport window (**Figure 6.22**).

   The Click/Countoff Options dialog box appears (**Figure 6.23**).

5. Select Click and Countoff options as desired.

Figure 6.19 The Click plug-in window.

Figure 6.20 In the MIDI controls panel of the Transport Window, click the Metronome Click button.

Figure 6.21 From the Click plug-in settings pop-up menu, select a click sound preset.

Figure 6.22 Double-click the Countoff button to open the Click/Countoff Options dialog box.

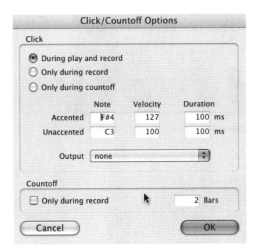

Figure 6.23 The Click/Countoff Options dialog box.

Figure 6.24 Tempo and Meter rulers in the Edit window.

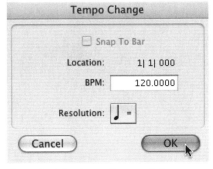

Figure 6.25 Double-click the Song Start Marker in the Edit window.

Figure 6.26 The Tempo Change window.

6. Begin Playback. A click is generated according to the Click/Countoff option settings and the current tempo and meter of the session.

Setting Click tempo and meter

The click plug-in follows the tempo and meter information displayed in the Tempo and Meter rulers at the top of the Edit window (**Figure 6.24**). When you open a new session, the Click plug-in automatically defaults to a tempo of 120 beats per minute (BPM) and a meter of 4/4 (4 beats per measure). You can, however, set the default click tempo and meter of your session as desired.

To set the default tempo:

1. Click the Tempo Ruler Enable button (Conductor) in the Transport window.

2. Double-click the Song Start Marker in the Edit window (**Figure 6.25**).

   The Tempo Change window appears (**Figure 6.26**).

3. Enter the desired BPM for the session.

4. Set Location to 1|1|000. This replaces the current default tempo with the new default tempo.

5. Set Resolution to the note value you want the tempo based on. The default note value is quarter note.

6. Click Apply to set the new tempo.

Using Manual Tempo Mode

In Manual Tempo mode, Pro Tools ignores events in the Tempo Track ruler and instead plays back at the tempo displayed in the Transport window. You can set the manual tempo with the tempo slider or by tapping in the tempo on the keyboard.

To set Manual Tempo mode:

1. Click the Tempo Enable button
   (Conductor) in the Transport window
   to disable the Tempo Ruler.

   The Tempo Enable button becomes
   unhighlighted and Manual Tempo
   mode is enabled.

2. Drag the tempo slider to set a manual
   tempo in the tempo field (**Figure 6.27**).

   or

   Click in the Tempo field until it is highlighted and press or tap "T" on your keyboard repeatedly for the tempo desired.

   Pro Tools calculates the tempo from the
   last eight taps (or fewer).

To set the default meter:

1. Double-click the Current Meter button
   in the Transport window (**Figure 6.28**).

   The Meter Change window appears
   (**Figure 6.29**).

2. Enter the desired meter for the session.

3. Set the Location to 1|1|000. This replaces
   the current default meter with the new
   default meter.

4. Set the Click note value to the desired
   number of clicks per measure. The
   default note value is quarter note.

5. Click Apply to set the new meter.

For additional information on tempo and
meter see *Using Rulers, Chapter 10: Editing
Basics*. For information on generating a click
track from a MIDI device, see *Chapter 18:
Recording MIDI*.

Figure 6.27 Set the manual tempo with
the tempo slider or with the Tap button.

Figure 6.28 Double-click the
Current Meter button in the
Transport window.

Figure 6.29 The Meter Change window.

RECORDING AND PLAYING BACK AUDIO

7

Now that you've configured a session and set audio input levels, it's time to lay down some tracks.

This chapter shows you the basics of recording and playing back audio in Pro Tools. We'll begin by discussing the Transport window—the control center for all recording and playback operations. You'll learn how to use various transport controls and features for punching, looping, and navigating tracks.

In addition, we'll show you how to record a single audio track, as well as how to record multiple audio tracks simultaneously. Then, we'll talk about overdubbing tracks using automated punch recording, loop recording, recording to playlists, and recording on the fly with QuickPunch.

Finally, we'll cover Pro Tools' playback features such as playback scrolling, loop playback, and scrubbing tracks to locate punches.

The Transport Window

Although the Transport window (**Figure 7.1**) features many of the basic controls you'll find on a CD player or tape deck, it also provides some advanced tools for punching, looping, and synching tracks.

The Transport window contains the following buttons:

Online: This button lets Pro Tools receive an external time code source for synchronization. Clicking the button puts Pro Tools online.

Return to Zero: This button locates to the session start point. Alternatively, you can press Return (Macintosh) or Enter (Windows).

Rewind: This button rewinds from the current play location.

Stop: This button stops playback or recording. Alternatively, you can press the spacebar.

Play: This button begins playback. If you're in *Record-Ready mode*, however, it begins recording from the timeline insertion point. (See tip later in this section.) Pressing the spacebar also works. For half-speed playback, press Shift-spacebar.

Fast Forward: This button fast-forwards from the timeline insertion point.

Go to End: This button locates to the end of the session. You can also press Option-Return (Macintosh) or Control-Enter (Windows).

Record: This button, which flashes when pressed, puts Pro Tools in Record-Ready mode. You can also press F12, Command-spacebar (Macintosh), or Control-spacebar (Windows).

Pre-Roll: This button specifies the amount of track that plays before a punch-in point. Click the button to enable pre-roll, and then enter a pre-roll value in the adjacent field.

Post-Roll: This button specifies the amount of track that plays after a punch-out point. Click the button to enable post-roll, and then enter a post-roll value in the adjacent field.

Transport Master: The Transport Master lets you drive (or *slave*) devices from the Pro Tools transport controls. Conversely, you can set Pro Tools to slave from the transport controls Transport Master. For more information on slaving devices to Pro Tools, see the *Pro Tools Reference Guide*.

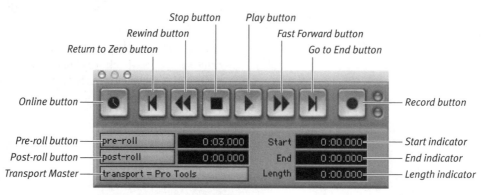

Figure 7.1 The Transport window.

The Transport window also contains these indicators:

Start: The Start indicator displays the start time of a record or play range. Enter a value in the field to set the start time.

End: The End indicator specifies the end point of a record or play range. Enter a value in the field to set the end time.

Length: The Length indicator displays the length of a record or play range. Enter a value in the field to set a new length.

✔ Tips

- You can play tracks at different speeds and in different directions by setting your keyboard's numeric keypad to Transport mode. To do this, choose Setup > Preferences. Click the Operation tab, and then select Transport from the Numeric Keypad options.

- To change the track playback speed, select a maximum of two tracks. Then press Control (Macintosh) or Start (Windows) and a number key (0–9). The higher the number, the faster the playback speed.

- To change the playback direction, press either the Plus key to go forward or the Minus key to go backward. For more information on Numeric Keypad modes, see the *Pro Tools Reference Guide*.

- Record-Ready mode is not to be confused with the Record-Enable button. The former is a built-in safety mode, common to most recording devices, that protects your tracks from inadvertent erasures. The latter is a channel strip track control that opens a track to audio signal input.

THE TRANSPORT WINDOW

Viewing the Transport window

You can expand or contract the Transport window as needed. If you're tight on screen space, you can condense it to a simple control strip (**Figure 7.2**).

To open the Transport window:

◆ Choose Window > Transport.

You can expand the Transport window to include the following views (**Figure 7.3**):

Counters: The Counters view includes the same Location indicator found in the Edit window. It displays the current play position in both Main and Sub Time Scales.

Expanded: The Expanded view includes pre- and post-roll buttons, and start, end, length, and transport master indicators.

MIDI Controls: The MIDI Controls view includes Wait for Note, Click, Countoff, MIDI Merge, Tempo, Meter, and Conductor. For information on using Pro Tools' MIDI-based click track feature, see *Chapter 6: Getting Ready to Record.* For more information on MIDI Transport controls, see *Chapter 18: Recording MIDI.*

To see the Transport window's Expanded view:

◆ Choose View > Transport > Expanded (**Figure 7.4**).

To see the Transport window's Counters view:

◆ Choose View > Transport > Counters.

To see the Transport window's MIDI Controls view:

◆ Choose View > Transport > MIDI Controls.

Figure 7.2 Condensed view of the Transport window.

Transport control strip

Expanded view   Counters view   MIDI view

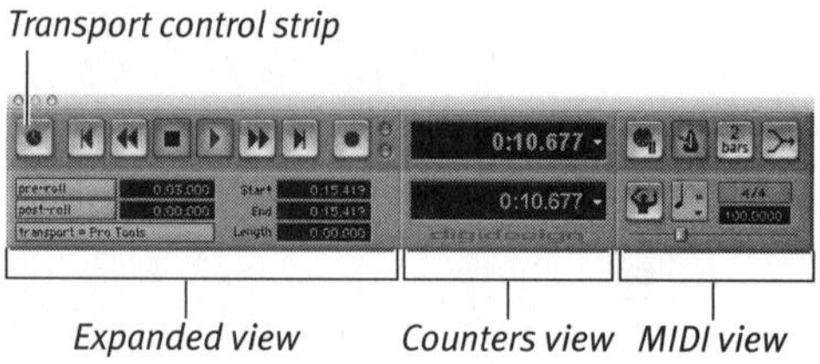

Figure 7.3 Expanded view of the Transport window.

Figure 7.4 Choose View > Transport > Expanded to view the Expanded Transport window.

THE TRANSPORT WINDOW

Figure 7.5 Click the Return to Zero button in the Transport window to return to the start of a track.

Figure 7.6 Click the Record button to put Pro Tools in Record-Ready mode.

Recording Audio Tracks

When you record audio into Pro Tools, it's saved on your hard disk as an audio file. Audio files are stored in the Audio Files folder inside the Session folder. In Pro Tools' default Non-destructive Record mode, audio files are protected from being accidentally overwritten or erased. For more information on audio files, see *Chapter 2: Software Basics* and *Chapter 8: File Management Basics.*

Pro Tools lets you record both mono and stereo audio tracks.

To record an audio track:

1. Choose Track > New.

2. Create a new mono or stereo audio track. (For instructions on creating new audio tracks, see *Chapter 5: Working with Tracks.*)

3. Assign an input to the track. (For information on assigning track inputs and outputs, see *Chapter 5: Working with Tracks.*)

4. Record-enable the track.

5. Set the audio input level. Ideally, input levels should top out in the yellow zone of the level meter. If levels are consistently hitting the red zone, the signal is *clipping* and the level should be turned down. (For information on setting audio input levels, see *Chapter 6: Getting Ready to Record.*)

6. Click the Return to Zero button in the Transport window to ensure that you start recording from the beginning of the track (**Figure 7.5**).

7. Click Record in the Transport window to put Pro Tools in Record-Ready mode (**Figure 7.6**).

continues on next page

8. Click Play in the Transport window or press the spacebar to begin recording (**Figure 7.7**).

9. Click Stop in the Transport window or press the spacebar to stop recording.

✔ Tips

■ To start recording, use these quick key commands: Press F12; press Command-spacebar (Macintosh) or Control-space-bar (Windows); or press 3 on the numeric keypad in Transport mode.

■ To cancel a take while recording, press Command-period (Macintosh) or Control-period (Windows). This removes the audio from your hard drive and deletes the region from the track's playlist.

■ To delete audio files from your hard drive, select the name of the audio file that you want to delete in the Regions list of the Edit window (**Figure 7.8**). Choose Clear from the Regions list pop-up menu (**Figure 7.9**), and then select Delete from the Clear Audio window.

Figure 7.7 Click the Play button to start recording.

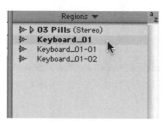

Figure 7.8 The Regions list on the right side of the Edit window.

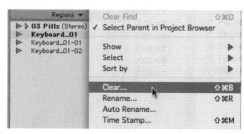

Figure 7.9 Use the Clear command in the Regions list pop-up menu to delete audio files from your hard drive.

What Is Feedback?

A *feedback* loop is created when an active microphone picks up its own signal from a loudspeaker and amplifies that signal again in a self-perpetuating cycle.

Feedback can be piercing and shrill, but like distortion, it has creative applications. In particular, when electric guitars are overdriven, they can produce a pleasing blend of feedback and distortion that can be rich in harmonic content and texture.

In the studio, however, unplanned feedback can occur suddenly and really zap your ears. Avoid feedback by keeping live mics isolated from the monitors—in another room, if possible.

Figure 7.10 Specify the number of audio tracks that you want to create in the New Tracks dialog box.

Figure 7.11 You can record-enable multiple tracks simultaneously. See "Record-Enabling Tracks" in Chapter 6.

Recording multiple audio tracks

You can record multiple tracks of audio simultaneously. This is useful for live band situations or any time you have multiple audio sources.

To record multiple audio tracks simultaneously:

1. Choose Track > New.

2. Specify the number of mono or stereo audio tracks you want, and then click Create (**Figure 7.10**).

3. Assign an input to each track.

4. Record-enable the tracks (**Figure 7.11**).

5. Set the audio input level.

6. Click Record in the Transport window.

7. Click Play in the Transport window or press the spacebar to begin recording.

8. Click Stop in the Transport window or press the spacebar to stop recording.

✔ Tips

- To append new material to the end of a track, press the Go to End button in the Transport window, and begin recording. The new audio is added to the end of the track.

  Note that in Non-destructive Record mode, appending new audio creates a new audio file and region. In Destructive Record mode, the new audio is added to the original audio file on the track.

- You may want to experiment with recording an instrument at half-speed. Reducing the speed can create some interesting sonic effects. To record audio at half-speed, press Command-Shift-spacebar (Macintosh) or Control-Shift-spacebar (Windows).

RECORDING AUDIO TRACKS

143

Punch-Recording Audio

If you have a great take with only a glitch or two, try fixing it with *punch recording*. Punch recording means literally pressing or *punching* the Record buttons into and out of Record mode at precise track locations.

Pro Tools' Zoom and Selection tools let you make incredibly precise punches—automatically. The Edit window's viewing features let you quickly zoom in on waveforms to accurately identify errors (**Figure 7.12**) and select audio regions to punch.

Once you've selected a region to punch, Pro Tools does the punching for you—entering Record mode at the punch-in point and leaving Record mode at the punch-out point. You can also set pre- and post-roll values to give the performer some lead-in time.

To punch-record audio:

1. Record-enable the track you want to punch.

2. Select Options > Link Timeline and Edit Selection (**Figure 7.13**).

3. Select a range to punch (**Figure 7.14**).

4. Set pre- and post-roll times (**Figure 7.15**). Be sure to give the performer enough time to get in the groove of the track.

5. Click the Record button in the Transport window.

6. When you're ready to record, click Play. If pre-roll is enabled, the track plays back until the punch-in point, and then switches into Record mode. If post-roll is enabled, the track switches back out of Record mode at the punch-out point and plays for the post-roll time.

   In Non-destructive Record mode, a new audio file is written to your hard drive and a new audio region appears in the Regions list.

Figure 7.12 Use the Edit window's Zoom tools to zoom in to the sample level on waveforms.

Figure 7.13 Select Options > Link Timeline and Edit Selection.

Figure 7.14 Use the Selector tool in the Edit window to select a range to punch.

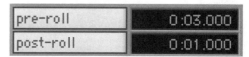

Figure 7.15 Set a pre-roll time in the Transport window to give yourself some lead time before the punch.

Figure 7.16 Select a record range in any Timebase ruler. The above ruler is minutes:seconds.

Figure 7.17 Drag the playback markers to select a record range.

Figure 7.18 The Memory Location dialog box lets you save and recall selections.

Figure 7.19 Use Destructive Record mode to permanently overwrite an audio file.

✔ Tips

- You can set the start and end points of a record range for punch- and loop-recording in the following ways:
  - ▲ Select a range in a track's playlist.
  - ▲ Select a range in a Timebase ruler (**Figure 7.16**).
  - ▲ Drag the playback markers in the ruler (**Figure 7.17**).
  - ▲ Enter start and end times in the Transport window.
  - ▲ Recall a memory location (**Figure 7.18**).

- Use Destructive Record mode if you want to overwrite the region of the audio file that you're punching. Choose Options > Destructive Record (**Figure 7.19**).

- When punching, use Auto Input Monitoring in the Track menu. This plays back the track until the punch-in point, when it switches to the audio input (so you can monitor what you're recording). At the punch-out point, it switches back to track playback.

PUNCH-RECORDING AUDIO

145

Using QuickPunch

You can use QuickPunch mode to make punches on the fly. QuickPunch lets you punch up to 200 times during one playback.

To punch on the fly with QuickPunch:

1. Select Options > QuickPunch (**Figure 7.20**).

   The letter P appears inside the Record button (**Figure 7.21**).

2. Set a QuickPunch crossfade length in the Editing Preferences window. Setting a crossfade length can help smooth the attack on punch-ins and punch-outs. (For instructions, see the next task.)

3. Record-enable the track you want to punch in on.

4. Locate a start point.

   Set pre- and post-roll times, if desired.

5. Start playback by clicking Play in the Transport window.

6. When you reach the punch-in point, click Record in the Transport window.

   or

   If you're using a Digi 002 or Digi 002 Rack system with a connected foot-switch, press the footswitch at the punch-in point.

7. To punch out, click the Record button (or press the footswitch) again.

Figure 7.20 Use QuickPunch Record mode to make punches on the fly.

Figure 7.21 In QuickPunch Record mode, the letter P appears inside the Record button.

USING QUICKPUNCH

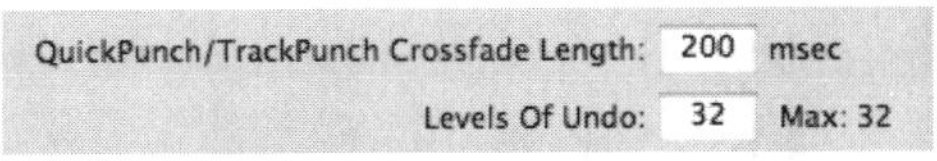

| QuickPunch/TrackPunch Crossfade Length: | 200 | msec |
| Levels Of Undo: | 32 | Max: 32 |

Figure 7.22 Enter a value (in milliseconds) for the QuickPunch Crossfade Length.

To set the QuickPunch crossfade length:

1. Choose Setup > Preferences.

2. Click the Editing Preferences window tab.

3. Enter a value (in milliseconds) for the QuickPunch crossfade length (**Figure 7.22**).

✔ Tip

■ A 32-track session is limited to sixteen simultaneous tracks of QuickPunch. If you want to QuickPunch on more tracks, reduce the session's total tracks. For more information on QuickPunch, see the *Pro Tools Reference Guide*.

USING QUICKPUNCH

Loop-Recording Audio

You can use Pro Tools' Loop Record mode to lay down successive nondestructive takes over the same section of a track. This can help a performer maintain focus and be more creative. For example, a songwriter could loop record while developing a melody to a song. Or a guitar player may want to loop record while developing a guitar part for a song. Or, loop-recording a vocalist can help them warm up, reduce performance anxiety, and help them stay in the flow of the music.

To loop-record audio:

1. Enable Loop Record Mode by selecting Options > Loop Record (**Figure 7.23**).

   The Record button displays a loop symbol (**Figure 7.24**).

2. Record-enable the track.

3. Select a recording range in the track's playlist (**Figure 7.25**).

4. Set a pre-roll time, if desired.

5. Click Record in the Transport window.

6. When you're ready to record, click Play.

   When the start point is reached, Pro Tools begins recording. When the end point is reached, the track loops back to the start point and continues recording.

7. When you've finished recording, click Stop.

   The recorded takes appear in the Regions list numbered sequentially. The most recently recorded take remains visible in the audio track.

Figure 7.23 Select Options > Loop Record.

Figure 7.24 In Loop Record mode, the Record button displays a loop symbol.

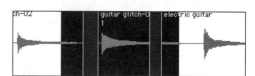

Figure 7.25 Select a recording range in the track's playlist.

Figure 7.26 Select a take to audition by clicking it with the Grabber tool.

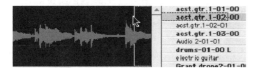

Figure 7.27 From the Regions list, Command-drag (Macintosh) or Control-drag (Windows) the take that you want to audition.

Auditioning Takes

Pro Tools provides some thoughtful ways to audition takes created with punch- and loop-recording. One easy way is to grab and drag individual takes from the Regions list onto the track.

To audition takes using the Regions list:

1. In the Edit window, select the current take by clicking it with the Grabber tool (**Figure 7.26**).

2. Command-drag (Macintosh) or Control-drag (Windows) from the Regions list the take you want to audition (**Figure 7.27**). The region replaces the previous take on the track and snaps to the correct location.

3. Repeat the preceding steps as desired to audition other takes.

The Takes List pop-up menu

You can also audition multiple takes on a track with the Takes List pop-up menu. This menu lets you choose from a list of takes with the same *user time stamp*, which means they have matching start times.

For more information on the Takes List pop-up menu, see the *Pro Tools Reference Guide*.

To audition takes using the Takes List pop-up menu:

1. Command-click (Macintosh) or Control-click (Windows) with the Selector tool at the precise beginning of the loop or punch range.

   or

   Select the track and Command-click (Macintosh) or Control-click (Windows) it.

   The Takes List pop-up menu appears with a list of takes with the same user time stamp (**Figure 7.28**).

2. Choose a region from the pop-up menu.

   The region replaces the previous take and snaps to the current location.

3. Repeat the preceding steps to audition other takes.

✔ Tip

- Use these Editing Preferences options to specify which takes are included in the Takes List pop-up menu (**Figure 7.29**):

   Take Region Name(s) That Match Track Names: When this option is selected, regions that share the same root name with the track appear in the Takes List pop-up menu.

   Take Region Lengths That Match: When this option is selected, takes matching the length of the current selection appear in the Takes List pop-up menu.

   "Separate Region" Operates on All Related Takes: When this option is selected, editing a region with the Separate Region command also affects all other takes with the same user time stamp.

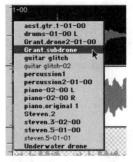

Figure 7.28 The Takes List pop-up menu displays a list of takes with the same user time stamp.

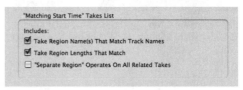

Figure 7.29 Use the "Matching Start Time" Takes List options in the Editing Preferences window to determine which takes appear in the Takes List pop-up menu.

Figure 7.30
Create new playlists for a track from the Playlist Selector pop-up menu.

Figure 7.31
Audition a playlist with the Playlist selector.

Recording to Playlists

Perhaps the best way to record multiple takes on a track is to record to playlists. All you do is create a new playlist, and then record. Use the Playlist selector to audition each playlist—each take—separately and identify the best one.

When you record to a new playlist, the audio file is written to disk and appears in the Audio Regions list. For more information on playlists, see *Chapter 2: Software Basics* and *Chapter10: Editing Basics*.

To record to a new playlist for a track:

1. From the track's Playlist Selector pop-up menu, choose New (**Figure 7.30**).

   Enter a name for the new playlist and click OK.

2. Record-enable the track.

3. In the Transport window, click the Return to Zero button.

4. Click Record in the Transport window.

   When you're ready to record, click Play.

5. When you've finished recording, click Stop.

   A new audio region appears in the track's region playlist.

   To audition a take, choose its playlist with the Playlist selector (**Figure 7.31**).

Recording from a Digital Source

Pro Tools lets you record from digital sources, such as DAT or ADAT, depending on your system's digital hardware inputs. Digi 002 and Digi 002 Rack users can choose from S/PDIF (RCA) inputs and ADAT optical inputs, whereas Mbox and Mbox 2 users are limited to S/PDIF (RCA) digital inputs.

For more information on connecting digital devices, see *Appendix A: Connecting Your Studio* and the *Pro Tools Reference Guide*.

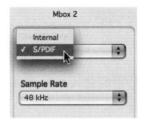

Figure 7.32 Choose the appropriate clock source in the Hardware Setup dialog box.

To record from a DAT or ADAT into a Pro Tools session:

1. Connect the digital output of the DAT or ADAT recorder to the appropriate digital inputs of your interface.

2. Choose Setup > Hardware.
   The Hardware Setup dialog box appears.

3. Select the appropriate sample rate.

4. Select the appropriate clock source (S/PDIF or Optical) and click OK (**Figure 7.32**).

5. Record-enable a track.
   Because this is a digital transfer, there's no need to set input levels.

6. Click Record in the Transport window.
   When you're ready to record, click Play.

7. Start playback on the DAT or ADAT recorder.

8. When you're finished recording, click Stop in the Transport window.
   Note: When you've finished recording from a digital source, return the sync mode to Internal. Failure to do so could result in record and playback errors.

✔ Tip

- The digital outputs of Pro Tools LE systems are active at all times. Thus, you can send digital audio to multiple external digital devices (such as an ADAT or DAT machine) simultaneously during mixdown.

RECORDING FROM A DIGITAL SOURCE

Figure 7.33 The Link Selection button in the Edit window.

Display	Operation	Ec

☐ Timeline Insertion Follows Playback
☐ Edit Insertion Follows Scrub/Shuttle
☐ Sends Default To "-INF"
☑ Audio During Fast Forward/Rewind
☐ Convert imported ".wav" files to AES31/Broad
☐ Automatically Copy Files on Import

Figure 7.34 To hear playback during fast forward and rewind operations, select Audio During Fast Forward/Rewind in the Operation Preferences window.

Playing Audio Tracks

Playback in Pro Tools is instantaneous: You can go immediately to any location in a recording without having to rewind or fast forward. Just click anywhere in a track with the Selector tool to begin playback from that point.

There are two cursors in the Edit window: The *playback cursor* is a solid line that shows the current playback location, and the *edit cursor* is a flashing line that shows the current edit location. The latter appears when you click on a track with the Selector tool.

By default, the playback and edit cursors are linked. To unlink them for editing purposes, just use the Link Selection button (**Figure 7.33**) in the Edit window.

To begin playback from a track location:

1. Select Options > Scrolling > None.

2. Select Options > Link Timeline and Edit Selection.

   or

   Enable the Link Selection button.

3. With the Selector, click in the track at the location at which you want playback to start.

4. Click Play in the Transport window to start playback

   or

   Press the spacebar to start playback.

5. Click Stop in the Transport window to stop playback

   or

   Press the spacebar to end playback.

✔ **Tip**

■ To hear playback during fast forward and rewind, select the Audio During Fast Forward/Rewind check box in the Operation Preferences window (**Figure 7.34**). This will help you cue up a track location by ear.

PLAYING AUDIO TRACKS

Setting playback scrolling

Pro Tools offers the following options for scrolling the contents of the Edit window during playback and recording (**Figure 7.35**):

None: The Edit window does not scroll during or after playback. The playback cursor moves across the Edit window, indicating the playback location.

After Playback: The Edit window scrolls to the final playback location after playback has stopped. The playback cursor moves across the Edit window, indicating the playback location.

Page: The Edit window scrolls during playback. The playback cursor moves across the Edit window, indicating the playback location.

To choose a playback scrolling option:

◆ Choose Options > Scrolling and select a scrolling option.

✔ Tip

■ You can set the edit cursor to appear at the precise location at which playback stops. To do so, select the Timeline Insertion Follows Playback check box in the Operation Preferences window (**Figure 7.36**). Then select Options > Link Timeline and Edit Selection.

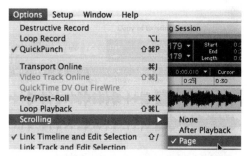

Figure 7.35 Select a playback scrolling option in the Options menu.

Figure 7.36 To set the edit cursor at the location where playback stops, select Timeline Insertion Follows Playback in the Operation Preferences window.

Figure 7.37 Select Options > Loop Playback.

Figure 7.38 The Play button displays a loop symbol when in Loop Playback mode.

Looping playback

Looping playback is a great way to create drum loops or loops of any other sound. Just select a playback range to loop, and then fine-tune the range until the loop fits the session. (Looping playback is also a useful, hands-free way to listen back to takes while making coffee.)

To loop-playback a selection:

1. Select Options > Link Timeline and Edit Selection.

2. With the Selector tool, choose the track range that you want to loop.

3. Select Options > Loop Playback (**Figure 7.37**).

   The Play button displays a loop symbol (**Figure 7.38**).

4. Click the Play button.

   Playback begins from the start point and continues until the selection's end point, where it loops back to the start point and repeats.

5. Click Stop in the Transport window to stop playback.

✔ Tip

■ You can also enable Loop Playback by Control-clicking (Macintosh) or right-clicking (Windows) the Play button in the Transport window. Or, with the numeric keypad set to Transport mode, press 4.

Locating the playback cursor

Pro Tools provides a handy Playback Cursor Locator, which lets you quickly find the playback cursor when it moves offscreen. This feature is mainly relevant when scrolling options are set to None.

If the playback cursor moves beyond the time visible in the Edit window, the Playback Cursor Locator appears at the right edge of the Main Timebase ruler. If the playback cursor is located before the time visible in the Edit window, the Playback Cursor Locator appears at the left edge of the Main Timebase ruler.

To locate the playback cursor:

◆ Click the Playback Cursor Locator in the Main Timebase ruler (**Figure 7.39**).

The moving playback cursor appears at its current time location in the center of the Edit window.

Scrubbing tracks

You can audition, or *scrub*, audio by running the Scrubber tool (**Figure 7.40**) back and forth over an audio region. Scrubbing is quite useful for locating punch or edit points that might be difficult to see in a waveform.

To scrub an audio track:

◆ Select and drag the Scrubber over the audio region that you want to audition (**Figure 7.41**).

The length and speed of audio played during scrubbing depends on the distance and speed at which you drag the Scrubber.

The resolution of the Scrubber is dependent on the zoom resolution of the track. Press Command (Macintosh) or Control (Windows) to scrub at finer resolutions.

Figure 7.39 Click the Playback Cursor Locator to center the moving playback cursor at its current location in the Edit window.

Figure 7.40 The Scrubber tool in the Edit window.

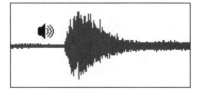

Figure 7.41 Drag the Scrubber over the region of audio that you want to audition.

PLAYING AUDIO TRACKS

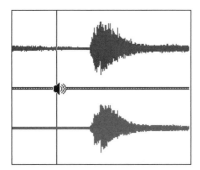

Figure 7.42 Drag the Scrubber between two adjacent tracks to audition both simultaneously.

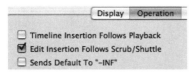

Figure 7.43 To locate to the point where scrubbing stops, select the Edit Insertion Follows Scrub/Shuttle check box in the Operation Preferences window.

To scrub two audio tracks simultaneously:

◆ Drag the Scrubber between two adjacent tracks (**Figure 7.42**).

or

◆ Scrub within a selection that contains multiple tracks.

(Only the first two tracks are scrubbed.)

✔ Tips

■ To scrub at fast speed, press Option (Macintosh) or Alt (Windows) while scrubbing.

■ To automatically locate to the point where scrubbing stops, select the Edit Insertion Follows Scrub/Shuttle check box in the Operation Preferences window (**Figure 7.43**).

Part III:
Audio File
Management

FILE MANAGEMENT BASICS

8

Pro Tools provides a number of smart file-management features that can help you work more efficiently and creatively. Mastering these tools for organizing, moving, and copying audio files will help you streamline your sessions and, most important, help you protect irreplaceable, one-of-a-kind sound recordings.

In Pro Tools most file-management functions mincorporate elements of DigiBase, a database-like utility that uses a powerful file-indexing protocol to keep track of audio files and session-related files on your hard drives. This chapter will show you how to use many of these basic but important file-management features. You'll learn how to locate missing files, import audio, and convert audio file formats (when necessary). In addition, we'll explain how to import entire tracks from a session using the import Session Data command. (We'll get more into the specifics of DigiBase in the next chapter.)

Next, we'll show you how to export audio files from a session; then we'll look at Pro Tools' features for saving hard drive space, including compacting and deleting audio files. We'll wrap things up with a brief but important discussion on why you should always back up your audio files.

Locating Audio Files

Each time you create a new audio file, Pro Tools tags it with a unique ID. This lets Pro Tools locate the file even if its name or location has changed. When you open a session, Pro Tools looks for all audio files belonging to that session. In Pro Tools 7, if any audio files (or other session-related files) are missing, Pro Tools opens a Missing Files warning.

The Missing Files warning indicates how many files are missing. It also gives you the option of manually finding and *relinking* missing files with their sessions (using the *Relink window*), or letting Pro Tools find and relink missing files automatically.

Pro Tools also distinguishes between files found on volumes suitable for record and playback (*Performance volumes*) and files found on nonsuitable volumes, such as CD-ROM or network servers (*Transfer volumes*). If Pro Tools determines that a file is located on a Transfer volume, a dialog appears prompting you to copy them to a suitable Performance volume.

For more information on the Relink window, Performance volumes, and Transfer volumes, see *Chapter 9: Managing Audio Files with DigiBase*.

To locate audio files:

1. Open a session.

   If any audio files are missing, the Missing Files warning appears (**Figure 8.1**).

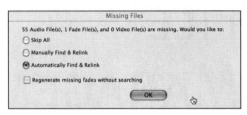

Figure 8.1 The Missing Files warning.

2. Choose one of the following options:

Automatically Find and Relink: Pro Tools searches all Performance volumes for matching files and automatically relinks matching files with the session.

or

Manually Find and Relink: The Relink window opens (**Figure 8.2**). In the Relink window you can search, compare, verify, and relink missing files.

or

Skip All: Ignores all missing audio files and fades. Missing files remain offline in the session.

or

Regenerate Missing Fades: Excludes fades from the relinking process and recalculates them instead.

For more information on relinking missing files, see *Chapter 9: Managing Audio Files with DigiBase*.

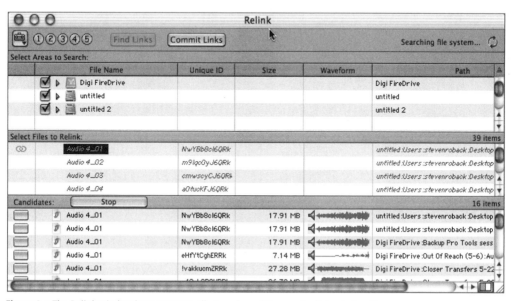

Figure 8.2 The Relink window lets you manually search, audition, and relink missing files.

To locate Transfer files:

1. Open a session.

   If any files are located on Transfer volumes unsuitable for playback, Pro Tools launches a warning.

2. Click Yes to open the Copy and Relink dialog box.

3. Specify a location for the copied files on a valid Performance volume.

4. Click OK.

✔ Tip

- A region whose parent audio file cannot be located is called an offline region. The name of an offline region appears italicized and dimmed in the Audio Regions list (**Figure 8.3**); it appears in blue italicized letters in track playlists. Offline regions can be edited like other regions, but they cannot be processed with Real Time AudioSuite (RTAS) plug-ins.

Figure 8.3 Offline regions appear italicized in the Audio Regions list.

Importing Audio

Pro Tools lets you import audio files and audio regions from other sessions or applications. You can use either the Import Audio to Track command or the Import Audio to Region List command. \Both commands open the Import Audio dialog box, which lets you audition, convert, and import audio files and regions.

When you use the Import Audio to Track command, Pro Tools automatically creates a new audio track and places the imported audio on it. When you use the Import Audio to Region List command, the audio file name appears in the Region list. You can then drag it onto a new or existing track.

You can also import audio by dragging it directly from a DigiBase browser into the Edit window of the current session.

You can import audio files in the following formats:

◆ AIFF

◆ WAV or BWF (.WAV)

◆ SDII

◆ SDI

◆ AAC audio (including audio with AAC, Mp4 and M4a file extensions)

Note: Pro Tools cannot import protected AAC or MP4 files with the .M4p file extension, as specified under digital copyright law.

◆ Sound Resource (AIFL), Macintosh only

◆ WMA (Windows Media), Windows only

◆ QuickTime (Macintosh only)

◆ RealAudio

◆ MXF Audio

◆ REX 1 and 2 files

◆ ACID files

Note: ACID files without slice data are imported as audio regions. Sliced ACID files and REX 1 and 2 files are imported as region groups.

IMPORTING AUDIO

Using the Import Audio dialog box

The Import Audio dialog box (**Figure 8.4**) includes the following options for handling imported audio files and regions:

Add: This option lets you add audio files that match the current session's sample rate and bit depth. Adding files does not require any additional hard drive space because the files are not copied; they remain in their existing location.

Audio files whose bit depths do not match the current session must be converted to the correct bit depths before they can be added to Pro Tools. The application *will* let you add audio files whose sample rates do not match the current session; however, they'll play at the wrong speed unless they're converted to the appropriate sample rate.

For more information on bit depth and sample rate, see *Chapter 4: Starting a New Session.*

Copy: This option creates a copy of the audio file and places it in the folder of your choice. The Copy option is useful for organizing and consolidating imported audio files in a new location.

Convert: If an audio file does not match the current session's sample rate, bit depth, and file type, the Import Audio dialog box displays a message prompting you to convert it (**Figure 8.5**). When you convert audio files, Pro Tools creates a new file with the correct attributes and places it in the folder of your choice.

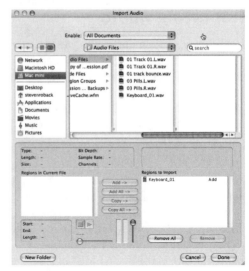

Figure 8.4 The Import Audio dialog box.

Figure 8.5 If an imported audio file's attributes (such as sample rate, bit depth, and file type) do not match the current session, you are prompted to convert it in the Import Audio dialog box.

Figure 8.6 Choose File > Import > Audio to Track.

Figure 8.7 Choose File > Import > Audio to Region Lists.

Figure 8.8 The Enable pop-up menu in the Import Audio dialog box.

To import audio files or regions into a session:

1. Choose File > Import > Audio to Track (**Figure 8.6**).

   or

   Choose File > Import > Audio to Region List (**Figure 8.7**).

   The Import Audio dialog box appears.

2. At the top of the Import Audio dialog box, click an audio file to display its properties and associated regions. Use the Enable pop-up menu to choose which audio file types are displayed (**Figure 8.8**).

3. Click the Play button to audition selected files.

   Use the horizontal slider to navigate to any location in the audio file. Use the vertical slider to adjust volume.

4. To place a file or region in the Import list, select the file (Shift-click to select multiple files) and click Add or Convert (**Figure 8.9**).

   You can also click Add All or Convert All to import all files and regions in the current directory.

   continues on next page

IMPORTING AUDIO

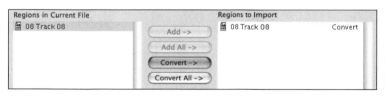

Figure 8.9 Click Add or Convert to place a file in the Import list.

167

5. To remove a file or region from the Import list, select it and click Remove.

To remove all files or regions, click Remove All.

6. Click Done.

7. If you're copying or converting files, you'll be prompted to choose a location for the new audio files.

Choose a folder on a valid audio drive.

If you choose File > Import > Audio to Track, the audio files and regions are converted (if applicable) and imported to individual audio tracks. They also appear as regions in the Audio Regions list.

or

If you choose File > Import > Audio to Region List, the files and regions appear as regions in the Regions list (**Figure 8.10**). You can then drag them to new or existing tracks.

Using drag and drop to import audio

In Pro Tools 7, you can drag and drop audio files and regions directly from a DigiBase browser, the Macintosh Finder, or Windows Explorer to a track, the Track list, the Regions list, or the Edit Window's Timeline (**Figure 8.11**).

To import audio using drag and drop:

1. Select the audio files or regions you want to import in a DigiBase browser, the Macintosh Finder, or Windows Explorer.

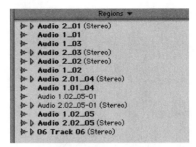

Figure 8.10 Imported audio files and regions appear in the Audio Regions list.

Figure 8.11 You can import selected audio files using drag and drop from a DigiBase browser.

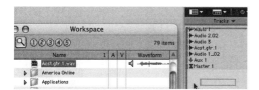

Figure 8.12 Importing audio files by dragging files onto the Track list.

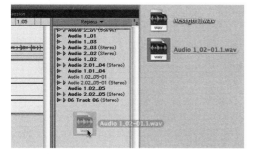

Figure 8.13 Importing audio files by dragging files onto the Regions list.

2. Do one of the following:

Click and drag the files or regions onto an existing track in the Edit window of the current session.

The imported audio files or regions appear within the existing track at the desired location.

or

Drag the files onto the Track list of the current session (**Figure 8.12**).

The imported audio files or regions appear in the Track list and a new track is created containing the imported audio file or region.

or

Drag the files onto the Regions list of the current session (**Figure 8.13**).

The imported audio files or regions appear in the Regions list. You can then drag the audio file or region from the Regions list to a track of your choice.

or

Drag the files onto any empty space in the Edit window (or Shift-drag the files anywhere in the Edit window) of the current session.

The imported audio files appear in new tracks inside the Edit window.

For more information on using DigiBase to import audio, see *Chapter 9: Managing Audio Files with DigiBase.*

✔ Tip

■ To batch-load multiple audio files into a session, open a Pro Tools session, and drag the audio files you want to import onto the Pro Tools icon (the bit depth, sample rate, and file type must match the current session). The batch-loaded audio files will appear in the open session's Audio Regions list. You can then drag them onto new or existing tracks.

IMPORTING AUDIO

Setting Sample Rate Conversion Quality

When you import audio files into Pro Tools, you may need to convert the sample rate to match the current session. Conversion quality settings include Low, Good, Better, Best, and TweakHead. The higher the quality, the longer the length of the conversion process. (TweakHead can take significantly longer than the other options.)

To set the sample rate conversion quality:

1. Choose Setup > Preferences.

2. Click the Editing tab.

3. From the Conversion Quality pop-up menu, select a sample rate conversion quality (**Figure 8.14**).

✔ Tips

■ Keep in mind that converting audio can degrade sound quality: While Good or Better conversion quality settings are generally adequate, consider using Best or TweakHead settings whenever practical. This will help you maintain the highest-quality audio possible.

■ When using the File > Import > Audio to Track command, interleaved (single-file) stereo files are automatically imported to stereo tracks. Split stereo files can also be imported to stereo tracks, but the split pair must be the same length, and they must be named "filename.L" and "filename.R." These files will have a three-letter file extension appended after the ".L" or ".R."

Figure 8.14 The Conversion Quality pop-up menu.

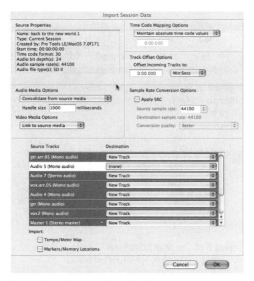

Figure 8.15 The Import Session Data dialog box.

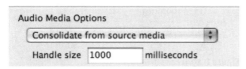

Figure 8.16 Audio Media Options offer alternatives for copying and consolidating audio files.

Importing Tracks

You can use the File > Import > Session Data command to import entire tracks from other sessions, including audio, MIDI, auxiliary input, instrument, and master fader tracks.

The Import Session Data dialog box lets you view the properties of the source session and select which tracks to import. It also gives you options for handling source media, placing imported tracks, and converting audio file type, sample rate, and bit depth to match the current session. (In Pro Tools HD systems, the Import Session Data dialog also lets you import track attributes, such as channel strip settings, track views, and automation.)

The Import Session Data dialog box (**Figure 8.15**) provides the following features:

Source Properties: The Source Properties area displays information about the source session, including source session name, type, start time, bit depth, and sample rate.

Audio Media Options (**Figure 8.16**): These options provide alternatives for copying and consolidating imported audio files. They include:

◆ **Consolidate from Source Media:** This option consolidates audio by copying only currently used portions of audio files. It also lets you set a *handle* value. A handle is a preserved segment of the original audio file before and after each region. It can be useful for fine-tuning the boundaries of a region.

◆ **Copy from Source Media:** This option copies all audio files related to the imported tracks from the source media to a new location.

◆ **Link to Source Media (Where Possible):** This option links the current session to the existing audio files, thus avoiding audio file duplication and saving hard drive space.

If the source files don't reside on "playable" media (such as CD-ROM) or if the files require conversion, the files are copied.

◆ **Force to Target Session Format:** This option copies and converts any files that do not match the current session's file format, bit depth, and sample rate.

Video Media Options (**Figure 8.17**): This lets you choose between copying video files to a new location or linking to them in their original location.

Time Code Mapping Options: These options provide alternatives for placing imported tracks in the current session. Options include:

◆ **Maintain Absolute Time Code Values:** This option places imported tracks at the same time location as in the source session.

◆ **Maintain Relative Time Code Values:** This option places imported tracks at the same time offset from the session start time as in the source session.

◆ **Map Start Time Code To:** This option lets you place imported tracks at a start time that you input in the Time Value field (**Figure 8.18**). Imported track start times are relative to start times in the source session.

Track Offset Options (**Figure 8.19**): This option lets you specify a track offset in addition to any offset incurred with the Time Code Mapping options. Any imported audio is offset in the current session's timeline by the specified amount.

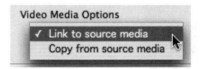

Figure 8.17 Video Media options offer alternatives for copying and consolidating video files.

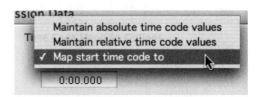

Figure 8.18 The Map Start Time Code To option lets you input a start time for imported tracks.

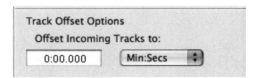

Figure 8.19 Track Offset options

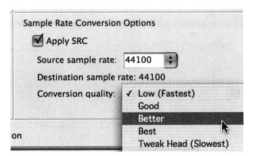

Figure 8.20 Sample Rate Conversion options.

Sample Rate Conversion Options
(**Figure 8.20**): These options let you convert the sample rate of imported audio files. If the source sample rate and the current session sample rate match, this area is dimmed. Sample Rate Conversion Options include:

◆ **Source Sample Rate:** This option lets you choose a sample rate from which to begin the conversion process.

◆ **Destination Sample Rate:** The Destination Sample Rate always displays the sample rate of the current session.

◆ **Conversion Quality:** This option lets you change the quality of the sample-rate conversion process. At lower quality settings audio processing is faster; at higher settings audio processing is slower. For more information, see *Setting Sample Rate Conversion Quality* earlier in this chapter.

Source Tracks: The Source Tracks area lets you select source tracks to import. Each source track has a corresponding Destination pop-up menu, which lists options for importing the track. The Destination pop-up menu provides the following options:

◆ **None:** The source track is not imported.

◆ **New Track:** The source track is imported to a new track. (On HD systems, selected track attributes are imported as well.)

Import Tempo/Meter Map: This check box lets you import meter and tempo tracks from the source session. Tempo and meter events in the destination session are replaced.

Import Markers/Memory Locations:
This check box lets you import markers and memory locations from the source session. Markers and memory locations in the destination session are retained.

IMPORTING TRACKS

To import tracks:

1. Open a session or create a new one.

2. Chose File > Import > Session Data
   (**Figure 8.21**).

3. Select a session and click Open.

   or

   Drag the session file whose tracks you
   want to import from a DigiBase browser
   into the track playlist area in the current
   session's Edit window.

   The Import Session Data dialog box
   appears.

4. Select the tracks to import in the Source
   Tracks list (**Figure 8.22**).

   Shift-click to select multiple contiguous
   files. Command-click (Macintosh) or Alt-
   click (Windows) to select multiple noncontiguous files.

5. Choose the time code mapping option
   for imported audio files.

6. If the sample rates of the current session
   and the source session do not match,
   choose the sample rate of the source
   session.

7. Choose options for imported audio and
   video media files (if applicable).

8. Select Import Tempo/Meter Map if you
   want to import the configured Tempo
   and Meter rulers from the source session.

9. Select Import Markers/Memory Locations
   if you want to import markers and memory locations from the source session.

10. Click OK.

11. If you are copying or consolidating
    media, choose a location to place the
    media files.

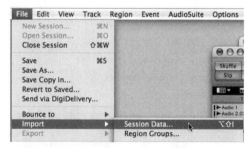

Figure 8.21 Choose File > Import > Session Data.

Figure 8.22 The Source Tracks list lets you select
tracks to import.

✔ Tip

■ Imported tracks are made inactive if
  their source media is unavailable or if
  the current session's I/O Setup has
  configuration conflicts.

IMPORTING TRACKS

Figure 8.23 The Export Regions as Files command in the Audio Regions list pop-up menu.

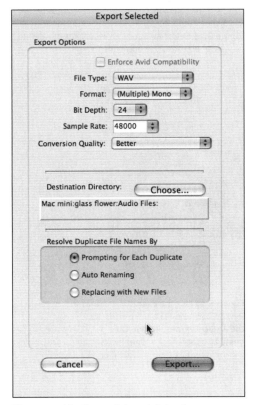

Figure 8.24 The Export Selected dialog box.

Exporting Audio

Pro Tools provides a variety of methods to export audio. The most straightforward way is to use the Export Regions as Files command in the Regions list pop-up menu (**Figure 8.23**).

You can also export audio by bouncing or consolidating audio tracks. For information on the Bounce to Disk command, see *Chapter 17: Mixdown and Mastering*. For information on the Consolidate Selection command, consult the *Pro Tools Reference Guide*.

Exporting a region as a new audio file

The Export Regions as Files command lets you export audio regions as new audio files. It also lets you convert the audio file type, bit depth, and sample rate. This command is helpful if you want to extract a region as a distinct new audio file for use with another session.

To export a region as a new audio file:

1. In the Regions list, select the audio regions you want to export.

2. From the Regions list pop-up menu, choose Export Selected As Files.

   The Export Selected dialog box appears (**Figure 8.24**).

   continues on next page

3. In the Export Options area, set a file type, format (mono or stereo), bit depth, and sample rate for the file you want to export (**Figure 8.25**).

4. Choose one of the following options for resolving duplicate file names (**Figure 8.26**):

   ▲ **Prompting for Each Duplicate:** If a file in the destination directory already has the name of the file you're trying to export, Pro Tools will prompt you to enter a new file name.

   ▲ **Auto Renaming:** This option automatically changes the name of a duplicate file by adding a number to its end (such as file-01).

   ▲ **Replacing with New Files:** This option replaces an existing audio file with a new audio file with the same name.

5. Click Export.

The new audio files are exported.

✔ Tip

■ If you want to reuse a region in another session, use the Export Region Definitions command in the Regions list pop-up menu (**Figure 8.27**). This command lets you export region information that points to the original audio on disk—without creating a new audio file.

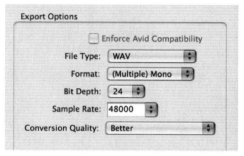

Figure 8.25 The Export Options area lets you set multiple parameters for exported files.

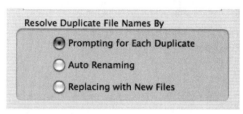

Figure 8.26 Select an option to resolve duplicate file names when exporting audio files.

Figure 8.27 Use the Export Region Definitions command in the Audio Regions list pop-up menu to export region definitions without creating a new audio file.

Figure 8.28 Select unused regions in a session by choosing Select > Unused Regions in the Audio Regions list pop-up menu.

Figure 8.29 The Clear Selected command lets you remove audio regions from a session or delete audio files from a hard disk.

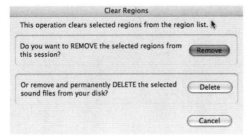

Figure 8.30 The Clear Regions dialog box.

Compacting and Deleting Audio Files

A good way to free up valuable hard disk space is to compact or delete audio files. The Regions list pop-up menu provides commands for both compacting and deleting unused or unwanted audio files.

Removing audio regions

The Compact Selected command helps you reduce the size of an audio file. It does this by permanently deleting unused portions of an audio file that are not referenced by any region definitions.

Before running the Compact Selected command, remove any unused regions from a session. This eliminates unwanted region references and ensures that the maximum amount of file compacting takes place.

To remove audio regions from a session:

1. In the Regions list pop-up menu, Click Select > Unused (**Figure 8.28**).

   The unused regions in the session are highlighted in the Regions list.

2. Choose the Clear command from the Regions list pop-up menu (**Figure 8.29**). The Clear Regions dialog box appears (**Figure 8.30**).

3. Click Remove.

   Unused audio regions are removed from the session, although the audio files they reference remain intact on the hard drive. For more information on managing regions with the Regions list, see *Chapter 10: Editing Basics.*

Compacting audio files

When you use the Compact command, the Compact Selected dialog box appears, which lets you *pad* regions (**Figure 8.31**). A pad is a small segment of audio before and after a region. It can be useful for creating fades or trimming region start and end times.

To compact an audio file:

1. Select the regions you want to compact in the Regions list.

2. Choose Compact from the Regions list pop-up menu (**Figure 8.32**).
   The Compact Selected dialog box appears.

3. Enter the amount of padding in milli-seconds.

4. Click Compact.

✔ Tip

■ Keep in mind that the Compact command is destructive: It permanently alters the original audio file and cannot be undone. Therefore, use the command only after you've finished editing and are certain that you don't need the audio data any longer.

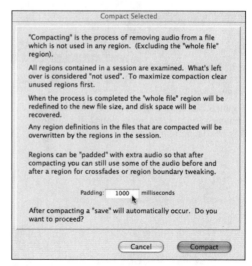

Figure 8.31 The Compact Selected dialog box.

COMPACTING AND DELETING AUDIO FILES

Figure 8.32 Choose Compact from the Regions list pop-up menu.

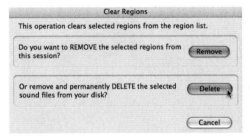

Figure 8.33 Click Delete to permanently delete audio files from the hard disk. Use this command with care!

Deleting audio files

The Clear command lets you permanently delete entire audio files from your hard disk.

To delete audio files from your hard disk:

1. Select the audio files you want to delete in the Regions list.

2. Choose Clear from the Regions list pop-up menu.

   The Clear Regions dialog box appears.

3. Click Delete (**Figure 8.33**).

   The Clear command is destructive and cannot be undone. Deleted files are permanently erased from the hard disk.

Importing Audio from Audio CDs

In Pro Tools 7, you can import audio tracks directly from an audio CD using File menu commands or drag and drop methods.

Keep in mind that CD audio is formatted at a resolution of 16 bits and a sample rate of 44.1 kHz. If your Pro Tools session is formatted at a sample rate of 48 kHz or higher, Pro Tools will convert the imported CD audio file format to match that of your session.

To import a CD audio track from the File menu:

1. Insert an audio CD into the CD drive.

2. Choose File > Import > Audio to Track
   or
   Choose File > Import Audio to Region List.
   The Import Audio dialog box opens.

3. Select the CD audio tracks to be imported (**Figure 8.34**).

4. Select Convert.

4. Click Done.

5. Navigate to a destination for the imported audio, and click Choose.
   Pro Tools converts the CD audio track to the session's audio file format, bit depth, and sample rate, and saves it on your hard drive.
   If you're using File > Import > Audio to Track, the imported CD audio track appears in a new track inside the Edit Window and in the Regions list.
   If you're using File > Import > Audio to Region List, the imported CD audio track appears in the Regions list. From there you can drag the audio region to an existing track.

Figure 8.34 To import a CD audio track, choose File > Import > Audio to Track.

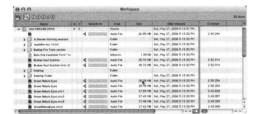

Figure 8.35 The Workspace Browser window.

To import a CD audio track using drag and drop:

1. Insert an audio CD into the CD drive.

2. Choose Window > Workspace.
   The DigiBase Workspace browser opens.

3. Click and drag the CD audio tracks you want to import from the Workspace Browser to either the Tracks list, the Regions list, or the anywhere in the Edit Window's Timeline.

4. The selected CD audio tracks are imported and converted to match the file format of the current session (**Figure 8.35**).

IMPORTING AUDIO FROM AUDIO CDS

Backing Up Your Files

No chapter on file management would be complete without a discussion of backup. You only need to lose an irreplaceable recording once to appreciate the value of backing up your audio files. Get in the habit of backing up all new audio files—and session files—to a different hard drive *immediately* after a session.

To back up session files and audio files:

1. Choose File > Save Copy In

The Save Session Copy In dialog box appears (**Figure 8.36**).

2. Select All Audio Files in the Items To Copy area.

3. Create a folder named Backup, followed by the current date.

4. Click Save.

or

1. On the desktop, navigate to the Pro Tools Session folder that you want to back up.

2. Copy the entire folder (including session files and the Audio Files and Fade Files folders) to a different hard drive.

✔ Tip

■ The Save Copy In command is the only way to change the sample rate of an existing session.

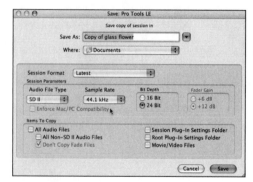

Figure 8.36 Use the Save Copy In dialog box to back up session files and audio files.

MANAGING AUDIO FILES WITH DIGIBASE

DigiBase is a database-like file-management utility designed especially for managing Pro Tools files. DigiBase's comprehensive file-management tools and smartly designed user interfaces (or *browsers*) make performing file-management tasks quick, easy, and painless.

This chapter shows you how to use DigiBase to manage your audio files. We'll start with an overview of DigiBase, including how DigiBase's database works. Then we'll take a closer look at DigiBase *browsers*. You'll learn how to use browsers to view audio file information, and you'll learn how to perform file-management tasks, such as searching, copying, auditioning, and importing audio files.

We'll conclude with a look at DigiBase's other windows, including DigiBase's Relink window, which helps you locate missing files; and DigiBase's Tasks window, which lets you regulate background file-processing tasks.

About DigiBase

DigiBase uses a file-indexing process to gather information about audio files and other session-related files. This file information, or *metadata,* includes basic file data (file name, file size, date created, etc.) and more complex data (audio file formats, waveforms, sample rate, bit depth, duration, etc.). DigiBase stores this metadata in database files on your system's *storage volumes* (hard drives).

Pro Tools uses stored file data to maintain *links* between audio files and their associated sessions. This data is also displayed in browsers, where you can perform file-management tasks (**Figure 9.1**).

For more information on browsers, see *About Browsers* later in this chapter, or see the *Pro Tools Reference Guide.* For more information on DigiBase's database features, see the *Pro Tools Reference Guide.*

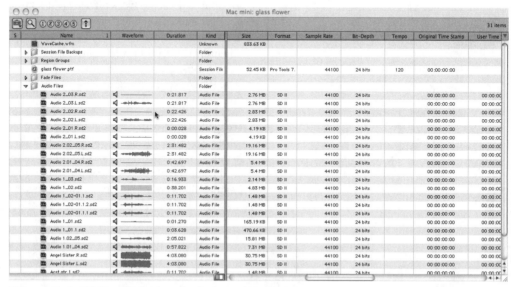

Figure 9.1 Typical DigiBase Project browser displaying the contents of a Pro Tools session folder, including audio waveforms and other file information.

New DigiBase features in Pro Tools 7

DigiBase in Pro Tools 7 includes the following new features:

◆ Support for Standard MIDI files, REX files, ACID files, and region group files

◆ Bar|Beat display of Duration for tick-based audio and MIDI files

◆ New Tempo Column

◆ Drag and Drop of audio files to plug-ins

◆ Drag and Drop import of Standard MIDI files, region group files, REX files, and ACID files.

DigiBase elements

DigiBase includes the following browsers and windows, or *elements*:

Workspace browser: The Workspace browser gives you access to all mounted storage volumes, as well as the folders and files they contain. It lets you search multiple volumes (and catalogs) and designate volume classifications (whether a drive is suitable for recording and playback of audio and video).

Volume browsers: Volume browsers let you manage files on local volumes and network volumes. Changes made using a Volume browser (such as copying, deleting, or moving files and folders) are mirrored on the actual volumes.

Project browsers: Project browsers display files associated with the current session. Project browsers give you tools for viewing, managing, auditioning, and spotting individual audio files.

ABOUT DIGIBASE

Catalogs (Pro Tools HD only): Catalog browsers let you organize files from multiple sources into libraries. Catalog browsers give you tools for searching and sorting audio files, and let you share files with other Pro Tools users.

Relink window: The Relink window gives you tools for locating missing files and reestablishing links (*relinking*) between audio files and their associated sessions.

Tasks window: The Tasks window lets you regulate background file-processing tasks, such as copying, searching, indexing, and fade creation.

For more information on DigiBase elements, see the corresponding sections of this chapter, or see the *Pro Tools Reference Guide*.

For more information on Workspace browsers, Volume browsers, and Project browsers, see the following sections of this chapter, or see the *Pro Tools Reference Guide*. For more information on Catalogs (TDM only), see the *Pro Tools Reference Guide*.

Understanding data flow

To manage your files effectively, it's important to understand how data flows between DigiBase's various elements (**Figure 9.2**).

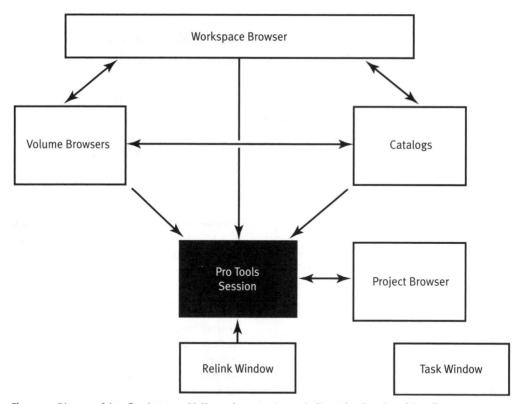

Figure 9.2 Diagram of data flow between DigiBase elements. Arrows indicate the direction of data flow.

ABOUT DIGIBASE

About Browsers

Much like your computer's operating system, DigiBase browsers give you access to the contents (folders and files) of your storage volumes. Browsers display your volumes, folders, and files, as well as information about this content (stored in the associated database file), including detailed information about your audio files. You can use browsers to organize your storage volumes, audition audio files, open sessions, and perform file-management tasks, such as indexing, searching, moving, copying, deleting, and relinking audio files.

In Pro Tools 7, DigiBase browsers have been enhanced to support the display of additional file formats, standard MIDI files, region group files, REX files, ACID files.

For more information on standard MIDI files, see *Part VI: MIDI Sequencing*. For more information on region group (.rgrp) files, see *Chapter 2: Software Basics and Chapter 12:*

Working with Regions. For more information on REX files and ACID files, *see the Pro Tools Reference Guide.*

The Browser window

Although each browser type has different features, the basic design of the browser window remains the same (**Figure 9.3**).

Browser windows include the following features:

Title bar: The Title bar shows the browser type and the name of its associated volume.

Toolbar: The Toolbar contains the Browser menu, Search icon, view presets, and browser navigation tools.

Items list: The Items list displays the contents of a volume, folder, or session.

Columns: Columns display metadata for volumes, folders, and files in the Items list. Columns can be resized, rearranged, and dragged between fixed and scrolling panes.

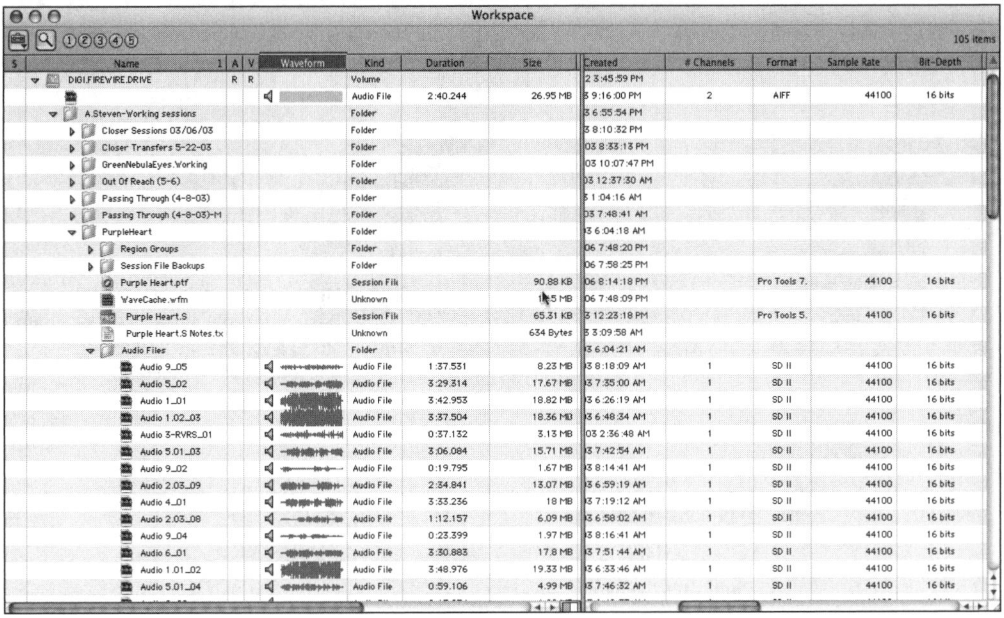

Figure 9.3 The Browser window's basic design is the same for all types of browsers. The Workspace browser is shown.

ABOUT BROWSERS

Search icon: The Search icon lets you search for files in volumes and folders.

View presets: View presets let you save up to five different browser layouts.

Sort toggle: The Sort toggle lets you shift the sort order between ascending and descending.

Browser menu: The Browser menu provides commands specific to each type of browser. For more information on the Browser menu, see *Browser menu commands*, later in this chapter.

Columns and metadata

The metadata gathered about items (volumes, folders, files) and stored in database files is displayed in columns inside the browser window (**Figure 9.4**). Each column displays a specific data field pertaining to the item. Columns display the following data:

Status: This column displays the status of each item. A **T** icon is displayed for items on Transfer volumes (**Figure 9.5**). No icon is displayed for online or offline items.

File Name: This column displays the name of the file, folder, volume, catalog (TDM only), or session. This text field is editable in all browsers except catalogs.

A: This column designates volumes for audio as R (Record), P (Playback), or T (Transfer) (**Figure 9.6**).

V: This column designates volumes for video as R (Record), P (Playback), or T (Transfer).

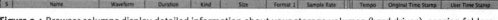

Figure 9.4 Browser columns display detailed information about your storage volumes (hard drives), session folders, and audio files.

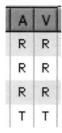

Figure 9.6 The Audio and Video Designator columns let you designate storage volumes as R (Record), P (Playback), or T (Transfer).

Figure 9.5 The Status column displays the status of each item. A T indicates the item is on a Transfer volume, such as a CD-ROM.

Kind: This column indicates whether a file is a session file, audio file, or other. This field cannot be edited.

Date Created: This column displays the creation date of an item. This field cannot be edited.

Date Modified: This column displays the last date the item was modified. This field cannot be edited.

Capacity: This column displays the capacity of a volume. This field cannot be edited.

Free: This column displays the amount of unused space on a volume. This field cannot be edited.

Duration: This column displays the duration, in absolute time, of a file, regardless of time code format. This field cannot be edited.

Number of Channels: This column indicates if a file is mono or stereo. This field cannot be edited.

Sample Rate: This column displays an audio file's sample rate.

Bit Depth: This column displays an item's bit depth. This field cannot be edited.

Tempo: This column displays the tempo associated with region group, MIDI, REX, ACID, and session files. This field cannot be edited.

Format: This column indicates the file format of an audio file, such as WAV, AIFF, or SDII. This field cannot be edited.

Waveform: This column displays an audio waveform of an audio file.

File Comment: This column displays any embedded comments associated with an audio file. (AIFF files are not supported.)

Database Comment: This column displays any user comments stored with the database. Available in Project browser only.

Path: This column displays the directory path to the item.

UID: This column displays the unique ID for a Pro Tools file.

Clip Name: This column displays the name of the file, or the Avid clip name when the file is an OMF file.

Tape: When DigiTranslator is installed, this column displays the original Avid tape name if the file is an OMF file. If the file was originally recorded into a Pro Tools session, the original session name is displayed.

FPS: When DigiTranslator is installed, this column displays the frame rate if the file is an OMF file.

Original Time Stamp: This column displays an audio file's original time stamp.

User Time Stamp: This column displays an audio file's user time stamp if one exists.

Link Path: This column displays the path to the file used for relinking. Available in Relink window only.

ABOUT BROWSERS

Browser menu commands

The Browser menu provides a slightly different set of commands for each type of browser, as specified below. Browser menu commands include the following:

Update Database for Selected: This command updates the database for the currently selected volumes or folders.

Calculate Waveform: This command calculates waveform displays for selected audio files or all files contained in a selected folder.

New Folder: This command creates a new folder on the current volume. In Volume browsers, a new folder is created on disk.

Reveal in Finder: This command opens the corresponding parent window in the Finder for the currently selected file.

Select Offline Files: This command selects all files currently offline.

Invert Selection: This command inverts (reverses) the current selection.

Copy and Relink: This command copies items currently selected in the Project browser to a chosen location and relinks the session to the copies (instead of the originals). Use this to easily move files from a *Transfer* to a *Performance* volume. For more information on Transfer and Performance volumes, see *The Workspace browser* later in this chapter.

Relink Offline: This command opens the Relink window; available in Project browsers only. For more information on the Relink Window, see *The Relink window* later in this chapter.

Relink Selected: This command opens the Relink window with all selected files from the current browser displayed and selected as Files to Match; available in the Project browser only.

Duplicate Selected: This command creates duplicates of selected items in the same location.

Lock Selected: This command locks all selected items. Currently locked files remain locked. Locking a folder locks all files and subfolders it contains.

Unmount: This command lets you unmount any online volume; available in the Workspace browser only.

Delete Selected: This command deletes any selected items. Deleted items are deleted from disk.

Figure 9.7 Click the Show/Hide icon to show or hide a browser window's scrolling pane.

Figure 9.8 To move a column between a browser's fixed pane and scrolling pane, click and drag the column header.

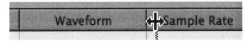

Figure 9.9 To resize a column, drag the column's boundary to the desired width.

Viewing Browsers

Browser windows provide flexible features for viewing the contents of your hard drives. Using these features will help you find and evaluate your session folders and audio files more effectively.

Using fixed and scrolling panes

A browser's Items list consists of columns that display information (such as file size, creation date, and sample rate). The Items list provides two panes for viewing these columns: a fixed pane and a scrolling pane.

To show or hide the scrolling pane:

◆ Click the Show/Hide icon in the lower-right corner of the fixed pane (**Figure 9.7**).

Arranging columns

You can move columns in the Items list between the fixed pane and scrolling pane. (You may want to place frequently used columns in the fixed pane and less frequently used columns in the scrolling pane.) In addition, you can resize and sort columns as desired.

To move columns from the fixed pane to the scrolling pane:

◆ Drag the column header to the desired pane (**Figure 9.8**).

To rearrange columns in a pane:

◆ Drag the column header to a new position.

To resize a column:

◆ Drag the column header boundary to the desired width (**Figure 9.9**).

Sorting items by columns

You can sort the contents of any column in ascending or descending order. This lets you view items (volumes, folders, and files) according to the data displayed in a column.

You can perform secondary sorts, as well, up to a maximum of four.

To sort items by columns:

◆ Click the column title header.

The number 1 appears in the column header (**Figure 9.10**).

To add a secondary sort:

◆ Option-click (Macintosh) or Alt-click (Windows) the column title for the secondary sort.

The number 2 appears in the column header (**Figure 9.11**).

To toggle a column sort order between ascending and descending:

◆ Click the Sort toggle arrow at the top of the vertical scroll bars (**Figure 9.12**).

Storing view presets

Browser windows provide five view presets (**Figure 9.13**), which let you save and recall customized browser configurations. You can save up to five preset views for each type of browser.

To store a view preset:

1. Open a browser.

2. Arrange columns and views as desired.

3. Command-click (Macintosh) or Control-click (Windows) one of the five view preset buttons.

Figure 9.10 To sort items by column data, click the column header. The number 1 appears in the column header, indicating that column is the primary sort column.

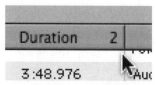

Figure 9.11 To perform a secondary sort, Option-click (Macintosh) or Alt-click (Windows) the desired column. The number 2 appears in the column header, indicating that column is the secondary sort column.

Figure 9.12 To toggle a sort column between ascending and descending order, click the arrow at the top of the vertical scroll bar.

Figure 9.13 Browser windows include five view preset buttons, which let you store customized browser configurations.

Group-01.rgrp

Figure 9.14 The (.rgrp) Region Group file icon.

DT_Drmlp_clipclop_140.rx2

Figure 9.15 The REX 2 file icon

PLP_Jungle_Beat_01.wav

Figure 9.16 A sliced ACID (Wave ACID) file icon

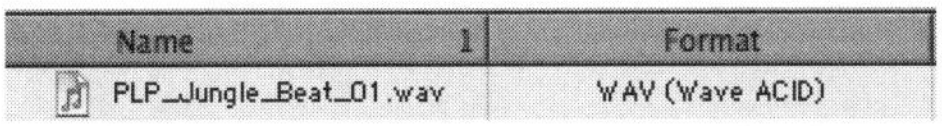

Name	1	Format
PLP_Jungle_Beat_01.wav		WAV (Wave ACID)

Figure 9.17 Sliced ACID files display WAV (Wave ACID) in the format column. ACID files with no slice data display WAV (WAVE) in the Format column.

Viewing region group files (.rgrp) in DigiBase browsers

In DigiBase browsers, region group files (.rgrp) display the Region Group file icon (**Figure 9.14**) and the following information:

Duration: Indicates the length of the region group file as specified in the last saved timebase.

Kind: Region group file.

Number of Channels (# Channels): Displays both stereo and multitrack region groups, indicated in the number of audio (nA), MIDI, and instrument tracks (nM).

Format: Region group.

Viewing Rex Files in DigiBase browsers

In DigiBase browsers, REX files display a REX file icon (**Figure 9.15**) and the following information:

Duration: Indicates the length for tick-based REX files in Bars|Beats as specified in the last saved timebase.

Kind: Audio file.

Format: AIFF (REX 1 files) or ReCycle (REX 2 files).

Viewing ACID Files in DigiBase browsers

In DigiBase browsers, ACID files display a unique icon (**Figure 9.16**) and the following information:

Duration: Indicates the length for tick-based ACID files in Bars|Beats as specified in the last saved timebase.

Kind: Audio file.

Format: Wav (Wave ACID) or WAV (WAVE).

Sliced ACID files display WAV (Wave ACID) in the format column (**Figure 9.17**). ACID files with no slice data display WAV (WAVE) in the Format column.

Using Browsers

DigiBase includes the following three types of browsers: the Workspace browser, Volume browsers, and Project browsers.

The Workspace browser gives you access to all storage volumes attached to your system; Volume browsers give you access to individual volumes only; and Project browsers give you access to the current session folder only. In effect, Volume browsers and Project browsers are subsets of the Workspace browser; you can launch Volume browsers and Project browsers by double-clicking the icon of a volume or session folder within the Workspace browser.

The Workspace browser

The Workspace browser (**Figure 9.18**) displays the contents of all storage volumes attached to your system, including all session folders, audio files, and non-Pro Tools files.

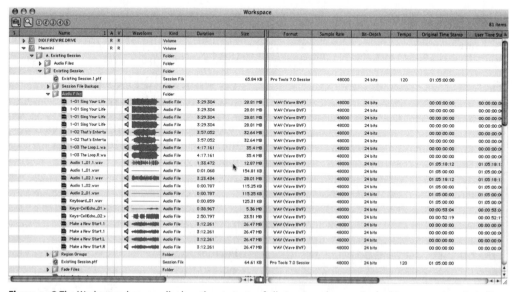

Figure 9.18 The Workspace browser displays the contents of all storage volumes attached to your system, including all session folders, audio files, and non-Pro Tools files.

Figure 9.19 To open the Workspace browser, choose Window > Show Workspace.

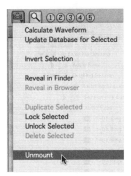

Figure 9.20 To unmount a volume, choose Unmount from the Browser menu.

The Workspace browser gives you access to the contents of all session folders: From within the browser you can open session files, audition and import audio files, and manage all of your Pro Tools session-related files. You can also mount and unmount storage volumes within the browser, and you can designate storage volumes as Record and Playback, Playback Only, or Transfer.

In addition, with its broad access to all volumes, the Workspace browser gives you the most comprehensive search capabilities available in Pro Tools. For more information on searches, see *Searching Items* later in this chapter.

To open the Workspace browser:

1. Launch Pro Tools.

2. Choose Window > Workspace (**Figure 9.19**).

   or

   Press Option-; (semi-colon) (Macintosh) or Alt-; (Windows).

   The Workspace browser appears.

Mounting and unmounting volumes

The Workspace browser lets you mount and unmount volumes while Pro Tools is launched.

To unmount a volume from within the Workspace browser:

1. Select a volume in the Workspace browser.

2. Choose Unmount from the Browser menu (**Figure 9.20**).

   The Workspace browser closes the database file for the selected volume, removes it from the Workspace browser, and then unmounts the disk from the computer. Removable volumes (such as a CD-ROM) are ejected.

Designating audio and video volumes

The Workspace browser provides audio and video designator columns, which let you classify whether storage volumes are *Performance volumes* (suitable for Record and Playback or Playback only) or *Transfer volumes* (suitable for storage only).

The audio and video volume designator columns provide the following volume designator options:

R (Record): R designates that a volume can record and play audio and video files.

P (Playback): P designates that a volume can play audio and video already on it but cannot have new files recorded to it.

T (Transfer): T designates that a volume can be used for storing, transferring, or auditioning files but cannot be used for recording or playback (such as CD-ROMs).

To designate an audio or video volume:

1. Open the Workspace browser.

2. Click in the desired Audio or Video Designator column (**Figure 9.21**).

3. From the Designator pop-up menu, choose the desired designation for the volume (R, P, or T) (**Figure 9.22**).

Figure 9.21 The Audio and Video Designator columns in the Workspace browser.

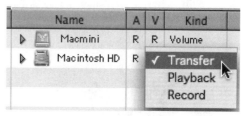

Figure 9.22 To designate an Audio or Video volume, choose R (Record), P (Playback), or T (Transfer) from the Designator pop-up menu.

Figure 9.23 To open a session from within a browser, double-click on the session file icon.

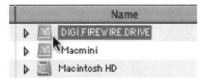

Figure 9.24 To open a volume in the Workspace browser, double-click the volume's icon.

✔ Tip

- Use the Workspace browser as the start point and end point for working in Pro Tools. This will help you become familiar with the file-management environment, and it will help you remember to back up your audio files.

  To start, launch Pro Tools from the application icon. Open the Workspace browser, then open your session files by double-clicking the session file icon inside the browser window (**Figure 9.23**). To end, close the session without quitting Pro Tools by pressing Shift-Command-W (Macintosh) or Shift-Control-W (Windows), and then back up your audio files and other session files from inside the Workspace browser.

Volume browsers

Volume browsers give you access to the contents of individual mounted hard drives, network storage, and CD-ROMs. You can use Volume browsers to manage, audition, and import individual items in the volume. You can also use a Volume browser to update the database for a volume.

To open a Volume browser:

- ◆ Double-click a volume or folder in the Workspace browser (**Figure 9.24**).

  or

- ◆ Click the Expand/Collapse icon next to the item. This displays the contents of the volume or folder within the current browser.

Project browsers

Project browsers (**Figure 9.25**) give you access to all files related to the current session regardless of what volume they reside on. Project browsers are useful for quickly viewing and auditioning audio files in the current session. Project browsers also provide a Copy and Relink command, which is useful for relinking Transfer files.

The Project browser displays the following:

Audio Files Folder: This folder contains all audio files referenced by the session.

Fade Files Folder: This folder contains all fade files referenced by the session.

Render Sources Folder: This folder contains all files that have been imported into the session, but are still being converted, copied, or processed.

Video Files Folder: This folder contains all video files referenced by the session.

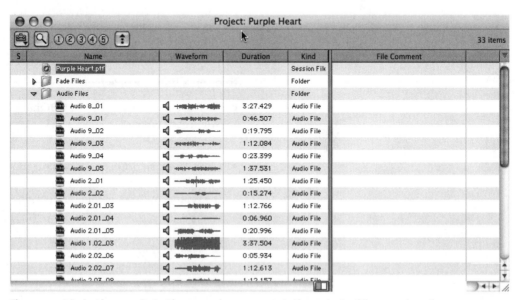

Figure 9.25 A Project browser. Project browsers give you access to the contents of the current session.

Figure 9.26 To open a Project browser for the current session, choose Window > Project.

Figure 9.27 The Copy and Relink command in a Project browser's Browser menu.

To open a Project browser:

1. Launch Pro Tools and open a session.

2. Choose Window > Project (**Figure 9.26**).
   or
   Press Option-O.
   The Project browser opens.

Copying and relinking files

The Copy and Relink command lets you copy files and relink the session to the copies rather than to the originals. This is useful for copying files from Transfer volumes to Performance volumes.

To copy files to a new location and relink to the copies:

1. In the Project browser, select the files you want to copy and relink.

2. Choose Copy and Relink from the Browser menu (**Figure 9.27**).
   The selected files are copied to the chosen location and relinked in the background.

For information on auditioning files, see *Waveforms and Auditioning* later in this chapter, or see the *Pro Tools Reference Guide*.

USING BROWSERS

Indexing

DigiBase uses an indexing process to extract metadata from files. It then stores that data in the associated database file and displays it in the columns of a browser. When you open a browser, Pro Tools automatically indexes the contents of each folder. You can manually index the entire contents of a volume or folder using the Update Database command in the Browser menu.

To manually index the contents of a volume or folder:

1. Select the volume, folder, or item in the Items list.

2. From the Browser menu, choose Update Database for Selected (**Figure 9.28**).

   The database for the entire contents of the selected volume or folder is updated.

For more information on indexing, see the *Pro Tools Reference Guide.*

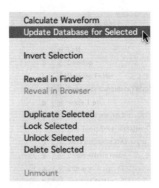

Figure 9.28 To index a volume, folder, or audio file, from the Browser menu, select Update Database for Selected.

Searching Items

DigiBase browsers include a powerful search tool. The Workspace browser gives you the broadest search capability, letting you access the content of all volumes attached to your system. All other browsers let you search the contents of that individual browser only.

When you perform a search, you can filter the contents of your volumes according to a number of *search criteria*, including file name (text), date and time, or time code; or you can select a search criterion from the Kind pop-up menu.

Search results are displayed in the Search Results pane, which appears below the Items list when you click the Search icon.

For more information on searching items, see the *Pro Tools Reference Guide*.

To search the current browser:

1. Click the Search icon.

    The Search Results pane appears (**Figure 9.29**).

continues on next page

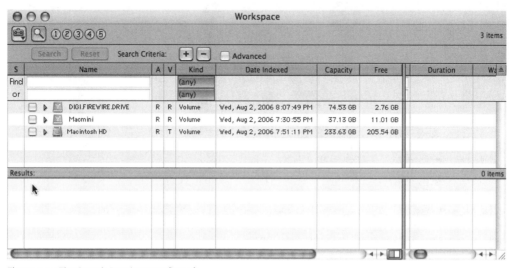

Figure 9.29 The Search Results pane (lower).

2. Enter text in the File Name field, or enter a date, or select search criteria from the Kind pop-up menu (**Figure 9.30**).

3. Click the Search button (**Figure 9.31**) or press Return (Macintosh) or Enter (Windows).

The search begins (indicated by the Search button becoming a Stop button). Results of the search are displayed in the Search Results pane (**Figure 9.32**).

Figure 9.30 The Kind pop-up menu lets you select additional search criteria.

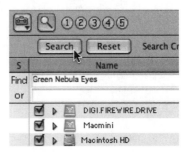

Figure 9.31 Click the Search button to begin a search.

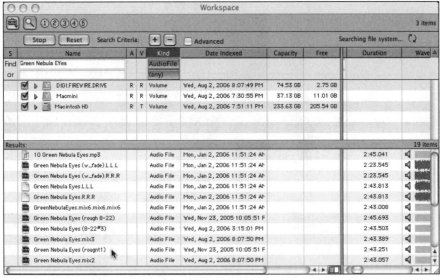

Figure 9.32 Search results appear in the Search Results pane.

Figure 9.33 Click the Stop button to stop an active search.

Figure 9.34 Click the Reset button to reset your search settings.

To stop a search:

◆ During a search, click the Stop button (**Figure 9.33**).

The search is stopped. Search results already found are displayed.

To reset your search settings:

◆ Click the Reset button (**Figure 9.34**).

All search fields are cleared and the main browser view (all items) returns.

To close the search pane:

◆ Click the Search icon to toggle the search pane closed/open.

The search is stopped. The Search pane is closed and the window returns to the main Browser view.

For more information on searching items, see the *Pro Tools Reference Guide*.

Waveforms and Auditioning

DigiBase lets you audition audio files by clicking directly on the audio file's waveform inside a DigiBase browser. When you open a session, DigiBase automatically calculates waveforms for each audio file in that session. DigiBase also calculates waveforms when you import audio into a session (**Figure 9.35**).

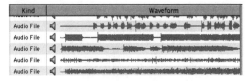

Figure 9.35 Audio file waveforms displayed in a browser.

Calculating waveforms

When browsing in DigiBase, you may encounter audio files (in folders other than the current session) that do not yet have waveforms calculated. In this case, a gray bar appears in the waveform column (**Figure 9.36**). These files have not yet been indexed by Pro Tools, and thus do not have waveforms calculated. In order to audition these files, you can, however, direct Pro Tools to calculate waveforms as follows:

Figure 9.36 If an audio file's waveform has not been calculated, a gray bar appears in the browser's Waveform column.

To calculate waveforms in a browser:

1. Select online audio files, or folders, in a browser.

2. Choose Calculate Waveform from the Browser menu (**Figure 9.37**).

   The audio file's waveform appears in the Waveforms column.

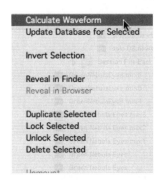

Figure 9.37 To calculate a selected audio file's waveform, choose Calculate Waveform from the Browser menu.

Figure 9.38 To audition an audio file, click and hold the Speaker icon.

Figure 9.39 To audition an audio file from a specific point, click and hold on the audio file's waveform at the desired location.

Auditioning audio files

You can audition audio files inside any browser. Auditioning is useful for identifying and evaluating audio files before importing, copying, or deleting them.

To audition an audio file:

1. Select an audio file in the browser's Items list.

2. Press the spacebar.

or

Click and hold the Speaker icon (to the left of the waveform display) (**Figure 9.38**).

To audition from a specific point within an audio file:

◆ Click and hold on the audio file's waveform display at the desired location (**Figure 9.39**).

To loop audition an audio file:

1. Select an audio file in the browser's Items list.

2. Press Option-spacebar.

or

Option-click (Macintosh) or Alt-click (Windows) in the waveform.

WAVEFORMS AND AUDITIONING

Moving, Copying, Duplicating, and Deleting Items

DigiBase follows the same protocol for moving, copying, duplicating, and deleting items as your computer's operating system. For example, moving an item from one volume to another volume copies the file, and Pro Tools warns you if an item is about to be overwritten.

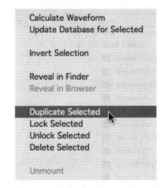

Figure 9.40 To duplicate selected items, choose Duplicate Selected from the Browser menu.

To move items:

◆ Select one or more items and drag them to a new location.

Moving an item to a new location on the same volume moves the item. Moving an item to a different volume copies the item.

To copy and move items:

◆ Select one or more items and Option-drag (Macintosh) or Alt-drag (Windows) them to a new location.

To duplicate one or more items:

1. Select one or more items.

2. Press Command-D (Macintosh) or Control-D (Windows).

   or

   Choose Duplicate Selected from the Browser menu (**Figure 9.40**).

Figure 9.41 To delete selected items, choose Delete Selected from the Browser menu.

To delete one or more items:

1. Select one or more items.

2. Press Delete.

   or

   Choose Delete Selected from the Browser menu (**Figure 9.41**).

   Pro Tools asks you to confirm that you want to permanently delete selected files from disk.

3. Click Delete.

   The files are deleted from disk.

To delete locked files:

1. Select one or more locked files.

2. Press Command-Delete (Macintosh) or Control-Delete (Windows).

   The locked files are deleted from disk.

Importing Audio Files Using Drag and Drop

Pro Tools lets you import audio files by dragging and dropping from a DigiBase browser into the Regions list, existing tracks, or new tracks. You can also spot audio at a desired location in a track.

If an imported audio file does not match the sample rate, bit depth, or file format of the current session, Pro Tools automatically converts the file to match the session upon import. For more information on file conversion, see *Chapter 8: File Management Basics*.

To import audio files into the Regions list:

1. Select the audio files in a browser.

2. Drag the files onto the Regions list of the current session (**Figure 9.42**).

   The imported audio files appear in the Audio Regions list.

To import audio files into an existing track:

1. Select the audio files in a browser.

2. Drag the files onto an existing track in the Edit window of the current session.

   The imported audio files appear within the existing track at the desired location.

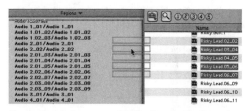

Figure 9.42 To import audio files into the Audio Regions list, drag and drop the files you want to import directly into the Audio Regions list.

Figure 9.43 Select Spot mode in the Edit Modes section of the Edit window.

Figure 9.44 The Spot Dialog box lets you select an exact location to place imported audio files.

Figure 9.45 To import and spot an audio file using its waveform, Command-click (Macintosh) or Control-click (Windows) at the approximate location you want the audio spotted. Drop the waveform into a track.

To import audio files into new tracks:

1. Select the audio files in a browser.

2. Drag the files onto any empty space in the Edit window.

   or

   Shift-drag the files anywhere in the Edit window.

   The imported audio files appear in new tracks inside the Edit window.

To import and spot audio into a track:

1. Enable Spot Mode (**Figure 9.43**).

2. Select an audio file in a browser.

3. Drag and drop the items into a Track playlist.

   The Spot Dialog box appears (**Figure 9.44**).

4. Enter the time location where you want to spot the item.

5. Click OK.

   The imported audio file appears in the track at the desired time location.

To import and spot an audio file using its waveform:

1. Command-click (Macintosh) or Control-click (Windows) in the audio file's waveform display at the approximate time location you want to spot the audio in the track (**Figure 9.45**).

2. While pressing Command-click or Control-click, drag and drop the waveform onto an existing audio track.

   The imported audio file appears in the track at the desired time location.

Importing region groups, REX, and ACID files using drag and drop

Pro Tools 7 lets you import Standard MIDI files, region group files, REX files, and ACID files into a session using drag and drop from a DigiBase browser.

To import a region group file:

1. Choose File > Import > Region Groups.

2. Select the desired region group to import.

3. Click Import

   or

   Drag and drop the desired region group file from a Digibase browser to the Regions list, a track, the Track List or the Timeline.

   Depending on where you drop the region group the following occurs:

   ▲ Dropping a region group in the Regions list adds the region group to the list. All audio, MIDI, and region groups contained with the dropped region group also appear in the Regions list.

   ▲ Dropping a region group in a track imports files contained within the region group directly to that track and spots the region group to the drop location. If multitrack files are contained within the region group, those files are imported to adjacent tracks.

   ▲ Dropping a region group in the Track List or Timeline creates new tracks for the imported region group.

To import a REX file into Pro Tools:

◆ Drag and drop the desired REX file from a DigiBase browser to the Regions list, a track, the Track List, or the Timeline.

   The REX file is converted to a region group when imported, and all its slices are converted into individual audio files and regions

To import an ACID file into Pro Tools:

◆ Drag and drop the desired ACID file from a DigiBase browser to the Regions list, a track, the Track List, or the Timeline.

   The ACID file is converted to a region group when imported, and all its slices are converted into individual audio files and regions. If no slice data is present, the ACID file is imported as a regular audio file.

For more information on importing audio files, see *Chapter 8: File Management Basics*. For more information on importing items with drag and drop in DigiBase, see the *Pro Tools Reference Guide*. For more information on region groups see *Chapter 13: Advanced Editing*. For more information on REX files and ACID files, see the *Pro Tools Reference Guide*.

Figure 9.46 The Missing Files dialog box.

Relinking Audio Files

When you open a session, Pro Tools attempts to locate all files linked to that session. When missing files or Transfer files (files on drives unsuitable for record and playback) are detected, Pro Tools prompts you to relink the files.

Relinking Transfer files

When a Transfer file is detected, a dialog box appears, prompting you to copy the Transfer file to a Performance volume (suitable for record and playback).

To relink Transfer files:

◆ In the Transfer files dialog box, click Yes.
Files are copied to the selected Performance volume. The copies are then relinked to the session.

Relinking missing files

When a missing file is detected, Pro Tools launches the Missing Files dialog box (**Figure 9.46**). The Missing Files dialog box gives you the following options:

Skip All: The Skip All option ignores all missing audio files and fades. Missing files remain offline in the session.

Manually Find and Relink: The Manually Find and Relink option opens the Relink window, where you can search, compare, verify, and relink missing files.

Automatically Find and Relink: The Automatically Find and Relink option searches all performance volumes and auto-matically relinks matching files with the ses-sion. Note: This option automatically commits relinked files without asking for verification.

Regenerate Missing Fades: The Regenerate Missing Fade option excludes fades from the relinking process and recal-culates them instead.

The Relink window

The Relink window (**Figure 9.47**) lets you search, compare, verify, and relink missing files. The Relink window includes the following:

Menu and Toolbar: This includes the Relink menu, view presets, and relinking buttons.

Select Areas to Search: This selects volumes on which to search for missing items.

Select Files to Relink: This lists missing files.

Candidates: This lists files that match the "relinking criteria" for a missing file. The link icon next to the candidate can be toggled to link (or unlink) the candidate to the selected missing file.

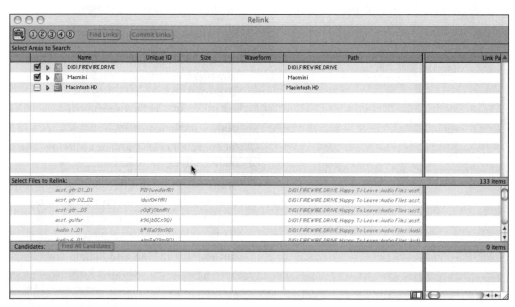

Figure 9.47 The Relink window.

Figure 9.48 To open the Relink window from inside a browser, in the Browser menu, select Relink Offline.

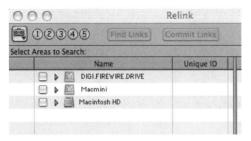

Figure 9.49 The Select Areas to Search pane of the Relink window.

Figure 9.50 In the Select Areas to Search pane, check the box next to the volumes and/or folders you want included in the search.

To open the Relink window:

1. From the Missing Files dialog box, select Manually Find and Relink.

or

In an open session, Choose Window > Project.

2. Choose Relink Offline from the Browser menu (**Figure 9.48**).

The Relink window appears.

Configuring areas to search

You can configure searches in the Relink window by selecting specific volumes and folders in the Select Areas to Search (**Figure 9.49**) pane. When you perform a search, only those volumes and folders selected are searched. Configuring the Select Areas to Search pane will help make your searches more accurate and less time-consuming.

To configure the Select Areas to Search pane:

◆ In the Select Areas to Search pane, click the Search column next to each volume or folder you want included in the search (**Figure 9.50**).

Relinking single and multiple missing files

The Relink window lets you relink missing files individually or in batches. When you relink files individually, you use the Find All Candidates button, which displays all candidate files. You can then select the best-suited file to relink.

Relinking multiple files in batches is handy if you need to relink numerous missing files in short order. When you relink files in batches, you use the Find Links button, which displays a link icon, indicating Pro Tools has found the best-suited candidate. You can then view that candidate file and commit the link. (Or, if you need further confirmation before committing a relink, you can view all candidates for an individual file, and select the best-suited candidate yourself.)

To relink a single missing file:

1. Configure the Select Areas to Search pane.

2. Select one item in the Select Files to Relink list (**Figure 9.51**).

3. Click Find All Candidates (**Figure 9.52**).
   Pro Tools searches the selected volumes and folders and displays all files with matching File Name and/or Unique ID in the Candidates list (**Figure 9.53**). (Link icons indicate if a file is already linked.)

4. Click the Link toggle next to the candidate you want to relink (**Figure 9.54**).

5. Click Commit Links (**Figure 9.55**). (Note: Committed links cannot be undone).

   or

   Repeat steps for additional missing files, leaving the Commit process until later.

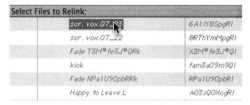

Figure 9.51 In the Select Files to Relink pane, select a single file.

Figure 9.52 The Find All Candidates button in the Relink window.

Figure 9.53 The Candidates list displays all candidate files matching search criteria for relinking.

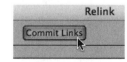

Figure 9.54 Click the Link toggle next to the candidate file you want to relink.

Figure 9.55 The Commit Links button.

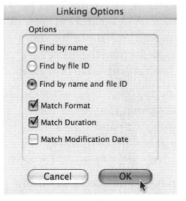

Figure 9.56 Click the Find Links button to search for multiple files to relink.

Figure 9.57 The Link Options dialog box.

To relink multiple missing files:

1. Configure the Select Areas to Search pane.

2. Select one or more items in the Select Files to Relink list.

3. Click Find Links (**Figure 9.56**).
   The Linking Options dialog appears (**Figure 9.57**).

4. Select the desired Linking options.

5. Click OK.
   Pro Tools searches the selected volumes and folders. A link icon appears next to each file in the Select Files to Relink list as Pro Tools identifies a suitable candidate for the link.

6. In the Select Files to Relink list, click an individual file to view the candidate file.

7. Click Commit Links.
   or
   Click Find All Candidates to view all candidate files, and select the best-suited candidate.

Committing links

Relinking cannot be undone. When using the Relink window to relink missing files, you must click the Commit Link button in order to finalize the relink. Once you have committed a relink, the old link is lost, and the relink cannot be undone.

To commit links:

1. Use the Relink window to find a relinking candidate.

2. Click Commit Link.
   The candidate file is relinked to the session.

Managing Background Processing with the Tasks Window

Pro Tools performs most file-management tasks (such as copying, indexing, and relinking) in the background, letting you record, edit, and mix without interruption. Background processing can, however, especially on slower computers, divert CPU power and impact a session.

To help you optimize CPU resources, the Tasks window (**Figure 9.58**) lets you monitor, pause, and cancel background processing. The Tasks window is also useful for checking the status of a task and for stopping unwanted tasks from being performed.

The Tasks window

The Tasks window includes the following features:

Active Tasks pane: The Active Tasks pane (upper) shows the tasks that are in progress or in queue to start. When a task is completed, it disappears from the queue. Incomplete tasks are moved to the Paused Tasks pane.

Paused Tasks pane: The Paused Tasks pane (lower) displays paused tasks. Tasks listed in this pane must be moved to the Active Tasks pane for processing to proceed.

Tasks Window menu: The Tasks window menu provides commands for Tasks window operation.

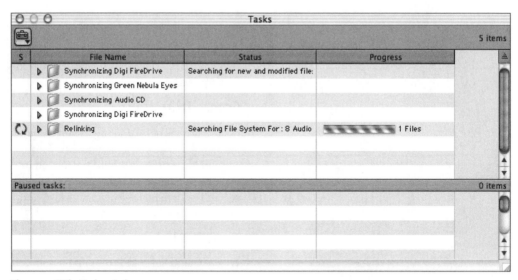

Figure 9.58 The Tasks window.

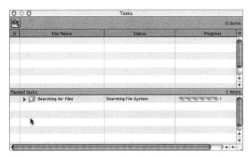

Figure 9.59 To pause a task, drag the task from the Active Tasks pane to the Paused Tasks pane.

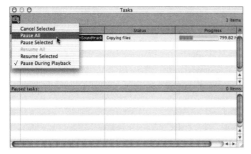

Figure 9.60 To pause all tasks, select Pause All from the Tasks window menu.

Columns: Columns display the following data:

◆ **Name:** This column indicates the name of the audio file or other affected item.

◆ **Status:** This column indicates the action being taken.

◆ **Progress:** This column indicates the progress of the task.

◆ **Progress Indicator:** This column indicates that the task is in process.

◆ **Quantification:** This column shows the percentage of progress of the current task.

◆ **Warning Message:** If a task does not complete successfully, this column displays a warning symbol and a message describing the problem.

To open the Tasks window:

◆ Choose Window > Task Manager.
The Tasks window opens.

To toggle between maximized and minimized views:

◆ Click the green View Toggle icon at the top of the Tasks window.

Pausing and canceling tasks

The Tasks window lets you pause, resume, and cancel tasks, as follows:

To pause a task:

◆ Drag the appropriate task from the Active Tasks pane to the Paused Tasks pane (**Figure 9.59**).
The task moves to the top of the Paused Tasks pane.

To pause all tasks:

◆ Choose Pause All from the Tasks window menu (**Figure 9.60**).

To resume a task:

◆ Drag a task from the Paused Tasks pane to the Active Tasks pane.

The task returns to its previous position in the queue.

To resume all paused tasks:

◆ Select Resume All from the Tasks window menu (**Figure 9.61**).

All tasks in the Paused Tasks pane (except failed tasks) are moved to the Active Tasks pane.

To cancel a task:

1. Select any task in either pane of the Tasks window.

2. Select Cancel Selected in the Tasks menu (**Figure 9.62**).

   or

   Press Delete.

   The task is canceled and removed from the Tasks window.

To cancel all tasks:

1. Select any task in either pane of the Tasks window.

2. Press Command-A (Macintosh) Control-A (Windows) to select all tasks in that pane.

3. Press Delete.

   All tasks are removed from the Tasks window. (This command cannot be undone.)

For more information on the Tasks window, see the *Pro Tools Reference Guide*.

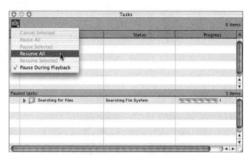

Figure 9.61 To resume all paused tasks, select Resume All from the Tasks menu.

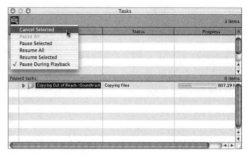

Figure 9.62 To cancel selected tasks, select Cancel Selected from the Tasks menu.

Part IV:
Editing Audio

EDITING BASICS

Using a visual interface to edit audio is perhaps the most powerful feature of hard-disk recording: You can use your eyes and ears to manipulate visual representations of audio with remarkable speed and precision. Pro Tools provides many tools for working in this visual environment. With a little practice, you'll be able to transform raw audio material into streamlined final mixes.

This chapter introduces you to the basics of editing audio in Pro Tools. We'll start off with some concepts such as non-destructive editing and playback editing. Next, we'll talk about regions, and we'll show you several tools for viewing and handling them.

We'll also get into playlist editing, a feature that lets you create multiple arrangements of audio regions on a single track. And we'll look at how Edit modes influence the movement of regions in a session. Lastly, we'll discuss the Edit window's rulers and the useful memory location feature.

Editing Audio in Pro Tools

Audio editing tasks in Pro Tools are performed in the Edit window. The Edit window provides versatile tools for viewing, auditioning, selecting, and assembling audio. For a detailed description of the Edit window, see *Chapter 3: The Mix and Edit Windows.*

What is non-destructive editing?

Editing in Pro Tools is *non-destructive*. This means that when you edit audio, the original audio file saved on disk is not altered. Instead, you perform edits on audio *regions*, which are visual representations of audio files. Audio regions can be whole audio files or segments of audio files, and are usually displayed during editing as audio waveforms.

Certain Pro Tools commands—such as those that delete or compact audio files—are *destructive*: They permanently alter the parent audio file on disk. Pro Tools generally warns you before completing a destructive command.

What is playback editing?

You can perform many editing tasks while Pro Tools is in playback mode. This makes the editing process highly interactive and can help increase your editing speed and productivity. You can perform the following tasks during playback:

◆ Capture, separate, or trim regions

◆ Place, spot, or rearrange regions

◆ Add fades or crossfades to audio regions

◆ Nudge audio regions

◆ Audition playlists

◆ Adjust automation data

◆ Process audio with AudioSuite plug-ins

Some editing commands (such as those for setting audio inputs, outputs, and sends) cannot be performed during playback.

EDITING AUDIO IN PRO TOOLS

Figure 10.1 A whole-file audio region.

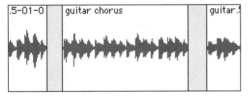

Figure 10.2 A region representing a segment of an audio file.

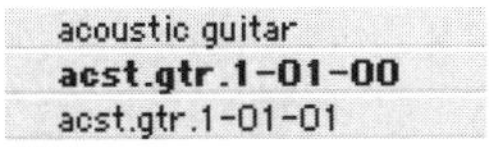

Figure 10.3 Whole-file audio regions are represented in bold in the Regions list.

Understanding Regions

An audio region is a visual representation of a parent audio file stored on disk. A region can represent a whole audio file (**Figure 10.1**) or a segment of an audio file (**Figure 10.2**). When track view is set to Waveform, regions are displayed as audio waveforms. There is no limit to the number of regions you can have in a track playlist.

When you edit audio, you're editing the regions that represent the audio, not the actual audio file. The original audio file is protected and remains unchanged on your hard disk. Regions can be edited, copied, looped, grouped, and arranged in any number of ways to create new parts, sections, or song structures.

Region types

Pro Tools has various types of regions, including:

Whole-File Audio Regions: These are created when you record or import audio, consolidate existing regions, or process audio non-destructively with an AudioSuite plug-in. Whole-file audio regions represent the entire audio file on hard disk, and are displayed in bold letters in the Regions list (**Figure 10.3**).

When you record audio into Pro Tools, it appears initially as a whole-file audio region. When you select segments of a whole-file audio region, you create new regions that reference only the selected portion of the parent audio file.

User-Defined Regions: These regions are created when you perform certain tasks, such as recording, capturing, separating, or consolidating audio regions. They are also created when you trim a whole-file audio region or rename an existing region.

Auto-Created Regions: These are automatically created when you edit regions or punch-record over existing regions. You can turn auto-created regions into user-defined regions by renaming them.

Offline Regions: These are regions whose parent audio file cannot be located when you open a session. Offline regions appear italicized and dimmed in the Regions list (**Figure 10.4**) and as light-blue regions with italicized names in a track's playlist. You can edit offline regions, but you cannot process them with AudioSuite plug-ins.

Stereo Regions: These are displayed as single regions in the Regions list. Click the triangle next to the multichannel file name to see its individual mono channels (**Figure 10.5**).

Region Groups: New in Pro Tools 7, a *region group* is a collection of audio regions and/or MIDI regions referenced by a single region group file (.rgrp file format). Region groups let you handle and perform some edits on multiple regions in one move. Region group files are displayed as single regions in the Regions list. Click the triangle next to the region group file icon in the Regions list to see the individual regions contained in the region group file (**Figure 10.6**). You can place region group files on audio, MIDI, and instrument tracks.

Figure 10.4 Offline regions are italicized and dimmed in the Regions list.

Figure 10.5 A stereo region displaying its associated mono regions.

Figure 10.6 Click the triangle next to a region group file to view the individual regions contained in the region group.

Figure 10.7 A Waveform track view.

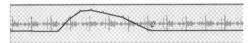

Figure 10.8 Volume track view. Use the Grabber tool to drag the breakpoints on the line graph.

Figure 10.9 The Track View pop-up menu.

Viewing Regions

The Edit window provides several features for viewing regions and their attributes.

Setting the track view

The track view determines which type of data is displayed in a track's playlist. You can select from Waveform, Volume, Pan, Mute, and Blocks. You can also view automated plug-in parameters. In most cases, you'll perform edits using Waveform view (**Figure 10.7**).

When track view is set to Volume, Pan, or Mute, a line graph representing the data appears against a dimmed waveform view. These line graphs include *breakpoints,* which you can edit by dragging with the Grabber tool. You can also draw new breakpoints with the Pencil tool (**Figure 10.8**).

When track view is set to Blocks, audio regions are displayed as empty blocks bearing the region's name. Blocks view is less CPU-intensive and can help accelerate screen redraws during playback scrolling.

To set the track view:

1. Click the Track View selector.

   The Track View pop-up menu appears (**Figure 10.9**).

2. Choose a track view from the pop-up menu.

✔ Tip

- To toggle between Waveform and Volume track views, click in the track you want to toggle. (If you want to toggle multiple tracks, Shift-click the additional tracks.) Then press Control-minus (Macintosh) or Start-minus (Windows) on the keyboard.

Setting the track height

You can display tracks in the Edit window at six different heights: Mini, Small, Medium, Large, Jumbo, and Extreme. Large track heights are useful for precise editing; smaller track heights help conserve screen space.

To set the track height:

1. Click the arrow next to the Track View selector (**Figure 10.10**).

   or

   Click in the area to the right of the track controls (**Figure 10.11**).

   The Track Height pop-up menu appears.

2. Select a track height from the pop-up menu (**Figure 10.12**).

✔ Tip

- Pro Tools provides an expanded track display, which lets you view volume, mute, and pan data separately for each channel of a stereo pair (**Figure 10.13**). To turn on expanded track display for a stereo track, select Expanded Track Display in the Track Height pop-up menu (**Figure 10.14**).

Figure 10.10 Click the arrow button to open the Track Height pop-up menu.

Figure 10.11 Click to the right of the track controls to open the Track Height pop-up menu.

Figure 10.12 The Track Height pop-up menu.

Figure 10.13 The expanded track display lets you view data separately on both tracks of a stereo pair.

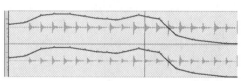

Figure 10.14 Choose Expanded Track Display from the Track Height pop-up menu on a stereo track.

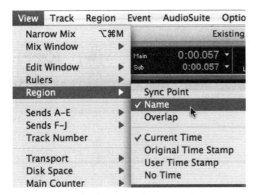

Figure 10.15 To display the region name, choose View > Region > Name.

Figure 10.16 To display region time locations, choose View > Region and then select from the time location display options.

Displaying region names and time locations

Region names and time locations are displayed in the upper-left corner of each region. Pro Tools lets you turn these displays on and off to prevent interference with waveform editing.

To display region names:

◆ Choose View > Region > Name (**Figure 10.15**).

To display region time locations:

1. Choose View > Region.

2. Select one of the following time location display options (**Figure 10.16**):

 Current Time: This option displays the start and end times of regions.

 Original Time Stamp: This option displays each region's original time stamp (the time location of the region when it was first created).

 User Time Stamp: This option displays each region's user time stamp. The user time stamp is identical to the original time stamp by default, but you can redefine it using the Time Stamp Selected command.

 No Time: This option disables the display of region times.

VIEWING REGIONS

Zooming

The Edit window gives you several tools for quickly zooming in and out on audio regions. These tools include Horizontal and Vertical Zoom buttons, the Zoomer tool, Zoom Preset buttons and Zoom Toggle. Learning these zooming features will help make editing fast and painless.

Using the Horizontal Zoom Buttons

The Horizontal Zoom buttons let you zoom in and out in the horizontal direction on audio tracks.

To zoom in and out horizontally on all tracks:

◆ To zoom in, click the right Horizontal Zoom button (**Figure 10.17**). To zoom out, click the left Horizontal Zoom button.

or

◆ To zoom in, press Command-] (Macintosh) or Control-] (Windows). To zoom out, press Command-[(Macintosh) or Control-[(Windows).

Using the Vertical Zoom Buttons

The Vertical Zoom buttons let you zoom in and out in the vertical direction on audio and MIDI tracks.

To zoom in and out vertically on all tracks:

◆ To zoom in, click the top Vertical Zoom button. To zoom out, click the bottom Vertical Zoom button (**Figure 10.18**).

or

◆ To zoom in, press Command-Option-] (Macintosh) or Control-Alt-] (Windows). To zoom out, press Command-Option-[(Macintosh) or Control-Alt-[(Windows).

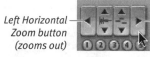

Left Horizontal Zoom button (zooms out) — Right Horizontal Zoom button (zooms in)

Figure 10.17 Horizontal Zoom buttons.

Top Vertical Zoom button (zooms in)   Bottom Vertical Zoom button (zooms out)

Figure 10.18 Vertical Zoom buttons.

ZOOMING

Figure 10.19 The Zoomer tool.

Figure 10.20 Click and hold on the Zoomer tool to select a Zoomer tool mode.

Figure 10.21 To zoom in horizontally, drag the Zoomer in any track.

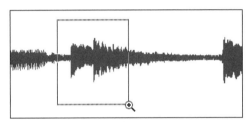

Figure 10.22 To zoom in vertically and horizontally, press Command (Macintosh) or Control (Windows) while dragging the Zoomer in any track.

Using the Zoomer Tool

The Zoomer tool lets you zoom in and out of a selected track point or a selected track area. The Zoomer tool offers two modes:

◆ **Normal Zoom mode**: In this mode the Zoomer tool remains selected after zooming.

◆ **Single Zoom mode**: In this mode the currently selected Edit tool automatically returns after zooming.

To set the Zoomer tool mode:

1. Click the Zoomer tool (**Figure 10.19**).

2. From the Zoomer tool pop-up menu, select Normal Zoom mode or Single Zoom mode (**Figure 10.20**).

To zoom around a selected track point:

1. Select the Zoomer tool.

2. Click once on the desired point within the track.

   All tracks are zoomed in one level and centered around the point.

3. To zoom out one level, Option-click (Macintosh) or Alt-click (Windows) with the Zoomer tool.

To zoom into a selected track area:

1. Select the Zoomer tool.

2. To zoom horizontally, drag with the Zoomer tool in the track's playlist (**Figure 10.21**).

   or

   To zoom horizontally and vertically, press Command (Macintosh) or Control (Windows) while dragging in the track's playlist (**Figure 10.22**).

ZOOMING

Using Continuous Zoom

Pro Tools 7 lets you zoom in and out on tracks continuously in both horizontal and vertical directions. When using continuous zoom, zoom levels expand and contract smoothly. Continuous zoom is helpful for maintaining your orientation when making precise edits.

To zoom continuously on an individual track:

1. Select the Zoomer tool.

2. Press Control (Macintosh) or Start (Windows) while dragging vertically in the track's playlist.

To zoom continuously on all tracks simultaneously:

1. Select the Zoomer tool.

2. Press Control-Shift (Macintosh) or Start-Shift (Windows) while dragging vertically across multiple tracks.

   or

   Press Control (Macintosh) or Start (Windows) while dragging horizontally in the track's playlist.

   All visible tracks zoom to the same zoom level.

Using Zoom Presets

The Edit window gives you five user-definable zoom preset buttons.

To store a zoom preset:

1. Navigate to a zoom level that you want to store.

2. Command-click (Macintosh) or Control-click (Windows) one of the five zoom preset buttons (**Figure 10.23**).

   The preset button flashes to indicate the zoom is being stored, and then remains highlighted.

Zoom preset buttons

Figure 10.23 To store a zoom preset, Command-click (Macintosh) or Control-click (Windows) on a zoom preset button.

Figure 10.24 To toggle between zoomed-in and zoomed-out views of a track selection, press Control-E (Macintosh) or Start-E (Windows).

To recall a zoom preset:

◆ Click a zoom preset button.

or

◆ While pressing Control (Macintosh) or Start (Windows), press the zoom preset number on the keyboard.

✔ Tips

■ To zoom in on a selection, press Option-F (Macintosh) or Alt-F (Windows).

■ To zoom so that all regions are visible in the Edit window, do one of the following:

■ Double-click the Zoomer tool in the toolbar.

■ Press Option-A (Macintosh) or Alt-A (Windows).

■ Press the F5 key twice.

■ To toggle between zoomed-in and zoomed-out views of a track selection, press Control-E (Macintosh) or Start-E (Windows). The selection is zoomed in to fill the Edit window, and tracks containing the selection are set to Large view (**Figure 10.24**).

ZOOMING

Using Zoom toggle

The Zoom Toggle button lets you switch back and forth between the current zoom view and a different user-defined zoom view. This is useful for making edit selections, examining glitches, or for any other task that requires quickly zooming in and out.

Figure 10.25 The Zoom Toggle button.

To define a Zoom Toggle view:

1. Make an edit selection.

2. Click the Zoom Toggle button. The Zoom Toggle button is highlighted, indicating it is enabled.

3. Adjust the following Zoom Toggle parameters as desired: Track Height, Vertical Zoom, Track View, and Grid.

4. Click the enabled (lit) Zoom Toggle button to store the new Zoom Toggle view and return to the previous zoom view.

5. Click the Zoom Toggle button to recall your new Zoom Toggle view.

To use Zoom Toggle:

1. Make a selection on one or more tracks.

2. Click the Zoom Toggle button (**Figure 10.25**).

   or

   Press Control-E (Macintosh) or Start-E (Windows).

   or

   With Commands Focus enabled, press E.

   The selection is zoomed to the stored Zoom Toggle view.

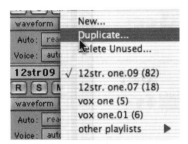

Figure 10.26 Choose Duplicate from the Playlist selector pop-up menu.

Figure 10.27 Enter a name for the duplicated playlist.

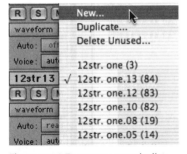

Figure 10.28 To create a new playlist, choose New from the Playlist selector pop-up menu.

Working with Playlists

An *edit playlist* is a snapshot of a track's current arrangement of regions. Pro Tools lets you create multiple edit playlists on each track, and switch quickly between them using the Playlist selector. This gives you the flexibility to experiment with different region-editing ideas. An edit playlist can contain a single region or multiple regions.

When you create a new track, its playlist is empty until you record or import audio onto it, or drag a region to it from the Regions list. It's a good practice to work from a duplicate of a track's original playlist: This preserves the track's region arrangement and frees you to try new edits.

To duplicate a track's current playlist:

1. Click the track's Playlist selector.

2. Choose Duplicate from the pop-up menu (**Figure 10.26**).

3. Enter a name for the duplicated playlist (**Figure 10.27**).

4. Click OK.

   The duplicated playlist appears and the track's name is changed to the name of the new playlist.

   You can also create a new playlist, and then record or drag regions to it.

To create a new playlist:

1. Click the track's Playlist selector.

2. Choose New from the pop-up menu (**Figure 10.28**).

3. Enter a name for the new playlist menu.

4. Click OK.

   An empty playlist appears in the track.

To assign a playlist:

1. Click the track's Playlist selector.

2. Choose an existing playlist from the pop-up menu (**Figure 10.29**).

   The selected playlist appears in the track and the track's name is updated to that of the selected playlist.

To delete a playlist:

1. Click the track's Playlist selector.

2. Choose Delete Unused from the pop-up menu.

3. Select the playlist you want to delete (**Figure 10.30**).

4. Click OK.

   The selected playlist is deleted. Caution: You cannot undo this action.

✔ Tips

- You can rename a playlist by renaming the track to which it is assigned: Double-click the track's name, enter a new name, and click OK.

- Each track also has a single automation playlist for each automated track control (such as volume, mute, and pan). For more information on automation playlists, see *Chapter 16: Automating a Mix.*

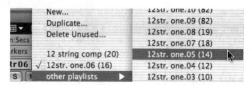

Figure 10.29 Choose a playlist from the pop-up menu.

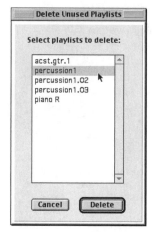

Figure 10.30 The Delete Unused Playlists dialog box.

WORKING WITH PLAYLISTS

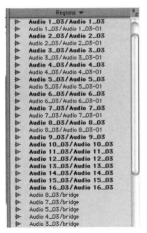

Figure 10.31 The Regions List.

Using the Regions List

When you record, import, or create a new audio region during editing, it appears in the Regions list (**Figure 10.31**). This list lets you manage the flow of audio regions in and out of a session. Whole-file audio regions are displayed in bold, and stereo and multichannel regions can be expanded to view individual channels. You can drag regions from the list directly onto any audio track.

In Pro Tools 7, the Regions list also displays MIDI regions and region group files.

The Regions list pop-up menu provides options for displaying, sorting, finding, and selecting audio regions. You can also use the list to import, export, compact, and delete audio files on disk. For information on managing audio files, see *Part III: Audio File Management.*

Displaying audio file info

The Regions list lets you display information about audio regions, including region names, color coding, timebase, and information about a region's parent audio file, including the parent audio file's name, the disk name on which it resides, and the file's full pathname.

To display audio file info:

1. Click the Regions list pop-up menu (**Figure 10.32**).

2. Choose Show.

3. Select from the following (**Figure 10.33**):

- ◆ Color

- ◆ Icon

- ◆ Time Base

- ◆ File Name

- ◆ Disk Name

- ◆ Full Path

✔ Tip

- ■ DigiBase's Project browser (and other DigiBase browsers) displays detailed audio file data, including sample rate, bit depth, file format, date created, date modified, and time stamp. You can also audition audio files and import them using drag and drop directly into the Regions list of the current session. Choose Window > Project. For more information on DigiBase browsers, see *Chapter 9: Managing Audio Files with DigiBase*.

Figure 10.32
The Regions list pop-up menu.

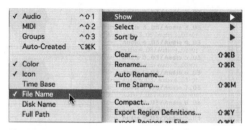

Figure 10.33 Choose an option from the Regions list pop-up menu to display information about a region's parent audio file.

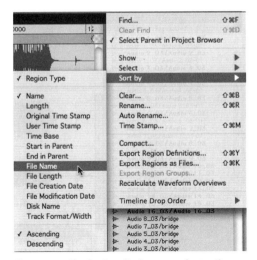

Figure 10.34 The Regions list lets you select options for sorting audio regions.

Sorting regions

The Regions list provides options for sorting audio regions. These options can help you manage regions, which can become quite numerous during a session. You can sort audio regions by name, length, time stamp, start time, and end time.

You can also sort regions by their parent audio file attributes, including creation date, disk name, and track format (stereo or mono).

To sort regions:

1. Click the Regions list pop-up menu.

2. Choose Sort by.

3. Select a sorting parameter (**Figure 10.34**). Audio regions are displayed in order according to the sorting parameter.

✔ Tip

■ To reverse the order of the displayed regions repeat steps 1 and 2 above, and then select Ascending or Descending from the pop-up menu.

Finding regions

The Regions list provides a Find command, which displays regions that match a word or phrase.

To find regions:

1. Click the Regions list pop-up menu and choose Find (**Figure 10.35**).

   or

   Press Command-Shift-F (Macintosh) or Control-Shift –F (Windows).

   The Find Regions dialog box appears.

2. Type the region name or portion of the region name you want to find (**Figure 10.36**).

3. Click OK.

   All regions matching the specified name appear in the Regions list. The name of the search also appears at the top of the list, indicating the found regions (**Figure 10.37**).

✔ Tip

- The Find Regions dialog box retains a history of your previous searches. Click the small arrow next to the search field to view your Find History, remove entries, or insert entries (**Figure 10.38**). Use this feature to minimize retyping your searches.

Figure 10.35 Choose Find from the Regions list pop-up menu.

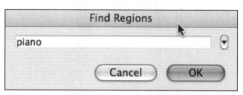

Figure 10.36 Type the name of the region you want to find in the Find Regions dialog box.

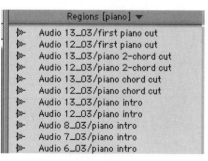

Figure 10.37 When displaying regions with the Find command, the name of the search appears at the top of the Regions list.

Figure 10.38 To view your search history in the Find Regions dialog box, click the small arrow next to the search field.

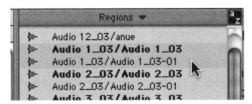

Figure 10.39 To select multiple regions, Command-click (Macintosh) or Control-click (Windows) their names in the Regions list.

| acst.gtr.1-01-01 |
| acst.gtr.1-02-00 |
| acst.gtr.1-03-00 |
| drums-01-00 L |
| grant.alien-01-00 |
| Grant.drone2-01-00 |

Figure 10.40 Drag the Marquee in the Regions list to select multiple regions.

Selecting in the Regions list

You can select single or multiple regions in the Regions list and drag them to tracks.

To select a single region:

◆ Click the region name that you want to select in the Regions list.

The selected region is highlighted and can be dragged to a track.

To select multiple regions:

◆ Command-click (Macintosh) or Control-click (Windows) each region that you want to select (**Figure 10.39**).

or

1. Move the cursor to the left of the region names until the Marquee cursor appears

2. Command-click (Macintosh) or Control-click (Windows) to the left of each region that you want to select.

The selected regions are highlighted and can be dragged to tracks.

To select a range of regions:

1. Move the cursor to the left of the region names until the Marquee appears.

2. Drag the Marquee over the regions you want to select (**Figure 10.40**).

or

Shift-click to the left of the first and last regions that you want to select.

All regions in the selected range are highlighted and can be dragged to tracks.

USING THE REGIONS LIST

239

To select unused regions:

1. Click the Regions list pop-up menu.

2. Choose Select > Unused (**Figure 10.41**).

   All unused audio regions are highlighted and can be dragged to tracks or cleared from the Regions list.

✔ Tip

- You can also select audio regions using the keyboard. To do this, click and hold on the a-z button in the upper right of the Audio Regions list pop-up menu (**Figure 10.42**), and then type the first few letters of the region name. The region name is highlighted and can be dragged to a track.

Clearing audio regions

You can remove unwanted audio regions from the Regions list using the pop-up menu. Periodically clearing unused regions will help you keep the Regions list manageable.

To clear unused audio regions:

1. Click the Regions list pop-up menu.

2. Choose Select > Unused.

   All unused regions are highlighted.

3. Choose Clear from the Regions list pop-up menu (**Figure 10.43**).

   The Clear Regions dialog box appears.

4. Click Remove (**Figure 10.44**).

   All unused regions are removed from the Regions list.

✔ Tips

- The parent audio files of a removed audio region remain untouched on disk.

- Caution: You cannot undo the Remove command.

Figure 10.41 To select unused regions in a session, choose Select > Unused in the Regions list pop-up menu.

Figure 10.42 You can select regions by clicking the a-z button, and then typing the first few letters of the region's name.

Figure 10.43 To remove regions from the Regions list, choose Clear from the Regions list pop-up menu.

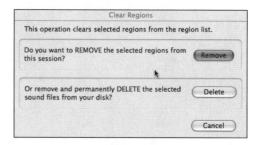

Figure 10.44 The Clear Regions dialog box.

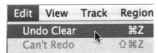

Figure 10.45 To undo the last operation, choose Edit > Undo.

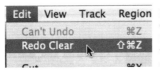

Figure 10.46 Choose Edit > Redo to recall the last undone operation.

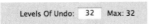

Figure 10.47 Choose Setup > Preferences > Editing and then input up to 32 levels of undo.

Using Multiple Undo

The Edit menu's Undo command lets you undo up to 32 previous sequential operations. Undo lets you quickly return to earlier editing configurations. After an operation is undone, you can use the Redo command to return to a later editing configuration.

Certain Pro Tools commands will clear the undo queue, such as those for deleting a track or playlist, or for clearing a region from the Regions list. Pro Tools will warn you before it clears the undo queue.

To undo the last operation:

◆ Choose Edit > Undo (**Figure 10.45**).

or

◆ Press Command-Z (Macintosh) or Control-Z (Windows).

To redo the last undone operation:

◆ Choose Edit > Redo (**Figure 10.46**).

or

◆ Press Shift-Command-Z (Macintosh) or Shift-Control-Z (Windows).

✔ Tip

■ If you're low on RAM, reducing the levels of undo can help save memory. Choose Setup > Preferences, and click the Editing tab. In the Levels of Undo field, enter a value between 1 and 32 (**Figure 10.47**). Click Done.

Using the Undo History Window

The Undo History window displays the current queue of undoable and redoable operations. You can use the Undo History window to return your editing session to a previous state.

To show the Undo History window:

◆ Choose Window > Undo History (**Figure 10.48**).

The Undo History window appears (**Figure 10.49**). Undoable operations appear in bold. Redoable operation appear in italics.

To undo an operation in the Undo History window:

◆ Click the operation you want to undo in the Undo History window.

The selected operation is undone, as well as all operations in the queue performed after the selected operation.

To redo an operation in the Undo History window:

◆ Click the operation you want to redo in the Undo History window.

The selected operation is redone, as well as all operations in the queue performed before the selected operation.

Figure 10.48 To show the Undo History window, choose Window > Undo History.

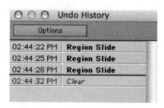

Figure 10.49 The Undo History window.

USING MULTIPLE UNDO

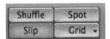

Figure 10.50 The Edit mode buttons in the upper-left corner of the Edit window.

Figure 10.51 The Spot dialog box.

Setting Edit Modes

Pro Tools has four Edit modes: Shuffle, Spot, Slip, and Grid. These modes control how regions are moved and placed in the Edit window. Using the appropriate Edit mode for a task can help make editing faster and more efficient.

To set the Edit mode:

◆ Select one of the four Edit mode buttons in the upper-left corner of the Edit window (**Figure 10.50**).

Edit modes affect the movement and placement of regions as follows:

Shuffle: In Shuffle mode, adjacent audio regions automatically snap together. This is useful for removing a segment from a continuous piece of audio— such as removing a section from a song. When a new region is created or placed on a track, it automatically snaps to the region to its left.

In Shuffle mode, you can rearrange the order of regions on a track, but regions can't overlap. When you change a region's start or end time, the other regions on the track are moved accordingly.

Spot: Spot mode lets you move a selected region to an exact time location. When you select a region in Spot mode, the Spot dialog box appears (**Figure 10.51**). You can then enter a precise start time for the selected region.

Spot mode is useful for precision tasks such as synchronization: You can enter SMPTE frame locations (HD only) or another time format, capture an incoming timecode address, or use a region's time stamp as a reference point.

continues on next page

Slip: Slip mode lets you move regions freely in a track with few constraints. Unlike Shuffle mode, Slip mode lets you overlap regions or separate regions with space (silence).

In Slip mode, you can use edit tools—the Trimmer, Selector, Grabber, and Pencil—without time restrictions. This freedom makes Slip mode ideal for use in most editing situations.

Grid: Grid mode lets you snap selected regions to a user-defined time grid. This mode is useful for placing regions cleanly on the beat. It's also good for making precise Edit and Timeline selections.

There are two types of Grid mode:

▲ **Absolute Grid mode:** Absolute Grid mode snaps a selection cleanly to the grid.

▲ **Relative Grid mode:** Relative Grid mode moves selections by the current grid unit. Relative mode is useful when working with regions that fall between boundaries.

To select Grid mode:

◆ Click the Grid mode button and select Absolute or Relative Grid mode (**Figure 10.52**)

To set the grid size, choose a time in the Grid Value pop-up menu (**Figure 10.53**).

To display grid lines in the Edit window, choose Setup > Preferences. Click the Display tab. Select "Draw Grids in Edit Window." You can also toggle the display of grid lines on and off by clicking the current Timebase ruler (**Figure 10.54**).

For more information on using Edit modes, see *Chapter 12: Working with Regions*.

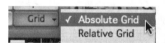

Figure 10.52 Click the Grid mode button to select Absolute or Relative Grid mode.

Figure 10.53 The Grid Value pop-up menu.

Figure 10.54 Toggle the display of grid lines on and off by clicking any Timebase ruler.

✔ Tips

■ To switch between Grid mode and Slip mode while dragging a region, press the Command key (Macintosh) or the Control key (Windows).

■ The Grid Value pop-up menu contains an option for Regions/Markers. This lets you snap a region to other region locations (start, end, and sync points), markers, and track selections.

■ To switch between Edit modes, use the following function keys: F1 (Shuffle), F2 (Slip), F3 (Spot), F4 (Grid).

SETTING EDIT MODES

Conductor rulers

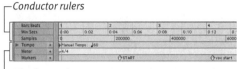

Timebase rulers

Figure 10.55 The Edit window's Timebase and Conductor rulers.

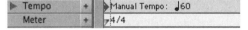

Figure 10.56 The Tempo and Meter rulers.

Using Rulers

Pro Tools provides two types of track rulers: Timebase and Conductor. These rulers appear directly above the track playlists, along the top of the Edit window (**Figure 10.55**).

Timebase rulers provide a timing reference for track material. You can also use them to make *Edit selections* of track material or *Timeline selections* of record and play ranges. When you make a selection in a Timebase ruler, all tracks in the Edit window are selected.

Pro Tools LE displays the following Timebase rulers:

◆ Bars:Beats

◆ Minutes:Seconds

◆ Samples

Conductor rulers indicate important track locations within a session. Pro Tools provides the following Conductor rulers:

◆ Tempo

◆ Meter

◆ Markers

The Tempo and Meter rulers indicate locations where tempo or meter (time signature) changes occur (**Figure 10.56**). You can use these rulers to map out a session's tempo and meter fluctuations. This is useful for aligning track material with a fixed time reference such as bars and beats.

The Markers ruler displays user-defined memory locations.

USING RULERS

To display all rulers:

◆ Choose View > Rulers > All.

or

1. Click the Ruler View selector (**Figure 10.57**).

2. Choose All.

   All Timebase and Conductor rulers appear along the top of the Edit window.

To display the Minutes:Seconds ruler (or any other specific ruler):

◆ Choose View > Rulers > Minutes:Seconds (**Figure 10.58**) (or any other ruler you want to display).

To remove a ruler from the display:

◆ Option-click the ruler's name to the left of the ruler display (**Figure 10.59**).

or

1. Click the Ruler View selector.

2. Deselect the ruler you want to hide.

To display only the Main Time Scale in the ruler:

◆ Choose View > Rulers > None.

or

1. Click the Ruler View selector.

2. Choose None.

✔ Tip

■ You can change the order of the ruler display by clicking and dragging on the name of any ruler.

Figure 10.57 The Ruler View selector.

Figure 10.58 Choose View > Rulers > Minutes:Seconds (or another ruler) to display the selected Timebase rulers.

Figure 10.59 Option-click a ruler's name to remove it from the ruler display.

Figure 10.60 To set the Main Time Scale, click the arrow next to the counter in the Location Indicators window and choose a time format.

Setting the Main Time Scale

The Main Time Scale (or Main Timebase Ruler) is the primary time format of a session. The Main Time Scale determines the time format used for the following:

◆ The Main Time Counter in the Transport and Edit windows

◆ Start, end, and length values

◆ Pre- and post-roll values

◆ Grid and Nudge values

You can set the Main Time Scale to the following time formats:

◆ **Bars:Beats**: Displays Main Time Scale in bars and beats as in musical notation.

◆ **Minutes:Seconds**: Displays the Main Time Scale in minutes, seconds, tenths, hundredths, and thousandths of a second.

◆ **Samples**: Displays the Main Time Scale in samples for precise sample-level editing.

◆ **Time Code**: Displays the Main Time Scale in SMPTE frames. Pro Tools supports frame rates of 23.976, 24, 255, 29.97 Drop, 30 Non-Drop, and 30 Drop frames per second (HD and LE with DV Toolkit 2 systems only).

◆ **Feet+Frames**: Displays the Main Time Scale in feet and frames for audio sync to 35 millimeter film format (HD and LE with DV Toolkit 2 systems only).

To set the Main Time Scale:

◆ In the Location Indicators window click the arrow next to the Main Time Scale counter (**Figure 10.60**).

The Main Time Scale changes to the selected time format.

For information on the Main Time Scale, see the *Location Indicators* section in *Chapter 3: The Mix and Edit Windows* or *The Pro Tools Reference Guide*.

SETTING THE MAIN TIME SCALE

247

Using Memory Locations

Pro Tools lets you set *memory locations*, which store information about specific edit points and selected track ranges. Memory locations are useful for recalling important locations in a session and quickly navigating to them.

You can recall memory locations by clicking them in the Memory Locations window (see *Recalling Memory Locations*, later in this chapter).

Setting memory locations

When you set a memory location, the New Memory Location dialog box appears (**Figure 10.61**). The New Memory Location dialog box lets you set time properties, place location markers, and store selections and other general properties for each memory location.

Time properties determine whether a memory location represents a specific edit point or a selected range. You can choose the following time properties in the New Memory Location dialog box:

Marker: This property recalls a specific time location in a session. When you create a *Marker memory location*, a yellow marker appears in the Markers ruler (**Figure 10.62**).

You can choose a timeline reference for each memory location using the Reference selector in the New Memory Location dialog box. Memory locations referenced to Bars:Beats appear as yellow chevrons in the Markers ruler, whereas those referenced to Absolute appear as yellow diamonds (**Figure 10.63**).

Selection: This property recalls a selected track range. Create a *Selection memory location* if you want to return to a selected record or play range.

None: This property recalls no time information. Memory locations created without a time property are called *General Properties memory locations*.

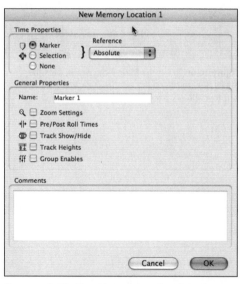

Figure 10.61 The New Memory Location dialog box.

Figure 10.62 A Marker memory location in the Markers ruler.

Figure 10.63 Memory locations referenced to Bars:Beats appear as yellow chevrons in the Markers ruler. Those that are referenced to Absolute appear as yellow diamonds.

Figure 10.64 To display the Markers ruler, select View > Rulers > Markers.

The New Memory Location dialog box also lets you save the following general properties with each memory location:

Zoom Settings: This recalls horizontal and vertical zoom values for audio and MIDI tracks. Zoom settings are useful for quickly moving between zoomed-in and zoomed-out track views.

Pre/Post-Roll Times: This recalls pre- and post-roll times. You can use this in conjunction with a Selection memory location to recall the pre- or post-roll values of a selected track range.

Track Show/Hide: This recalls which tracks are hidden in a session. You can use this to recall different groups of tracks during editing or mixing.

Track Heights: This recalls all of the session's current track heights. This is useful in conjunction with zoom settings for quickly switching between different track views.

Group Enables: This recalls which Edit and Mix groups are enabled. Use this option if you want to recall a particular group for editing or mixing.

To create a Marker memory location:

1. Configure any settings you want to save along with the Marker memory location (such as zoom settings, pre/post-roll times, Show/Hide tracks, track heights, or Edit and Mix Group enables).

2. Select Options > Link Edit and Timeline Selection. (This makes all selections apply to both Timebase rulers and track playlists.)

3. Select View > Rulers > Markers (**Figure 10.64**).

continues on next page

4. Click with the Selector tool at the desired location in any track or ruler.

5. Click the Marker/Memory Location button (**Figure 10.65**).

or

Press Enter on the numeric keypad.

or

Control-click (Macintosh) or Start-click (Windows) in the Markers ruler at the desired location.

The New Memory Location dialog box appears.

6. Select the Marker option.

7. Click the Reference selector and select Bar | Beat or Absolute (**Figure 10.66**).

8. Enter a name for the new marker and select any general properties you want to save with the marker.

9. Click OK.

A marker appears at the designated location in the Markers ruler and in the Memory Locations window.

✔ Tip

■ To move a marker to a new location, drag it to the new location in the Markers ruler (**Figure 10.67**).

or

Click with the Selector in the Markers ruler (or any Timebase ruler or track). In the Memory Locations window or in the Markers ruler, Control-click (Macintosh) or right-click (Windows) the Marker memory location you want to redefine. Enter a new name for the marker. Click OK.

Figure 10.65 Click the Marker/Memory Location button to the left of the Markers ruler to create a Marker memory location at the current track location.

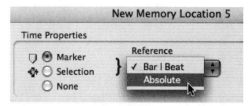

Figure 10.66 Click the Reference pop-up menu to choose a time reference (Bar | Beat or Absolute) for a new memory location.

Figure 10.67 Drag a marker to move its location in the Markers ruler.

Figure 10.68 Click Name to open the Memory Locations window's pop-up menu.

To create a Selection memory location:

1. Configure any settings you want to save with the Marker memory location (such as zoom settings, pre/post-roll times, Show/Hide tracks, track heights, or Edit and Mix Group enables).

2. Select Options > Link Edit and Timeline Selection. (This makes all selections apply to both Timebase rulers and track playlists.)

3. Select a range of material in one or more tracks.

4. Press Enter on the numeric keypad.

   or

   Choose Add Memory Location from the Memory Location pop-up menu at the top of the Memory Locations window (**Figure 10.68**). (Click Name to open the pop-up menu.)

   The New Memory Location dialog box appears.

5. Choose the Selection option.

6. Click the Reference selector and select Bar | Beat or Absolute.

7. Enter a name for the new memory location and select any general properties you want to save with it.

8. Click OK.

   The Selection memory location is created and appears in the Memory Locations window.

✔ Tip

- To change a selection stored with a memory location, select a range of material in one or more tracks. In the Memory Locations window, Control-click (Macintosh) or right-click (Window) the memory location you want to redefine. Enter a name for the memory location and click OK.

To create a General Properties location:

1. Configure any settings you want to save with the Marker memory location (such as zoom settings, pre/post-roll times, Show/Hide tracks, track heights, or Edit and Mix Group enables).

2. Press Enter on the numeric keypad.

   The New Memory Location dialog box appears.

3. Select None.

4. Enter a name and select any general properties you want to save with it.

5. Click OK.

   The General Properties memory location is created and appears in the Memory Locations window.

✔ Tip

■ To redefine general properties stored with a memory location, make the changes you want to the session's configuration. In the Memory Locations window, Control-click (Macintosh) or right-click (Windows) the memory location that you want to redefine; or Control-click (Macintosh) or right-click (Windows) the marker in the Markers ruler. Select the general properties you want to save in the New Memory Location dialog box and click OK.

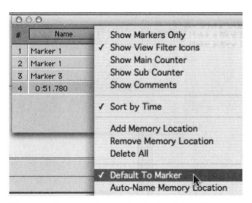

Figure 10.69 Select Default to Marker in the Memory Locations window pop-up menu to create a memory location on the fly.

To create a memory location on the fly:

1. Select Default to Marker in the Memory Locations window pop-up menu (**Figure 10.69**).

2. Select Auto-Name Memory Location in the Memory Locations window pop-up menu.

3. Click Play in the Transport window.

4. Press Enter at the desired location.

   A marker is automatically created and appears in the Markers ruler.

   Note that the New Memory Location dialog box does not appear when creating memory locations on the fly.

✔ Tips

- To rename a memory location, double-click it in the Memory Locations window or double-click the marker in the Markers ruler. Enter a new name in the New Memory Location dialog box and click OK.

- To change a memory location's time properties, double-click it in the Memory Locations window or double-click the marker in the Markers ruler. Select Marker, Selection, or None, and then click OK.

Recalling memory locations

You can recall memory locations by clicking them in the Memory Locations window (**Figure 10.70**). You can also recall them from the numeric keypad.

The Memory Locations window pop-up menu provides options for viewing, sorting, creating, and deleting memory locations. The menu has the following options:

Show Markers Only: This displays only Marker memory locations in the Memory Locations window.

Show View Filter Icons: This extends the Memory Locations window to include an icon-based view filter, which lets you show or hide memory locations based on their properties (**Figure 10.71**). To show or hide memory locations containing a specific property, click the appropriate icon.

Figure 10.70 To recall a memory location, click its name in the Memory Locations window.

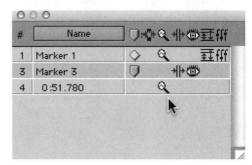

Figure 10.71 View filter icons in the Memory Locations window.

USING MEMORY LOCATIONS

Figure 10.72 The Main and Sub Counters display the location of Marker memory locations and the start time of Selection memory locations.

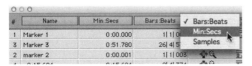

Figure 10.73 Click the top of each Main and Sub Counter column to select a Main and Sub Time Scale.

Show Main and Show Sub Counter: These options extend the Memory Locations window to include columns displaying the location of Marker memory locations and the start times for Selection memory locations (**Figure 10.72**). Click at the top of each column for a pop-up menu that lets you change the Main and Sub Time Scale (**Figure 10.73**).

Sort by Time: This option sorts markers by their order in the timeline, followed by Selection memory locations and General Properties memory locations, which are listed in the order in which they were created.

Add Memory Location: This command creates a new memory location.

Remove Memory Location: This command removes the currently selected memory location in the Memory Locations window.

Delete All: This command deletes all memory locations from the session.

Default to Marker: This option causes all new memory locations to default to Marker memory locations.

Auto-Name Memory Location: This option lets you create a memory location without opening the Memory Locations dialog box. When the Default to Marker option is selected, a Marker memory location is automatically created.

To recall a memory location:

1. Choose Window > Memory Locations.
   The Memory Locations window appears.

2. Click the memory location you want to recall.

   or

   With the Numeric Keypad mode set to Classic, press the memory location number on the keypad followed by the period key.

   or

   With the Numeric Keypad mode set to Transport, press the period key, the memory location number, and the period key again.

   or

   Click a Marker memory location in the Markers ruler.

   In all the preceding cases, the playback cursor locates to the chosen memory location and any general properties stored with it are recalled.

✔ Tips

- To delete a marker from the Markers ruler, Option-click (Macintosh) or Alt-click (Windows) the marker you want to delete.

- To delete a memory location, in the Memory Locations window, Option-click (Macintosh) or Alt-click (Windows) the memory location.

   or

   In the Memory Locations window, select the memory location and choose Delete Memory from the pop-up menu.

USING MEMORY LOCATIONS

SELECTING REGIONS

When you edit audio in Pro Tools, you don't alter the original audio files saved on disk. Rather, you edit regions (usually displayed as waveforms) that represent the original audio files. Editing regions involves two steps:

Selecting regions (choosing the portion of recorded material you want to edit),

Working with regions (performing edit functions such as moving, duplicating, trimming, aligning, and so forth on selected regions).

This chapter covers selecting regions in Pro Tools. We'll introduce you to three selection types: Edit selections, Timeline selections, and Track selections. You'll learn how to make each type of selection, and you'll learn how to link and unlink Edit selections with Timeline and Track selections to make your editing session more productive.

Then you'll learn a few tricks for fine-tuning your selections, including how to extend, nudge, and change the length of a selection.

In addition, we'll show you how to select waveforms at locations of minimal volume to avoid adding unwanted noise (pops and clicks) or jarring transitions to your recordings.

About Selections

Selections in Pro Tools are classified in two ways: *Edit selections* and *Timeline selections*. An Edit selection refers to the actual audio region and/or track space that becomes highlighted when you make a selection (**Figure 11.1**). Edit selections can include a single region or multiple regions, and can include the space before, after, and in between regions. You can make Edit selections on single tracks or across multiple tracks.

When you make a Timeline selection, you select a range of time in any Timebase ruler (**Figure 11.2**). Timeline selections automatically apply across all tracks in a session.

Timeline selections are indicated in the ruler by blue arrows called *Playback markers* (**Figure 11.3**). Playback markers turn red during recording. *Pre-* and *post-roll flags* accompany Playback markers. These indicate the current pre- and post-roll times and turn green when the Pre- or Post-Roll buttons in the Transport window are enabled.

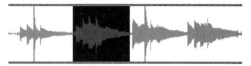

Figure 11.1 An Edit selection. Edit selections apply only to the selected track. Shift-click on additional tracks to extend the Edit selection.

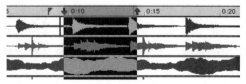

Figure 11.2 A Timeline selection. Timeline selections automatically apply across all tracks.

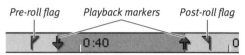

Figure 11.3 Playback markers with pre- and post-roll flags in the Min:Secs ruler.

Edit markers

Figure 11.4 Edit markers, which indicate an Edit selection, appear when Edit and Timeline selections are unlinked.

Figure 11.5 The Link Selection button.

Linking and Unlinking Edit and Timeline Selections

Edit and Timeline selections are linked by default. This means that when you select inside a track, the corresponding range in the timeline is also selected.

You may, however, want to unlink Edit and Timeline selections to perform certain editing tasks. For instance, if you're working with video, you may want to retain a Timeline selection of video while you search for sounds to accompany it elsewhere in the session. Once you've found the desired sound, you can return to the current Timeline selection and apply the sound to the video.

When Edit and Timeline selections are unlinked, Edit selections are displayed in the ruler as *Edit markers*, which appear as black brackets (**Figure 11.4**).

To unlink Edit and Timeline selections:

◆ Deselect Options > Link Edit and Timeline Selection.

or

◆ Click the Link Selection button in the upper left area of the Edit window (**Figure 11.5**).

The Link Selection button is unhighlighted, and the Link Edit and Timeline Selection function is disabled.

LINKING AND UNLINKING SELECTIONS

Linking and Unlinking Track and Edit Selections

11.6 To link and unlink Track and Edit selections, click the Link Track and Edit selection button in the upper left corner of the Edit window.

You can link and unlink Track and Edit selections in the Edit window. When you link Track and Edit selections, selecting material in the Edit window automatically selects all associated tracks. This way you can quickly change track parameters (such as track height or track view) on multiple tracks during a session.

Unlinking Track and Edit selections disables the automatic selection of tracks when selecting material in the Edit window.

To link or unlink Track and Edit selections:

◆ Select or deselect Options > Link Track and Edit Selection.

or

◆ Click the Link Track and Edit Selection button in the upper left of the Edit window (**Figure 11.6**).

The Link Track and Edit Selection button becomes highlighted and Track and Edit selections are linked.

LINKING AND UNLINKING SELECTIONS

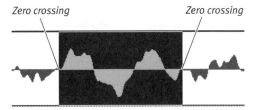

Zero crossing   *Zero crossing*

11.7 An Edit selection that begins and ends at a zero crossing.

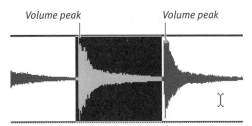

Volume peak   *Volume peak*

Figure 11.8 An Edit selection that begins before one volume peak and ends before another volume peak.

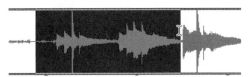

Figure 11.9 Drag the Selector over a portion of a region to make an Edit selection.

Selecting Regions

The Selector tool in the Edit window lets you select portions of audio regions within individual tracks. Using the proper technique to select regions is key to making smooth, noise-free edits.

Editing waveforms

When you select a portion of an audio region in Waveform view, make sure that your selection does not begin or end at a point of high waveform amplitude. This can introduce audible clicks and pops at the boundaries of a newly created region. Instead, make sure your selections begin and end as close as possible to a *zero crossing*. A zero crossing is a point where the waveform crosses its center line, and the waveform's amplitude is zero (**Figure 11.7**).

In addition, try to begin your selections immediately before a volume peak, and end them immediately before another volume peak (**Figure 11.8**). Selecting at zero crossings and before volume peaks—both points of low volume—will help ensure that your edits flow seamlessly and are free of clicks and pops.

To select a portion of a region:

◆ Drag the Selector tool over the portion of the region you want to select (**Figure 11.9**). The selected portion is highlighted.

To select an entire region:

◆ Click the region with the Grabber.

 or

◆ Double-click the region with the Selector.

To select two regions and the time range between them:

1. Click with the Grabber on the first region.

2. Shift-click the second region.

   Both regions and the time range between them (including any other regions) are highlighted (**Figure 11.10**).

To select an entire track:

1. Click in the track with the Selector.

2. Choose Edit > Select All.

   or

   Triple-click in the track with the Selector.

To select all regions in all tracks:

1. Select All in the Groups list (**Figure 11.11**).

2. Click in any track with the Selector.

3. Choose Edit > Select All.

   or

   Triple-click with the Selector in any track.

To make a selection on the fly:

1. Use the Selector to click in the track before the start location of the range you want to select.

2. Click Play in the Transport window.

3. When playback reaches the start location, press the Down Arrow key.

4. When playback reaches the end location, press the Up Arrow key.

   The selected range is highlighted.

5. Click Stop.

Figure 11.10 A selection including two regions and the time range between them.

Figure 11.11 Click All in the Edit Groups list to group all tracks in a session.

Figure 11.12 Drag the Playback markers in the ruler to move a selection's start or end point.

Changing a Selection's Length

You can make an existing selection longer or shorter by pressing the Shift key while clicking or dragging (or by dragging the Playback markers in the ruler).

To change the length of a selection:

◆ Shift-click or Shift-drag with the Selector to the left or right of the existing selection.

or

◆ In the ruler, drag the Playback markers for a selection's start or end point (**Figure 11.12**).

Nudging Selections

Nudging is useful for fine-tuning the boundaries of a region selection. You can nudge a selection by the current Nudge value. You can also nudge the start and end points for a selection by the current Nudge value.

To nudge a selection range:

1. Make a selection with the Selector.

2. Enter a Nudge value in the Nudge Value field, located in the upper right area of the Edit window (**Figure 11.13**).

3. Hold down the Shift key, and press the Plus or Minus key on the numeric keypad.

   The selected range moves by the Nudge value (**Figure 11.14**).

To nudge a selection's start point:

1. Make a selection with the Selector.

2. Enter a Nudge value in the Nudge Value field, located in the upper right area of the Edit window.

3. Hold down Option-Shift (Macintosh) or Alt-Shift (Windows), and press the Plus or Minus key on the numeric keypad.

   The selection's start point moves by the Nudge value (**Figure 11.15**).

To nudge a selection's end point:

1. Make a selection with the Selector.

2. Enter a Nudge value in the Nudge Value field, located in the upper right area of the Edit window.

3. Hold down Command-Shift (Macintosh) or Control-Shift (Windows), and press the Plus or Minus key on the numeric keypad.

   The selection's end point moves by the Nudge value.

Figure 11.13 The Nudge Value field.

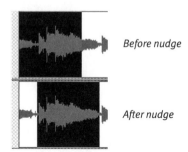

Before nudge

After nudge

Figure 11.14 To nudge a selection forward or backward, hold down the Shift key, and press the Plus or Minus key on the numeric keypad.

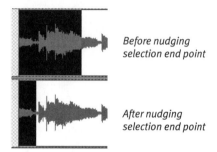

Before nudging selection end point

After nudging selection end point

Figure 11.15 To nudge a selection's end point, hold down Command-Shift (Macintosh) or Control-Shift (Windows), and press the Plus or Minus key on the numeric keypad.

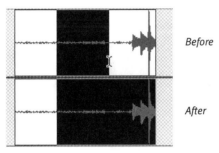

Before

After

Figure 11.16 To extend a selection to a region's end point, select a portion of the region and press Shift-Tab.

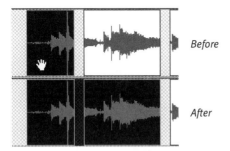

Before

After

Figure 11.17 To extend a selection to include the next region, select a region with the Grabber, and then press Shift-Control-Tab (Macintosh) or Shift-Start-Tab (Windows).

Extending a Selection

You can extend a selection in three ways: to region start and end points, to include an adjacent region, or to markers and memory locations.

To extend a selection to a region's start point:

1. Select a portion of a region with the Selector.

2. Press Shift-Option-Tab (Macintosh) or Shift-Start-Tab (Windows).

    The selection extends to the region's start point.

To extend a selection to a region's end point:

1. Select a portion of a region with the Selector.

2. Press Shift-Tab.

    The selection extends to the region's end point (**Figure 11.16**).

To extend a selection to include an adjacent region:

1. Select a region with the Grabber.

2. Press Shift-Control-Tab (Macintosh) or Shift-Start-Tab (Windows).

    The selection extends to include the next region (**Figure 11.17**).

    or

    Press Shift-Control-Option-Tab (Macintosh) or Shift-Start-Control-Tab (Windows).

    The selection extends to the previous region.

EXTENDING A SELECTION

To extend a selection to a marker or memory location:

1. Make a selection with the Selector or Grabber.

2. Shift-click a marker in the Markers ruler (**Figure 11.18**).

   or

   Shift-click a memory location in the Memory Locations window.

   The selection is extended from the original insertion point to the marker or memory location.

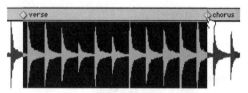

Figure 11.18 To extend a selection to a marker, Shift-click the marker in the Markers ruler.

✔ Tip

■ If a long selection doesn't fit in the Edit window, press the Left Arrow key to jump to the beginning of the selection, or the Right Arrow key to jump to the end of it.

EXTENDING A SELECTION

Figure 11.19 The selection indicator in the Transport window.

Using Selection Indicators

The selection indicators at the top of the Edit window let you make precise edit selections. They use the time format of the session's Main Time Scale.

To make a selection using the selection indicators:

1. Click in the track you want to select.

2. Enter a value for the selection start point in the selection indicator's Start field (**Figure 11.19**).

3. Enter a value for the selection end point in the selection indicator's End field.

4. Press Enter.

   The selected range of track is highlighted.

Tabbing to Transients

The Tab to Transients button automatically locates the cursor to the next *transient peak* in an audio waveform. A transient is a sound —such as a drum hit, a piano note, or a guitar strum—that occurs for a brief time period. The transient peak is the instance of strongest attack in the transient. For example, a snare drum hit consists of a strong initial attack—a transient peak— followed by a period of decay.

Tabbing to transients is quite handy for locating the precise start and end point of audio regions.

To set the start and end points of a selection using Tab to Transients:

1. Click the Tab to Transients button to enable it (**Figure 11.20**).

2. Click in the audio track before the material you want to select.

3. Press the Tab key repeatedly until the cursor locates to the transient at the start of the selection (**Figure 11.21**). If necessary, press Option-Tab (Macintosh) or Control-Tab (Windows) to return the cursor to the previous transient peak.

4. Press Shift-Tab until the cursor locates to the end of the selection. If necessary, press Shift-Option-Tab (Macintosh) or Shift-Control-Tab (Windows) to move the selection end point to the previous transient.

✔ Tip

■ Use the Edit window's Smart tool (**Figure 11.22**) whenever possible during editing. It lets you quickly access the Selector, Grabber, and Trimmer tools, and create fades, all from within a region. The Smart tool is very intuitive, and will save you time and reduce fatigue in your mousing hand.

Figure 11.20 The Tab to Transients button.

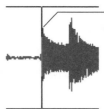

Transient peak

Figure 11.21 Press the Tab key to locate the cursor to the next transient.

Figure 11.22 The Smart tool in the Edit window.

Figure 11.23 A Timeline selection. To make a Timeline selection, drag with the Selector in any Timebase ruler.

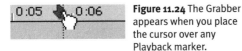

Figure 11.24 The Grabber appears when you place the cursor over any Playback marker.

Figure 11.25 Drag the second Playback marker to make a Timeline selection.

Making Timeline Selections

When you make a Timeline selection, you select a range of time in a Timebase ruler. The current Timeline selection (as indicated by the Playback markers) always determines the range for playback and recording.

When Edit and Timeline selections are linked, edit selections are mirrored in the timeline. When Edit and Timeline selections are unlinked, however, you can make Timeline selections that are distinct from Edit selections.

To make a Timeline selection:

◆ Drag with the Selector in any Timebase ruler (**Figure 11.23**).

All tracks in the session are highlighted within the selected range.

or

1. Place the cursor over the first Playback marker (down arrow).

The Grabber appears (**Figure 11.24**).

2. Drag the first Playback marker to set the desired start point.

3. Drag the second Playback marker (up arrow) to set the desired end point (**Figure 11.25**).

All tracks in the session are highlighted within the selected range.

To move a Timeline selection in the ruler:

◆ Hold down Option (Macintosh) or Alt (Windows), and drag either Playback marker to the left or right.

The Timeline selection slides backward or forward along the timeline while the selection's length is maintained.

MAKING TIMELINE SELECTIONS

WORKING WITH REGIONS

Once upon a time, recording engineers performed edits by cutting and splicing back together analog tape. Cutting tape with a razor blade is a destructive process: The original audio recording is altered permanently. In Pro Tools, however, editing is non-destructive: Edits are performed on audio regions that visually represent your audio files. Your original audio files remain untouched on disk. Editing audio regions non-destructively makes it easy to clean up rough spots on tracks, and it frees you to experiment with different arrangements and generate new musical ideas.

This chapter covers the fundamentals of editing audio regions. Using the techniques for selecting audio regions presented in the previous chapter, you'll learn how to create new regions by capturing portions of larger regions. You'll learn various methods of sliding regions within tracks and between tracks, and how to place regions, align regions, and trim regions, too.

We conclude with a look at ways to manage regions including how to rename, hide, and delete them from a session. You'll also learn how to create region groups, which let you handle multiple regions represented by a single region group file.

Creating New Regions

Pro Tools provides several commands for
creating new regions from selected portions
of regions. When you create a new region,
it's displayed in the track's playlist and in the
Regions list.

Capturing regions

The Capture Region command lets you
define a selection as a new region and automatically adds it to the Regions list. You can
then drag the new region from the list to
any track.

To capture a new region:

1. Select the portion of the existing region
   you want to capture with the Selector tool.

2. Choose Region > Capture (**Figure 12.1**).

3. Enter a name for the new region and
   click OK.

   The new region appears in the Regions
   list. The selected portion of the region
   remains selected.

✔ Tip

■ To set Pro Tools to automatically name
  new regions, select a newly created
  region in the Regions list. In the pop-up
  menu, choose Auto Rename Selected
  (**Figure 12.2**). Enter the desired auto-
  name parameters in the Auto Rename
  dialog box.

Figure 12.1 To capture a new region, choose Region >
Capture.

Figure 12.2
Choose Auto
Rename in the
Regions list
pop-up menu.

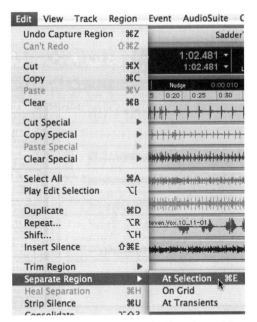

Figure 12.3 To separate a selected region, choose Edit > Separate Region > At Selection.

New region   *Separated region*   *New region*

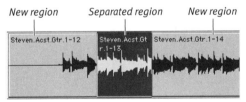

Figure 12.4 New regions with new start and end times are created on either side of a separated region.

Separating regions

The Separate Region command lets you define a selection as a new region and separate it from adjacent audio data. You can separate edit selections made within a single region, across adjacent regions in the same track, or across multiple tracks.

In Pro Tools 7 the Separate Region command includes new options for separating regions quickly into many smaller regions.

◆ **At Selection:** At Selection creates one new separate region at the exact start and end points of your region selection.

◆ **On Grid:** On Grid creates separate new regions between each grid line within your edit selection, according to the current grid value.

◆ **At Transients:** At Transients creates separate new regions between each transient peak (audio level spike) contained within your edit selection.

If no selection is made, the region is split at the edit cursor's insertion point.

To separate a region:

1. Select the portion of the existing region you want to separate.

   or

   Click with the Selector at the point where you want to split the region.

2. Choose Edit > Separate Region > At Selection (or select On Grid or At Transients to create the desired number of smaller separate regions) (**Figure 12.3**).

   A new, separate region is created and appears in the Regions list. New regions with new start and end times are created on either side of the separated region (**Figure 12.4**).

To separate a region using the Separation Grabber:

1. With the Selector, select the region you want to separate.

2. Choose the Separation Grabber from the Grabber pop-up menu (**Figure 12.5**).

3. Drag the separated region to the desired location on any track (**Figure 12.6**).

   A new, separate region is created and appears at the desired location. New regions with new start and end times are automatically created on either side of the separated region.

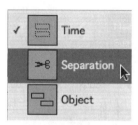

Figure 12.5 Click and hold the Grabber tool and choose the Separation Grabber from the Grabber pop-up menu.

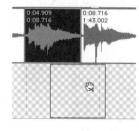

Figure 12.6 You can drag a separated region to a new location on any track.

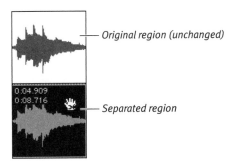

Original region (unchanged)

Separated region

Figure 12.7 To separate a selected region without altering the original region, choose the Separation Grabber. Then, while pressing Option (Macintosh) or Alt (Windows), drag the selection to a new location on any track.

Edit	View	Track	Region	Ev
Undo Region Slide			⌘Z	
Redo Heal Separation			⇧⌘Z	
Cut			⌘X	
Copy			⌘C	
Paste			⌘V	
Clear			⌘B	
Cut Special			▶	
Copy Special			▶	
Paste Special			▶	
Clear Special			▶	
Select All			⌘A	
Play Edit Selection			⌥[	
Duplicate			⌘D	
Repeat...			⌥R	
Shift...			⌥H	
Insert Silence			⇧⌘E	
Trim Region			▶	
Separate Region			▶	
Heal Separation			⌘H	
Strip Silence			⌘U	
Consolidate			⌥⇧3	

Figure 12.8 To restore separated regions, choose Edit > Heal Separation.

To separate a selection without altering the original region:

1. Select the region you want to separate.

2. Choose the Separation Grabber from the Grabber pop-up menu.

3. Hold down Option (Macintosh) or Alt (Windows), and drag the selection to the desired location on any track.

   A new, separate region is created and placed at the desired location. The original region remains intact (**Figure 12.7**).

✔ Tip

■ You can restore a separated region with the Heal Separation command: Select part of the first region, the entire separation between the regions, and part of the second region. Choose Edit > Heal Separation (**Figure 12.8**). (Regions must remain adjacent, with start and end points unchanged, for the Heal Separation command to work.)

CREATING NEW REGIONS

Placing Regions in Tracks

Once you've created a new region, you can place it in a track by dragging it within the same track, dragging it from another track, or dragging it from the Regions list. The exact placement of a region in a track is affected by the current Edit mode (**Figure 12.9**) as follows:

Shuffle mode: In this mode, adjacent regions automatically snap together and cannot overlap. When you place a new region at the start point of an existing region, the existing region is pushed to the right and snaps to the end of the new region.

Spot mode: In this mode, you can move a region to an exact time location on a track. Spotting is useful when working with film and video, or whenever you need to move a region to a precise time location. When you place a new region while in Spot mode, the Spot dialog box prompts you to enter a time location.

Grid mode: In this mode, the dragged region snaps to the nearest Grid boundary. You can choose a Grid value in the Grid Value pop-up menu in the upper right of the Edit window.

Slip mode: In this mode, you can move and place regions anywhere in a track. Slip mode is useful for moving regions quickly within and between tracks.

For more information on Edit modes, see *Sliding Regions,* later in this chapter; or see *Chapter 10: Editing Basics.*

Figure 12.9 The Edit mode buttons: Shuffle mode, Spot mode, Grid mode, and Slip mode. Edit modes give you different ways to place regions on tracks.

Figure 12.10 You can place regions on tracks by dragging them from the Regions list.

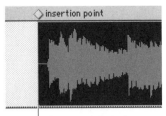

Region start point

Figure 12.11 To place the start of a region in the same track at the edit insertion point, Control-click (Macintosh) or Start-click (Windows) with the Grabber.

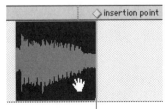

Region end point

Figure 12.11 To place the start of a region in the same track at the edit insertion point, Control-click (Macintosh) or Start-click (Windows) with the Grabber.

To place a region in a track:

1. Select a region in the Regions list.

2. Drag the selected region to the desired track location (**Figure 12.10**).

   The region is placed in the track at the desired location, as determined by the current Edit mode.

To place the start of a region at the edit insertion point:

1. Use the Selector to click in the track at the desired insertion point.

2. Hold down Control (Macintosh) or Start (Windows) and drag the region from a track, the Regions list, or a DigiBase browser to the destination track.

   or

   If the region is already in the track, Control-click (Macintosh) or Start-click (Windows) the region with the Grabber.

   The region appears in the track with its start at the edit insertion point (**Figure 12.11**).

To place the end of a region at the edit insertion point:

1. Use the Selector to click in the track at the desired time location.

2. Hold down Command-Control (Macintosh) or Control-Start (Windows) and drag the region from either another track or from the Regions list to the destination track.

   or

   If the region is already in the track, Command-Control-click (Macintosh) or Control-Start-click (Windows) the region with the Grabber.

   The region appears in the track with its end at the edit insertion point (**Figure 12.12**).

Sliding Regions

You can slide regions (or groups of regions) within a track or between tracks using the Edit window's Grabber tool. Sliding is a useful and intuitive way to move audio regions: You can slide regions into rough arrangements quickly by eye; or you can move them to precise time locations.

Pro Tools offers a number of sliding methods, which depend on the current Edit mode.

Slipping regions

In Slip mode, you can move regions freely with the Grabber tool within a track or between tracks. You can slip a region between other regions, or you can slip a region so that it overlaps or completely covers another region.

To slip regions:

1. In the Edit window, set the Edit mode to Slip (**Figure 12.13**).

2. Click the Grabber tool (**Figure 12.14**).

3. With the Grabber, drag the region you want to slip.

   The region moves freely to any location on any track.

Figure 12.13 Click Slip to set the Slip Edit mode.

Figure 12.14 The Grabber tool in the Edit window.

SLIDING REGIONS

Figure 12.15 Set the Edit mode to Shuffle.

Region start point

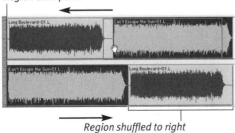

Region shuffled to right

Figure 12.16 Drag a region to the start point of another region. The dragged region snaps to the start point of the other region. The other region is shuffled to the right and snaps to the end point of the dragged region.

Space between regions

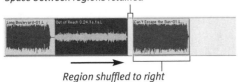

Slide region between two regions

Figure 12.17 Drag a region between two other regions.

Space between regions retained

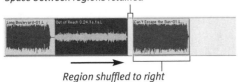

Region shuffled to right

Figure 12.18 The dragged region snaps to the end of the existing region on the left. The region to the right is displaced to the right by the length of the dragged region. The space between the two regions is retained.

Shuffling regions

In Shuffle mode, adjacent regions automatically snap together and cannot overlap. When you place a new region at the start point of an existing region, the existing region is pushed to the right and snaps to the end of the new region.

To shuffle regions:

1. In the Edit window, set the Edit mode to Shuffle (**Figure 12.15**).

2. With the Grabber tool, drag a region to the start point of another region.

   The dragged region appears at the existing region's start point. The existing region is shuffled to the right and snaps to the end of the newly placed region (**Figure 12.16**).

   or

   With the Grabber tool, drag a region between two existing regions (**Figure 12.17**).

   The dragged region snaps to the end of the existing region on the left. Any regions to the right are displaced to the right by the length of the newly placed region (**Figure 12.18**).

SLIDING REGIONS

Spotting regions

In Spot mode, you can place regions at exact time locations in a track. Spotting is useful for accurately placing regions dragged from the Regions list. It's also useful for fixing timing problems between tracks of music and for accurately synchronizing dialog or sound effects during video post-production.

To spot a region:

1. In the Edit window, set the Edit mode to Spot (**Figure 12.19**).

2. Drag a region from the Regions list to an existing track.

   or

   Click a region already in a track with the Grabber tool.

   The Spot dialog box appears (**Figure 12.20**).

3. In the Spot dialog, select the desired time format from the Time Scale pop-up menu (**Figure 12.21**).

Figure 12.19 Click Spot to set the Edit mode.

Figure 12.20 The Spot dialog box.

Figure 12.21 Select a time format from the Time Scale pop-up menu.

Figure 12.22 Click the Up arrow next to the Original Time Stamp or User Time Stamp to enter those values in the currently selected field.

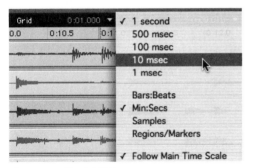

Figure 12.23 The Grid Value pop-up menu.

Figure 12.24 Click the Grid mode button, and then choose Absolute or Relative from the pop-up menu.

4. Click in the field for Start, Sync Point, or End and type in a new time location.

or

Click the Up arrow next to Original Time Stamp or User Time Stamp to enter those values into the currently selected field (**Figure 12.22**). For more information on time stamps, see *Chapter 10: Editing Basics,* or see the *Pro Tools Reference Guide.*

The region is moved to the new location specified for its start or sync point. (If a region does not have a sync point defined, the Sync Point field in the Spot Dialog functions the same as the Start field.)

Using Grid modes

In Grid mode, a dragged region snaps to the nearest Grid boundary. You can choose a Grid value in the Grid Value pop-up menu, to the right of the Grid Value indicator (**Figure 12.23**).

Pro Tools provides two different Grid modes, as follows:

Absolute Grid mode: In Absolute Grid mode, moving any region snaps the region to the nearest Grid boundary.

Relative Grid mode: In Relative Grid mode, you can move regions by the amount of the current Grid value, retaining the region's relative position.

To select Absolute or Relative Grid mode:

◆ In the Edit window, click Grid mode and choose Absolute or Relative from the pop-up menu (**Figure 12.24**).

SLIDING REGIONS

To place or move a region while in Grid mode:

1. In the Edit window, select a Grid value from the Grid Value pop-up menu.

2. Drag a region from the Regions list to an existing track.

   or

   With the Grabber, drag an existing region within a track to a new location.

   In Absolute Grid mode, the region snaps to the nearest Grid boundary (**Figure 12.25**). In Relative Grid mode, the region moves by the amount of the current Grid value (**Figure 12.26**).

   For more information on Grid mode, see *Chapter 10: Editing Basics*, or see the *Pro Tools Reference Guide*.

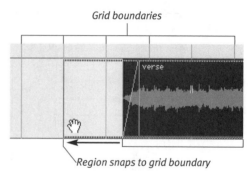

Grid boundaries

Region snaps to grid boundary

Figure 12.25 In Absolute Grid mode, regions snap to grid boundaries only.

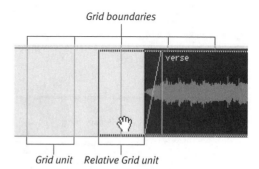

Grid boundaries

Grid unit   *Relative Grid unit*

Figure 12.26 In Relative Grid mode, regions move by the amount of the current Grid value from their current location.

SLIDING REGIONS

Region start point

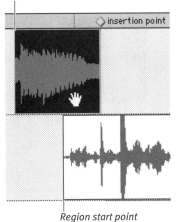

Region start point

Figure 12.27 To align the start point of regions on different tracks, click with the Grabber on the region you want to align to. Control-click (Macintosh) or Start-click (Windows) on the region you want to align.

Region start point

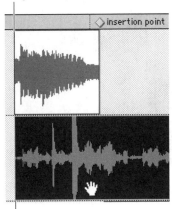

Region start point

Figure 12.28 The start point of the second region aligns to the start point of the first region.

Aligning Regions

You can align a region to the start, end, or sync point of another region on a different track. This is useful for bringing regions on different tracks into alignment for playback.

To align the start points of regions on different tracks:

1. Use the Grabber to select the region you want to align to (**Figure 12.27**).

2. Control-click (Macintosh) or Start-click (Windows) with the Grabber on the region you want to align.

   or

   Control-drag (Macintosh) or Start-drag (Windows) a region from the Regions list to another track.

   The start point of the second region aligns to the start point of the first region (**Figure 12.28**).

To align the end point of a region to the start point of another region on a different track:

1. Use the Grabber to select the region you want to align to (**Figure 12.29**).

2. Command-Control-click (Macintosh) or Control-Start-click (Windows) with the Grabber on the region you want to move.

   or

   Command-Control-drag (Macintosh) or Control-Start-drag (Windows) a region from the Regions list to another track.

   The end point of the second region aligns to the start point of the first region (**Figure 12.30**).

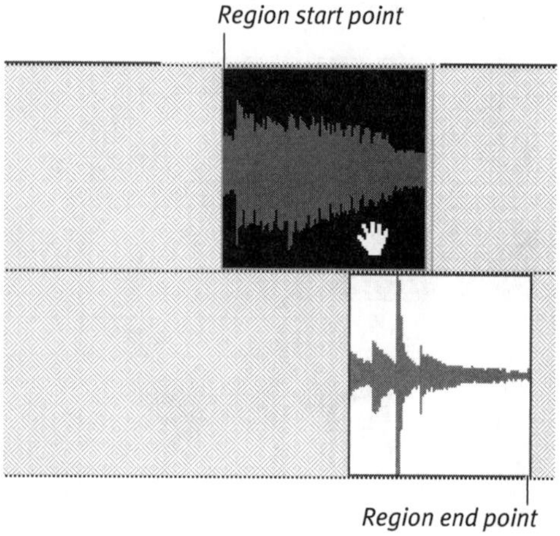

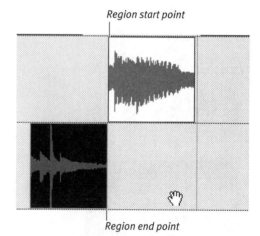

Region start point

Region end point

Figure 12.29 To align the end point of a region to the start point of a region on another track, click with the Grabber on the region you want to align to. Command-Control-click (Macintosh) or Control-Start-click (Windows) on the region you want to move.

Region start point

Region end point

Figure 12.30 The end point of the second region aligns to the start point of the first region.

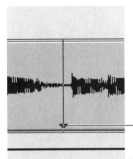

Figure 12.31 To identify a region sync point, choose Region > Identify Sync Point.

— *Region sync point*

Figure 12.32 An arrow appears in the region at the sync point.

Identifying Sync Points

When you identify a region sync point, you define a specific point within a region. You can then align the sync point with an exact time location in a session.

Sync points are particularly useful in film and video work, where sound effects must occur at an exact moment. For instance, a video of a car crash might call for a sound effect consisting of a screech and a crash. By placing a sync point at the peak volume of the crash, you can easily spot the sound effect to the precise instant of the crash.

To create a sync point in a region:

1. Click the Slip Edit mode button in the top left of the Edit window.

2. Click with the Selector on the location at which you want to place the sync point.

3. Choose Region > Identify Sync Point (**Figure 12.31**).

   An arrow appears in the region indicating the sync point's location (**Figure 12.32**).

To place the sync point of a region at the edit insertion point:

1. Click with the Selector in the track to define an edit insertion point.

2. Hold down Shift-Control (Macintosh) or Shift-Start (Windows) and drag the region from either the Regions list or from another track to the destination track.

or

If the region is already in the track, Shift-Control-click (Macintosh) or Shift-Start-click (Windows) on the region with the Grabber.

The region appears in the track with its sync point at the edit insertion point (**Figure 12.33**).

To align the sync point of a region to the start point of another region on a different track:

1. Click with the Grabber to select the region you want to align to.

2. Shift-Control-click (Macintosh) or Shift-Start-click (Windows) with the Grabber on the region you want to move.

or

Shift-Control-drag (Macintosh) or Shift-Start-drag (Windows) a region from the Regions list to another track.

The sync point of the second region aligns to the start point of the first region (**Figure 12.34**).

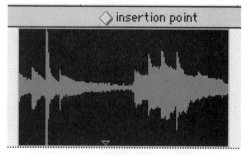

Figure 12.33 A region with its sync point at the edit insertion point.

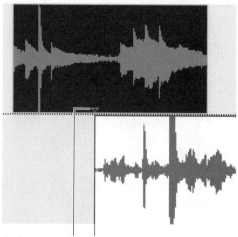

Region sync point   Region start point

Figure 12.34 The sync point of one region aligns to the start point of another region on a different track.

Trimming Regions

Trimming is a quick way to condense or expand regions. Pro Tools gives you a number of trimming options, including a versatile Trim tool and a set of Trim commands.

Using the Trimmer tool

The Edit window's Trim tool includes the following modes:

Standard Trim tool: The Standard Trim tool lets you move region boundaries without moving the region. This is useful for hiding unwanted audio segments or for revealing currently hidden audio segments. (Think of the Standard Trim tool as opening and closing a curtain of invisibility over audio region boundaries—the trimmed part of the region does not disappear, it is merely rendered invisible and inactive).

The Standard Trim tool lets you shorten regions or lengthen them up to the full length of the original audio file on disk.

Time Compression/Expansion (or TCE) Trim tool: The TCE Trim tool lets you compress or expand the duration of audio regions. Unlike the Standard Trim tool, which lets you change region boundaries only, the TCE Trim toolstretches or shrinks the actual audio currently displayed within a region. The TCE Trim tool processes the audio with the Time Compression/Expansion (AudioSuite) plug-in, which creates a new file.

The TCE Trim tool is useful for correcting audio segments that are too short or too long. It's also useful for matching the length of audio segments on separate tracks. For example, when you record harmonies or multiple vocal tracks, out-of-sync phrasing is common. With the TCE Trim tool, you can compress or expand a region to match the phrasing of the other vocal parts.

A word of caution: The TCE Trim tool can alter the sonic character of an audio region—as always, trust your ears. For more information on trimming regions, see the *Pro Tools Reference Guide*.

To trim a region with the Standard Trim tool:

1. Click the Standard Trim tool in the Edit window (**Figure 12.35**).

2. Move the cursor near the start or end of the region until the Standard Trim cursor appears.

3. Drag the Standard Trim cursor to the left or right to shorten or lengthen the region, respectively (**Figure 12.36**).

   The region boundaries move, and the region is shortened or lengthened by the desired amount. If you're trimming a stereo region, both channels are trimmed.

To compress or expand a region with the Time Compression/Expansion (TCE) Trim Tool:

1. Select the TCE Trim tool in the Edit window (**Figure 12.37**).

2. Move the cursor near the start or end of the region until the Time Trimmer cursor appears (**Figure 12.38**).

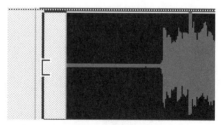

Figure 12.35 The Trimmer tool.

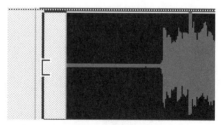

Figure 12.36 Drag with the Trimmer to shorten or lengthen a region.

Figure 12.37 Click the Trimmer tool and choose the Time Trimmer from the pop-up menu. The Time Trimmer is labeled "TCE" for Time Compression/Expansion.

Figure 12.38 Move the cursor near the start or end of a region until the Time Trimmer cursor appears.

TRIMMING REGIONS

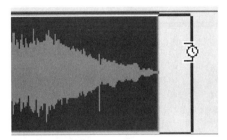

Figure 12.39 To compress or expand a region's time length, drag the Time Trimmer to the left or right of the region.

3. Drag the Time Trimmer cursor to the left or right to compress or expand the region, respectively (**Figure 12.39**).

   The Time Compression/Expansion (AudioSuite) plug-in processes the audio, and the region is compressed or expanded by the desired amount. A new audio file is created, which appears in the Regions list.

✔ Tips

- In Grid mode, the Time Trimmer cursor lets you compress or expand regions by precise grid increments. In Spot mode, the Time Trimmer cursor lets you compress or expand regions to a specified time location.

- To reverse the direction of the Time Trimmer cursor, press Option (Macintosh) or Alt (Windows).

Using the Trim command

The Edit window's Trim command offers the following options for trimming selections:

Trim to Selection: This removes all audio in a region except the selected portion. It's useful if you want to create a new region and clear the remaining unused part of the region from a track.

Trim Start to Insertion: This removes all audio in a region from the start point to the edit insertion point. It's useful for quickly clearing audio at the beginning of a take.

Trim End to Insertion: This removes all audio in a region from the end point to the edit insertion point. It's useful for quickly clearing audio at the end of a take.

Trim Start to Fill Selection: This command is designed to fill gaps between regions by trimming (expanding) from the start of one region toward the end of another region. Regions not filling the entire gap will be revealed to their original start point.

Trim End to Fill Selection: This command is designed to fill gaps between regions by trimming from the end point of one region toward the start point of another region. Regions not filling the entire gape will be revealed to their original end point.

To Fill Selection: This command is designed to fill gaps between regions by trimming (expanding) from the start point of one region and trimming (expanding) from the end point of the other region.

To trim a selection:

1. Select a portion of a region.

2. Choose Edit > Trim Region > To Selection (**Figure 12.40**).

   The selected portion of a region becomes a new region, and the unselected portion is removed from the track (**Figure 12.41**).

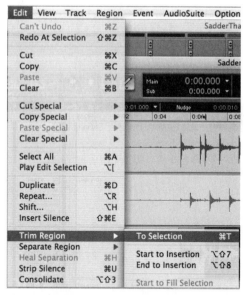

Figure 12.40 To trim a selection, choose Edit > Trim Region > To Selection.

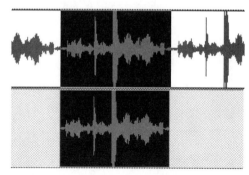

Figure 12.41 The selected portion of the region becomes a new region, and the unselected portion is removed from the track.

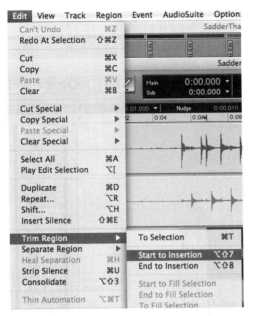

Figure 12.42 To trim a region from the start point to the edit insertion point, choose Edit > Trim Region > Start To Insertion.

To trim a region from the start point to the insertion point:

1. Click in the track with the Selector to designate an edit insertion point.

2. Choose Edit > Trim Region > Start To Insertion (**Figure 12.42**).

   The edit insertion point becomes the region's new start point (**Figure 12.43**).

To trim a region from the end point to the insertion point:

1. Click in the track with the Selector to designate an edit insertion point.

2. Choose Edit > Trim Region > End To Insertion (**Figure 12.44**).

   The edit insertion point becomes the region's new end point.

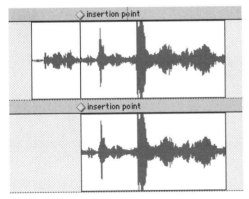

Figure 12.43 The edit insertion point becomes the region's new start point.

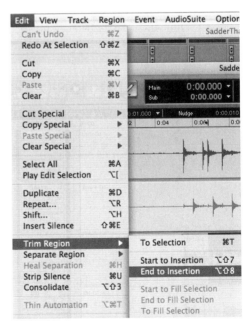

Figure 12.44 To trim a region from the end point to the insertion point, choose Edit > Trim Region > End To Insertion.

TRIMMING REGIONS

To fill gaps between regions using Trim to Fill:

1. With the Selector tool, select across the gap between to regions (**Figure 12.45**).

Figure 12.45 With the Selector tool, select across the gap between to regions.

2. Choose Edit > Trim Region and then select from the three Trim to Fill command options (discussed previously) (**Figure 12.46**).

The selected regions are trimmed (expanded) to fill the gap between the regions.

✔ Tips

- You can trim the start and end point of a region by nudging: Define a Nudge value in the upper right of the Edit window. Then use the Grabber to select the region you want to trim.

- To trim a region's start point, hold down Option (Macintosh) or Alt (Windows) and press Plus or Minus on the numeric keypad. To trim a region's end point, hold down Command (Macintosh) or Control (Windows) and press Plus or Minus on the numeric keypad.

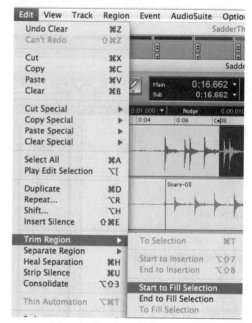

Figure 12.46 To fill the gap between two regions, choose Edit > Trim Region > Start to Fill Selection.

TRIMMING REGIONS

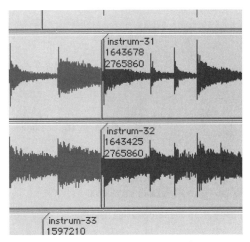

Figure 12.47 Choose View > Region > Overlap. Regions overlapping adjacent regions display a "dog-ear" corner.

Displaying Region Boundary Overlap/Underlap

Pro Tools makes it easy to perform edit-intensive tasks, such as creating *composite performances* (creating one good performance on a single track from pieces of multiple performances on different tracks). It's easy to copy and paste audio regions from multiple tracks onto a single "comp" track.

When you place separate audio regions tightly together on a track, the boundaries of adjacent regions overlap or underlap. It's important to keep tabs on region overlap, because it is easy to inadvertently click-on an underlapping region, bringing it forward to overlap neighboring regions.

If the previously underlapping region has been edited, had its tempo changed, or had its length altered with time-compression/expansion effects, bringing it forward into overlap position could disrupt the seamless flow of composite regions and produce unwanted, jarring noise at region transitions.

To display the region overlap indicator:

◆ Choose View > Region > Overlap.

A thin diagonal line (or "dog-ear) appears at the corner of regions currently overlapping the boundaries of adjacent regions (**Figure 12.47**).

To change region overlap or underlap:

1. Select the reason you want to change.

2. Choose Region > Bring to Front.

The selected region changes to overlap neighboring regions.

or

Choose Region > Send to Back.

The selcted region changes underlap neighboring regions.

Nudging Regions

You can nudge selected regions by precise increments using the numeric keypad's Plus and Minus keys. Nudging is very helpful for fine-tuning the placement of a region.

To set the Nudge value:

1. In the Nudge Value pop-up menu, choose a time scale for the Nudge value (**Figure 12.48**).

2. Select a Nudge value from the pop-up menu.

   or

   Type a number into the Nudge Value field (**Figure 12.49**).

To nudge a region:

1. Set the Nudge value, following the preceding instructions.

2. Select the region you want to nudge using the Grabber or Selector.

3. Press the Plus key on the numeric keypad to move the selection forward by the Nudge value. Press the Minus key to move the selection back by the Nudge value.

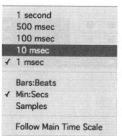

Figure 12.48 The Nudge Value pop-up menu.

Figure 12.49 The Nudge Value field.

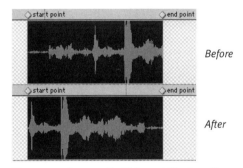

Figure 12.50 Press and hold Control (Macintosh) or Start (Windows), and then press Plus or Minus on the numeric keypad to nudge the contents of a selected region without changing its start or end points.

Nudging a region's contents

You can nudge a region's contents without changing its start or end point. This is useful if a region is placed at the correct location (such as a precise time location), but the material within the region is situated too early or late.

To nudge a region's contents without changing its start or end points:

1. Set the Nudge value, following the instructions in the *To set the Nudge value* section.

2. With the Grabber, select the region whose contents you want to nudge.

3. Hold down Control (Macintosh) or Start (Windows) and press Plus or Minus on the numeric keypad to move the audio waveform by the Nudge value.

   The region's contents are moved by the Nudge value. The region's start and end times remain unchanged (**Figure 12.50**).

Using Edit Commands

You can use these standard Edit menu commands to manipulate audio regions in Pro Tools:

Copy: The Copy command duplicates the selected region and places it on the clipboard.

Cut: The Cut command places a selection on the clipboard and removes it from a track.

Paste: The Paste command places a cut or copied region from the clipboard onto a track at the edit insertion point. Pasted regions will overwrite preexisting audio regions on the track.

Clear: The Clear command removes a region from a track without placing it on the clipboard.

When you cut or copy a selection, the current track view determines what is placed on the clipboard. For example, in Waveform view, cutting or copying a selected region places any volume, pan, mute, send, or plug-in automation on the clipboard, along with audio region data.

If a track displays automation data (such as in Volume, Mute, or Pan view), cutting or copying places only the automation data on the clipboard. For more information on editing automation, see *Chapter 16: Automating a Mix*.

To cut or copy a selected region:

1. Set the track view for the tracks you want to edit (**Figure 12.51**).

2. Select the audio material you want to cut or copy.

3. Choose Edit > Copy to place the selection on the clipboard without removing it from the track (**Figure 12.52**).

   or

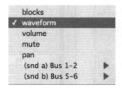

Figure 12.51 Click the Track View selector to set the track view.

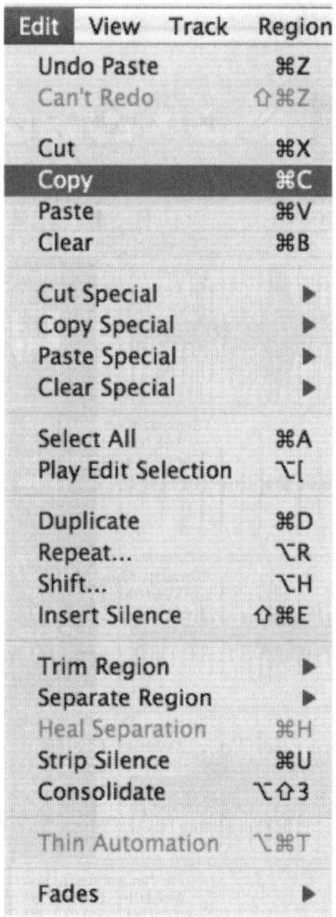

Figure 12.52 To place a copy of a selection on the clipboard, choose Edit > Copy.

Figure 12.53 To place a selection on the clipboard and remove it from the track, choose Edit > Cut.

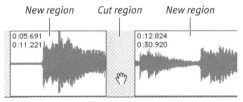

New region *Cut region* *New region*

Figure 12.54 New regions are automatically created on either side of cut regions.

Figure 12.55 To place a region from the clipboard onto a track at the edit insertion point, choose Edit > Paste.

Choose Edit > Cut to place the selection on the clipboard and remove it from the track (**Figure 12.53**).

If the selected region was cut or copied, the selection appears as a new region in the Regions list. If the selected region was cut, new regions are automatically created on either side of the selection (**Figure 12.54**).

To paste a selected region:

1. Click in the track with the Selector to set an edit insertion point.

   Press Tab to move the insertion point to the end of a region. Press Option-Tab (Macintosh) or Control-Tab (Windows) to move the insertion point to the start of a region.

   or

   Select a region with the Grabber or Selector.

2. Choose Edit > Paste (**Figure 12.55**).

   The cut or copied selection appears in the track at the edit insertion point.

To clear a selected region:

1. Set the track view for the tracks you want to edit.

2. Select the audio material you want to clear.

   or

   Use the Grabber to select one or more regions.

3. Choose Edit > Clear (**Figure 12.56**).

   The selected region is removed from the track. If a portion of a region was cleared, new regions are automatically created on either side of the selection.

✔ Tips

■ You can quickly slide a copy of a region to another location by pressing Option (Macintosh) or Alt (Windows) while dragging the region (**Figure 12.57**). The original region remains unchanged.

■ You can retain the timeline location of a dragged region by pressing Control (Macintosh) or Start (Windows) while dragging the region.

Edit	View	Track	Region
Undo Paste			⌘Z
Can't Redo			⇧⌘Z
Cut			⌘X
Copy			⌘C
Paste			⌘V
Clear			⌘B
Cut Special			▶
Copy Special			▶
Paste Special			▶
Clear Special			▶
Select All			⌘A
Play Edit Selection			⌥[
Duplicate			⌘D
Repeat...			⌥R
Shift...			⌥H
Insert Silence			⇧⌘E
Trim Region			▶
Separate Region			▶
Heal Separation			⌘H
Strip Silence			⌘U
Consolidate			⌥⇧3
Thin Automation			⌥⌘T
Fades			▶

Figure 12.56 To remove a selected region from a track, choose Edit > Clear.

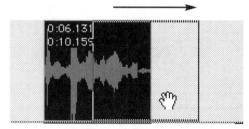

Figure 12.57 To slide a copy of a region from one location to another without changing the original region, press Option (Macintosh) or Alt (Windows) while dragging the region.

USING EDIT COMMANDS

Using Special Edit Commands

Special Edit commands are identical to regular Edit commands except they act only upon the automation data (volume, pan, mute, and plug-in automation) on audio, auxiliary input, master fader, and instrument tracks. You can also use Special Edit commands to edit MIDI controller data.

Each Special Edit command includes a submenu containing options for applying the command as follows:

Copy Special

◆ **All Automation:** Copies all automation data, shown or not.

◆ **Pan Automation:** Copies only pan automation data or MIDI pan data, shown or not.

◆ **Plug-in Automation:** Copies only plug-in automation data that is shown.

Cut Special

◆ **All Automation:** Cuts all automation data or MIDI data, shown or not.

◆ **Pan Automation:** Cuts only pan automation data or MIDI pan data, shown or not.

◆ **Plug-in Automation:** Cuts only plug-in automation data that is shown.

Paste Special

◆ **Merge:** Pastes MIDI note data in the clipboard to a selected destination and merges it with preexisting MIDI note data.

◆ **Repeat to Fill Selection:** Pastes unlimited copies of audio and MIDI regions, automation data, or MIDI controller data from the clipboard to fill a selected location.

◆ **To Current Automation Type:** Pastes automation or MIDI controller data from the clipboard to a selected destination as the "current" automation type. This lets you use automation data interchangeably between all types of automation; you can use MIDI data interchangeably between all MIDI functions.

Clear Special

◆ **All Automation:** Clears all automation and MIDI controller data, shown or not.

◆ **Pan Automation:** Clears only pan automation data or MIDI pan data, shown or not.

◆ **Plug-in Automation:** Clears only plug-in automation data that is shown.

USING SPECIAL EDIT COMMANDS

To copy automation data from one track to another track using Copy Special:

1. Click the Track View selector to view track automation (volume, pan, mute).

2. Using the Selector tool, select the track playlist (or portion of a track's playlist whose automation you want to copy) (**Figure 12.58**).

3. Choose Edit > Copy Special > All Automation (**Figure 12.59**).

   All automation data in the playlist selection is copied to the clipboard.

4. Choose Edit > Paste Special > Repeat to Fill Selection.

   All automation in the clipboard is pasted to the selected track. If your track selection exceeds the length of the inserted automation, the automation is repeated (multiple times if necessary) to fill the entire selection (**Figure 12.60**).

   For additional information on Special Edit commands, see the *Pro Tools Reference Guide*.

Figure 12.58 Set Track View to the desired automation type. Then, in the track's playlist, select the portion of automation you want to copy.

Figure 12.59 To copy selected automation, choose Edit > Copy Special > All Automation.

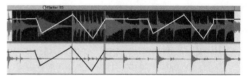

Figure 12.60 Choose Edit > Paste Special > Repeat to Fill Selection; Pasted automation repeats until the entire length of the selection is filled.

Start	4:23.343
End	7:45.263
Length	3:21.920

Figure 12.61 The Event Edit area (at top of Edit window). Enter start and end time to make a selection.

Edit	View	Track	Region
Undo Paste			⌘Z
Can't Redo			⇧⌘Z
Cut			⌘X
Copy			⌘C
Paste			⌘V
Clear			⌘B
Cut Special			▶
Copy Special			▶
Paste Special			▶
Clear Special			▶
Select All			⌘A
Play Edit Selection			⌥[
Duplicate			⌘D
Repeat...			⌥R
Shift...			⌥H
Insert Silence			⇧⌘E
Trim Region			▶
Separate Region			▶
Heal Separation			⌘H
Strip Silence			⌘U
Consolidate			⌥⇧3
Thin Automation			⌥⌘T
Fades			▶

Figure 12.62 To duplicate a region, choose Edit > Duplicate.

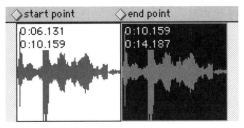

Figure 12.63 A duplicated region is placed immediately after the selection's end point.

Duplicating and Repeating Regions

The Duplicate command copies a selected region and places the copy at the end of the region. Duplicating is useful for quickly making back-to-back copies of a region. For example, you might want to duplicate a measure or two of drums to create a drum loop. Duplicate is similar to the Copy and Paste commands, only faster and more convenient.

The Repeat command is similar to Duplicate except the Repeat dialog box prompts you to specify the exact number of copies to create.

To duplicate a selected region:

1. With the Selector, select the region you want to duplicate.

   or

   Click in the track and enter the start and end points for the selection in the Event Edit area (**Figure 12.61**).

2. Choose Edit > Duplicate (**Figure 12.62**).

   The selected region is placed immediately after the selection's end point (**Figure 12.63**).

To repeat a selected region:

1. With the Selector, select the region you want to repeat (**Figure 12.64**).

   or

   Click in the track and enter the start and end points for the selection in the Event Edit area.

2. Choose Edit > Repeat.

   The Repeat dialog box appears.

3. Enter the number of times you want to repeat the selected region (**Figure 12.65**).

4. Click OK.

   The selected region is placed immediately after the selection's end point and duplicated the specified number of times (**Figure 12.66**).

Figure 12.64 To repeat a region, select a region to repeat, and then choose Edit > Repeat.

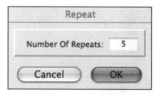

Figure 12.65 The Repeat dialog box. Enter the number of times you want to repeat the selected region.

Figure 12.66 The selected region repeats the specified number of times.

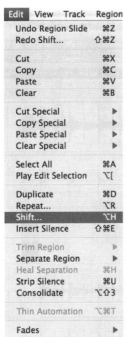

Edit	View	Track	Region
Undo Region Slide			⌘Z
Redo Shift...			⇧⌘Z
Cut			⌘X
Copy			⌘C
Paste			⌘V
Clear			⌘B
Cut Special			▶
Copy Special			▶
Paste Special			▶
Clear Special			▶
Select All			⌘A
Play Edit Selection			⌥[
Duplicate			⌘D
Repeat...			⌥R
Shift...			⌥H
Insert Silence			⇧⌘E
Trim Region			▶
Separate Region			▶
Heal Separation			⌘H
Strip Silence			⌘U
Consolidate			⌥⇧3
Thin Automation			⌥⌘T
Fades			▶

Figure 12.67 To shift a selected region, choose Edit > Shift.

Shifting Regions

The Shift command lets you move a selected region backward or forward in a track by a specified amount. Shifting is useful for moving regions by precise distances in a track.

To shift a selected region:

1. With the Selector or Grabber, select the region you want to shift.

2. Choose Edit > Shift (**Figure 12.67**). The Shift dialog box appears.

3. Click the Earlier or Later radio button.

4. Type a value in one of the Timebase fields to specify the amount by which the selection will be shifted (**Figure 12.68**).

5. Click OK. The selected region is shifted backward or forward in time by the specified amount.

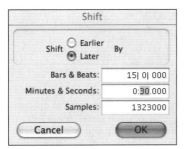

Figure 12.68 The Shift Dialog box. Enter the shift amount in a Timebase field.

Quantizing Regions

The Quantize Regions command aligns the start points (or sync points) of selected audio and MIDI regions to the nearest grid boundary. Quantizing is useful for adjusting the rhythmic timing of regions in a session. You can simultaneously quantize selected regions on multiple tracks. Keep in mind, however, that a region cannot be quantized unless the entire region is selected.

To quantize regions:

1. Define a Grid value in the upper right of the Edit window (**Figure 12.69**).

2. Select the regions you want to quantize (**Figure 12.70**).

3. Chose Region > Quantize to Grid (**Figure 12.71**).

   The selected region is moved so its start point aligns with the nearest grid line (**Figure 12.72**).

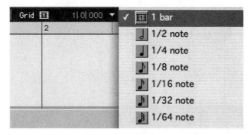

Figure 12.69 Define a Grid value for quantizing regions in the Grid Value pop-up menu.

Figure 12.70 Select a region to quantize.

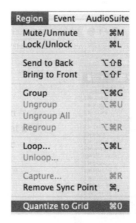

Figure 12.71 To quantize regions, choose Edit > Quantize to Grid.

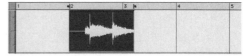

Figure 12.72 A quantized region: The start point moves to align with nearest grid line.

Region	Event	AudioSuite
Mute/Unmute		⌘M
Lock/Unlock		⌘L
Send to Back		⌥⇧B
Bring to Front		⌥⇧F
Group		⌥⌘G
Ungroup		⌥⌘U
Ungroup All		
Regroup		⌥⌘R
Loop...		⌥⌘L
Unloop...		
Capture...		⌘R
Remove Sync Point		⌘,
Quantize to Grid		⌘0

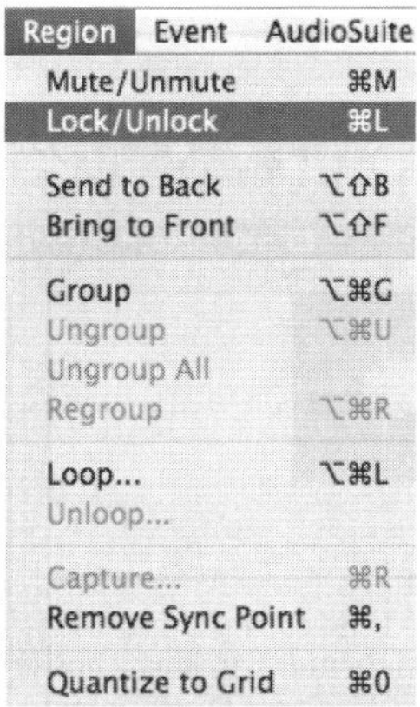

Figure 12.73 To lock or unlock regions, choose Region > Lock/Unlock.

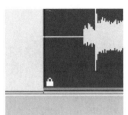

Figure 12.74 A locked region displays a small lock icon.

Locking Regions

Locking a region anchors it to its current location. This is a good way to ensure that carefully spotted regions are not accidentally moved in a session.

To lock a region:

1. With the Grabber, select the regions you want to lock.

2. Choose Region > Lock/Unlock (**Figure 12.73**).

   A small lock icon appears in the region, indicating that it has been locked (**Figure 12.74**).

Muting/Unmuting Regions

The Region menu's Mute/Unmute command lets you mute playback of a selected region. You can mute regions simultaneously on multiple tracks. Muted regions appear dimmed in track playlists.

To mute regions:

1. With the Grabber, select the regions you want to mute.

2. Choose Region > Mute/Unmute (**Figure 12.75**).

   The selected regions are muted and dimmed in the track playlist (**Figure 12.76**). Selected regions that were previously muted become unmuted.

✔ Tip

■ You can mute a single region (or any portion of a track by recording Mute *automation*. You can record Mute automation (as well as volume, pan, and plug-in automation) in two ways:

  In Mute, Volume, Pan, and Send (to DSP plug-ins) Track view, you can graph parameter changes over a track's waveform (**Figure 12.77**).

  Or, you can "write" mute, volume, pan, and Send automation in real-time during playback using the mute button (or volume fader, pan slider, and Sends Output window). Pro Tools "reads" (automatically performs) your recorded track control manipulations during playback.

  For more information on "Automation" Pro Tools, see *Chapter 16: Automating a Mix* or see the *Pro Tools Reference Guide*.

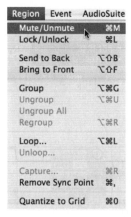

Figure 12.75 To mute or unmute regions, choose Region > Mute/Unmute.

Figure 12.76 Muted regions are dimmed in the track playlist.

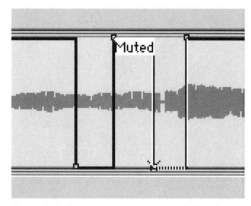

Figure 12.77 Mute or unmute any portion of a track by graphing mute automation settings in Mute Track view.

MUTING/UNMUTING REGIONS

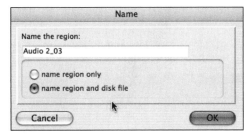

Figure 12.78 The Name (region) dialog box.

Managing Regions

Anytime you cut, separate, or otherwise break an audio region into two or more segments, Pro Tools *auto-creates* new regions from the remaining segments. As a result, the number of regions in a session can multiply like rabbits. This multitude of regions tends to crowd the Regions list and makes it difficult to find the regions you want.

Fortunately, Pro Tools provides the following features to help you manage regions and to help you keep the number of regions in a session to a minimum.

Renaming regions

Renaming regions with more descriptive or memorable names can make them easier to identify. Pro Tools lets you rename regions by double-clicking on them with the Grabber tool, or by selecting a region, and then choosing the Rename command in the Regions list's pop-up menu.

To rename a region using the Grabber tool:

1. In the Edit window, select the Grabber tool.

2. With the Grabber, double-click on the region you want to rename.

    The Name dialog box appears (**Figure 12.78**).

3. Enter the new name of the region. If you selected a whole audio file, specify whether to rename just the region or both the region and the audio file on disk.

4. Click OK.

    The region is renamed.

To rename one or more regions in the Regions list:

1. Select Show > Auto-Created from the Regions list pop-up menu (**Figure 12.79**). This displays all auto-created regions in the Regions list.

2. In the Regions list, select one or more regions to rename.

   or

   With the Editing preference for "Region List Selection Follows Track Selection" enabled, select a region in a track.

3. Choose Rename from the Regions list pop-up menu (**Figure 12.80**).

   or

   Double-click on a region name in the Regions list.

   The Name dialog box appears.

4. In the Name dialog box, enter a new name for the region. If you selected a whole audio file, specify whether to rename just the region or both the region and the audio file on disk.

5. Click OK.

   The selected region is renamed. If you're renaming more than one region, the Name dialog box prompts you for each successive region.

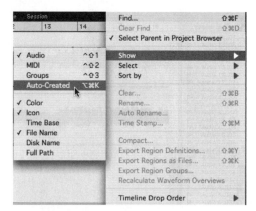

Figure 12.79 In the Regions list pop-up menu, select Show > Auto-Created.

Figure 12.80 To rename a region, choose Rename in the Regions list pop-up menu.

MANAGING REGIONS

Figure 12.81 To set auto-name parameters, choose Auto Rename in the Regions list pop-up menu.

Figure 12.82 The Rename Selected Regions dialog box.

Setting auto-name parameters

When new regions are auto-created during editing, Pro Tools also *auto-names* these new regions. By default, Pro Tools names these new regions numerically in sequential order. This can lead to a lengthy Regions list full of numbered regions that are difficult to identify.

To help you better differentiate regions (and avoid a mind-boggling list of numbered regions), Pro Tools lets you create a naming scheme for auto-created regions.

To set auto-name parameters for a region:

1. Select a region in the Regions list.

2. Choose Auto Rename from the Regions list pop-up menu (**Figure 12.81**).

   The Rename Selected Regions dialog box appears (**Figure 12.82**).

3. In the Rename Selected Regions dialog, enter the text you want used when naming new regions created from the selected region. You can input the following auto-name parameters:

   Name: This parameter determines the root name for the auto-created region.

   Starting Number: This parameter sets the start number for the sequentially numbered new regions.

   Number of Places: This parameter determines the number of zeros that occur before the auto numbers.

   Suffix: This parameter specifies the text to be appended to the end of the name, following the auto-numbering.

4. Click OK.

   Regions created from the selected region will be auto-named according to the set parameters.

Hiding auto-created regions

Pro Tools lets you hide auto-created regions in the Regions list while *user-defined* regions continue to be displayed. This can help you keep the Regions list down to a manageable length.

To hide auto-created regions:

◆ Deselect Show > Auto-Created (**Figure 12.83**).

Auto-created regions are removed from the Regions list. User-defined regions remain visible in the Regions list. User-defined regions include the following:

▲ Whole-file audio regions

▲ Regions created during recording

▲ Imported regions

▲ Renamed regions

▲ Regions created during AudioSuite plug-in processing

▲ New regions created with Capture Regions and Separate Region commands

▲ Regions created by trimming whole-file audio regions

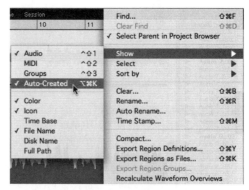

Figure 12.83 To hide auto-created regions in the Regions list, deselect Show > Auto-Created.

Figure 12.84 To select unused regions, in the Regions list pop-up menu, choose Select > Unused Regions.

Figure 12.85 To remove unused regions, choose Clear from the Regions list pop-up menu.

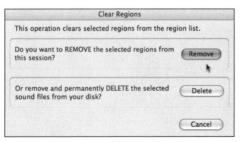

Figure 12.86 The Clear Regions dialog box.

Removing unused regions

Removing unused regions, when possible, can help you keep the number of regions in your session from getting out of hand. You can locate and remove unused regions in a session with the Clear Selected command.

To find and remove unused audio regions:

1. In the Regions list pop-up menu, under Select, choose one of the following (**Figure 12.84**):
   - ▲ All
   - ▲ Unused
   - ▲ Unused Audio Except Whole Files
   - ▲ Offline
   The desired unused regions are selected.

2. Choose Clear from the Regions list pop-up menu (**Figure 12.85**).
   The Clear Regions dialog box appears (**Figure 12.86**).

3. Click Remove.
   The unused regions are removed from the session.
   or
   If you're clearing a whole-file audio region and you want to permanently remove the audio file from your hard drive, click Delete.
   CAUTION: Be certain before you click Delete: The audio file is permanently erased from your hard drive.
   For more information on managing regions, see *Chapter 13: Advanced Editing* or see the *Pro Tools Reference Guide* and the *DigiBase Guide*.

MANAGING REGIONS

13

ADVANCED EDITING

Now that you've mastered the basics of editing in Pro Tools, it's time to learn a few advanced editing features. The features covered in this chapter are easy to learn. With a bit of practice, they'll help you produce even smoother and more pristine-sounding audio.

We'll begin with Region Groups, a new feature in Pro Tools 7, which lets you create collections of regions and handle them as one file. Next, we'll look at fades and crossfades. You'll learn when to use them and how to create them in Pro Tools. We'll also look at the Batch Fade feature, which lets you apply multiple fades or crossfades across several regions simultaneously.

Next, we'll explore repairing audio waveforms. We'll show you how to quickly locate problematic glitches in your audio waveforms, and how to easily reshape the waveform with the Pencil tool to eradicate the unwanted noise.

Lastly, we'll explore silence—that is, Pro Tools' Strip Silence feature, which removes portions of audio files that fall below a user-defined volume threshold. We'll sign off with the Insert Silence feature, which lets you add silence to a selected audio region.

Region Groups

A *region group* is a collection of regions, brought together and handled as a single region group file (.rgrp file format). You can use a region group just like you would a regular region: You can place region groups in tracks, edit them, view and manage them in the Regions list, and export and import them between Pro Tools sessions. (Region group file names are given the .rgrp extension upon export).

Region groups are useful for managing large numbers of similar small regions. For example, complex vocal arrangements, such as three part harmonies, are well suited for using region groups (multiple takes, redos, touch ups, edits composites can cause an explosion in the Regions list population). Creating a region group for each harmony part (or section of a harmony part) will help

you keep your arrangements clean and organized. You can also nest region groups within region groups, which lets you organize your subsets of regions with region groups.

Creating region groups

To create a region group, you must first select the regions you want in the group. Region group selections can start and end anywhere in a track, including within a region, on a region boundary, or in empty space. Selections placed within region boundaries will separate the region at the selection boundaries. Blank space included in the selection will become part of the region group.

To create a region group:

1. Select one or more regions in a track playlist (**Figure 13.1**).

Figure 13.1 Select one or more regions to place in a region group.

Figure 13.2 A single region group appears in the track playlist and in the Regions list.

Figure 13.3 The region group icon is displayed in the lower left corner of the region group.

Figure 13.4 Select a region group to ungroup.

Region	Event	AudioSuite
Mute/Unmute	⌘M	
Lock/Unlock	⌘L	
Send to Back	⌥⇧B	
Bring to Front	⌥⇧F	
Group	⌥⌘G	
Ungroup	⌥⌘U	
Ungroup All		
Regroup	⌥⌘R	
Loop...	⌥⌘L	
Unloop...		
Capture...	⌘R	
Remove Sync Point	⌘,	
Quantize to Grid	⌘0	

Figure 13.5 To ungroup a region group and all nested region groups it contains, choose Region > Ungroup All.

2. Choose Region > Group.

A single region group appears in the track playlist and in the Regions list (**Figure 13.2**). The region group icon is displayed in the lower left corner of the region group in the track (**Figure 13.3**).

To ungroup a region group:

1. Select a region group to ungroup (**Figure 13.4**).

2. Choose Region > Ungroup

The first level of region groups is ungrouped (nested region groups are maintained).

or

Choose Region > Ungroup All (**Figure 13.5**).

All region groups, including nested region groups, are ungrouped.

To regroup a region group:

1. Select any region from the ungrouped region group (**Figure 13.6**).

2. Choose Region > Regroup (**Figure 13.7**).

   Region groups (ungrouped with the Ungroup All command) are restored tracks (**Figure 13.8**).

Editing Region Groups

Region groups are edited using the same standard editing commands used to edit regular regions: Cut, Copy, Paste, Clear, Trim, Lock, Mute, Name, Duplicate, Repeat, Spot, and so on.

When you apply an edit command to a region group it also applies to the regions it contains, with a few noteworthy exceptions: The Trim command, for example, applies to the boundaries of the region group only.

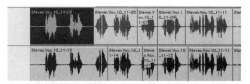

Figure 13.6 To regroup a region group, first select any ungrouped region.

Figure 13.7 Choose Region > Regroup.

Figure 13.8 A restored region group. The Region > Regroup command restores region groups ungrouped with the Ungroup All command.

REGION GROUPS

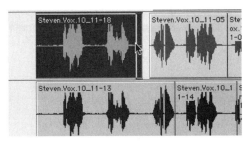

Figure 13.9 You can trim individual ungrouped regions.

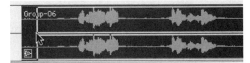

Figure 13.10 The TCE Trim tool lets you trim region group boundaries.

Figure 13.11 Trimming a region group with the TCE Trim tool creates a new region over the region group.

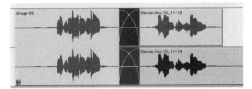

Figure 13.12 A crossfade between a region group and individual regions.

- Fade and crossfades can be created between two audio region groups and between an audio region group and a regular audio region (**Figure 13.12**). Ungrouping a region group removes any group level fades or crossfades. Fades and crossfades are restored by the Regroup command.

To trim individual regions within a region group:

1. Choose Region > Ungroup All.

   The region group is ungrouped. Individual regions appear in tracks.

2. Trim individual regions as desired (**Figure 13.9**).

3. Choose Region > Regroup.

   The region group is restored with trim edits to individual regions saved.

In addition, certain edit commands create new regions over region groups, as follows:

- Trimming a region group with the TCE Trim tool applies to region group boundaries only (**Figure 13.10**) and creates a new region over the region group (**Figure 13.11**).

- AudioSuite processing of a grouped region creates a new region over the region group.

- Consolidating a selection including a grouped region creates a new audio file and region over the region group.

- Recording into a region group creates a new audio file and region over the region group.

- Pencil tool waveform redraw creates a new region over the region group.

✔ Tips

- With Tab to Transients enabled, the Tab key moves the location cursor to transients and region boundaries within a region group; with Tab to Transients disabled, the Tab key moves the location cursor to region group boundaries and the sync point, if present, only.

Looping Regions

New in Pro Tools 7, the Region Loop command lets you create loops of selected audio and MIDI regions and region groups (**Figure 13.13**).

Figure 13.13 A region loop.

Creating region loops

Creating region loops is an excellent way to quickly generate full-song rhythm sections (drum or percussion parts) or to extend a sound effect or a one-of-a-kind riff for fading in and out as desired throughout a song.

Figure 13.14 Select the audio (or MIDI) region you want to loop.

To loop a region:

1. Select an audio or MIDI region, or region group (**Figure 13.14**).

2. Choose Region > Loop.

   The Region Looping dialog box appears (**Figure 13.15**).

3. In the Region Looping dialog box, do one of the following:

   ▲ Select the Number of Loops option and enter the number of times to loop the region.

   ▲ Select the Loop Length option and enter the duration according to the Main Time Scale. If the length is not an exact multiple of the source loop's duration, the last loop will be truncated.

   ▲ Select the Loop Until End of Session or Next Region option. The looped region will repeat until the end of the session or until the next region on the track. If necessary, the last loop will be truncated to fit.

4. To create a crossfade at the loop point, choose Enable Crossfade. Select Settings. Configure the crossfade as desired (**Figure 13.16**). Click OK.

5. In the Region Looping dialog, click OK.

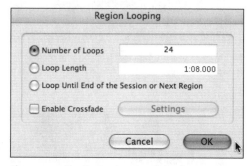

Figure 13.15 The Region Looping dialog box.

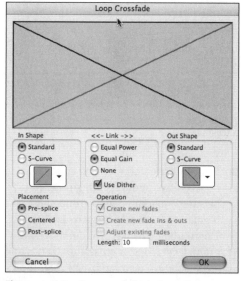

Figure 13.16 Creating crossfades between loops helps to smooth transitions between individual loop iterations.

LOOPING REGIONS

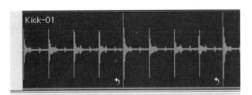

Figure 13.17 The region loop appears in the track playlist. Each loop iteration displays the loop icon.

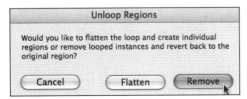

Figure 13.18 The Unloop Regions dialog box.

Figure 13.19 Click Remove in the Unloop Regions dialog box to remove all loop iterations except the originally selected source region.

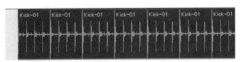

Figure 13.20 Click Flatten in the Unloop Regions dialog box to unloop the region loop and create individual regions.

The loop appears on the track (as specified in the Region Looping dialog box) with each region of the loop displaying the loop icon (**Figure 13.17**).

To unloop looped regions:

1. Select the looped region.

2. Choose Region > Unloop.
   The Unloop Regions dialog box opens (**Figure 13.18**).

3. In the Unloop Regions dialog box, select one of the following:
   ▲ **Remove:** This option unloops and removes all loop iterations except the source loop iteration (**Figure 13.19**).
   or
   ▲ **Flatten:** This option unloops the region loop and creates individual regions from loop iterations (**Figure 13.20**).

To unloop region loops and ungroup region groups:

1. Select a looped region that contains one or more region groups.

2. Choose Region > Ungroup All.
   The selected loop is unlooped and region groups are ungrouped (individual regions reappear).

Editing Looped Regions

You can apply edits to an entire region loop (edits apply to all regions in a loop), or you can edit the individual regions within a region loop. Clicking on the region loop with the Grabber tool, Smart Tool, or Selector tool selects the entire region loop; clicking the icon of an individual region in a loop selects that region only.

When you move a region loop, all regions in that loop are moved along with the source loop. However, individual regions in a region loop cannot be moved separately from the region loop.

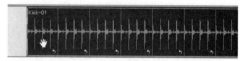

Figure 13.21 Select a loop by clicking on it with the Grabber tool.

Figure 13.22 Select an individual loop iteration by clicking its loop icon.

To select a looped region:

◆ Using the Grabber tool or Smart tool, click the looped region (**Figure 13.21**).

or

◆ Using the Selector tool, double-click the looped region.

The entire region loop is selected, including the source region and all its loop iterations.

To select an individual source region or loop iteration:

◆ Using the Grabber tool or Smart tool, click the loop icon of a source region or the desired individual loop iteration (**Figure 13.22**).

or

◆ Using the Selector tool, double-click the loop icon of a source region or the desired individual loop iteration.

The individual source region or individual loop iteration is selected.

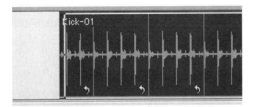

Figure 13.23 Use the Standard Trim tool to trim region loop boundaries.

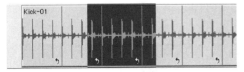

Figure 13.24 Make an edit selection of the area you want to keep within a region loop.

Figure 13.25 To trim a region loop to a selected area, choose Edit > Trim Region > To Selection.

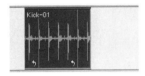

Figure 13.26 The region loop is trimmed on both sides of the edit selection.

Trimming looped regions

Looped regions can be trimmed using the Standard Trim tool, Trim Region commands, or the Loop Trim tool. The Standard Trim tool lets you trim the boundaries of entire region loops. Trim Region commands let you trim an entire region loop down to a selected area or from the start or end point of a region loop to the edit insertion point.

The Loop Trim tool lets you quickly alter the source loop selection by trimming individual loop iterations. All iterations in the region loop are then updated automatically to match the individual trimmed region. The number of loops in the region loop either increases or decreases to fill the space of the entire region loop. The Loop Trim tool appears when you move the Standard Trim tool over the loop icon of any loop iteration in the region loop.

To trim region loop boundaries:

1. Choose the Standard Trim tool.

2. Trim the start or end of the region loop.

   Region loop boundaries move to reveal additional loop iterations or to conceal existing loop iterations (**Figure 13.23**).

To trim a region loop to a selection:

1. Choose the Selector tool.

2. Make the desired edit selection within the region loop (**Figure 13.24**).

3. Choose Edit > Trim Region > To Selection (**Figure 13.25**).

   The region loop is trimmed on both sides of the edit selection (**Figure 13.26**).

To trim a region loop using the Loop Trim tool:

1. Choose the Standard Trim tool.

2. Move the Standard Trim cursor over an individual region's loop icon (**Figure 13.27**).

3. Trim the boundaries of the individual region as desired (**Figure 13.28**).

   All loops in the region loop are updated automatically to match the new boundaries (of the individual region trimmed with the Loop Trim tool) (**Figure 13.29**).

✔ Tips

- To trim region loops in one loop iteration increments, press Control (Macintosh) or Start (Windows) while trimming with the Standard Trim tool.

- With Tab to Transients enabled, the Tab key moves the location cursor to transients and region boundaries in a looped region; with Tab to Transients disabled, the Tab key moves the location cursor to start and end boundaries of the entire region.

- The TCE Trim tool unloops and consolidates the entire region loop. A new region appears over the region loop and in the Regions list.

- Looping audio regions does not loop automation. To copy and apply a selected segment of automation to a region loop, choose Edit > Copy Special to copy the automation to the clipboard. Then choose Edit > Paste Special > Repeat to Fill Selection.

For more information on Trim tools in Pro Tools 7, see *Chapter 12: Working with Regions* or see *The Pro Tools Reference Guide*. For more information on Looping Regions, see *The Pro Tools Reference Guide*.

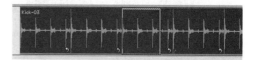

Figure 13.27 Drag the Standard Trim tool over the loop icon of any individual iteration in the loop.

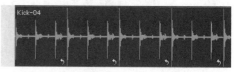

Figure 13.28 Trim the individual region of the loop as desired.

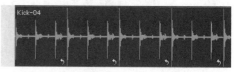

Figure 13.29 All loops in the region loop are updated to match the trim performed on the individual loop iteration.

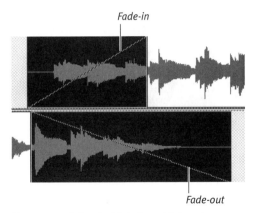

Fade-in

Fade-out

Figure 13.30 A standard fade-in and fade-out.

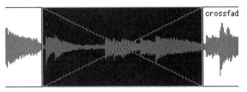

crossfad

Figure 13.31 A crossfade is an overlapping fade-out and fade-in placed between two adjoining audio regions.

Creating Fades and Crossfades

Pro Tools lets you add *fades* and *crossfades* to audio regions. A fade is a volume curve that controls the rate of increase (*fade-in*) or decrease (*fade-out*) of a region's volume. Fade-ins are placed at the start of regions; fade-outs are placed at the end (**Figure 13.30**). You can add fades and crossfades to regular audio regions, region groups, and looped regions.

Fades let you smooth the entrance and exit of audio during a mix. You can use fades on final mixes (such as a fade-out at the end of a song). Or, you can use fades to blend individual elements into a mix. For example, you may want to embellish a song chorus with a sample or instrumental part. Fades can help you smoothly incorporate these sounds.

A crossfade is an overlapping fade-out and fade-in placed between two adjoining audio regions (**Figure 13.31**). Crossfades let you smooth transitions between separate audio regions on a track. You can use crossfades to reduce noise (such as clicks and pops) or to reduce distracting changes in sound character that can occur between regions during playback.

You can assign different volume curves to the fade-out and fade-in portion of a cross-fade. The type of volume curve you assign determines the crossfade's character. Crossfade types include:

Centered: Centered crossfades extend across both sides of the splice point—the location where two cross-faded regions join (**Figure 13.32**). In a centered crossfade, the first region must contain audio material beyond its end point, and the second region must contain audio material before its start point.

Pre-Crossfade: Pre-crossfades are created before the splice point (**Figure 13.33**). This maintains the volume at the very beginning of the second region, which is useful if you want to preserve a strong attack at the beginning of the region.

Post-Crossfade: Post-crossfades are created after the splice point (**Figure 13.34**). They're useful if you want to maintain the volume of the first region until its end.

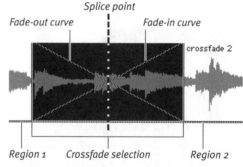

Figure 13.32 A centered crossfade.

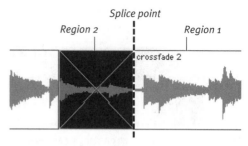

Figure 13.33 A pre-crossfade. The selection range extends just up to the beginning of Region 2.

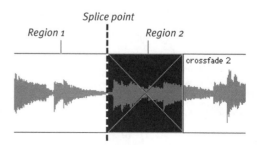

Figure 13.34 A post-crossfade. The selection range begins just after the end of Region 1.

About the Fades dialog box

The Fades dialog box (**Figure 13.35**) lets you select, view, audition, and edit fade volume curves. It includes the following buttons:

Audition: This button lets you preview a fade or crossfade.

View First Track: If a fade includes multiple tracks, this button lets you view the first pair of adjacent tracks.

View Second Track: If a fade includes multiple tracks, this button lets you view the second pair of adjacent tracks.

View Both Tracks: This button displays the waveforms of the first two adjacent tracks in a multitrack fade.

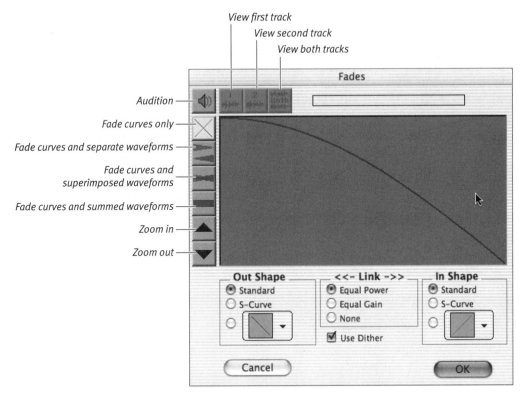

Figure 13.35 The Fades dialog box.

Fade Curves Only: This button displays the fade curves without showing the audio waveforms (**Figure 13.36**).

Fade Curves and Separate Waveforms: This button displays fade curves along with separate views of the fade-in and fade-out waveforms (**Figure 13.37**).

Fade Curves and Superimposed Waveforms: This button displays fade curves along with superimposed views of the fade-in and fade-out waveforms (**Figure 13.38**).

Fade Curves and Summed Waveform: This button displays the fade curves along with a single waveform representing the summation of the cross-faded audio.

Zoom In: This button zooms in on the audio waveform.

Zoom Out: This button zooms out on the audio waveform.

Figure 13.36 The Fade Curves Only button in the Fades dialog box displays the fade curves without showing the audio waveforms.

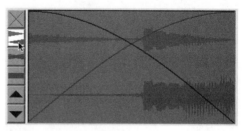

Figure 13.37 The Fade Curves and Separate Waveforms button displays fade curves and separate views of the fade-in and fade-out waveforms.

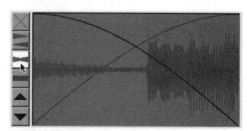

Figure 13.38 The Fade Curves and Superimposed Waveforms button displays the fade curves along with superimposed views of the fade-in and fade-out waveforms.

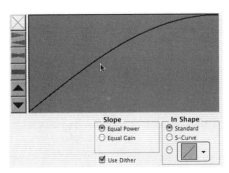

Figure 13.39 The Standard fade curve.

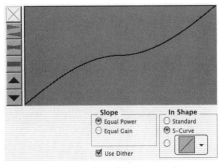

Figure 13.40 The S-shaped fade curve. Drag on the curve to adjust its shape.

Figure 13.41 The Preset Curves pop-up menu.

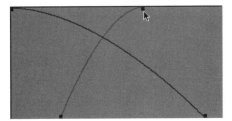

Figure 13.42 You can adjust preset curves used as crossfades by dragging their end points.

The Fades dialog box provides the following fade-in and fade-out curve shapes:

Standard: This is an all-purpose fade curve. You can adjust its shape by dragging it (**Figure 13.39**).

S-Curve: The S-shaped fade curve inverts at the start and end to make fade-ins faster and fade-outs slower (**Figure 13.40**). You can adjust its shape by dragging it.

Preset Curves: The Preset Curves pop-up menu (**Figure 13.41**) lets you choose from seven curves. You can adjust preset curves by dragging their end points (**Figure 13.42**).

Linking curves can help smooth the transition between fade-ins and fade-outs of a crossfade. When fades are linked, adjusting one fade curve automatically adjusts the other. The Fades dialog box offers the following options for linking fade-in and fade-out curves (**Figure 13.43**):

Equal Power: The Equal Power option is useful when cross-fading between audio regions that are out of phase or differ in sound character. It can also help prevent volume drop-outs that can occur with an Equal Gain crossfade. Option-click (Macintosh) or Alt-click (Windows) on the fade curve to reset it to its default shape.

Equal Gain: The Equal Gain option is useful when cross-fading between audio regions that are in phase or have similar or identical sound character (such as a drum loop). It can also help prevent the clipping that can occur when using an Equal Power crossfade. Option-click (Macintosh) or Alt-click (Windows) on the fade curve to reset it to its default shape.

None: This option disables linking between the fade-out and fade-in curves. This lets you adjust the curves separately and create custom crossfade shapes. To adjust the fade-in curve, press Option (Macintosh) or Alt (Windows) while dragging the curve. To adjust the fade-out curve, press Command (Macintosh) or Control (Windows) while dragging the curve.

The Fades dialog box also provides a Use Dither option (**Figure 13.44**), which lets you add *dither* to fades. Dither is a form of randomly generated noise that helps smooth out fade-ins or fade-outs from silence. Dither can also help smooth crossfades between low-level audio regions.

For more information on fades, see the *Pro Tools Reference Guide.*

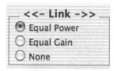

Figure 13.43 You can link fade-in and fade-out parameters in the Fades dialog box.

Figure 13.44 Select the Use Dither check box in the Fades dialog box to add dither to a fade.

CREATING FADES AND CROSSFADES

Figure 13.45 A fade-in selection. The selection must extend to the exact beginning of the region or a blank area prior to the region in the track.

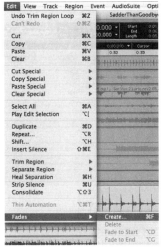

Figure 13.46 To create a fade-in or fade-out, choose Edit > Fades > Create.

Figure 13.47 You can adjust a fade curve by dragging it.

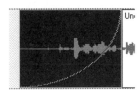

Figure 13.48 Pro Tools calculates the selected fade curve, and it appears in the region.

To create a fade-in:

1. With the Selector, select the beginning of the region you want to fade in. The selection must extend to the exact beginning of the region or a blank area prior to the region in the track (**Figure 13.45**).

2. Choose Edit > Fades > Create (**Figure 13.46**).
   The Fades dialog box appears.

3. Choose an In Shape.

4. Click the Audition button to play the fade. If desired, adjust the curve by dragging it in the Fades dialog box (**Figure 13.47**).

5. Select a Link option.

6. Click OK.
   Pro Tools calculates the fade-in and writes it to disk. The chosen fade curve appears in the region (**Figure 13.48**).

CREATING FADES AND CROSSFADES

To create a fade-out:

1. Select the end of the region you want to fade out. The selection must extend to the exact end of the region or a blank area after the region in the track.

2. Choose Edit > Fades > Create.

   The Fades dialog box appears.

3. Choose an Out Shape.

4. Click the Audition button to play the fade. If desired, adjust the curve by dragging it in the Fades dialog box.

5. Select a Link option.

6. Click OK.

   Pro Tools calculates the fade-out and writes it to disk (**Figure 13.49**). The chosen fade curve appears in the region.

To create a crossfade between two regions:

1. With the Selector, drag from where you want the crossfade to begin (in the first region) to where you want it to end (in the second region) (**Figure 13.50**).

2. Choose Edit > Fades > Create.

3. Use the view buttons to adjust the view of the crossfade.

4. Choose an Out Shape and an In Shape.

5. Select a Link option.

6. Audition the crossfade.

7. Click OK.

   Pro Tools calculates the crossfade and writes it to disk. The crossfade appears between the two selected regions.

Figure 13.49 Fade files are stored in the Fade Files folder inside the Session folder.

Figure 13.50 A crossfade selection between two regions.

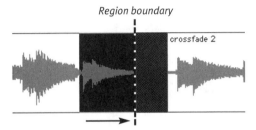

Region boundary

crossfade 2

Figure 13.51 Shift-drag or press Shift-Tab to extend a selection forward to the next region boundary.

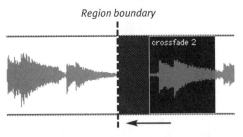

Region boundary

crossfade 2

Figure 13.52 Press Option-Shift-Tab (Macintosh) or Control-Shift-Tab (Windows) to extend the selection back to the previous region boundary.

To create a pre- or post-crossfade:

1. Click with the Selector in the track you want to cross-fade.

2. Press Tab to move forward to the next region boundary.

   or

   Press Option-Tab (Macintosh) or Control-Tab (Windows) to move back to the previous region boundary.

3. Shift-drag or press Shift-Tab to extend a selection forward to the next region boundary (**Figure 13.51**).

   or

   Press Option-Shift-Tab (Macintosh) or Control-Shift-Tab (Windows) to extend the selection back to the previous region boundary (**Figure 13.52**).

4. Choose Edit > Fades > Create.

5. Choose an In Shape and Out Shape for the crossfade.

6. Audition the crossfade.

   Adjust the fade-in and fade-out curves, if desired, by dragging them in the Fades dialog box.

7. Click OK.

   A pre- or post-crossfade appears between the selected regions.

CREATING FADES AND CROSSFADES

To remove a crossfade:

1. Select the area of the track containing the crossfade you want to delete.

2. Choose Edit > Fades > Delete (**Figure 13.53**).

   or

1. Select the crossfade with the Grabber or Selector.

2. Press Delete (Macintosh) or Backspace (Windows).

   The crossfade is removed and the regions are returned to their previous state.

To trim a crossfade:

1. Select the crossfade with the Grabber or Selector.

2. Drag the Trim tool at the start or end of the crossfade to lengthen or shorten it (**Figure 13.54**).

   The crossfade is recalculated and a new crossfade appears.

✔ Tips

- When making selections for crossfades that occur on the border of two regions, use the Tab key to move the cursor to the exact beginning or end of a region.

- Disabling the Use Dither function when editing fades and crossfades can help speed previews and fade recalculations.

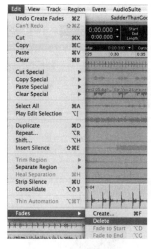

Figure 13.53 To remove a crossfade, choose Edit > Fades > Delete.

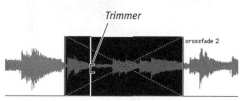

Figure 13.54 To trim a crossfade, drag the Trimmer at the start or end of a crossfade.

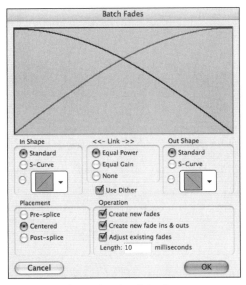

Figure 13.55 The Batch Fades dialog box.

Figure 13.56 A multiple region selection.

Figure 13.57 Multiple crossfades created with the Batch Fades dialog box.

Creating Fades and Crossfades in Batches

Pro Tools lets you create multiple fades and crossfades simultaneously. Creating fades and crossfades in batches lets you quickly smooth transitions between multiple regions.

To create batch fades you must first make a selection across multiple regions, and then choose the Create Fades command. This launches the Batch Fades dialog box (**Figure 13.55**), which provides options for creating multiple fades and crossfades.

To create crossfades between multiple regions at once:

1. Drag with the Selector from the first region you want to cross-fade to the last region you want to cross-fade (**Figure 13.56**).

2. Choose Edit > Fades > Create.
   The Batch Fades dialog box appears.

3. Select a Batch Operation.

4. Select a crossfade type (pre-splice, centered, or post-splice).

5. Enter a crossfade length in milliseconds.

6. Click OK.
   Fades and crossfades appear in the selected regions (**Figure 13.57**).

✔ Tip

- To smooth region transitions for an entire audio track, select Create New Fades and Create New Fade-Ins and -Outs from the Operation area of the Batch Fades dialog box. This creates a fade-in at the start of the first selected region, crossfades between subsequent regions, and a fade-out at the end of the last region.

Repairing Waveforms with the Pencil Tool

Pro Tools lets you make destructive edits to waveform data using the Edit window's Pencil tool. This is useful for repairing pops, clicks, or other sharp volume spikes in a waveform. The Pencil's waveform repair feature only functions when the waveform is zoomed-in to the sample level.

To edit an audio waveform with the Pencil tool:

1. Use the Zoomer or Horizontal Zoom buttons to zoom in to the sample level where the waveform appears as a thin line (**Figure 13.58**).

2. Using the Pencil tool, drag over the area of the waveform you want to reshape (**Figure 13.59**).

✔ Tips

- Limit your edits to small problem areas, and be careful not to overedit. Too much reshaping can alter the sound or add noise.

- Repairing waveforms with the Pencil tool is destructive: It permanently alters the underlying audio file. Always back up an audio region before repairing it. To do this, select the region you want to repair, and then choose AudioSuite > Duplicate. In the Duplicate plug-in window, select Playlist and Use In Playlist (**Figure 13.60**), and click the Process button. The Audio-Suite plug-in creates a duplicate audio file. The duplicate replaces the region on the track and the suffix .DUPL is added to the region name.

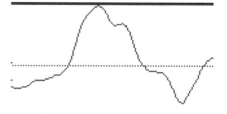

Figure 13.58 The Waveform view zoomed in to the sample level.

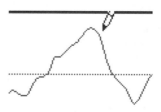

Figure 13.59 To repair a waveform, drag the Pencil tool over the area of the waveform you want to reshape.

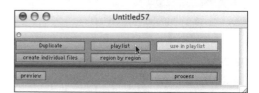

Figure 13.60 The Duplicate AudioSuite plug-in lets you quickly back up a region's underlying audio file.

- When working with the Pencil tool, use Zoom Preset buttons or memory locations to quickly recall a sample-level zoom setting. For information on zoom presets and memory locations, see *Chapter 10: Editing Basics*.

Figure 13.61 The Strip Silence window.

Stripping Silence from Regions

The Strip Silence command removes portions of audio regions that fall below a user-defined volume threshold. This process divides audio regions into separate regions.

Stripping silence is useful for quickly breaking larger audio regions into smaller, more manageable regions. For example, stripping silence from a sound effect makes it easier to locate it to a specific point. It's also useful for condensing regions in preparation for compacting audio. For information on compacting audio, see *Chapter 8: File Management Basics.*

About the Strip Silence window

The four sliders in the Strip Silence window (**Figure 13.61**) let you determine how Pro Tools defines silence in audio regions.

Strip Threshold: This slider determines the volume threshold below which audio is considered silence (-48 dB to 0).

Minimum Strip Duration: This slider sets a minimum time period (0 to 1,000 ms) below which audio is considered silence.

Region Start Pad: This slider sets a time value that is added to the start of new regions. Use this to preserve audio that falls below the volume threshold.

Region End Pad: This slider sets a time value that is added to the end of new regions.

The Strip Silence window includes a Rename button, which, when clicked, opens the Rename Selected Regions dialog box (**Figure 13.62**). Here, you can set the following parameters for automatically naming regions created with the Strip Silence command:

Name: The Name field lets you enter a base name for all regions created with Strip Silence.

Starting Number: The Starting Number field lets you enter a start number for sequential auto numbering.

Number of Places: The Number of Places field lets you enter the number of numeric places (zeros) that will precede the auto-numbers.

Suffix: The Suffix field lets you append text to the end of the name (after the auto-numbering).

To strip silence from an audio selection:

1. Select one or more regions (Shift-click to select multiple tracks).

2. Choose Edit > Strip Silence (**Figure 13.63**).

3. Click the Rename button to establish a naming scheme for regions created with Strip Silence.

4. Adjust the Strip Threshold and Minimum Strip Duration sliders until rectangles appear, which indicate areas of audio above the threshold (**Figure 13.64**).

5. Adjust the Region Start Pad and Region End Pad sliders to fine-tune the Strip Silence region selections.

6. Click the Strip button.

   The selection is removed from the track (**Figure 13.65**). New regions are created and appear in the Audio Regions list.

✔ Tip

- Use the Undo command or Heal Separation command to restore stripped silence.

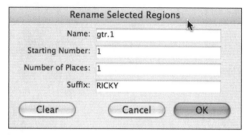

Figure 13.62 The Rename Selected Regions dialog box.

Figure 13.63 To show the Strip Silence window, choose Edit > Strip Silence.

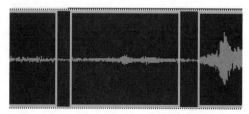

Figure 13.64 Adjust the sliders for Strip Threshold and Minimum Strip Duration until the strip rectangles appear in the selection.

Figure 13.65 Strip Silence removes the selected audio from the track and creates new regions in the Audio Regions list.

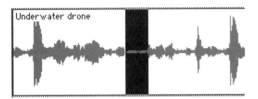

Figure 13.66 Select the segment of the region in which you want to insert silence.

Figure 13.67 To insert silence, choose Edit > Insert Silence.

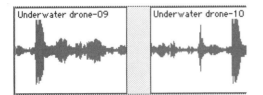

Figure 13.68 In Slip mode, inserting silence clears all audio data and automation data from the selected range.

Inserting Silence

The Insert Silence command lets you add silence to an audio region selection. The command is affected by the current Edit mode as follows:

Slip mode: In Slip mode, if a selected track is displaying audio data, the selected range is cleared of the audio data, as well as all underlying automation data on all selected tracks.

If a selected track is displaying automation data (such as volume, mute, or pan), then silence is inserted into the automation type visible on each track. Press Control (Macintosh) or Start (Windows) while choosing the Insert Silence command to insert silence on all automation playlists for all selected tracks.

Shuffle mode: If a selected track is displaying audio data in Shuffle mode, silence is inserted into the selected range and existing audio regions are shuffled. If a selected track is displaying automation data, only the visible automation type is cleared, and a blank gap appears. Regions are not shuffled.

Grid mode: In Grid mode, inserting silence clears all audio and automation data within a selected range.

To insert silence into a track:

1. Select the portion of a region in which you want to insert silence (**Figure 13.66**).

2. Choose Edit > Insert Silence (**Figure 13.67**).

   Silence is inserted into the selected audio range. In Slip mode, all audio data and automation data is cleared from the selected range (**Figure 13.68**). In Shuffle mode, silence is inserted in the selected range, and existing audio regions are shuffled.

Part V:
Mixing Audio

MIXING BASICS

Mixing is a process of slowly building and shaping multiple tracks of audio into a balanced and coherent presentation. There are no absolute rules in mixing—following your own ears and tastes is essential. There are, however, a few important basics that you need to know if you want to turn a rough mix into an exciting sound production.

This chapter starts with an in-depth look at creating stereo mixes. We'll describe how stereo imaging is used to simulate a three-dimensional acoustic space and explain how panning, equalization, and spatial effects can create the perception of width, height, and depth in a stereo mix.

We'll also discuss how audio signal flows through individual channel strips, as well as how to assign track inputs and outputs. Next, we'll cover inserts: how they operate, how signal flows through them, and the basics of mono and stereo DSP effects plug-ins. Then we'll show you how to assign sends and how to use send and track Output windows.

Last up, we'll cover the useful trick of creating submixes, which can help conserve track space and system resources.

Creating Stereo Mixes

A stereo mix refers to mixing multiple tracks of audio down to two channels (a left channel and a right channel). Stereo mixes are designed for listening over two speakers (a left speaker and a right speaker).

When we create a stereo mix, we're actually constructing a simulation or "image" of a three-dimensional acoustic space. To construct this *stereo image*, we use various techniques to trick our binaural (two-ear) auditory system into perceiving sound in the three dimensions of width, depth, and height. These techniques include left/right panning, *spatial effects* (reverb, delay, chorus, and flange), and EQ shaping (**Figure 14.1**).

The process of creating a stereo image begins during recording: The size, shape, and reflectivity of the recording space all contribute to the character of the sound. Various miking techniques, such as close miking, distant miking, ambient miking, and stereo miking, let you capture the three-dimensional character of the recording space. For more information on miking techniques, see the *Microphone Placement Techniques* sidebar in *Chapter 6: Getting Ready to Record.*

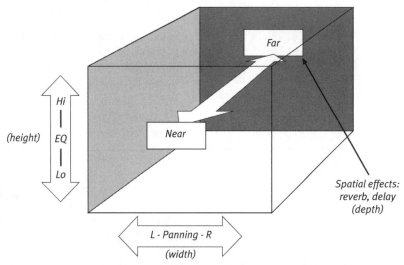

Figure 14.1 A stereo image is a simulation of a three-dimensional acoustic space: Left/right panning simulates width, EQ shaping simulates height, and spatial effects simulate depth.

Creating width

When we create a stereo mix, we use left/right panning to spread tracks out across the stereo image. This *separation* lets us hear tracks with more clarity and introduces the perception of width in the stereo image (**Figure 14.2**). Panning tracks tastefully is key to making mixes sound balanced and spacious.

Left/right panning gives sound a location within the stereo image as a result of the *precedence effect*. The precedence effect describes how we locate sounds in a three-dimensional space: Whichever of your ears first hears a sound perceives it as significantly louder than your other ear does. Our binaural (two-ears) auditory system uses this difference in perceived loudness to automatically triangulate the location of the sound source.

Panning a track to the left or right changes the proportional level of the track in each speaker. Due to the precedence effect, we can create the illusion that a sound is coming from any point between the left and right speakers. When the level of a track is equal in both speakers, we perceive it as coming from straight ahead.

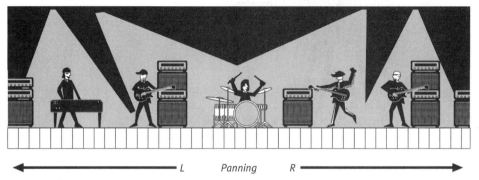

Figure 14.2 Left/right panning lets you simulate the acoustic spread of a band on stage. The perception of width is created by panning elements from left to right.

CREATING STEREO MIXES

Creating depth

When a sound occurs within an acoustic space, we hear both *direct sound* and *reflected sound*. Direct sound emanates from the sound source and travels unimpeded to the listener. Reflected sound bounces off surfaces such as floors, ceilings, and walls; thus, it takes longer to reach the listener (**Figure 14.3**). The time delay between direct sound and reflected sound, combined with their relative volumes, lets us perceive depth (front to back) within an acoustic space.

In stereo mixing, we use spatial effects to simulate the characteristics of acoustic spaces. Most reverbs provide pre-set room shapes with adjustable parameters (including room size, reverb decay time, and number of reflections), so you can define the character of the acoustic space.

We then mix the direct sound (*uneffected signal*) with the reflected sound (*effected signal*) to place the sound at the desired depth within the stereo image. For example, a sound placed in a large hall with many reflections (high *diffusion*), slow reverb decay, and no direct sound mixed in will sound distant. The same sound placed in a small room with few reflections, quick reverb decay, and lots of direct sound mixed in will sound "in your face."

For more information on spatial effects, see *Chapter 15: Adding Effects to a Mix.*

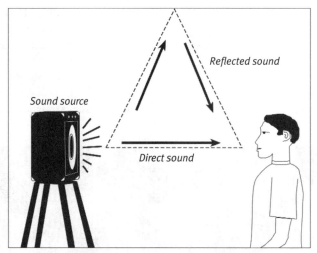

Figure 14.3 The direct sound and reflected sound from an audio source reach the ear at different times. This time delay creates the perception of depth.

Creating height

Humans hear sounds in a frequency spectrum between 20 Hz and 20 kHz. In audio production, this spectrum is generally broken down into four frequency bands: low (20 Hz–200 Hz), low-middle (200 Hz–1 kHz), high-middle (1 kHz–5 kHz), and high (5 kHz–20 kHz). Every instrument occupies a different range in this spectrum (**Figure 14.4**). Low-pitched instruments such as bass and tuba tend toward the lower end of the spectrum, whereas higher-pitched instruments such as flute and piccolo tend toward the higher end.

When we talk about creating height in a stereo mix, we're referring to using equalization, or *EQ*, to open up spaces within these frequency ranges to enhance the clarity and separation of sounds within the stereo image.

Most instruments have fundamental frequencies within the low-mid range. Making small decreases (or *cuts*) or increases (or *boosts*) in this frequency range can dramatically alter the character of an instrument's sound. Higher-pitched instruments have more frequencies in the high-mids. Boosting these frequencies can help enhance clarity, brightness, and definition.

Keep in mind that most instruments also generate harmonics up into the highs. Boosting these high harmonics can add sparkle and brilliance to a track.

For more information on EQ, see *Chapter 15: Adding Effects to a Mix.*

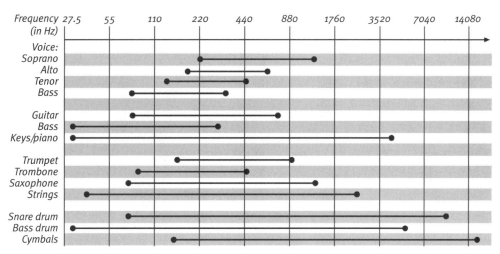

Figure 14.4 Frequency ranges of common instruments.

CREATING STEREO MIXES

About mono compatibility

Many people still listen to music over car radios that have only one speaker. So, before you call the mix a wrap, listen to it for mono compatibility. If you notice a decrease in clarity, or if lower frequencies seem unstable, you may have some *phase cancellation* in the stereo mix. Phase cancellation occurs when sound waves overlap in such a way that they cancel each other out. This can cause frequencies to lose clarity or drop out entirely.

If you hear phase cancellation, try reversing the phase on any stereo-pair microphones. It's not uncommon for improperly placed stereo microphones to introduce phasing problems. Several Pro Tools plug-ins provide phase invert buttons, including the DigiRack EQ and delay plug-ins (**Figure 14.5**). Also, double-check any stereo effects in the mix— some stereo effects processors can introduce out-of-phase signals.

Phase Invert button

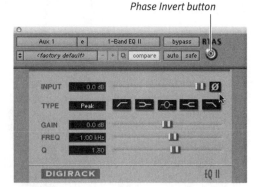

Figure 14.5 The Phase Invert button on the DigiRack EQ plug-in.

The Mixing Process

Most producers and engineers follow the general mixing process outlined below. Remember, there's no absolute order to these steps. Mixing is a fluid process: Through repeated listening and tweaking, you'll gradually approach an ideal blend of audio elements.

Finish recording: Before you start mixing, make sure you have all your ideas recorded. Then give yourself some time—however much you need—to gain some perspective on the tracks before you begin mixing. You might realize that you forgot to record a bass part, or that the track really needs a background vocal to bring it all together. You can always record a take during mixing should the inspiration hit you, but don't start mixing with tired ears—you won't be able to hear accurately and your mixes may suffer.

Choose tracks: Choose the best takes for your final mix. Arrange them in the Mix window in as ergonomic a fashion as possible.

Clean up tracks: Remove any unwanted regions from the tracks. Then listen to each track individually and erase any distracting noises such as glitches, bad punches, chair creaks, and voices. Perform any additional editing tasks you desire.

Prepare tracks: Assign track outputs to the main mix. Create master faders and auxiliary inputs as needed. Create submixes and mix groups. Set all track faders as close to unity level (0 dB) as possible.

Create a rough balance: Set initial track volumes and pan placements.

Apply effects: Add internal DSP plug-in effects or external hardware effects. Begin with sparing amounts of EQ, subtracting frequencies, when possible, to clear space for sounds. Then add *dynamic effects* (such as compressors, limiters, gates, or expanders) to smooth out spiking volumes or minimize background noise. Finally, add spatial effects to add depth to the mix. For additional information see *Chapter 15: Adding Effects to a Mix.*

Check gain staging: Check levels on each gain stage in your system. Optimize levels on all inserts, sends, inputs, and outputs. Avoid clipping audio signals. For more information on gain staging, see *Chapter 4: Starting a New Session.*

Set the final balance: Adjust the final volume levels and pan settings. Practice any mix moves on faders, mutes, solos, and plug-in controls that you want to automate.

Record automation: Record mix moves on faders, sends, mutes, solos, and plug-in controls. If necessary, do multiple passes—Pro Tools saves the automation and you can add to it later.

Bounce the mixes to hard disk: Bounce the mix to disk using Pro Tools' Bounce feature. Convert audio file type, sample rate, or bit depth, if necessary.

Check the mix: Copy the mix to CD or DAT tape. Listen to it on a variety of systems, including a shelf-size system, a car stereo, and a home stereo—the more, the better. Make sure the mix retains the same overall balance of audio elements across all systems. Repeat as many of the preceding steps as many times as needed.

Monitoring a Mix

Many factors influence the way we hear a mix, including the type of speakers, the acoustics of the room, and the playback volume. Although a mix may sound great on your studio monitors, the same mix can sound dramatically different on another system.

Knowing the performance specifications of your speakers, as well as the acoustics of the mixing space, can help you avoid introducing compensation errors into the mix. For example, knowing that the room tends to exaggerate bass will keep you from removing too much bass from the mix.

To make sure your mixes sound good on as many systems as possible, do the following:

Use alternate speakers: Listen to the mix on different size speakers: small, medium, and large. Make sure you can hear all the elements of the mix clearly over each type of speaker.

Use reference CDs: Play some CDs that you know well over the monitor system as a sonic reference point. This gives you something to compare your mixes to, and can help you identify the acoustic tendencies of your monitors and mixing room.

Use consistent levels: Monitor your mixes at consistent levels—ideally, between 70 and 90 decibels. Monitoring at overly loud levels will quickly fatigue your ears (especially in the mid-range). This can lead to mid-range heavy mixes that lack spaciousness and clarity.

Listen on alternate systems: Burn a CD of the mix and listen to it on as many systems as possible—from boomboxes to home stereos to the best audiophile components you can find. Also, try listening to the mix in both large and small spaces, and play it on a car stereo while driving to see if the low-end is audible over the engine hum. Listening on a range of systems will give you excellent perspective on the mix and alert you to any consistent problems that need fixing.

Understanding Audio Signal Flow

Audio signal flow refers to the path that audio takes through the Pro Tools mixer. Generally, this path is fixed, moving from top to bottom through audio track, auxiliary input, and master fader channel strips.

Don't confuse audio signal flow with I/O Setup—they're related but not identical. Audio signal flow refers to the path audio takes within channel strips, whereas I/O Setup determines the specific channel assignments for inputs, outputs, inserts, and busses. For more information on I/O Setup, see *Chapter 2: Software Basics,* and *Chapter 4: Starting a New Session.*

About audio tracks and auxiliary inputs

Audio tracks and auxiliary inputs have the same top-to-bottom audio signal flow: Audio travels first to any inserts, then to sends and faders, and lastly to the outputs. The main difference between audio tracks and auxiliary inputs is the audio input source: Audio tracks receive input from external audio sources or from audio files playing back on disk (**Figure 14.6**). Auxiliary inputs receive audio signal from internal busses or external hardware sources (**Figure 14.7**).

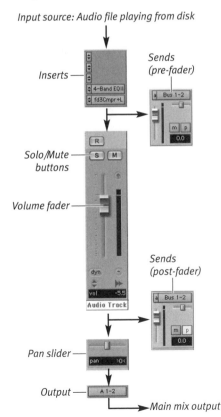

Figure 14.6 Audio signal flow through an audio track channel strip.

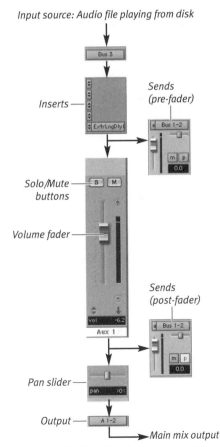

Figure 14.7 Audio signal flow through an auxiliary input channel strip.

Audio tracks and auxiliary inputs are designed for different mixing tasks. Audio tracks let you control the playback parameters (such as mute, solo, pan, volume level, and automation) of individual audio files as they play back from disk.

Auxiliary inputs are designed for creating *submixes*. A submix is created when you bus an audio signal from multiple audio tracks to a single auxiliary input. For instance, you can create a stereo submix of drums and bass by busing their tracks to an auxiliary input. This lets you control the entire rhythm section using one fader. Or, you can use an auxiliary input to create a *send-and-return* submix, also called an *effects loop*, which lets you add an effect to multiple tracks of audio simultaneously. For more information on submixes, see *Creating Submixes* later in this chapter. For more information on effects loops, see *Chapter 15: Adding Effects to a Mix.*

For additional information on audio tracks and auxiliary inputs, see *Chapter 3: The Mix and Edit Windows.*

About master faders

Master faders control the main volume levels of outputs and bus paths. You can use master faders for many purposes, such as to control the main mix output, submix levels, send levels, or bus levels, or to apply effects to a main mix.

Master fader inserts are always *post-fader* (unlike the inserts for audio tracks and auxiliary inputs, which are always *pre-fader*). This means the Main Mix fader always comes before the Inserts section (**Figure 14.8**). Thus, you can insert an effect (such as dither or an aural exciter) on the final main mix output. But use effects on the main outputs cautiously. Adding compression to a main mix is not a good idea—this is better left until mastering. Compressing the main

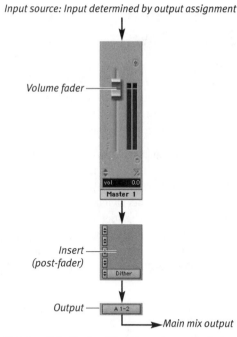

Input source: Input determined by output assignment

Volume fader

Insert (post-fader)

Output

Main mix output

Figure 14.8 Audio signal flow through a master fader.

Figure 14.9 To create a new master fader, select File > New Track. Select Master Fader from the pop-up menu.

Figure 14.10 Set the outputs of each track in the mix to the main mix outputs (typically 1–2).

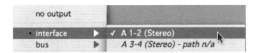

Figure 14.11 Set the output of the master fader to the main mix output (typically 1–2).

outputs can reduce the openness of a mix and limit a mastering engineer's options for enhancing the final output. For more information on compression and other effects, see *Chapter 15: Adding Effects to a Mix*.

For more information on master faders, see *Chapter 3: The Mix and Edit Windows*.

To use a master fader as a master volume control for the main mix:

1. Select Track > New.
   The New Track dialog box appears.

2. Select Mono or Stereo from the pop-up menu.

3. Select Master Fader from the pop-up menu (**Figure 14.9**).

4. Enter the number of master faders and click Create.

5. Set the outputs of all audio tracks in the session to the main mix outputs (typically 1–2) (**Figure 14.10**).

6. Set the panning position of each track.

7. Set the output of the master fader to the main mix output (**Figure 14.11**).

✔ Tip

- You can make audio tracks, auxiliary inputs, and master faders inactive. Making these tracks inactive can help you conserve your system's overall mixer and DSP resources. For more information on making tracks inactive, see *Chapter 5: Working with Tracks*. Or, see the *Pro Tools Reference Guide*.

UNDERSTANDING AUDIO SIGNAL FLOW

351

Assigning Inputs and Outputs

Audio tracks and auxiliary inputs have *Input selectors* and *Output selectors* that let you route audio to and from their respective channel strips.

Input selectors let you assign audio input from external sources (via the Pro Tools interface) or from internal busses. Output selectors let you route audio output to external destinations (via the Pro Tools interface) or to internal busses.

Master faders, on the other hand, have only Output selectors, which let you route audio output to the main mix or to internal busses.

For more information on assigning inputs and outputs, see *Chapter 5: Working with Tracks*.

To assign inputs to audio tracks or auxiliary inputs:

◆ In the Mix or Edit window, click the track Input selector and choose from the available audio interface channels and busses (**Figure 14.12**).

Select No Input to remove all the input assignments on that track.

To assign outputs to an audio track or auxiliary input:

◆ In the Mix or Edit window, click the track Output selector and choose from the available audio interface channels and busses (**Figure 14.13**).

Select No Output to remove all the output assignments on that track.

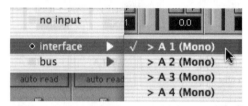

Figure 14.12 Click the track Input selector and choose from the available audio interface channels and busses.

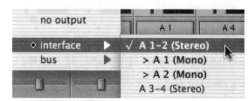

Figure 14.13 Click the track Output selector and choose from the available audio interface channels and busses.

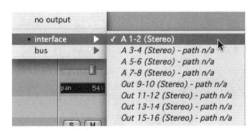

Figure 14.14 Click the master fader Output selector and choose from the available audio interface channels and busses.

To assign outputs to a master fader:

◆ In the Mix or Edit window, click the master fader Output selector and choose from the available audio interface channels and busses (**Figure 14.14**).

✔ Tip

■ You can make output paths inactive. Making a track output inactive silences output while maintaining all automation and playlist data. Pre-fader sends continue to feed audio signal to their assigned destination. This can help you conserve your system's overall mixer resources while maintaining your track configuration and effects output.

■ To make an output inactive/active: Command-Control-click (Macintosh) or Control-Start-click (Windows) on the desired output. Or, uncheck/check the inactive/active box for the desired output in the I/O Setup window.

■ For more information on making outputs inactive, see the *Pro Tools Reference Guide*. For information on making tracks inactive, see *Chapter 5: Working with Tracks* or the *Pro Tools Reference Guide*.

ASSIGNING INPUTS AND OUTPUTS

About Inserts

Pro Tools provides five insert slots on each audio track, auxiliary input, and master fader channel strip. Inserts can be either *hardware inserts* or *software plug-in inserts*.

In terms of audio signal flow, audio travels through the inserts section of a channel strip sequentially from top to bottom (**Figure 14.15**). Therefore, a plug-in inserted in a higher position will deliver an effected audio signal to a plug-in inserted in a lower position. For example, if you insert a reverb below a delay, the audio signal entering the reverb will already have delay on it. You can change the order of inserts by dragging them up or down (**Figure 14.16**).

Figure 14.15 Audio flows through the Inserts section of a channel strip sequentially from top to bottom.

Figure 14.16 You can change the order of inserts by dragging them up or down.

When you insert a stereo plug-in on a mono channel strip, all subsequent mono plug-ins convert to their stereo equivalents, and the mono channel strip becomes a stereo channel strip (**Figure 14.17**). This lets Pro Tools quickly accommodate stereo effects during a mix. For more information on using inserts, see *Chapter 3: The Mix and Edit Windows* or *Chapter 15: Adding Effects to a Mix.*

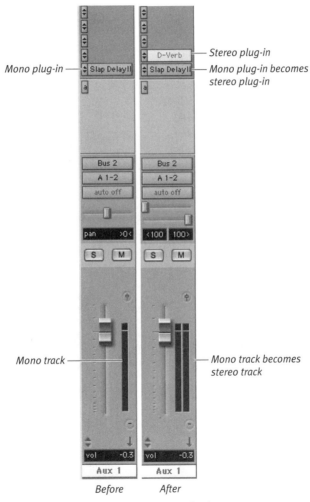

Mono plug-in — Slap Delay II

Stereo plug-in — D-Verb
Mono plug-in becomes stereo plug-in — Slap Delay II

Mono track

Mono track becomes stereo track

Before　　　*After*

Figure 14.17 When you insert a stereo plug-in on a mono track, all subsequent mono plug-ins convert to their stereo equivalents, and the mono track becomes a stereo track.

ABOUT INSERTS

Assigning Sends

Pro Tools 7 provides up to ten mono or stereo sends on each audio track and auxiliary input (**Figure 14.18**). Sends let you route audio to internal busses or external outputs. You can send audio via internal busses to auxiliary inputs to create submixes or to add plug-in effects, or you can send audio via external outputs to a headphone mix, or to external hardware effects. Sends always receive audio after it passes through the Inserts section of a channel strip.

You can set a send to either Pre- or Post-Fader mode (**Figure 14.19**). When a send is in Pre-Fader mode, audio signal first passes through the send, and then goes to the fader. In Post-Fader mode, the signal first passes through the fader, and then travels to the send. Post-fader sends are frequently used for effects processing; pre-fader sends are used for headphone and monitor mixes.

You can control send parameters (including level, pan, mute, and pre- and post-fader) through a send Output window or by using individual send controls that appear within the Sends view. For more information on sends, see *Chapter 3: The Mix and Edit Windows.* or *Chapter 15: Adding Effects to a Mix.*

To assign a send to a track:

1. Click a Send button and choose an output or bus path (**Figure 14.20**).

2. Set the output level of the send in the individual send control or in a send Output window.

To open a send Output window:

◆ Click a Send button.

A send Output window appears (**Figure 14.21**).

Figure 14.18 Pro Tools 7 provides up to ten mono or stereo sends on each audio track and auxiliary input.

— *Pre/Post-Fader button*

Figure 14.19 Post-fader sends are frequently used for effects processing; pre-fader sends are used for headphone and monitor mixes.

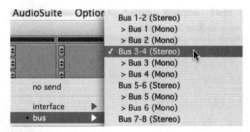

Figure 14.20 To assign a send to a track, click a Send button and choose an output or bus path.

Figure 14.21 A stereo send Output window.

Figure 14.22 To open individual send controls, select View > Sends A–E or Sends F–J. Select any individual send (Send A through Send J).

Figure 14.23 An individual send control.

Figure 14.24 To display send level meters for individual send controls, select Setups > Preferences, click the Display tab, and then select Show Meters in Sends View.

 — Bus path

Figure 14.25 Naming bus paths in the I/O Setup can help you keep track of bus assignments.

To open individual send controls:

1. Select View > Mix Window > Sends A–E and/or Sends F–J.

   The selected Sends view appears in the channel strip.

2. Select View > Sends A–E or Sends F–J and choose the desired send (**Figure 14.22**).

   Send controls appear for the chosen send (**Figure 14.23**).

To display send level meters for individual send controls:

1. Choose Setup > Preferences.

2. Click the Display tab.

3. Select Show Meters in Sends View (**Figure 14.24**).

4. Click OK.

✔ Tips

- If you're using a slow computer, try hiding send level meters to improve screen redraw times. Also, making a send inactive releases its processing resources and helps improve system performance.

- To quickly set the send output level to zero, Option-click (Macintosh) or Alt-click (Windows) the Send fader.

- To set the default level for new sends to 0 dB (unity gain), choose Setup > Preferences > Operations. Deselect Sends Default to "-INF."

- Naming bus paths in the I/O Setup can help you keep track of send assignments (**Figure 14.25**). For more information on I/O Setup, see *Chapter 4: Starting a New Session.*

Using Output Windows

Pro Tools provides dedicated Output windows for tracks and sends. Output windows look just like channel strips, but are larger and can hover independently over the Mix and Edit windows. This lets you easily access the output controls of the track or send during editing or mixing.

Track Output windows provide Track Volume faders, Pan sliders, Mute and Solo buttons, and automation controls (**Figure 14.26**). Send Output windows provide Send Volume faders, Pan sliders, Mute and Solo buttons, and automation controls (**Figure 14.27**).

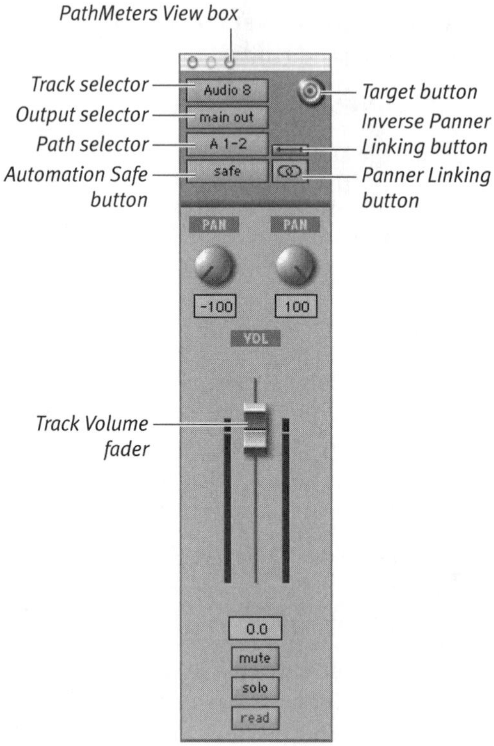

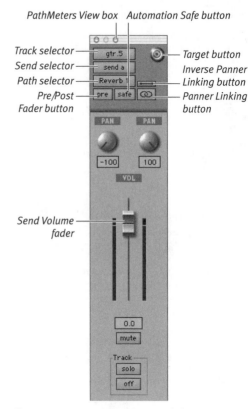

Figure 14.26 A stereo audio track Output window.

Figure 14.27 A stereo send Output window.

Meters View box

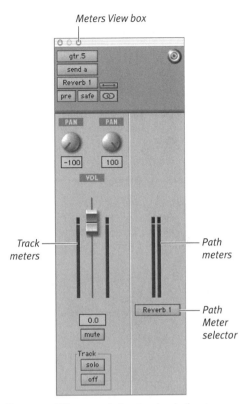

Track meters

Path meters

Path Meter selector

Figure 14.28 The expanded meter view in the stereo send Output window lets you view path level meters.

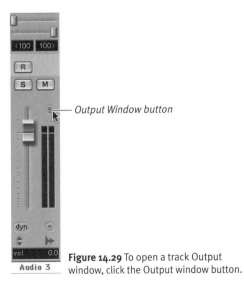

Output Window button

Audio 3

Figure 14.29 To open a track Output window, click the Output window button.

All Output windows have these additional controls:

Track selector: The Track selector lets you choose any audio track, auxiliary input, or master fader in the session.

Output selector: The Output selector lets you access any existing outputs.

Send selector: The Send selector lets you access any existing sends on the track.

Path selector: The Path selector lets you assign the Output path for the current track or send.

Panner Linking button: The Panner Linking button lets you link and unlink the left and right pan knobs of stereo Output windows.

Target button: The Target button lets you keep the current Output window open when you open a new Output window. Clicking the target changes it from red to gray and anchors it to its current location and output assignment.

Automation Safe button: The Automation Safe button places the track in Safe mode and prevents existing automation from being overwritten.

Meter View box: The Meter View box opens an expanded Output window that includes path level meters (**Figure 14.28**).

To open a track Output window:

◆ Click the Output Window button of an audio track, auxiliary input, or master fader channel strip (**Figure 14.29**).

The track Output window appears.

To open a sends Output window:

◆ When the Sends view is showing assignments, click on the send (**Figure 14.30**).
   or

◆ When the individual send controls are showing, click the send Output selector button.

   A sends Output window appears.

Figure 14.30 To open a send Output window, click the send itself.

Linking stereo pans

Stereo Output windows provide a Panner Linking button that lets you move left and right pan knobs simultaneously. When linked, left and right pan knobs move in the same direction in unison.

Pro Tools also provides Inverse Panner Linking, which lets you move the pans in mirror opposite directions.

Figure 14.31 The Panner Linking button. Click this button to move stereo pans in unison.

Inverse Panner Linking button

Figure 14.32 The Inverse Panner Linking button. Click this button to move stereo pans in mirror opposite directions.

Figure 14.33 The Target button.

To enable Panner Linking:

◆ Click the Panner Linking button (**Figure 14.31**).

   The Panner Linking button becomes highlighted. The stereo pans now move together in unison.

To enable Inverse Panner Linking:

1. Click the Panner Linking button.

2. Click the Inverse Panner Linking button (**Figure 14.32**).

   The Inverse Panner Linking button becomes highlighted. The stereo pans now move in mirror opposite directions.

✔ Tips

■ To open multiple track or sends Output windows, Shift-click any Output button or send assignment.

■ To keep an Output window open, click the red Target button (**Figure 14.33**). The Output window remains open when other output windows are opened.

Creating Submixes

When you create a *submix*, multiple tracks of audio are merged into a single track. Submixing is useful if you're running low on tracks and you want to free up additional track space. Submixes also let you control groups of instruments from a single set of track controls. For instance, creating a stereo submix of multiple drum tracks lets you control the entire drum section from a single stereo fader.

When you create a submix, audio is routed from either sends or track outputs to available busses. The audio is then received by audio tracks or auxiliary inputs whose track inputs are assigned to the same bus. To merge source tracks into a single destination track, you must record the combined signals to a new audio track.

When creating a *stereo* submix, make sure the sound quality, relative levels, and stereo panning are how you want them to be in the final mix. It's a good idea to save the original audio files in case you decide later that you don't like the submix—this way you can import the original files and start over.

You can also create submixes to add effects to multiple audio tracks simultaneously. This is called an effects loop. When you create an effects loop, you *send* the audio (on a bus) to an auxiliary input. The signal is then routed through any effects inserted on the auxiliary input. The auxiliary input then *returns* the effected signal to the main mix. For more information on creating effects loops, see *Chapter 15: Adding Effects to a Mix*. For more information on creating submixes, see the *Pro Tools Reference Guide*.

To create a submix of multiple audio tracks to a single audio track:

1. Choose Track > New.

2. Create a stereo audio track.

   A new stereo audio track appears. This is the destination audio track for the submix.

3. Assign a send or track output to a bus path for each source track you want in the submix (**Figure 14.34**).

4. Assign the destination track inputs to the same bus path assigned to the source tracks (**Figure 14.35**).

5. Assign the outputs of the destination audio track to the main mix (**Figure 14.36**).

6. Record-enable the destination audio track.

7. Using either the sends output controls (for sends) or track controls (for track outputs), adjust the relative volumes and stereo panning of the source tracks. (To accurately monitor the submix when using sends, make sure the source track's outputs are set to the main mix outputs.)

8. In the Transport window, click Record-Play to record the submix to the destination stereo audio track.

9. Listen to the submix.

   Make any necessary volume or panning adjustments to the source track's output controls. Repeat as many times as necessary.

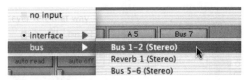

Figure 14.34 When creating a submix, assign send or track outputs to a bus path for each track you want in the submix.

Figure 14.35 Assign the inputs of the destination track to the same bus path assigned to the source tracks.

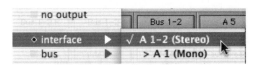

Figure 14.36 Assign the outputs of the destination audio track to the main mix.

✔ Tips

■ If you've used up all available tracks in a session, you can still free up tracks by bouncing a submix to disk. Bouncing to disk does not require any additional tracks. You can bounce as many or as few tracks as you want, including the entire final mix (with effects and automation). For more information on bouncing to disk, see *Chapter 17: Mixdown and Mastering*.

■ An advantage of using sends instead of track outputs to bus audio is that each send has separate output controls. This lets you adjust volume, pan, and mute for each track without changing the track control settings on the actual audio track.

■ If you have open tracks (and don't need to merge tracks into a submix for effects processing or any other reason), consider creating mix groups. Mix groups let you control the parameters (such as volume, solos, mutes, send levels, and automation) for all grouped tracks from a single set of track controls. For more information on mix groups, see *Chapter 5: Working with Tracks*.

ADDING
EFFECTS TO A MIX

Adding effects can help you transform a flat and lifeless rough mix into a spacious and exciting sound production. Effects let you shape a mix in many ways: You can balance track levels with compression or open up frequency ranges with equalization (EQ). You can even place tracks inside spacious sonic landscapes with reverb and delay.

Pro Tools lets you use both internal software effects, called *DSP plug-ins*, and external hardware effects. Third-party vendors offer numerous RTAS plug-ins, many of which use the same algorithms as their hardware ancestors. And if you have a roomful of vintage gear that you're aching to use, it's a snap to patch in external hardware.

Think of this chapter as a primer on effects. We'll cover plug-in and external hardware effects, and we'll introduce you to three useful types of effects: EQ, dynamic effects, and spatial effects. With a little practice you'll be sending your mixes into new dimensions... literally.

What Is a DSP Plug-in?

A DSP (digital signal processing) plug-in is software that lets you add effects such as reverb, compression, and EQ to audio signals within the Pro Tools environment.

Real-time and non-real-time DSP plug-ins

Real-time DSP plug-ins process audio signals non-destructively while a session is playing (the original audio file is unchanged). Real-time plug-ins can receive existing audio signals playing back from disk, or live audio signals as they are being recorded to disk.

You can monitor the output and adjust the parameters of a real-time plug-in at any point during the production process until you are satisfied with the effect. The effect is not recorded into the session until you mix it down to an external 2-track recording machine or bounce it to hard disk in Pro Tools.

Non-real-time effects operate independently of session playback. These effects alter the original audio file and replace it with a new audio file containing the effect.

Maintaining Perspective on the Mix

The ability to monitor and adjust a real-time effect gives you a high degree of creative control over the sound and placement of an effect within a mix.

But, a note of caution: Be careful not to spend too much time "perfecting" your effects. Many great mixes have been tweaked to death by endless fine-tuning of effects parameters. And many great songs have become comic due to the overapplication of a "cool" effect.

This doesn't mean you should ignore adjusting your effects —just maintain perspective on the mix context. The effect must work with other sonic elements.

Ask yourself honestly: Is this effect making it sound better? Or, does it obscure, cloud, phase out, or busy the mix? Don't be afraid to "move on" to your next mixing task. Chances are you won't come back to the item you are obsessing on.

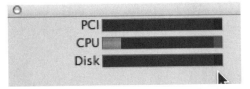

Figure 15.1 The DigiRack RTAS 1-Band EQ III plug-in.

Figure 15.2 The System Usage window can help you manage CPU resources.

Adding by Subtracting

Use effects to take away sounds that diminish the clarity of your mix. Open up the stereo image when possible to create an expansive and listenable sound space. For example, use EQ to subtract frequencies that cause blatant ear fatigue. Use dynamic effects (such as compression, gates, limiters) to reign in transient peaks and frequencies to tighten and add punch. Always consider what you can remove to make the mix sound better.

Pro Tools 7 systems support the following real-time and non-real-time DSP plug-ins:

RTAS (Real-Time AudioSuite): (Pro Tools LE and HD systems) RTAS plug-ins use your computer's CPU to process audio non-destructively in real time (**Figure 15.1**). Pro Tools LE ships with Digidesign's DigiRack RTAS plug-ins.

Using large numbers of RTAS plug-ins can tax CPU resources and hamper the performance of other Pro Tools features such as track count, edit density, graphics, and automation. Keeping an eye on the System Usage window (**Figure 15.2**) can help you manage CPU resources and get the most out of RTAS plug-ins.

TDM (Time-Division multiplexing): (Pro Tools HD systems only) Unlike RTAS plug-ins that rely entirely on a host computer's processor, TDM plug-ins use dedicated DSP processing chips provided with higher-end Pro Tools HD. For more information on TDM plug-ins, see the *Pro Tools Reference Guide* or the *DigiRack Plug-ins Guide*.

AudioSuite: (Pro Tools LE and HD systems) Pro Tools ships with a diverse set of non-real-time AudioSuite plug-ins. You can configure AudioSuite plug-ins to either destructively alter the original audio file on disk or to create an entirely separate new audio file containing the effect.

WHAT IS A DSP PLUG-IN?

About Plug-ins as Inserts

Pro Tools lets you use up to five real-time DSP plug-ins as inserts on each track. You can use these inserts in two ways:

Line Inserts (single tracks): You can use plug-ins as *line inserts* on individual audio tracks, auxiliary inputs, and master faders (**Figure 15.3**). A line insert applies its effect only to the track on which it's inserted. For example, you can add compression to a lead vocal by simply inserting a compressor on the lead vocal track. Inserts on audio tracks and auxiliary inputs are always pre-fader. Inserts on master faders are always post-fader.

Line insert

Figure 15.3 A 1-Band EQ III plug-in used as a line insert. A line insert applies its effect only to the track on which it's inserted.

Explore Effects Fearlessly— Use Effects Cautiously

Try playing with effects and keep track of the results: try ultra-short, medium, and long delay effects; try massive hall reverbs and tiny cave spaces; try routing delays through reverbs; try putting compression on bass, drums, voice, and other effects; try using pre-fader sends. Turn knobs, press buttons, move faders, pans, and levers all the way up, down, right, left: Listen to what your effects can do.

If your experiments produce some never-before-heard textures, rhythms, and spaces, identify their unique character in the context of your creation. Then use them with utmost minimalism and subtlety: Overtly audible effects are usually too loud.

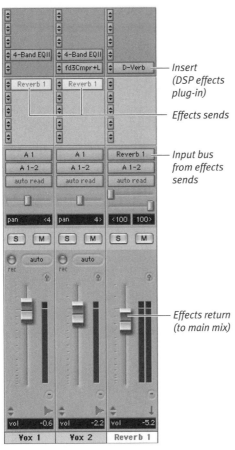

Insert
(DSP effects
plug-in)

Effects sends

Input bus
from effects
sends

Effects return
(to main mix)

Figure 15.4 An effects loop. The effects sends on each track bus audio to the auxiliary input. The auxiliary input's volume fader acts as the effects return. For an example of an effects loop, see Figure 15.32.

Effects Loop (multiple tracks): You can use a plug-in in a send-and-return submix, known as an *effects loop* (**Figure 15.4**). An effects loop lets you add an effect to multiple tracks simultaneously. To create an effects loop, you insert a plug-in on an auxiliary input, and then bus as many tracks as you want to the auxiliary input for simultaneous processing. The auxiliary input then *returns* the processed audio to the main mix outputs. Because effects loops process multiple tracks simultaneously, they can help you conserve CPU resources. For more information on effect loops, see *Creating Effects Loops* later in this chapter.

Understanding plug-in formats

Pro Tools lets you use the following plug-in formats:

Mono plug-ins: Mono plug-ins are designed for use on mono tracks. They have mono (one-channel) outputs.

Mono/stereo plug-ins: Mono/stereo plug-ins are designed for use on mono tracks; however, they have stereo (two-channel) outputs. When a mono/stereo plug-in is inserted on a track, all subsequent inserts (and the track itself) become stereo.

Multi-channel (stereo) plug-ins: Multi-channel plug-ins are designed for use on stereo or larger multi-channel tracks. In Pro Tools LE, all multi-channel plug-ins are stereo.

Multi-mono plug-ins: Multi-mono plug-ins are designed for use on stereo or larger multi-channel tracks when a multi-channel version of the plug-in is not available. Parameters for all channels are linked by default. You can, however, unlink parameters using the Master Link button. Unlinking parameters lets you control the parameters for each channel separately.

Inserting Plug-ins on Tracks

In order to use an RTAS plug-in in Pro Tools, you must first insert it on a track. You can do this in the Inserts view of either the Mix or Edit window. Both windows display all currently inserted plug-ins (**Figure 15.5**).

To insert a plug-in on a track:

1. Choose View > Mix Window > Inserts.

2. Click an Insert selector on the track and choose the desired plug-in (**Figure 15.6**). The plug-in window appears.

Inserting plug-ins during playback

You can insert plug-ins during playback, with the following restrictions:

◆ Plug-ins cannot be inserted or removed during recording.

◆ Plug-ins that change a track's format cannot be inserted or removed during playback. (For instance, when you insert a stereo plug-in on a mono track, the track automatically becomes a stereo track.)

◆ Plug-ins that contain automation cannot be removed during playback.

◆ Plug-in automation cannot be enabled during playback.

◆ Side-chain inputs cannot be created during playback.

Figure 15.5 The Inserts view displays all currently inserted plug-ins.

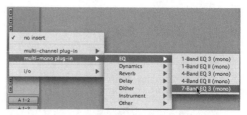

Figure 15.6 To choose a plug-in, click an Insert selector and choose from the plug-ins menu. Multi-channel plug-ins offer 2-track L/R (stereo) output. Multi-mono plug-ins are one track (mono).

Figure 15.7 You can move inserts by dragging them between slots in the Inserts view.

Figure 15.8 When a line insert is lit, the corresponding plug-in window is open.

Moving and duplicating inserts

You can move or duplicate already inserted plug-ins by dragging them to open insert slots on the same track or on another track. When you move or duplicate inserts, they retain their original settings and automation.

To move an insert:

◆ Drag the insert to the desired location (**Figure 15.7**).

The moved insert appears in the new location.

To duplicate an insert:

◆ Option-drag (Macintosh) or Alt-drag (Windows) the insert to the desired location.

A copy of the insert appears in the new location.

For more information on inserts, see *Chapter 14: Mixing Basics and Chapter 3: The Mix and Edit Windows.*

✔ Tip

■ A lit Insert button in the Inserts view indicates that the corresponding plug-in window is open (**Figure 15.8**).

Organizing the Plug-ins menu

The Plug-ins menu is displayed when you click on insert selectors and plug-in window selectors. You can organize the Plug-ins menu by selecting an option from the "Organize Plug-In Menus By" pop-up menu, in the Display tab of the Preferences menu, as follows:

◆ **Flat List:** Flat List organizes all plug-ins available in alphabetical order.

◆ **Category:** Category organizes the Plug-in menu according to effects type, including EQ, Dynamics, Delay, Reverb, Pitch Shift, Noise Reduction, Modulation, Dither, Hardware, Instrument, and Other. Plugs-ins can appear in more than one category.

◆ **Manufacturer:** Manufacturer organizes the Plug-in menu by the company that makes the plug-in, such as Digidesign, Propellerheads, Eventide, and so on.

◆ **Category and Manufacturer:** Category and Manufacturer organizes plugs-in on two levels. The top level orders them according to effect type, and the second level places them under manufacturer headings (**Figure 15.9**).

To organize the Plug-ins menu:

1. Choose Setup > Preferences.

2. Click the "Organize Plug-in Menus By" pop-up menu and select an option (**Figure 15.10**).

3. Click Done.

   The Plug-ins menu will organize plug-ins according to the selected option.

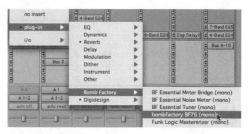

Figure 15.9 The Plug-ins menu organized by Category and Manufacturer.

Figure 15.10 To organize the Plug-ins menu, choose Setup > Preferences. Then select an option from the "Organize Plug-in Menus By" pop-up menu.

✔ Tip

■ The insert selector in the Mix and Edit window also functions as a "clip indicator" for certain plug-ins. When a plug-in's processed signal has clipped, the indicator turns red. To clear the clip indicator, click the LED in the plug-in header.

Using Plug-in Windows

When you click on an insert, a window for the assigned plug-in appears. This window lets you adjust the parameters of the corresponding DSP plug-in.

By default, Pro Tools displays one plug-in window at a time, but for convenience, you can display multiple plug-in windows. You can also open and adjust parameters on individual channels of multi-mono plug-ins.

Plug-in windows share the following parameters (**Figure 15.11**):

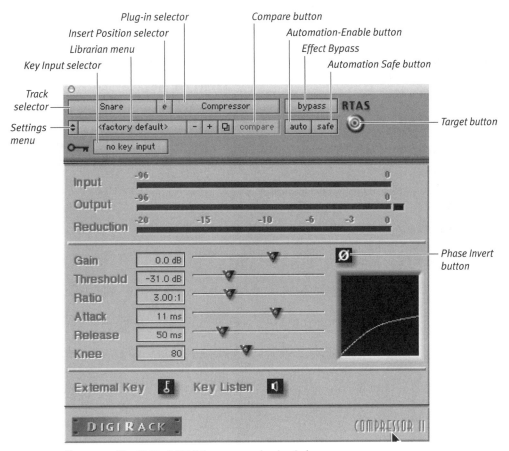

Figure 15.11 The DigiRack RTAS Compressor plug-in window.

Key Input selector: The Key Input selector lets you select audio on a particular input or bus and route it to the plug-in. This menu only appears on plug-ins that feature side-chain processing.

Librarian menu: The Librarian menu lets you recall settings files saved in the plug-in's root settings folder or in the current session's Settings folder.

Settings menu: The Settings menu lets you copy, paste, save, and import plug-in settings.

Track selector: The Track selector lets you choose any non-MIDI track in the session.

Insert Position selector: The Insert Position selector lets you choose any insert on the current track.

Plug-in selector: The Plug-in selector lets you choose any real-time plug-in from the Plug-ins folder.

Compare button: The Compare button toggles between the original saved plug-in setting and the current plug-in setting.

Effect Bypass: The Effect Bypass disables the currently displayed plug-in. This lets you hear the track with and without the plug-in.

AutomationEnable button: This feature lets you enable automation recording for individual plug-in parameters.

Automation Safe button: The Automation Safe button protects plug-in automation from being overwritten.

Link Enable buttons: The Link Enable buttons let you link channels of a multi-mono plug-in. Each square represents a channel. (The Master Link button must be disabled to use the Link-Enable buttons.)

Channel selector: The Channel selector lets you access specific channels within a multi-channel track. This feature appears on multi-mono plug-ins only. Shift-click the Channel selector to open a separate plug-in window for each channel.

Master Link button: The Master Link button links the parameter controls on all channels of a multi-mono plug-in. This lets you adjust multiple channels simultaneously.

Target button: The Target button lets you select a plug-in as the target for any keyboard commands.

Phase Invert button: The Phase Invert button lets you invert the phase polarity of the input signal.

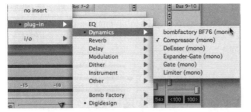

Figure 15.12 To open a plug-in window, click the insert in the Inserts view.

Figure 15.13 The red Target button.

Figure 15.14 To select a different plug-in on the same track, click the Plug-in selector and choose a plug-in from the pop-up menu.

To open a plug-in window:

◆ Click on an insert (**Figure 15.12**).

The selected plug-in window appears.

To open multiple plug-in windows:

◆ Click the red Target button on each plug-in window that you want to remain open (**Figure 15.13**).

The Target button becomes grayed out and the window remains open when other plug-in windows open.

or

◆ Shift-click the Insert button of the desired plug-in.

The selected plug-in window opens, and any open plug-in windows remain open.

To select a different plug-in on the same track:

◆ Click the Plug-in selector and choose a plug-in from the pop-up menu (**Figure 15.14**).

The window for the new plug-in appears.

To select a plug-in on a different track:

◆ Click the Track selector and choose a track from the pop-up menu (**Figure 15.15**).

To open plug-in windows for each channel of a multi-mono plug-in:

1. Option-click (Macintosh) or Alt-click (Windows) the Channel selector in the plug-in window of the desired plug-in (**Figure 15.16**).

2. Select the desired channel.

   The plug-in window of the desired channel appears.

Figure 15.15 To select a plug-in on a different track, click the Track selector and choose a track from the pop-up menu.

Figure 15.16 To open plug-in windows for left and right channels of a multi-mono plug-in, Option-click (Macintosh) or Alt-click (Windows) the Channel selector.

Figure 15.17 An Effect Bypass button.

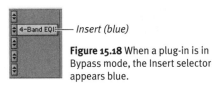

Insert (blue)

Figure 15.18 When a plug-in is in Bypass mode, the Insert selector appears blue.

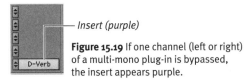

Insert (purple)

Figure 15.19 If one channel (left or right) of a multi-mono plug-in is bypassed, the insert appears purple.

Bypassing Plug-ins

Pro Tools lets you bypass a plug-in by clicking its Effect Bypass button (**Figure 15.17**). Bypassing a plug-in lets you compare the effected signal with the original dry signal. When a plug-in is in Bypass mode, the Insert appears blue (**Figure 15.18**). If one channel (left or right) of an unlinked multi-mono plug-in is bypassed, the Insert appears purple (**Figure 15.19**).

Bypass is different from using the *Compare* button, which lets you compare the original saved effect settings with the current plug-in setting configuration.

To bypass a plug-in:

◆ Click the plug-in window's Bypass button.
  or

◆ Command-click (Macintosh) or Control-click (Windows) the plug-in's Insert button.

Adjusting Plug-in Parameters

One nice thing about real-time plug-ins is that you can adjust them in real time—in other words, you can make changes to their parameters during playback. You can edit a plug-in's parameters by dragging its controls or by typing values into its value fields.

For instructions on adjusting individual RTAS plug-ins, see the *DigiRack Plug-ins Guide*, or consult the documentation that came with your third-party plug-in.

To adjust a plug-in parameter:

1. Begin audio playback so you can hear parameter changes in real time.

2. Adjust the parameters of the plug-in to achieve the desired effect.

To fine-tune plug-in parameter settings:

◆ Command-drag (Macintosh) or Control-drag (Windows) on the desired parameter control.

To return a control to its default value:

◆ Option-click (Macintosh) or Alt-click (Windows) on the desired parameter control.

Figure 15.20 Use the computer keyboard to input values directly into the value field of any plug-in parameter.

✔ Tips

■ If you have multiple plug-in windows open, click the Target button of the plug-in window that you want to make active.

■ You can use the computer keyboard to make the following edits:

Click in the value field of the parameter that you want to edit. Enter the desired value (**Figure 15.20**).

In fields that support values in kilohertz, typing "k" after a number value will multiply the value by 1000. For example, for 4000, enter 4k.

To increase a value, press the Up Arrow key on your keyboard. To decrease a value, press the Down Arrow key.

To move downward through the different parameter fields, press the Tab key. To move up, press Shift-Tab.

Types of Effects

Audio effects act upon the basic properties of a sound wave to create a new sound wave with different characteristics. Effects influence audio frequencies, volume, pitch, and duration, and simulate acoustic spaces that reflect and absorb sound waves. The most common types of audio effects are

Equalization (EQ): Equalizers let you adjust the volume of selected frequencies of a sound wave.

Dynamics: Dynamic effects (such as compressors, expanders, limiters, and noise gates) let you control the volume of a sound at specific threshold volume levels.

Delay: Delay effects (echo) let you repeat a sound at select delay times.

Reverb: Reverbs simulate the complex reflections (reverberations) of a sound within an acoustic space.

Other common audio effects include the following:

Pitch Shift: Pitch Shift changes the tuning of a musical part by percentages of a musical octave.

Time Compression/Expansion: Time Compression/Expansion effets change an audio signal's duration (length) without changing its pitch.

Dither: Dither uses a technique known as "noise-shaping" to minimize digital quanitization error and the resultant noise it can produce.

What Is DSP?

In Pro Tools, DSP refers to the manipulation or processing of digital audio. DSP occurs during many Pro Tools tasks, from simple volume changes to complex effects processing.

DSP is measured in terms of how much processing power a Pro Tools system has. In Pro Tools LE systems, all DSP tasks are handled by the host computer's CPU. The system's total DSP power thus depends on the processing power of the host computer. (Pro Tools HD systems have dedicated sound cards with embedded DSP chips. This gives HD systems a big DSP boost.)

Pro Tools lets you insert up to five real-time DSP plug-in effects on each audio track. Pro Tools LE ships with Digidesign's DigiRack RTAS plug-ins, which include 1- and 4-Band parametric EQ, dynamic effects, and delay and reverb effects.

In addition, there are a wide variety of third-party DSP plug-ins available, including reverbs, compressors, equalizers, pitch shifters, and mic and amp simulators. For a list of third-party DSP plug-ins, see *www.digidesign.com*.

What Is EQ?

Equalization (EQ) refers to *cutting* or *boosting* the volume level of specific frequencies of an audio signal. EQ is used to open up frequency ranges, and thus enhance the clarity, spaciousness, and blending of sounds in a mix.

Every instrument occupies its own frequency range (**Figure 15.21**). When you record multiple tracks of audio, the frequency ranges of various instruments overlap, often creating a unique blend of sound. But overlapping frequencies can also interfere with each other and produce frequency build-ups that make a mix sound unbalanced, cloudy, and flat.

This is where EQ enters. EQ lets you adjust the volume level of specific audio frequencies. Using EQ, you can turn down the volume of interfering frequencies and open up spaces for the main frequencies of instruments in the mix. This *EQ carving* enhances the clarity, spaciousness, and perceived height of the stereo image. For more information on stereo images, see *Chapter 14: Mixing Basics.*

EQ effects are most frequently used as line inserts on individual tracks. When you apply EQ to a track, it's a good idea to begin by gently cutting (or *subtracting*) frequencies on other tracks that may be interfering with the track you want to bring out. Subtracting EQ opens up space for the desired frequency range without adding new frequencies and boosting the overall mix volume.

You can then (sparingly) boost the frequency range of the track you want to bring out. For example, if you're mixing bass and kick drum, you may want to cut the kick and boost the bass at 100 Hz, and also boost the kick and cut the bass at 60 Hz. This will bring out each instrument's primary frequency ranges and add definition to both the kick and bass.

Remember, you don't want to "box" sounds into narrow frequency ranges by cutting off all their highs and lows. The interplay of harmonics and blending of frequency ranges gives a mix much of its unique character.

For more information on EQ, see the *Plug-ins Guide* that comes with your system.

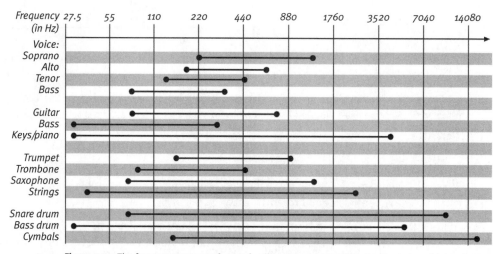

Figure 15.21 The frequency ranges of some familiar instruments. All instruments have high harmonics that contribute to the character of a sound.

Low pass
Notch
Hi shelf

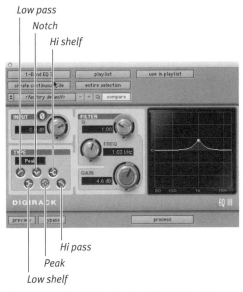

Hi pass
Peak
Low shelf

Figure 15.22 The DigiRack 1-Band EQ III plug-in lets you apply a single EQ filter to an audio signal.

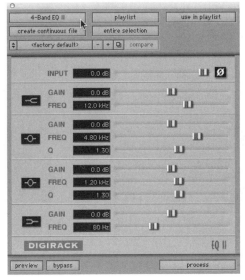

Figure 15.23 The DigiRack EQ II 4-Band EQ plug-in lets you apply up to four different EQ filters simultaneously.

Using EQ

Pro Tools' DigiRack plug-ins provide both one-band and four-band *parametric* EQs. A parametric EQ lets you choose the specific range of frequencies that you want to change. When you use a parametric EQ, you dial in a specific frequency, and then set the range around that frequency. This range is referred to as Q. The Q represents the number of octaves that the applied EQ affects. You can usually adjust Q to affect frequencies between one-half and two octaves wide.

The DigiRack 1-Band EQ (**Figure 15.22**) lets you apply a single EQ filter to an audio signal. The DigiRack 4-Band EQ (**Figure 15.23**) lets you apply up to four different EQ filters simultaneously. The DigiRack 7-Band EQ (**Figure 15.24**) lets you apply up to seven different EQ filters to a signal.

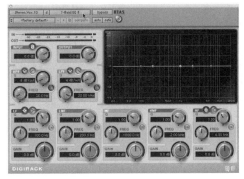

Figure 15.24 The DigiRack EQ III 7-Band EQ lets you apply seven different EQ filters simultaneously.

DigiRack EQ plug-ins include the following EQ filters:

Hi Pass/Low Pass: Pass filters are useful for eliminating unwanted high- or low-frequency ranges. A hi-pass filter lets high frequencies pass through, but cuts off low frequencies. A low-pass filter lets low frequencies pass through, but cuts off high frequencies.

Hi Shelf/Low Shelf: Shelf filters let you cut or boost both high- and low-frequency ranges. A hi-shelf filter lets you cut or boost frequencies above a chosen target frequency. A low-shelf filter lets you cut or boost frequencies below a chosen target frequency.

Hi Notch/Low Notch: Notch filters let you cut or boost an ultra-narrow band of frequencies. The Q button lets you set the width notch filter's frequency range. The Notch filter is found on the DigiRack EQ III plug-in only.

Peak: Peak filters let you cut or boost frequencies around a selected frequency. The Peak filter's Q button lets you set the frequency range that the Peak filter affects.

USING EQ

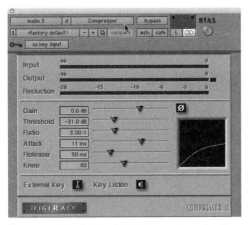

Figure 15.25 The DigiRack RTAS Compressor plug-in.

Using Dynamic Effects

Dynamic effects such as compressors, limiters, gates, and expanders let you control the *dynamic range* of an audio signal. The dynamic range is the difference between the softest and the loudest volume produced by a sound source. Controlling the dynamic range lets you smooth out performances that have erratic spikes in volume. It also lets you eliminate unwanted background noise.

Pro Tools' DigiRack RTAS plug-ins include the following dynamic effects:

Compressor: The Compressor plug-in (**Figure 15.25**) lets you reduce the dynamic range of signals that exceed a specified volume threshold. This lets you reduce extreme volume peaks on tracks that are prone to erratic levels (such as vocals and bass). For example, you can use compression to smooth out a vocal track that has both overly loud and overly soft moments. Once the extreme volume peaks are tempered, you can then turn up the volume of the track. This helps even out the volume of the vocal track, and in some cases, adds more presence and punch to a track.

The DigiRack RTAS Compressor plug-in has the following adjustable parameters:

- ◆ **Threshold:** The threshold is the level at which compression kicks in.

- ◆ **Ratio:** Ratio is the amount that a signal's volume is decreased (relative to the signal's original volume).

- ◆ **Attack:** Attack refers to the speed at which the compressor reacts to a loud signal.

- ◆ **Release:** The release is the speed at which the compressor lets go of the compression.

- ◆ **Knee:** The knee refers to the rate at which the compressor reaches full compression once the threshold has been exceeded.

Limiter: The Limiter plug-in (**Figure 15.26**) is a compressor that removes (rather than reduces) all signal exceeding the specified volume threshold. Limiters eliminate extreme volume spikes and thus prevent clipping. Because they eliminate loud volume peaks, limiters, like compressors, let you turn up the overall volume of a track. The DigiRack RTAS Limiter plug-in has the same adjustable parameters as the DigiRack RTAS Compressor plug-in.

Gate: The Gate plug-in (**Figure 15.27**) lets audio signals above a selected volume threshold pass through, whereas signals below the threshold are attenuated (decreased) by a specified amount. Gates (or noise gates) are the opposite of limiters: Rather than limit how loud a sound can get, they limit how soft a sound can get. Gates are useful for removing unwanted background noise on tracks. When recording drums, for instance, gates are often applied to each drum track to eliminate extraneous low-level noise coming from other drum mics. This not only helps make drum tracks less noisy, but can also increase their punch.

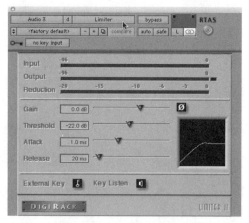

Figure 15.26 The DigiRack RTAS Limiter plug-in.

Figure 15.27 The DigiRack RTAS Gate plug-in.

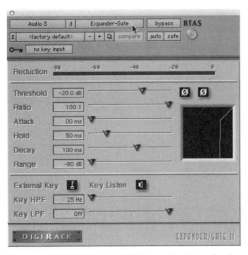

Figure 15.28 The DigiRack RTAS Expander-Gate plug-in.

The DigiRack RTAS Gate plug-in has the following parameters:

◆ **Threshold:** Threshold refers to the volume level below which the gate closes and attenuates the signal.

◆ **Attack:** Attack refers to the speed at which the gate reacts to a signal below the threshold.

◆ **Range:** Range is the amount (in decibels) that the gate attenuates the signal. For example, a range of 50 dB decreases any signal below the threshold by 50 dB.

◆ **Decay:** Decay determines the rate at which the gate closes after the signal reaches the threshold.

◆ **Hold:** Hold refers to the length of time that the gate stays open after the signal falls below the threshold. When the hold time is reached, the gate slams shut. This can sometimes produce a chopped-off sound.

Expander-Gate: The Expander–Gate plug-in (**Figure 15.28**) attenuates any signal falling below a specified volume threshold by a user-defined ratio. Compared to a gate alone, which reduces sounds below a set threshold by a specified amount, an expander's ratio changes the signal gradually. This makes the resulting signal sound more natural. Expanders are useful when you want to subtly reduce noise from a track rather than completely filter it out. For example, when dealing with a singer's breaths, you may want to use an expander rather than a gate. The expander will reduce the volume of the breath gradually, creating a more natural breathing sound than a gate, which would chop off the breath entirely.

The DigiRack RTAS Expander-Gate plug-in has the same parameters as the Gate plug-in.

Using Key Inputs for Side-chain Processing

Many RTAS plug-ins let you set up *side-chain processing*. Side-chain processing occurs when an effect on a track is triggered by audio from a different track. The audio source used to trigger the effect is called the *key input*. In Pro Tools you can use any bus or input as the key input.

Side chains and key inputs are typically used with dynamic effects such as compressors and noise gates (although you can no doubt find many other creative uses for them). For example, a kick drum can be used as the key input to trigger gating on a bass guitar.

To use a key input for side-chain processing:

1. From the Key Input menu, choose the input or bus carrying the audio that you want to trigger the plug-in (**Figure 15.29**).

2. Click External Key to activate side-chain processing (**Figure 15.30**).

3. Click Key Listen to audition the key input audio source (**Figure 15.31**).

4. Begin playback.

   The plug-in uses the key input to trigger its effect. Adjust plug-in parameters, if necessary, to achieve the desired effect.

✔ Tip

- Certain plug-ins feature key input filters (such as hi- and low-pass filters), which let you define specific frequency ranges as key inputs to trigger the plug-in effect. This is useful for filtering instruments so that only specific high frequencies (such as a hi hat) or low frequencies (such as a kick drum) trigger the effect. For more information on key input filters, see the *DigiRack Plug-ins Guide*.

Figure 15.29 To activate a plug-in from a side chain, click the Key Input selector and choose a bus or input.

Figure 15.30 The External Key button activates side-chain processing.

Figure 15.31 The Key Listen button lets you audition the key input audio source.

Creating Effects Loops

Pro Tools lets you create send-and-return submixes, known as *effects loops* (**Figure 15.32**). Effects loops are used to process multiple tracks of audio simultaneously through a single effect. For example, you might route several band tracks (such as drums, vocals, piano, and guitars) through a reverb to create the impression that a song is being played live inside a large hall. Effects loops can also help save DSP resources by minimizing the number of plug-ins used in a session.

When you create an effects loop, you bus audio from multiple tracks to an auxiliary input. (This is called an *effects send*.) A plug-in or hardware effect inserted on the auxiliary input then adds the desired effect to the signal. You then return the output of the auxiliary input to the main mix. (This is called an *effects return*.)

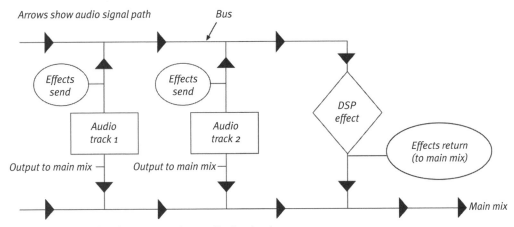

Figure 15.32 An effects loop. Arrows show audio signal path.

To create an effects loop:

1. Create an effects send: Assign a send on each source track to a mono or stereo bus path (**Figure 15.33**).

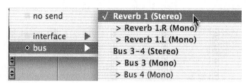

Figure 15.33 Create an effects send by assigning audio tracks to busses.

2. Assign each track's main output to the main mix outputs.

3. Choose Track > New.

   The New Track dialog box appears.

4. Choose Auxiliary Input (stereo or mono), and click Create.

5. Insert a real-time plug-in or external hardware effect on the auxiliary input (**Figure 15.34**).

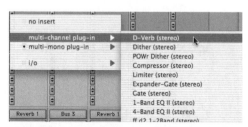

Figure 15.34 On the destination auxiliary input, insert the real-time effect that you want to use in the effects loop.

6. Set the plug-in or external effect to 100% Wet, and configure any other parameters as needed.

7. Click the Input selector of the auxiliary input and assign it to the same bus path as the source tracks.

8. Click the Output selector of the auxiliary input and choose the main mix outputs (**Figure 15.35**).

   This turns the auxiliary input into an effects return.

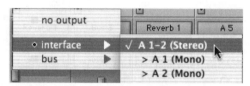

Figure 15.35 Create an effects return by assigning the outputs of the auxiliary input to the main mix outputs. Use the effects return to mix varying amounts of the treated signal into the mix.

9. Adjust the level of the auxiliary input to balance the effects return in the mix.

Using Delay Effects

Delay effects let you add depth and dimension to sounds in a mix. All delay effects are created the same way—by repeating sounds at various delay times. But small changes in delay time can produce very different sounding delay effects (**Figure 15.36**).

Many delay effects such as doubling, slapback, and echo simply repeat a signal at a specified delay time. Shorter delay times are useful for thickening sounds; longer delay times help reinforce rhythms, or create the perception of large spaces.

Some delay effects such as phase shifting, flanging, and chorus use short delay times together with *modulation*. Modulation occurs when the delay time is changed over time. When you add modulation to a delayed signal, slight pitch variations occur. These modulating delays can produce pretty far-out effects—from disembodied voices in desolate windscapes to shimmering choral effects.

Of course, take care not to oversaturate the mix with delay and reverb—a little takes you pretty far. Sometimes, spaces are best defined by what's not there. Like everything else in mixing (and recording), there are no absolutes with adding delay. As always, it's important to follow your ears.

DigiRack RTAS Mod Delay II plug-ins let you create the following delay effects:

Doubling: Doubling uses a single delay repeat at delay times between 30 and 80 ms. Repeats with delay times less than 50 ms are not discernable as discrete echoes; instead, they're perceived as additional voices or instruments. Doubling can help make a track sound thicker.

Slapback: Slapback usually consists of one or two repeats at delay times between 75 and 120 ms. Slapback is good for creating punchy vocal tracks or reinforcing the beat or tempo of a song.

Echo: Echo refers to one or more discretely audible repeats of the original source sound. Repeated signals with delay times longer than 50 ms are usually audible as discrete signals. Echoes produced by medium and long delay times (120–1000 ms or more) are useful for simulating large spaces. For example, adding a long delay to a guitar lead can make it sound like it's in a huge, cavernous space.

Phase shifting: Phase shifting uses very short delay times (1–3 ms) and modulation. Mixing the delayed signal with its original nondelayed source signal produces a slightly out-of-phase effect with a subtle yet distinctive "whooshing" sound.

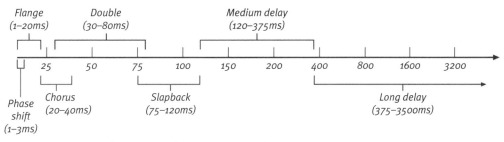

Figure 15.36 Delay times (in milliseconds) of common delay effects.

Flanging: Flanging uses short delay times (1–20 ms) and modulation. This produces a more dramatic "whoosh" than phase shifting, which makes it good for creating frightening voices and otherworldly sound effects.

Chorus: Chorus uses short delay times (20–40 ms) and modulation. By modulating repeated signals at these times and mixing them with the source signal, you can create the perception of multiple instruments and voices.

The DigiRack RTAS Mod Delay II plug-ins (**Figure 15.37**) include the following user-adjustable parameters:

Delay: Delay lets you set the delay time of the effect.

Feedback: Feedback controls the number of delay repeats. The higher the feedback level, the greater the number of delay repeats.

Depth: Depth lets you adjust the amount of modulation applied to the delayed signal.

Rate: Rate lets you adjust the speed of the modulation applied to the delayed signal.

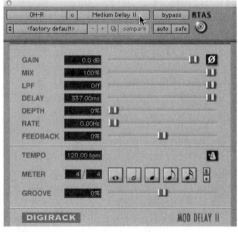

Figure 15.37 The DigiRack RTAS Mod Delay II plug-in.

Simulating Space

When you yell across the Grand Canyon, your voice bounces (or *echoes*) back to you ... back to you. The time it takes for your voice to return is the *delay time*. The delay time tells us how big a space is. For example, because it takes a long time for your voice to return from across the Grand Canyon, we know the space is pretty big.

In mixing, we use delay times to create the illusion of depth in the stereo image. The longer it takes for a delayed signal to *repeat*, the larger the perceived space.

For more information on stereo imaging, see *Chapter 14: Mixing Basics*.

What Is Reverb?

Reverb is a natural property of any enclosed room that occurs when sound waves bounce off walls, ceilings, and floors. You've probably experienced reverb, even if you're not familiar with the term—it's what makes singing in the shower sound so good. Reverb effects let you simulate acoustic spaces of all sizes, shapes, and reflectivity.

Reverb has three basic sound components (**Figure 15.38**):

Direct sound: Direct sound is what you hear when sound waves travel unimpeded from the source to your ears. Direct sound cues you to the location of the sound source in a three-dimensional space.

Early reflections: Early reflections are the first reflected sound waves to reach your ears after bouncing off the primary surfaces in a given room. Early reflections cue you to the size and shape of a room.

Reverberations: Reverberations are the final reflected sound waves to reach your ears. They consist of multiple sound reflections traveling from surface to surface within the confines of a room. The delay times of these reflected sound waves are so close together that you hear them as one long, decaying signal.

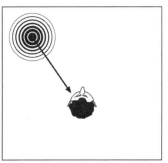
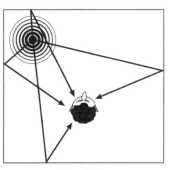
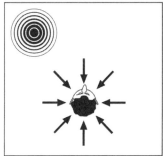

Direct sound   *Early reflections*   *Reverberation*

Figure 15.38 The three basic sound components of reverb.

Using Reverb

When you apply reverb to a sound, you're essentially bouncing that sound off the walls, floors, and ceilings of a simulated room. Adjusting reverb parameters (such as room size, decay, pre-delay, diffusion, and density) lets you create the illusion that a sound is inside of a space of almost any size or shape. For instance, if you want to place a pipe organ sound into a cathedral space, you'd run the organ through a reverb with long decay times and long pre-delay times. Then, by returning more of the reverb signal than the original signal to the main mix, you can create the distant vastness of a cathedral.

You can also combine delays and reverbs to create even more spacious sounds. For example, by adding short delay (doubling) to a background vocal, and then sending the delayed signal into a big reverb, you can create the illusion of a choir in a large hall.

In addition to its preset room algorithms such as halls, churches, plates, and rooms, Pro Tools' RTAS D-Verb reverb plug-in has the following user-adjustable parameters (**Figure 15.39**):

Size: The Size button lets you choose from three room sizes: small, medium, and large.

Decay: Decay is the length of time that the reverb lasts. Use longer decay times to simulate larger rooms.

Pre-delay: Pre-delay determines the amount of time between the beginning of an audio signal and the beginning of its reverberations. It lets you add definition to the source sound by separating it from its reverb.

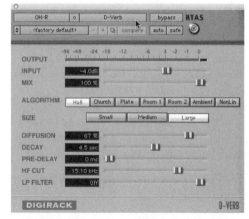

Figure 15.39 Digidesign's D-Verb reverb plug-in.

Diffusion: Diffusion determines the rate of increase of sound reflections in the room. You can use diffusion to adjust the perceived reflectivity of a room. Higher diffusion simulates a more reflective room; lower diffusion simulates a less reflective room.

Hi Frequency Cut: The Hi Frequency Cut filter lets you control the decay of high-frequency components in the reverb. Use it with the Low Pass filter to shape the overall high-frequency contour of the reverb.

Low Pass: The Low Pass filter controls the volume of high frequencies in the reverb. The Low Pass filter attenuates by 6 dB all sounds above a user-defined frequency.

Many third-party reverb plug-ins include these additional adjustable parameters:

Room size: In addition to preset room sizes, many reverbs let you adjust the actual room size in meters or feet. This gives you more control over the size of a reverb space.

Density: Density refers to the level of early sound reflections that a room produces. Because early reflections reach your ear before the main body of reverb, density can cue you to the size of the space. The higher the density setting, the larger the apparent space.

USING REVERB

Using External Hardware Effects

You can use external hardware effects such as reverbs or delays as in-line inserts or as send-and-return effects loops. To use external hardware, you must map the insert's inputs and outputs to audio interface channels in the I/O Setup dialog box. You must also connect the external hardware device to the corresponding inputs and outputs of the audio interface.

For more information on I/O Setups, see *Chapter 4: Starting a New Session.* For information on connecting external hardware devices, see *Appendix A: Connecting Your Studio* or the *Pro Tools Reference Guide.*

To define hardware inserts:

1. Choose Setup > I/O.

    The I/O Setup dialog box appears (**Figure 15.40**).

2. Click Insert.

3. Select an insert path (**Figure 15.41**).

    or

    Click New Path to create a new insert path.

4. Set the insert to the correct format (mono or stereo).

5. Map inserts in the Channel Grid as needed.

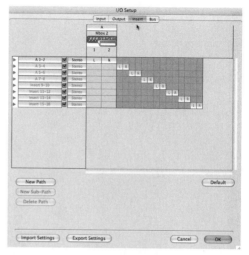

Figure 15.40 The I/O Setup dialog box.

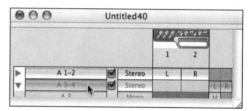

Figure 15.41 To define hardware inserts, select an insert path in the I/O Setup dialog box.

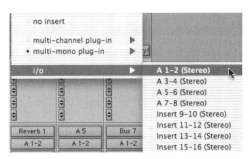

Figure 15.42 To assign a hardware insert to a track, choose an insert from the track Insert selector.

To assign a hardware insert to a track:

◆ Select an insert from the track Insert selector (**Figure 15.42**).

✔ Tip

■ To save DSP resources, make external hardware inserts inactive. Inactive inserts retain their routing assignments but do not let signal pass through.

■ To make an insert inactive: Command-Control-click (Macintosh) or Control-Start-click (Windows) on the insert you want to make inactive. Inactive inserts appear shaded and italicized.

■ Making inserts inactive can also work as a mute or bypass for hardware inserts that don't have their own Bypass button.

■ For more information on Active and Inactive modes, see *Chapter 21: Optimizing Performance.*

USING EXTERNAL HARDWARE EFFECTS

Using AudioSuite Plug-ins

Unlike RTAS (and TDM) plug-ins, AudioSuite plug-ins do not process audio in real time. Instead, they process audio directly to disk, creating a new audio file that includes the effected signal.

When using an AudioSuite plug-in, you must first select the audio region that you want to process. Keep in mind that delay or reverb effects will add additional material at the end of the selected audio region (a delay repeat or a reverb decay, respectively). For this reason, it's important to make the selection longer than the source audio. If there isn't enough room to write the effect into the audio file, the effect will be unceremoniously chopped off.

For more details on AudioSuite plug-ins, see the *DigiRack Plug-ins Guide* that came with your system.

To process audio with an AudioSuite plug-in:

1. Select the regions that you want to process.

2. Choose the desired AudioSuite plug-in from the AudioSuite menu (**Figure 15.43**).

3. Click the Preview button to audition the effect (**Figure 15.44**).

4. Adjust the plug-in parameters to achieve the desired effect.

5. Click the Process button.

    The selected audio is processed. Pro Tools appends an acronym to the region's name, indicating the AudioSuite process that has been applied. The new audio file then appears in the session.

Figure 15.43
The AudioSuite plug-in menu.

Figure 15.44 To audition an AudioSuite plug-in, click the Preview button.

✔ Tips

- To configure the plug-in for destructive processing, choose Overwrite Files from the File Mode pop-up menu. This will overwrite and permanently modify the original source audio files.

- To configure the plug-in for non-destructive processing, choose Create Individual Files from the File Mode pop-up menu. This will create a new audio file for each region that has been processed with the AudioSuite plug-in and leave the original source audio files unaltered.

- To process the selected region only in the track in which it appears, choose Playlist from the Selection Reference pop-up menu.

- To process and update every occurrence of the selected region throughout the session, enable the Use In Playlist button (and also choose Regions List from the Selection Reference pop-up menu).

- For additional AudioSuite processed-file handling options, see the *DigiRack Plug-ins Guide* that came with your system.

Improving RTAS Plug-in Performance

Pro Tools 7 adds support for multiprocessor computers. If you have a multiprocessor computer, you can boost your performance by dedicating additional processors to RTAS plug-in processing.

To specify the number of RTAS processors:

1. Choose Setup > Playback Engine.

2. From the RTAS Processing pop-up menu, choose the number of available processors you want to dedicate to RTAS plug-in processing.

You can also improve the performance of RTAS plug-ins by increasing Pro Tools' hardware buffer size and CPU usage limit. This will dedicate more processing power to RTAS plug-ins and other host processor tasks.

To set CPU Usage Limit for RTAS plug-in processing:

1. Choose Setup > Playback Engine.

2. From the H/W Buffer Size pop-up menu, select the desired hardware buffer size.

3. From the CPU Usage Limit pop-up menu, select the percentage of CPU power you want to dedicate to RTAS plug-ins and host processor tasks (**Figure 15.45**).

For more information on improving system performance, see *Chapter 21: Optimizing Performance* or the *Pro Tools Reference Guide*.

Figure 15.45 To improve RTAS plug-in performance, choose Setup > Hardware. Increase the CPU usage limit to dedicate more processing power to RTAS plug-ins. Multi-processor computers can select additional RTAS Processors from the pop-up menu.

16

AUTOMATING A MIX

Not long ago engineers, producers, and band members alike engaged in a Twister-like ritual known as "performing" the final mix on the board. Pulling off such a mix was no easy feat: For instance, if one person failed to turn up a guitar or vocal on the mixing board, the entire mix had to be scrubbed— and performed again from scratch. Needless to say, more than a few good mixes (and tempers) were lost in this process.

Thankfully, computer automation has made this arduous mix choreography a thing of the past. Pro Tools automation remembers your mix moves and plays them back exactly as you performed them. This can save you a huge amount of time. You can build mixes in logical stages, and, if you make a mistake, a simple tweak fixes it—no more redoing mixes from scratch.

This chapter shows you how to use Pro Tools automation. You'll learn how to write an automation pass, and how to edit and view automation data. We'll also discuss how to thin unneeded automation data— a trick that enhances both automation and CPU performance.

About Automation Modes

Each channel strip in the Pro Tools Mix and Edit windows provides an Automation Mode selector (**Figure 16.1**), which lets you choose how track automation is written and played back. Choose from the following automation modes:

Off Mode: Off mode turns off automation for all automation parameters.

Read Mode: Read mode plays back automation that was previously written for a track.

Touch Mode: Touch mode writes automation data only when you click on an automation parameter with the mouse. When you release the mouse, automation writing stops and the parameter returns to its previously automated position.

Latch Mode: Latch mode is similar to Touch mode: It writes automation only when you click on an automation parameter with the mouse. Latch mode, however, continues to write automation until you stop playback. This mode is particularly useful for automating pan controls and plug-ins, since it doesn't revert to its previous position when you release a control.

Write Mode: Write mode writes automation data during playback. It erases any preexisting automation data on the track. After you record automation data in Write mode, Pro Tools automatically switches to Touch mode. This prevents you from accidentally overwriting automation data on further playback.

Figure 16.1 The Automation Mode selector lets you choose how track automation is written and played back.

Figure 16.2 The Automation Enable window.

Figure 16.3 To open the Automation Enable window, choose Window > Automation Enable.

Figure 16.4 To suspend automation writing on all tracks, click the Auto Suspend button in the Automation Enable window.

Enabling Automation

The Automation Enable window (**Figure 16.2**) lets you enable (or suspend) automation writing for the following automation parameters:

◆ Volume

◆ Pan

◆ Mute

◆ Send Level (Volume)

◆ Send Pan

◆ Send Mute

◆ Plug-in parameters

To enable automation writing on all tracks:

1. Choose Window > Automation Enable (**Figure 16.3**).

   The Automation Enable window appears.

2. Select the automation parameters that you want to automate.

To suspend automation writing on all tracks:

1. Choose Window > Automation Enable.

2. To suspend automation writing on all tracks, click the Auto Suspend button (**Figure 16.4**).

   or

   To suspend automation writing of a specific parameter on all tracks, click the button for that parameter.

To suspend automation writing and playback on individual tracks:

1. In the Edit window, set the Track View selector to show the automation parameter that you want to suspend.

2. To suspend automation writing and playback for the displayed parameter, Command-click (Macintosh) or Control-click (Windows) on the name of the displayed parameter in the Track View selector (**Figure 16.5**).

   or

   To suspend writing and playback of an automation parameter on all tracks, Command-Option-click (Macintosh) or Control-Alt-click (Windows) on the name of the automation parameter in the Track View selector.

Figure 16.5 Command-click (Macintosh) or Control-click (Windows) the name of the displayed parameter in the Track View selector to suspend automation writing and playback.

Figure 16.6 Enable the track parameters that you want to automate in the Automation Enable window.

Figure 16.7 Select an automation mode for each track that you want to automate.

Writing Automation

Pro Tools lets you write automation in real time by simply moving the controls for the desired parameter during playback. As you move the controls, Pro Tools records (or writes) these moves. This is called an *automation pass*.

To write automation on a track:

1. Choose Window > Automation Enable.

2. Enable the track parameters that you want to automate (**Figure 16.6**).

3. Select an automation mode for each track that you want to automate (**Figure 16.7**). For the initial automation pass, select Write mode.

4. Click Play to begin writing automation. Move the controls that you want to automate.

5. When you've finished writing automation, click Stop.

After the first automation pass, you can write additional automation to the track without erasing the previous pass. To do so, set the automation mode to Touch or Latch.

To write additional automation to a previous automation pass:

1. Link the Edit and Timeline selections.

2. In the Edit window, make a selection or place the cursor in the location where you want to write automation (**Figure 16.8**).

3. Select Touch or Latch mode (**Figure 16.9**) on the tracks that you want to automate.

4. Click Play and begin writing automation. Move the controls that you want to automate.

5. When you've finished writing automation, click Stop.

✔ Tip

- You can use the Pencil tool (**Figure 16.10**) to draw automation directly into an automation playlist. The Pencil tool provides seven shapes: Free Hand, Line, Triangle, Square, Random, parabolic and S-curve (**Figure 16.11**). Experiment with them and see which one works for you. For more information on drawing automation, see the *Pro Tools Reference Guide*.

Figure 16.8 Make a selection or place the cursor in the location where you want to write automation.

Figure 16.9 To write additional automation to a previous automation pass, select Touch or Latch from the Automation mode selector.

Figure 16.10 The Pencil tool in the Edit window lets you edit automation by moving points along a line graph.

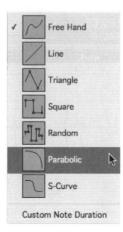

Figure 16.11 The Pencil tool's seven shapes.

WRITING AUTOMATION

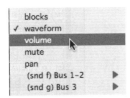

Figure 16.12 To view an automation parameter, click the Track View selector and choose from the pop-up menu.

Figure 16.13 The Volume automation playlist as an editable line graph.

Viewing Automation

Pro Tools creates a separate *automation playlist* for each automation parameter that you write. Unlike track playlists, which can display multiple region configurations, an automation playlist displays only a single automation line graph for each parameter. The Track View selector lets you view automation playlists.

To show automation data:

◆ Click the Track View selector and choose the automation playlist that you want to view (**Figure 16.12**).

The selected automation playlist appears in the track. The automation playlist displays an editable line graph representing the value of the automation parameter against time. Waveforms are displayed behind the line graph and appear lighter in color (**Figure 16.13**).

✔ Tip

■ To toggle between Waveform and Volume views, select the track that you want to toggle, and then press Control-Minus (Macintosh) or Start-Minus (Windows).

Automating Sends

Pro Tools lets you write automation for send volume, send mute, and send pan (for stereo and multichannel sends only). This lets you precisely control effects levels and placement during a mixdown.

Figure 16.14 Select the send parameters that you want to automate from the Automation Enable window.

To write send volume, mute, or pan automation:

1. Choose Window > Automation Enable.

2. Enable the send automation parameters that you want to automate (**Figure 16.14**).

3. Choose Write mode as the automation mode for the initial pass.

4. Display an individual send control, or display a send Output window.

5. Click Play and begin writing automation. Move the send controls that you want to automate.

6. When you've finished writing automation, click Stop.

✔ Tip

■ You can apply send volume and send mute automation to all members of a group. For more information, see *Appendix B: Setting Preferences*.

Figure 16.15 To enable plug-in automation, click the Automation-Enable button in the plug-in window.

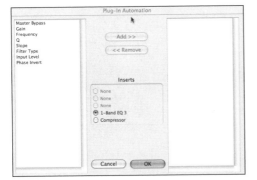

Figure 16.16 The Plug-in Automation dialog box lets you select plug-in parameters to automate.

Automating Plug-ins

Pro Tools lets you write automation for most plug-in parameters. First, however, you must enable the parameters that you want to automate using the Plug-in Automation dialog box.

To enable plug-in automation:

1. Open the window of the plug-in that you want to automate.

2. Click the AutomationEnable button (**Figure 16.15**).

   The Plug-in Automation dialog box appears (**Figure 16.16**).

3. Select the parameters to automate.

4. Click Add.

5. Click OK.

   The selected parameters become lit, indicating automation is active on those parameters.

To enable all plug-in parameters simultaneously:

1. Open the window of the plug-in you want to automate.

2. Control-Option-Command-click (Macintosh) or Control-Alt-Start-click (Windows) on the plug-in's Auto button.

   All plug-in parameters become lit, indicating plug-in automation is active.

To write plug-in automation:

1. Make sure the desired parameter is automation-enabled.

2. Choose an automation mode on the track in which the plug-in is inserted. For an initial pass, choose Write mode.

3. Click Play to begin writing automation.

4. Move the controls that you want to automate.

5. When you've finished writing plug-in automation, click Stop.

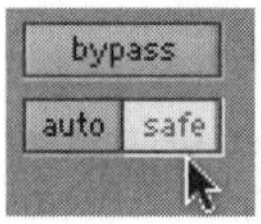

Protecting Written Automation with Automation Safe mode

Once you've written plug-in automation, use the Automation Safe button to protect it from being overwritten.

To place plug-in automation in Safe mode:

1. Open the window for the plug-in.

2. Select the Automation Safe button (**Figure 16.17**).

   The plug-in is placed in Automation Safe mode: Plug-in automation becomes inactive and cannot be overwritten.

Figure 16.17 The Automation Safe button protects plug-in automation from being overwritten.

Figure 16.18 To create a breakpoint, click with the Grabber (or the Pencil) on the automation playlist's line graph.

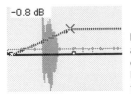

Figure 16.19 To move a breakpoint, click an existing point on the line graph and drag it to a new position.

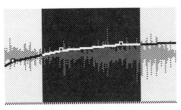

Figure 16.20 Select a range in the automation playlist that contains the breakpoints that you want to move.

Editing Automation

Pro Tools displays automation data as a line graph with editable breakpoints. You can graphically edit automation data by moving these breakpoints within a track's automation playlist. Dragging breakpoints up or down increases or decreases their value, respectively, whereas dragging them to the left or right makes the automation event occur earlier or later on the timeline.

Pro Tools lets you use standard Edit commands (Cut, Copy, and Paste) to edit automation data. In addition, Pro Tools 7 provides Special Edit commands (Special Cut, Special Copy, and Special Paste), specifically for editing automation data.

Graphically editing automation breakpoints

To graphically edit automation breakpoints, display the automation parameter that you want to edit by choosing it from the Track View selector. Then do one of the following:

To create a breakpoint:

◆ Click with the Grabber (or the Pencil) tool on the automation playlist's line graph (**Figure 16.18**).

To move a breakpoint:

◆ Click an existing point on the line graph with the Grabber tool and drag it to a new position (**Figure 16.19**).

To move several breakpoints at once:

1. Select a range in the automation playlist that contains the breakpoints that you want to move (**Figure 16.20**).

2. Press the Plus key to nudge the breakpoints to the right (later in the timeline) or the Minus key to nudge them to the left (earlier in the timeline). The breakpoints move by the current nudge value.

EDITING AUTOMATION

To change all breakpoint values in a region:

◆ Click in the region with the Trimmer and drag the breakpoints up to increase their value or down to decrease their value (**Figure 16.21**).

Cutting, copying, and pasting automation

You can also use traditional Cut, Copy, and Paste commands to edit automation data.

When you cut a selected range of automation data (**Figure 16.22**), Pro Tools adds anchor breakpoints to the data's beginning and end points. This preserves the value and slope of the breakpoints on the line graph inside the cut selection. It also preserves a portion of the slope of the line graph before and after the cut region (**Figure 16.23**). When you paste the cut selection, the anchor break-points are also pasted (**Figure 16.24**).

Copying automation data does not affect the selected region. When you paste a copied selection, however, anchor break-points are also pasted.

Deleting automation

To delete automation data, display the automation parameter that you want to edit by selecting it from the Track View selector. Then do one of the following:

To delete a single breakpoint:

◆ With the Grabber or Pencil tool, Option-click (Macintosh) or Alt-click (Windows) the breakpoint.

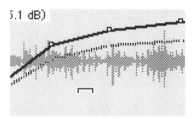

5.1 dB)

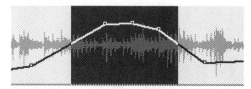

Figure 16.21 Click in the region with the Trimmer and drag breakpoints up or down to increase or decrease their value.

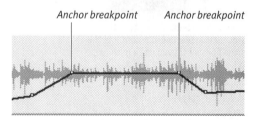

Figure 16.22 A selected range of automation data.

Anchor breakpoint   *Anchor breakpoint*

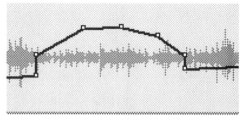

Figure 16.23 After the selected automation is cut, Pro Tools adds anchor breakpoints at the beginning and end of the cut region.

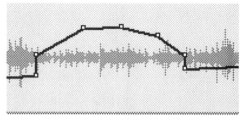

Figure 16.24 When a cut (or copied) selection is pasted, the anchor breakpoints are also pasted.

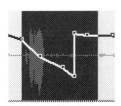

Figure 16.25 Select the range of automation data you want to delete.

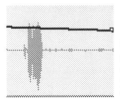

Figure 16.26 Deleting a selection of automation data erases any breakpoints contained within the selection.

To delete several breakpoints:

1. Use the Selector to select a range that contains the breakpoints (**Figure 16.25**).

2. Press Delete (Macintosh) or Backspace (Windows).

   All breakpoints within the selected range are erased (**Figure 16.26**).

To delete all automation data of the displayed parameter:

1. Click with the Selector in the track and choose Edit > Select All.

2. Press Delete (Macintosh) or Backspace (Windows).

To delete all automation data in all automation playlists on a track:

1. Use the Selector to select a range of data to be removed.

2. Press Control-Delete (Macintosh) or Start-Backspace (Windows).

   Pro Tools removes all automation data within the selected range on each of the track's automation playlists.

✔ Tips

- In Waveform view, cutting or copying a section of an audio track's waveform will also cut or copy any automation data associated with it.

- On auxiliary inputs, Instrument tracks, or master faders, only displayed automation data is cut or copied. To cut or copy all automation data on these track types, press Control while cutting or copying.

- Don't confuse cutting automation data with deleting it. When you delete a selected range of automation, all automation data is removed and no anchor breakpoints are created. This can alter the shape of the automation line graph.

EDITING AUTOMATION

Using Special Edit commands to edit automation

Special Edit commands (new in Pro Tools 7) are identical to regular Edit commands except they act only upon automation data (volume, pan, mute, and plug-in automation) on audio, auxiliary input, master fader, and instrument tracks. You can also use Special Edit commands to edit MIDI controller data.

Special Edit commands can be used to edit track automation data regardless of the track view. For example, you can edit volume, pan, and mute automation on a track without switching out of Waveform view. This reduces the steps involved in editing automation, and thus can speed up and simplify certain automation editing tasks.

Each Special Edit command includes a submenu, containing options for applying the command as follows:

Copy Special

- ◆ **All Automation:** Copies all automation data or MIDI controller data, shown or not.

- ◆ **Pan Automation:** Copies only pan automation data or MIDI pan data, shown or not.

- ◆ **Plug-in Automation:** Copies only plug-in automation data that is shown.

Cut Special

- ◆ **All Automation:** Cuts all automation data or MIDI controller data, shown or not.

- ◆ **Pan Automation:** Cuts only pan automation data or MIDI pan data, shown or not.

- ◆ **Plug-in Automation:** Copies only plug-in automation data that is shown.

Paste Special

- ◆ **Merge:** Pastes MIDI note data in clipboard to a selected destination and merges it with preexisting MIDI note data.

- ◆ **Repeat to Fill Selection:** Pastes unlimited copies of audio and MIDI regions, automation data, or MIDI controller data from the clipboard to fill the selected location.

- ◆ **To Current Automation Type:** Pastes automation or MIDI controller data from the clipboard to the selected destination as the "current" automation type. This lets you use automation data interchangeably between all types of automation; and you can use MIDI data interchangeably between all MIDI functions.

Clear Special

- ◆ **All Automation:** Clears all automation and MIDI controller data, shown or not.

- ◆ **Pan Automation:** Clears only pan automation data or MIDI pan data, shown or not.

- ◆ **Plug-in Automation:** Clears only plug-in automation data that is shown.

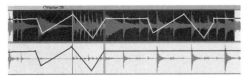

Figure 16.27 Select the automation data that you want to copy.

Figure 16.28 To copy the selected automation data, choose Edit > Copy Special > All Automation.

Figure 16.29 To paste the copied automation data to a selected track area, choose Edit > Paste Special > Repeat to Fill Selection. The automation is copied to the selected area of the region loop and repeated as many times as necessary to fill the selected area.

To copy automation data from one track to another track using Copy Special:

1. Click the Track View selector to view track automation (volume, pan, mute).

2. Using the Selector tool, select the track playlist (or portion of a track's playlist whose automation you want to copy) (**Figure 16.27**).

3. Choose Edit > Copy Special > All Automation (**Figure 16.28**).

   All automation data in the playlist selection is copied to the clipboard.

4. Choose Edit > Paste Special > Repeat to Fill Selection.

   All automation in the clipboard is pasted to the selected track. If your track selection exceeds the length of the inserted automation, the automation is repeated (multiple times if necessary) to fill the entire selection (**Figure 16.29**).

For additional information on Special Edit commands, see the *Pro Tools Reference Guide*.

EDITING AUTOMATION

Automating Looped Regions

Looping an audio region does not loop any automation data associated with the source region. This lets you add new automation across any portion of the loop (and it frees you from automation cleanup tasks).

You can copy and paste automation from the source region to individual loop iterations using the Special Copy and Special Paste Repeat to Fill Selection commands.

To copy and paste automation from the source regions to individual loop iterations:

1. Select the source region (**Figure 16.30**).

2. Choose Edit > Copy Special > All Automation or Pan Automation, or Plug-in Automation, depending on the automation you want to copy.

3. Select the looped region.

4. Choose Edit > Paste Special > Repeat to Fill Selection.

   The automation data from the source region is pasted and repeated to fill the loop iterations (**Figure 16.31**).

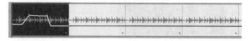

Figure 16.30 Select the source region of the region loop containing the automation data you would like to extend over the region loop.

Figure 16.31 To paste the copied automation from the source region to individual loop iterations, choose Edit > Paste Special > Repeat to Fill Selection. The automation data from the source region is pasted to the selected loop iterations.

AUTOMATING LOOPED REGIONS

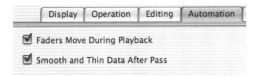

Figure 16.32 The Smooth and Thin Data After Pass option in the Automation Preferences window.

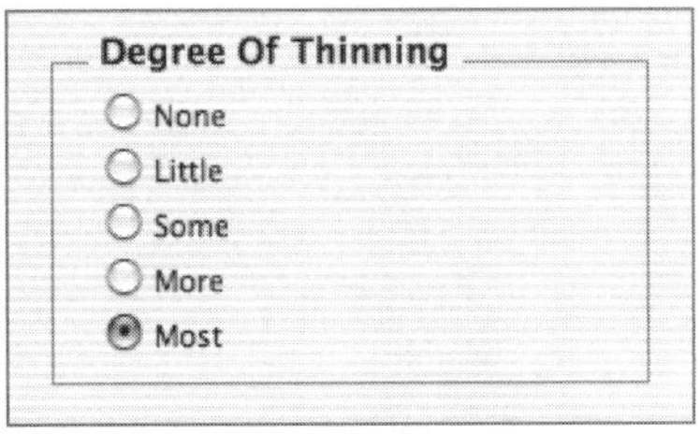

Figure 16.33 Select the amount of automation thinning from the Degree of Thinning option in the Automation Preferences window.

Thinning Automation

Pro Tools lets you reduce, or *thin*, the density of automation data written during an automation pass. This helps clear memory allocated to automation, which can enhance automation-writing efficiency and improve CPU performance.

Pro Tools provides two ways to thin automation data: The Smooth and Thin Data After Pass option in the Automation Preferences window and the Thin Automation command.

When the Smooth and Thin Data After Pass option is selected (**Figure 16.32**), Pro Tools automatically thins the automation breakpoint data after each automation pass. You can also select the amount of thinning from the Degree of Thinning option in the Automation Preferences window, including None (no thinning), Little, Some, More, and Most (maximum thinning) (**Figure 16.33**). For additional automation preferences, see *Appendix B: Setting Preferences*.

The Thin Automation command lets you selectively thin areas in a track where automation data is too dense.

To use the Thin Automation command:

1. In the Edit window, click the Track View selector to display the automation parameter that you want to thin.

2. With the Selector, highlight the automation data that you want to thin.

3. Choose Edit > Thin Automation to thin the selected automation.

   The selected automation data is thinned by the amount set in the Degree of Thinning option in the Automation Preferences window.

THINNING AUTOMATION

MIXDOWN AND MASTERING

Now that you've built and shaped your mix to your liking (and, you hope the liking of others), just one mixing step remains: final mixdown. This is where you combine all tracks, edits, effects, and automation events into a final two-track stereo master.

There are two basic ways to save a final mixdown in Pro Tools: You can output the main stereo mix to a two-track digital or analog recording machine such as a DAT or 1/4-inch tape machine. Or, you can *bounce* the final mix directly to hard disk, where it's saved as a new audio file.

This chapter shows you how to perform a final mixdown using the latter method. We'll cover the correct method for bouncing, as well as how to configure bounce output options according to your needs. We've also thrown in a brief discussion of mastering, which will help you understand how individual mixes are processed to create a sonically consistent final album.

Bouncing to Disk

Pro Tools' Bounce to Disk command lets you mix down multiple tracks of audio (along with all DSP effects and automation events) directly to a stereo mix on your hard disk. In the process, a brand new file is created, which you can save to the location of your choice.

Bouncing to disk is a fast and efficient way to generate a final mix. Should you later decide that you don't like the mix, no big deal—just make the desired adjustments to the mix and bounce it to disk again...as many times as you like.

When you bounce to disk, Pro Tools plays the mix back in real time so you can hear it as it's being bounced. You can't, however, make any adjustments at this point.

Bounced mixes include the following:

Audible tracks: All audible tracks are included in the bounce, including soloed tracks or regions. Muted tracks are not included.

Automation: All read-enabled automation is played back and incorporated into the bounced mix.

Inserts and sends: All active inserts (including real-time plug-ins and hardware inserts) and sends are applied to the bounced mix.

Selection or track length: If you make a selection in a track, only the selected area of the session will be bounced to disk. If no selection is made, the bounce will be the length of the longest audible track in the session.

Figure 17.1 If you want to include a track's automation in the bounced mix, set the track's automation mode to Read.

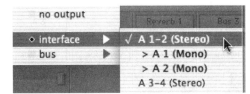

Figure 17.2 Assign the output of each track that you want to include in the bounce to the main mix outputs.

Time stamp information: Bounced material is automatically time-stamped so you can drag it to the same track location as in the original material.

Delay compensation: Pro Tools compensates for any bus delays due to a bounce. This means that if you import a bounced file back into a session and place it directly in time against the source mix, it will be phase accurate with the original source mix.

To bounce a final mix to disk:

1. Finalize all output levels and mix automation.

2. If you want to include a track's automation in the bounced mix, set the track's automation mode to Read (**Figure 17.1**).

3. Make sure that all of the tracks you want to include in the bounce are audible (not muted or inactive).

4. Assign the output of each track that you want to include in the bounce to the main mix outputs (**Figure 17.2**).

5. Do one of the following:

    To bounce a portion of a file, link Edit and Timeline selections. Select the portion of the file that you want to include in the bounce.

    or

    To bounce the entire session, don't make any selections. Press Return (Macintosh) or Enter (Windows) to go to the beginning of the session. The bounce will be the length of the longest audible track in the session.

continues on next page

BOUNCING TO DISK

6. Select File > Bounce to > Disk
(**Figure 17.3**).

The Bounce dialog box appears
(**Figure 17.4**).

7. Choose a Bounce Source option to set
the audio source for the bounced mix
(**Figure 17.5**).

8. Configure other Bounce options as
needed.

For detailed information on Bounce
options, see *Setting Bounce Options* later
in this chapter.

9. Click Bounce.

10. Select a destination for the new audio
file, enter a name, and click Save.

Pro Tools bounces the mix in real time and
performs Bounce option processing tasks.

Figure 17.3 Select File > Bounce
to > Disk.

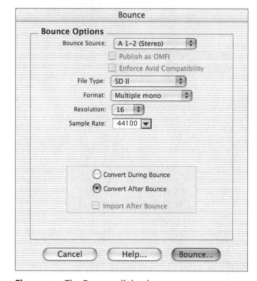

Figure 17.4 The Bounce dialog box.

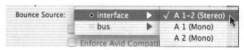

Figure 17.5 The Bounce Source option lets you choose
the audio source for the bounced mix.

BOUNCING TO DISK

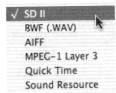

Figure 17.6 The File Type option lets you select a file type for the bounced mix.

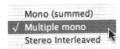

Figure 17.7 The Format option lets you select the number of channels that a bounced file has.

Setting Bounce Options

The Bounce to Disk command provides several options for converting and processing bounced tracks:

Bounce Source: The Bounce Source option lets you choose the main output or bus path that supplies the audio source for the mix. All currently active paths (as defined in the I/O Setup) are available as the Bounce Source.

File Type: The File Type option (**Figure 17.6**) lets you select a file type for the bounced mix. Choose from the following:

◆ SDII (Sound Designer II)

◆ BWF (.WAV) (Broadcast .WAV Format)

◆ AIFF (Audio Interchange File Format)

◆ MP3 (MPEG-1 Layer 3)

◆ QuickTime

◆ Sound Resource (Macintosh only)

◆ Windows Media (.asf, .wma, or .swmv file extensions) (Windows only)

Format: The Format option (**Figure 17.7**) lets you select the number of channels that a bounced file has. Choose from these file formats:

◆ **Mono (summed):** This format combines mix elements to create a single mono disk file.

◆ **Multiple mono:** This format creates the same number of mono files as the source path. For example, if the source is stereo, Multiple mono creates two mono files appended with ".L" (left) and ".R" (right) suffixes.

◆ **Stereo interleaved:** This format creates a single stereo interleaved file containing all of the bounced mix elements.

Resolution (or bit depth): The Resolution selector (**Figure 17.8**) lets you choose the bit depth of the bounced file:

Figure 17.8 The Resolution option lets you choose the bit depth of the bounced file.

- ◆ **8-bit:** Some multimedia applications and dialogue-only recordings still use 8-bit resolution. Use this setting only if high-quality audio is not required.

- ◆ **16-bit:** This is the standard resolution for audio CDs.

- ◆ **24-bit:** Use this setting when you want to maintain the highest possible sound quality. The setting is also good for archiving master stereo mixdowns for future use.

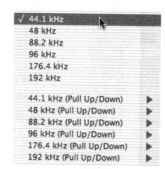

Figure 17.9 Choose a sample rate for the bounced mix.

Sample rate: You can convert bounced files to several sample rates. Generally, the higher the sample rate, the better the audio quality. There may be times, however, when smaller file size takes precedence over audio quality.

You can convert bounced files to the following sample rates (**Figure 17.9**):

- ◆ 44.1 kHz

- ◆ 48 kHz

- ◆ 88.2 kHz

- ◆ 96 kHz

- ◆ 176.4 kHz

- ◆ 192 kHz

- ◆ Custom sample rate

- ◆ Pull Up/Down sample rates

SETTING BOUNCE OPTIONS

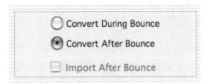

Figure 17.10 Choose a conversion quality setting for your bounced mix.

Figure 17.11 Select Convert After Bounce for more plug-in automation accuracy. Select Convert During Bounce for faster conversion, but less accuracy.

To set sample rate conversion quality:

◆ Choose Setup > Preferences. In the Editing preferences window, select from the Conversion Quality pop-up menu (**Figure 17.10**). Generally, the higher the conversion quality, the longer it takes for Pro Tools to convert the sample rate. Choose from five conversion quality settings: Low (Fastest), Good, Better, Best, and TweakHead (Slowest).

Convert During or After Bounce: Pro Tools can process bounce options either during or after the bounce. Select Convert After Bounce (**Figure 17.11**) for the highest level of plug-in automation accuracy. Select Convert During Bounce for faster conversion, but less accuracy.

Import After Bounce: The Import After Bounce option automatically imports a newly bounced file into the current session's Audio Regions list. This option applies only when you're using the Bounce to Disk command to create submixes for use within the current session.

Mastering Basics

Mastering is the point at which you prepare your mixes for duplication. It's also when you stop thinking about individual mixes and start thinking about how your mixes sound as a group.

Mastering usually involves optimizing dynamics and tonal balance, as well as matching the volume levels of all of your songs. Thus, EQ, compression, limiting, and other effects processing are frequently applied during this step.

If you're mastering mixes for an album release, we strongly recommend hiring a professional mastering engineer. A good mastering engineer has the ears, the experience, the right gear, and perhaps most important, the perspective (usually in short supply at the end of a recording process) to make your mixes sound good together. You'll be amazed how much better your mixes can sound after being professionally mastered.

Some of the basic steps involved in mastering include:

Song sequencing: Placing your songs in a sequence that flows is crucial to the listening experience. Think of a sequence theatrically, as if you're taking listeners on a sort of musical odyssey. Be aware of how different rhythms, lyrics, textures, and fade-ins and fade-outs affect the mood. Begin with tracks that draw listeners in. Then take them through different moods and emotions as you move toward a musical and thematic climax.

Equalization: EQ is often used in mastering to help balance frequencies within the aural spectrum. Most good mixes are mastered with relatively flat EQ across the frequency spectrum, with some roll-off at the very top and bottom. Listen carefully to the tonal balance of your songs. If you hear any frequencies that sound too loud or soft, you may want to try gently cutting or boosting them. Keep in mind, however, that if a particular instrument is too loud, you can't individually EQ it without affecting the entire mix. Thus, you may need to return to the mixing stage to correct it.

Compression and limiting: Dynamic effects, such as compression and limiting, are sometimes used in mastering to reduce transient volume peaks and boost a track's overall volume. Be careful not to overuse these effects: A touch of compression or limiting gives a track a nice volume boost while retaining clarity and dynamic range. But too much compression or limiting diminishes dynamic range and contrast, making a mix sound thin, dull, and flat. If you want to bring out individual instruments in a mix, consider using a multiband compressor, which compresses only specific frequency ranges. For more information on dynamic effects, see *Chapter 15: Adding Effects to a Mix*.

Balancing levels: After you EQ and optimize the dynamics of each song, make sure the relative volume levels of your mixes are similar. This will keep listeners from having to make repeated trips to the volume knob. To balance levels, simply listen to your tracks and compare their volumes. If you hear any noticeable differences, just turn their levels up or down until they're roughly the same.

Dither and noise shaping: Dither is a form of random noise that helps minimize *quantization distortion* in digital recordings. Quantization distortion is noise that occurs as a result of errors introduced when sampling low-level audio signals, or when digital audio is converted from higher to lower bit depths (such as when converting 24-bit audio to 16-bit for CD mastering). The DigiRack Dither and POWr Dither plug-ins use *noise shaping* to further reduce noise. Noise shaping uses digital filters to move noise from audible frequencies to less-audible frequencies. To use dither in Pro Tools, insert a Dither plug-in on the main mix's master fader.

Part VI:
MIDI Sequencing

18

RECORDING MIDI

This chapter helps you to record MIDI into Pro Tools. You'll learn how to set up MIDI interfaces and devices so Pro Tools can use them, and how to select inputs and outputs for MIDI tracks. Next, you'll learn how to record single and multiple MIDI tracks into Pro Tools, and how to punch record MIDI. We'll also cover two types of loop recording as well as how to import and export MIDI files to exchange data with other programs.

What Is MIDI?

The MIDI (Musical Instrument Digital Interface) communication protocol was originally designed to allow synthesizers created by different manufacturers to communicate with each other. MIDI became the glue that held together multiple keyboard and sound module setups. From very early in the computer music era, it also served as the protocol between computers and keyboards. Today, MIDI is most commonly used to record and play parts performed on a keyboard to trigger sounds in a synthesizer.

You can also use MIDI to:

◆ Send time code for synchronization

◆ Send Beat Clock information so all synthesizers receive the same tempo

◆ Modify parameters in synthesizers, samplers, and effects via controller information

◆ Send program and patch change commands to recall sounds and settings in external boxes.

MIDI terms

The following are some common terms relating to MIDI equipment and software.

MIDI channels: Each MIDI cable is capable of sending and receiving data on up to 16 channels. Each channel is generally reserved for a different instrument sound. For example, channel 10 is often reserved for drum sounds.

MIDI interface: A MIDI interface is a hardware device that connects to a computer to send and receive MIDI. MIDI interfaces can be simple devices that have 16 channels of MIDI send and receive, or complex devices that move hundreds of channels of MIDI to and from a computer. Many MIDI interfaces use USB connections, which provide self-powering (no AC connection required) and faster data transfer.

Controller: A controller is any device that's used to send MIDI without necessarily making a sound on its own. A keyboard controller, for example, can be used to trigger drum sounds in a sampler. As another example, a wind controller mimics the playing technique of a reed instrument but is connected via MIDI to control the sounds of another MIDI sound generator.

Sampler: A sampler is a sound generator that takes individual sounds, or *samples*, and plays them back when triggered by a MIDI note. Many samplers can be used to both mimic real instruments, such as a piano, and to radically modify sounds in creative ways. Samplers are often used to trigger loops as well.

Synthesizer: A synthesizer is an electronic instrument used to make sounds. There are many different kinds of synthesizers and different methods for synthesizing sounds, including analog, sample playback, wavetable, granular, physical modeling, and virtual analog synthesis.

MIDI keyboard: A MIDI keyboard is a device with piano- or organ-style keys that sends MIDI information when played. Keyboards often include onboard sounds in a synthesizer or sampler. In such cases, they can be used to play back the internal sounds as a synthesizer or as a MIDI controller for other instruments.

Sound module: A sound module is a MIDI synthesizer without a keyboard. A module can include any of the capabilities of a synthesizer but must be triggered by an external MIDI device to make sounds.

Sequencer: A sequencer is a recorder that records MIDI instead of audio. Sequencers can be hardware devices or computer programs that are used to record, edit, and play back MIDI data. Sequencers can work with not only MIDI notes but controller and sysex (system exclusive) data as well.

Keyboard workstation: A keyboard workstation is a keyboard that includes an onboard synthesizer, sequencer, and effects, and often, a sampler. Originally conceived as "one-stop shopping" for full audio production, keyboard workstations are more often used today as hot-rod controllers and for onstage performance.

Virtual instrument: A virtual instrument is a software version of an instrument, often a plug-in, that can be controlled with an external MIDI device. A virtual instrument might simulate an acoustic instrument or a hardware synthesizer, play samples, or be a completely original instrument.

WHAT IS MIDI?

The Difference Between MIDI and Audio

MIDI data is merely a set of instructions that tells any MIDI-compatible device what notes to play. MIDI data is represented in Pro Tools by a piano-roll style matrix of notes, or by a list of events, which can be converted into sound by a MIDI instrument such as a synthesizer. Audio data is a reproduction of actual sounds. Audio is represented in Pro Tools by a waveform.

MIDI offers several powerful advantages over audio. MIDI is a tempo-based protocol. Unlike an audio sample, a MIDI note is not recorded at a specific moment in time; rather, it's recorded at a particular bar and beat location (such as bar 34, beat 3, tick 117). This means that if you change the tempo or meter of a project, the tempo and meter of the MIDI tracks automatically change as well.

MIDI tracks are also much more pitch and sound independent than audio tracks. An audio file in a bass track, for example, will always play back exactly as it was recorded. A MIDI track, however, contains a series of separate events that the computer plays back at a certain time and place, according to your instructions, such as, "at bar 35, beat 1, send a C# out of port 3." With a few mouse clicks, you can make that C# play back a completely different sound on a different synthesizer. Or, you can transpose the note or copy it to a different track so it plays back two different sounds at the same time. This flexibility is part of the charm of MIDI: Because it's so easy to make changes, you can quickly try out different ideas.

While plenty of music is still made without MIDI or synthesizers, each year sees more MIDI in all stages of production. MIDI-based notation programs have become indispensable songwriting tools. Most dance, hip-hop, and techno music begins with a sequencer and MIDI. And as production techniques from styles like sampling and looping work their way into pop and rock productions, MIDI and sequencing are along for the ride. In addition, nearly all digital effects units have deep MIDI implementation, giving MIDI-savvy musicians new creative control regardless of the kind of music they make.

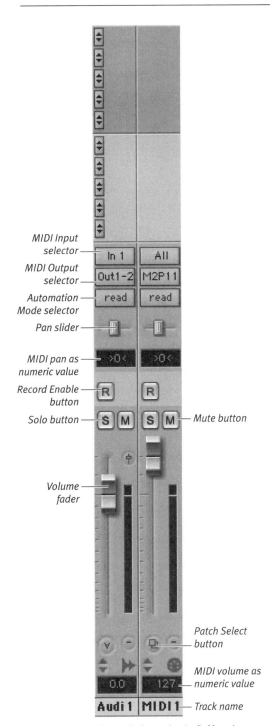

MIDI Input selector

MIDI Output selector

Automation Mode selector

Pan slider

MIDI pan as numeric value

Record Enable button

Solo button

Mute button

Volume fader

Patch Select button

MIDI volume as numeric value

Track name

Figure 18.1 An audio track channel strip (left) and MIDI track channel strip (right) in the Mix window.

MIDI in Pro Tools

Although MIDI and audio are quite different, working with MIDI in Pro Tools feels much like working with audio in Pro Tools. If you understand Pro Tools' audio features, you'll find the MIDI functions to be intuitive.

MIDI tracks

Like audio tracks, MIDI tracks are displayed in the Mix window as channel strips (**Figure 18.1**). Although both channel strips have a number of similar controls, such as solo, pan, and mute, MIDI track channel strips do have some differences. For example, MIDI tracks have no audio to send or bus, so their channel strips don't have controls for audio interface sends, RTAS plug-ins, or audio buses. Instead, MIDI track channel strips include controls for selecting MIDI inputs and outputs.

MIDI IN PRO TOOLS

Instrument tracks

An instrument track is a combination of a
MIDI track and an auxiliary input track
(**Figure 18.2**). An instrument track lets
you route MIDI input to virtual instrument
plug-ins inserted on the track, and route the
plug-in to the session's audio outputs. Before
Pro Tools 7, you needed a separate MIDI
track for the MIDI input and an auxiliary
input track for the plug-in output.

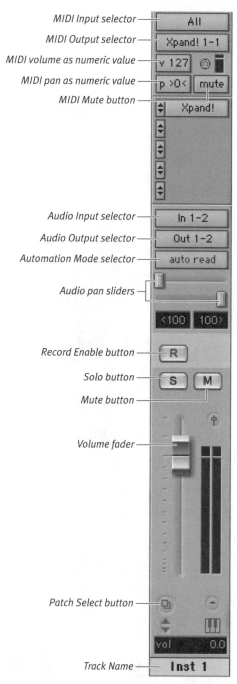

MIDI Input selector
MIDI Output selector
MIDI volume as numeric value
MIDI pan as numeric value
MIDI Mute button

Audio Input selector
Audio Output selector
Automation Mode selector

Audio pan sliders

Record Enable button
Solo button
Mute button

Volume fader

Patch Select button

Track Name

Figure 18.2 An instrument track channel strip in the
Mix window.

MIDI and instrument tracks in the Edit window

The Edit window displays MIDI and instrument tracks horizontally with MIDI notes running from left to right, sort of like a player piano roll (**Figure 18.3**). The buttons to the left of the tracks (**Figure 18.4**) serve many of the same functions as their audio track counterparts, such as the ability to resize, solo, mute, and name tracks.

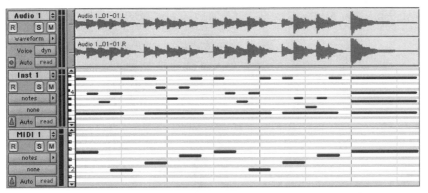

Figure 18.3 The Edit window displays audio tracks (top), instrument tracks (middle), and MIDI tracks (bottom) horizontally.

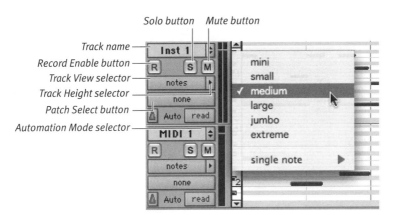

Figure 18.4 Track controls for MIDI and instrument tracks in the Edit window.

MIDI Event List

You can also view and edit MIDI data in the MIDI Event List. The MIDI Event List lets you make precise, numeric-based edits on all MIDI tracks data. In the MIDI Event List you can trigger notes by selecting them, and you can enter notes and other MIDI controller data using the MIDI Event List's Insert pop-up menu.

To open the Event List editor:

◆ Select Event > MIDI Event List, or press Option-Equal (Macintosh) or Alt-Equal (Windows).

The MIDI Event List window opens (**Figure 18.5**).

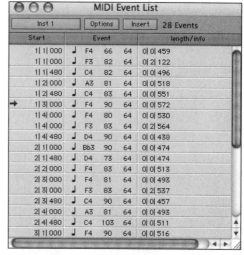

Figure 18.5 The MIDI Event List editor.

Figure 18.6 The Audio MIDI Setup window in Mac OS X.

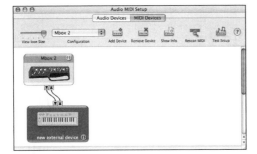

Figure 18.7 A configured MIDI device in Audio MIDI Setup.

MIDI Setup in Mac OS X

Mac OS X includes Apple's audio setup utility called Audio MIDI Setup (AMS), which automatically finds your audio and MIDI interfaces and devices (**Figure 18.6**).

Most MIDI interfaces and devices connect directly to the Mac through USB ports, and the interfaces do not require external power because the USB port supplies the power. That means you simply plug in the device and the Mac's Audio MIDI Setup detects the connection.

To set up a MIDI device on Mac OS X:

1. In Pro Tools, choose Setup > MIDI > MIDI Studio.

   The Audio MIDI Setup window opens.

2. In the Audio MIDI Setup window, click MIDI Devices. If the drivers are installed properly, connected MIDI interfaces or devices appear on the MIDI Devices page.

   If your MIDI device is a keyboard controller, it automatically appears as an input device for MIDI and instrument tracks, and your setup is complete.

   If your MIDI device is a MIDI interface (such as Mbox 2), you can add other devices that are connected to it.

3. Click Add Device.

4. Connect the new device to the MIDI interface by dragging a connection from the input and output of the interface icon to the output and input of the new device icon (**Figure 18.7**).

Once your device is in the MIDI setup, you can exit Audio MIDI Setup and begin recording MIDI into Pro Tools.

MIDI SETUP IN MAC OS X

MIDI Setup in Windows XP

Windows XP includes an application called MIDI Studio Setup (MSS), which lets you configure MIDI interfaces and devices connected to your system (**Figure 18.8**).

To set up a MIDI device in Windows XP:

1. In Pro Tools, choose Setup > MIDI > MIDI Studio.

   The MIDI Studio Setup window opens.

2. Click Create to add a new instrument.

3. Enter a name in the Instrument Name field.

4. Choose the Input Port and Output Port that you've used to connect your MIDI instrument (**Figure 18.9**).

5. Close the MIDI Studio Setup window.

Once your device is in the MIDI setup, you can exit MIDI Studio Setup and begin recording MIDI into Pro Tools.

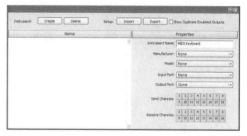

Figure 18.8 The MIDI Studio Setup window in Windows XP.

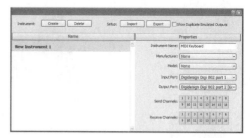

Figure 18.9 A configured MIDI device in MIDI Studio Setup.

Setting Up a MIDI Track

If you are controlling an external MIDI device or a softtware synthesizer application that can accept MIDI inputs, you'll record to a MIDI track in Pro Tools.

To add a MIDI track to your session:

1. Select Track > New, or press Shift-Command-N (Macintosh) or Shift-Control-N (Windows).

   The New Track dialog box appears.

2. Select MIDI Track from the pop-up menu (**Figure 18.10**).

3. Enter the number of tracks and click Create.

Figure 18.10 Create a new MIDI track.

Setting Up an Instrument Track

If you are using a virtual instrument plug-in, you can record to an Instrument track instead of a MIDI track.

To add an instrument track to your session:

1. Select Track > New, or press Shift-Command-N (Macintosh) or Shift-Control-N (Windows).

    The New Track dialog box appears.

2. Select Instrument Track from the pop-up menu (**Figure 18.11**).

3. Enter the number of tracks and click Create.

4. Choose View > Mix Window > Instruments to show the Instruments view in the track.

5. Click an Insert selector on the instrument track and choose an instrument plug-in. In this example, Digidesign's free Xpand! synthesizer plug-in is used.

The MIDI Output of the instrument track is automatically set to the instrument plug-in.

Figure 18.11 Create a new instrument track.

MIDI Input Enable

☑ MIDI Keyboard, Port 1
☑ Sound Module

Cancel   OK

Figure 18.12 In this window, two input devices are active.

Selecting MIDI Inputs

In order to record MIDI into Pro Tools, you must first enable your MIDI devices for input, and then select a particular channel on the device for recording.

To enable MIDI inputs for use with Pro Tools:

1. Select Setup > MIDI > Input Devices.
   The MIDI Input Device panel opens.

2. Select the check box next to each input device that you want to use, and click OK (**Figure 18.12**).

The devices that you selected are now available for recording MIDI into Pro Tools.

Once you enable a MIDI input, you must select an input source for each track that you will record.

To choose a MIDI input for a MIDI or instrument track:

1. In the Mix window, click the MIDI Input selector on the MIDI track (**Figure 18.13**) or instrument track (**Figure 18.14**) channel strip.

    The MIDI Input pop-up menu opens. You can use it to browse to any channel of any input in your MIDI studio.

2. Choose an input from a MIDI input device on the pop-up menu.

    The device becomes the input for the selected track.

✔ Tips

- Pro Tools has a unique MIDI Input setting called All. While many MIDI studios have a large number of MIDI devices that can send and receive on any of 16 channels, often only one device will really ever send MIDI. This device, called a master controller, is usually a keyboard or synthesizer that's used to play back all of the other MIDI equipment in the studio. Selecting All as the input is often the easiest way to select your master controller when no other devices are sending MIDI.

- Depending on how you want to route MIDI data in your studio, you might want to select Options > MIDI Thru. The MIDI Thru command echoes all incoming MIDI data back to the same device and channel from which it came. This is often the easiest way to set up MIDI, since parts will automatically trigger on the correct device and channel. MIDI Thru often works best with simple MIDI setups.

- If you use MIDI Thru, turn the local setting on your synthesizer to Off. This keeps you from hearing the same note twice—once when you press a key on your synthesizer and again when that same MIDI note is echoed by Pro Tools with MIDI Thru.

Figure 18.13 The MIDI Input selector on a MIDI track.

Figure 18.14 The MIDI Input selector on an instrument track (Instrument view).

Selecting MIDI Inputs

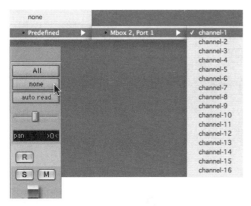

Figure 18.15 The MIDI Output selector pop-up menu lets you select where MIDI is sent out of Pro Tools.

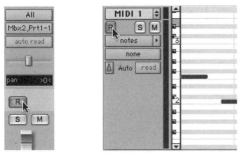

Figure 18.16 Click the Record Enable button in either the MIDI track channel strip (left) or the Edit window's Track controls (right) to monitor MIDI output.

Sending MIDI Out of Pro Tools

If you are using an external device to play back a MIDI track, you must select the output channel for that track to send MIDI to the device.

To send MIDI from Pro Tools to an external MIDI device:

1. In the Mix window, click the MIDI Output selector on the MIDI track channel strip.

   The MIDI Output pop-up menu displays the available outputs (**Figure 18.15**).

2. Choose the output to which you want to send MIDI information.

   The device becomes the output for the selected track.

✔ Tips

- If you send MIDI from Pro Tools to another device and the device sends it back to Pro Tools, a MIDI feedback loop can result—and it can sound nearly as awful as audio feedback. There are a number of ways to fix feedback loops, but this is one situation where you shouldn't use the All input setting mentioned earlier. If you're getting MIDI feedback loops, look carefully at things like MIDI Thru, local settings on your synthesizers, and general MIDI routing. Usually, you'll be able to find where the loop originated and fix it by changing input, output, or thru settings.

- Most sequencers assume that when a MIDI channel is active, it should be routing MIDI in and out of the program. Pro Tools, however, treats MIDI more like audio than most sequencers do: In order for a MIDI input to send to an output in Pro Tools, you must click the Record Enable button in either the MIDI track channel strip or in the Edit window's Track menu (**Figure 18.16**). Think of it like Record monitoring, but for MIDI.

Monitoring external MIDI instruments without a mixer

You can monitor an external MIDI instrument by connecting its audio output directly into the line-level inputs of your audio interface.

To monitor the audio output of your external MIDI device in Pro Tools:

1. Select Track > New, or press Shift-Command-N (Macintosh) or Shift-Control-N (Windows).

2. Create a mono or stereo auxiliary input track.

3. Click the input selector of the auxiliary input track, and choose the input to which your MIDI device audio output is connected (**Figure 18.17**).

4. Adjust the input level with the volume fader on the auxiliary input track.

5. To record the incoming signal, reassign the output of the auxiliary input channel to a bus and create an audio track whose input is assigned to the same bus.

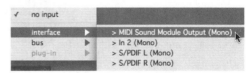

Figure 18.17 Click the Input selector of the auxiliary input track, and select the audio input for your external MIDI device.

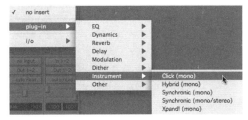

Figure 18.18 Insert the Click plug-in on the auxiliary input track.

Figure 18.19 The Click options determine when the click track is heard.

Creating a Click Track for Recording

Any time you are recording bar- and beat-based material, it's helpful to record with a click track. By recording to a click, your performance is more likely to line up with the beats, making it easier to edit and arrange later. Pro Tools makes it easy to set up a click track.

To set up a click track:

1. Select Track > New, or press Shift-Command-N (Macintosh) or Shift-Control-N (Windows).

2. Create a mono auxiliary input track.

3. Click an Insert selector on the track and choose the Click plug-in (**Figure 18.18**).

4. Select Options > Click to enable the click.

5. Click Play in the Transport window to start playback.

6. Adjust the click level with the volume fader on the auxiliary input track.

✔ Tip

- You can choose whether to play the click during playback, recording, or both by choosing Setup > Click and selecting from the available options (**Figure 18.19**).

Recording MIDI

After all of this configuring, clicking, and meandering about in Pro Tools, you can finally record MIDI onto your MIDI or instrument track.

✔ Tip

- Put Pro Tools in Non-Destructive Record mode (**Figure 18.20**) whenever you are recording MIDI. Although it doesn't directly affect MIDI, using Non-Destructive Record mode will prevent you from inadvertently messing up an audio track.

To record on a single MIDI or instrument track:

1. As described earlier, select a MIDI channel input in the Mix window to record, select the device and output, and then click the Record Enable button on the track.

2. Click the Record and Play buttons in the Transport window (**Figure 18.21**).

   Play your MIDI controller, synthesizer, or other MIDI data-generating equipment.

3. When you're finished recording, click Stop.

Figure 18.20 Be sure to deselect Destructive Record mode when you record MIDI.

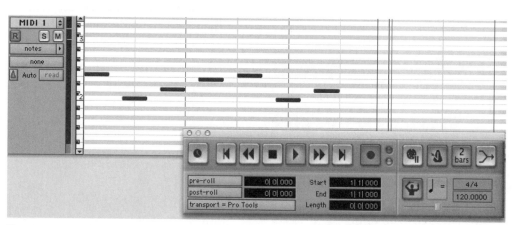

Figure 18.21 Recording on a MIDI track.

Figure 18.22 Don't panic! The All MIDI Notes Off command should make your gear stop squawking.

✔ Tip

■ If you wind up with a MIDI feedback loop, a stuck note in a synthesizer or sampler, or some other MIDI disaster, clicking Stop won't always fix the problem. Instead, choose Event > All MIDI Notes Off (**Figure 18.22**). This sends a command to all MIDI devices to immediately silence them.

Recording Multiple MIDI Tracks

While MIDI tracks are recorded individually more often than audio tracks are, sometimes it's necessary to track multiple MIDI tracks simultaneously—for instance, when you're recording more than one musician, when you're transferring parts from one sequencer to another, or when a keyboard is split so that it plays back on different channels on different parts of the keyboard.

Let's use the latter scenario as an example: The bottom two octaves of a keyboard are playing a bass sound on MIDI channel 1 while the right hand plays a keyboard sound on the top octaves transmitting on MIDI channel 2.

To record two MIDI tracks simultaneously:

1. Create two new MIDI tracks as described earlier.

2. Set the inputs to different MIDI channels. In this example, the first track records MIDI channel 1 of the controller, and the second track records MIDI channel 2 of the controller (**Figure 18.23**).

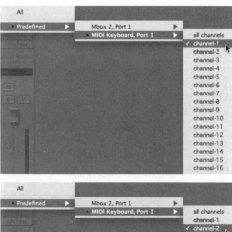

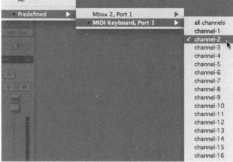

Figure 18.23 Select a different input for each MIDI track.

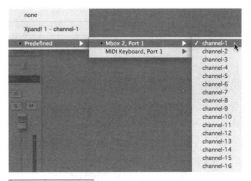

Figure 18.24 Set the MIDI outputs to play different sounds.

3. Send each MIDI channel output to a different device.

In this case, send the first track to channel 1 of the Mbox 2 MIDI out, and send the second track to the Xpand! virtual instrument plug-in (**Figure 18.24**).

4. Record-enable both tracks.

To record-enable multiple MIDI tracks, hold down the Shift key while clicking the Record Enable buttons on all of the channels you want to record.

5. In the Transport window, click the Record and Play buttons.

6. When you're finished recording, click Stop.

✔ Tips

■ Splitting inputs to their own tracks is also useful for keeping controller, MIDI automation, or other MIDI information on its own track. It's just easier to follow that way.

■ You can also record one input to two tracks. Why would you want to do this? Each track can trigger different sounds from the same notes by routing them to different synthesizers or different patches on the same synthesizer. For example, a single MIDI performance copied on multiple tracks can trigger an electric piano sound while also playing a string sound.

RECORDING MULTIPLE MIDI TRACKS

Punch-Recording MIDI

Punch-recording MIDI is similar to punch-recording audio. When punching MIDI, however, you use the MIDI Merge feature to determine how new MIDI data is recorded. You can turn this feature on and off with the MIDI Merge button, located in the Transport window (**Figure 18.25**).

How MIDI Merge works

When MIDI Merge is on, incoming MIDI data is *added* to the existing MIDI on the track. The existing recorded data remains unchanged. When MIDI Merge is off, incoming MIDI data *overwrites* the MIDI data on the track.

MIDI Merge is useful, for example, if you have a drum pattern that you like and want to record another kick drum in some places. On the other hand, turning MIDI Merge off is helpful if you have a drum track that you like overall, but you want to redo a bar or two.

To punch-record MIDI:

1. Create a new MIDI or instrument track, if necessary, and record-enable it.

   If you want to punch-record an existing track, record-enable that track.

2. With the Selection tool, select the section of the track where you want to record (**Figure 18.26**).

3. Set the MIDI Merge button to either On or Off.

MIDI Merge button

Figure 18.25 The MIDI Merge button is located on the right side of the Transport window.

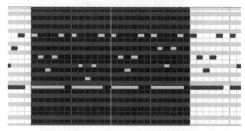

Figure 18.26 Select the part of the MIDI track that you want to punch-record.

4. Set the pre-roll amount in the Transport window and turn pre-roll on. Do the same for post-roll, if you'd like (**Figure 18.27**).

5. Click Record and then Play in the Transport window.

✔ Tips

■ To punch-record multiple MIDI tracks simultaneously, select all the tracks you want to punch and record-enable all of them. (The MIDI Merge setting applies to all punched tracks.) Remember to set the track inputs correctly.

■ Because MIDI is a tempo-based protocol, it's almost always best to work with it in Grid mode. Whether you're selecting, editing, moving, or recording MIDI tracks, stay in Grid mode unless there's a good reason to do otherwise.

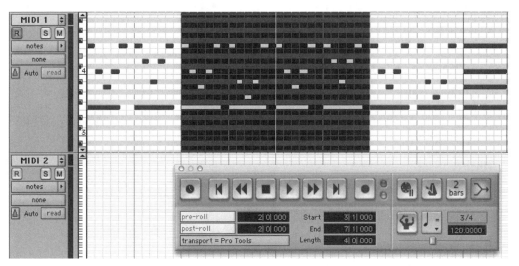

Figure 18.27 All set to punch. The track is record-enabled, four bars are selected, MIDI Merge is on, and pre- and post-roll are set to two bars.

Loop Recording MIDI

Pro Tools offers two distinct modes for loop recording MIDI. The first, called Loop Playback, lets you add individual parts or notes to a looped section, building a full MIDI part over many passes. This method is most commonly used to program drum parts. On the first pass, you record the kick drum; on the next pass, the snare; then the closed hi-hats; and finally, the open hi-hats on select beats. Looping in real time is an intuitive and creative way to program drum loops.

The second loop recording mode, called Loop Record, is more akin to the way Pro Tools is used to record audio in Loop mode. In Loop Record mode, the same section is looped, and each performance becomes its own MIDI region. This is generally used to work out parts or try new things. Because there's no need to start and stop the recording process, the creative juices can keep flowing, and you can retrieve the serendipitous events later. We'll cover both methods.

To build a part in Loop Playback mode:

1. Create a new MIDI or instrument track, or select an existing track in your session.

2. In the Edit window, select the bars to be looped with the Selection tool (**Figure 18.28**).

3. Record-enable the track either in the MIDI track channel strip or the Edit window, and select the MIDI input and output.

4. If you want to hear a lead in, set the pre-roll amount in the Transport window. Click the Pre-Roll button to activate it.

5. Select Options > Loop Playback to activate loop playback (**Figure 18.29**).

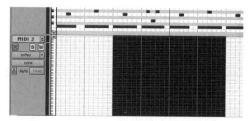

Figure 18.28 The selected bars will be loop-recorded. Note that record-enable is active.

Figure 18.29 To build a MIDI part by looping, activate Loop Playback in the Options menu.

LOOP RECORDING MIDI

Figure 18.30 The Transport window is set for loop-recording: MIDI Merge is on, the Play button displays the Loop Playback indicator, and pre-roll is set.

Figure 18.31 Activate Loop Record in the Options menu.

Figure 18.32 The Transport window set for loop-recording.

6. Click the MIDI Merge button to activate it (**Figure 18.30**).

   Each looped pass will add notes to the selected part in the MIDI track.

7. Click Record and then Play in the Transport window.

   You can now add new MIDI notes and other data with each pass.

8. When you're finished recording, click Stop.

To record multiple MIDI takes in Loop Record mode:

1. Create a new MIDI track or select an existing track in your session.

2. Select a section for the looped takes with the Selection tool.

3. Record-enable the track, and select inputs and outputs.

4. Turn pre-roll on and set the pre-roll amount in the Transport window, if you'd like.

5. Select Options > Loop Record to activate loop-recording (**Figure 18.31**).

   The Record button displays the Loop indicator (**Figure 18.32**).

6. Click Record and Play to begin tracking.

LOOP RECORDING MIDI

Each pass creates a new numbered MIDI region in the Regions list (**Figure 18.33**). (We'll cover MIDI regions more in *Chapter 19: Editing MIDI.*)

✔ Tips

■ You can move, edit, copy, or paste into the session any MIDI regions created by loop-recording. It edits like audio, but it's MIDI. It is very helpful to do this in the Edit window with your track view set to Regions. In Regions view, you can cut and copy regions aligned to your Grid (Grid mode), which is easier to manage than in the Notes view.

■ Because new MIDI regions are created with each loop in Loop Record mode, it's impossible to merge MIDI data; therefore, MIDI Merge is disabled in Loop Record mode.

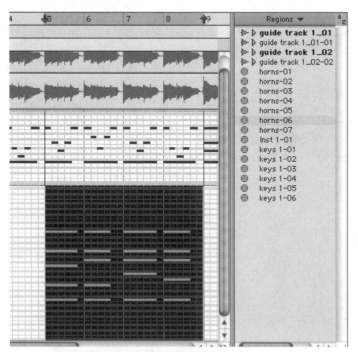

Figure 18.33 Each loop-recorded take is now in the MIDI Regions list. Take 6 has been dragged to the playlist and is selected.

Figure 18.34 Select Setup > MIDI > Input Filter.

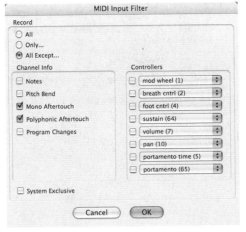

Figure 18.35 Confirm that sysex will not be filtered out and can be recorded.

Sysex Data and Pro Tools

Many MIDI parameters are defined in the MIDI protocol. Volume, for instance, is always on controller 7. Although this standardization can be helpful for various tasks, vendors can define MIDI events and meszThis specialized MIDI data is called system exclusive, or *sysex*, data.

Sysex has all manner of uses for those willing to deal with it. One of the more common uses is to do a sysex dump, in which a MIDI device sends all of its current settings as sysex data. After it's recorded into a Pro Tools session, the sysex data can be played back to the device to reset it to the correct state when you next work on that session.

To record sysex data into Pro Tools:

1. Create a new MIDI track or select the track in which you want to record the sysex data.

2. Select the correct input in the Mix window for the device that will be sending sysex data.

3. Record-enable the track.

4. Select Setup > MIDI > Input Filter (**Figure 18.34**).
   The MIDI Input Filter dialog box appears.

5. By default, Pro Tools allows sysex data to record.
   Confirm that the System Exclusive option is deselected in the dialog box, and then click OK to close it (**Figure 18.35**).

6. Click the Return to Zero button in the Transport window.
   Sysex is almost always used to set up a MIDI device. Sysex data should be at the beginning of a track.

continued on next page

7. Click Record and then Play to begin recording.

8. Initiate a sysex dump on the MIDI device.

9. Click Stop when the device is finished sending MIDI.

✔ Tips

- Sysex data does not automatically display in the track where it's recorded. Click the Track View pop-up menu and select sysex to see the data on the track (**Figure 18.36**).

- Every MIDI device has a different way of initiating a sysex dump. Many have a Vulcan Death Grip kind of thing where three buttons on different parts of the device have to be pushed at the same time. Many devices also have a command on their Global or MIDI menu. Check your device's manual.

- Part of the beauty of sysex is that it gets around the need for saving presets or writing down parameters for an effect or a synthesizer. You can take your project to a different studio with the same gear, drench the studio with sysex, and voila! The devices in the studio are now set up just like your home studio was when the sysex was recorded.

- Sysex data can be extremely dense, and not all MIDI devices and interfaces deal with it very well. If, after a few tries, sysex isn't recording correctly, you may need to resort to pencil and paper for parameter settings.

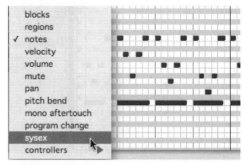

Figure 18.36 Setting a track to view sysex data is the only way to confirm that everything was recorded properly.

Figure 18.37 Select File > Import > MIDI to Track.

Figure 18.38 Choose which tempo to use and which tracks to keep in the current session.

Working with MIDI Files

At some time, you may need to work with another sequencer—perhaps to transfer a part written in a different program or on a keyboard workstation into Pro Tools. Or, you might need to move Pro Tools MIDI tracks into a live situation or export MIDI from a Pro Tools session into another program.

To do this, you need to use a Standard MIDI File (SMF). There are two kinds of SMFs: Type 0 and Type 1. Type 0 SMFs save all MIDI channel data from a session into one MIDI track. When imported, a Type 0 SMF shows up as a single MIDI track. Type 1 SMFs save each channel of MIDI data from a session to a separate MIDI track. When imported, a Type 1 SMF is "exploded" to individual MIDI tracks.

Type 1 SMFs are by far the more popular way to move MIDI files around, but Type 0 files can be more efficient in some cases. For example, some hardware sequencers work better with Type 0 SMF files.

To import a MIDI file to a session:

1. Select File > Import > MIDI to Track (**Figure 18.37**).

   A standard dialog box opens.

2. Navigate to the file that you want to import.

3. Click Open.

   The Import MIDI Settings dialog box opens.

4. Choose whether you want to use the tempo from the file you're about to import or use the tempo of the current Pro Tools session. Also, choose whether you want to keep or remove existing instrument tracks, MIDI tracks, and MIDI regions in the session (**Figure 18.38**).

continued on next page

WORKING WITH MIDI FILES

5. Click OK.

Pro Tools imports the MIDI file. If the file includes multiple tracks in a Type 1 SMF, each track will get its own MIDI track in the session. A MIDI region for each track appears in the Regions list.

6. Select the proper playback device and channel for each MIDI track in the Mix window.

✔ Tips

■ In some situations, you will not want to create new tracks for each track in a Type 1 SMF. For example, if you've created 32 drum patterns on a MIDI drum machine and want to try out a few of them, you can import a file directly to the Regions list without making a new track (**Figure 18.39**). After you import the file, you can drag the individual regions to tracks and edit them like any other MIDI region.

■ In Pro Tools 7, you can import MIDI files by dragging them from a DigiBase browser in the same ways you can import audio files: Drag MIDI files to an empty space in the Edit window to create new tracks or drag them into the Regions list to import them without creating new tracks.

■ As you import an SMF, it may require a little more effort to get it to play right. If you import an SMF with 16 instrument tracks, you'll need to reassign each track to the proper MIDI device and the proper patch (sound). It's a good idea to name the track with the sound and device/channel in the exporting program.

Figure 18.39 You can add a MIDI file to the Region list without creating a new track.

WORKING WITH MIDI FILES

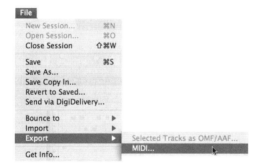

Figure 18.40 Select File > Export > MIDI.

Figure 18.41 Choose which type of SMF to export.

To export MIDI from Pro Tools:

1. Select File > Export > MIDI (**Figure 18.40**).
   A standard dialog box opens.

2. Name the file and navigate to the folder where you want to save it.

3. Select an SMF file option from the pop-up menu (**Figure 18.41**):

   Select 0 if you want to export the MIDI in your session as a single-track file.

   or

   Select 1 if you want to export the MIDI in your session as a multiple-track file.

4. Click Save.

✔ Tip

- It's a good idea to name the track to be exported with the sound and device/channel in Pro Tools. That way, the importing program will know how to assign the MIDI channel and sound.

Editing MIDI

If you're new to MIDI sequencing, Pro Tools MIDI may be all you'll ever need. If you're an experienced sequencing geek accustomed to another application, you'll still find a lot to work with in Pro Tools. Pro Tools 7 adds the ability to mirror MIDI edits in copied or looped MIDI regions and to edit a number of MIDI properties during playback.

In this chapter, you'll learn to edit MIDI to correct mistakes made with previously recorded MIDI tracks and to enter new tracks from scratch. We'll show you how to enter MIDI data manually and transform it directly in the Edit window. We'll also explore how the MIDI Operations tools can automatically edit MIDI data. Finally, we'll look at the MIDI Event List, which offers the deepest level of MIDI control in Pro Tools.

MIDI Regions

When you edit audio in Pro Tools, you must often create regions or move regions within a session. Editing MIDI also requires the use of regions. You can string MIDI regions together to form a playlist, just as you can when working with audio.

MIDI regions are displayed in the Regions list (**Figure 19.1**) along with audio regions and region groups. You can use this list to add regions to a session, as well as move and rename them.

To add a MIDI region to a MIDI track:

1. In the Regions list, select the MIDI region you want to add to the session.

2. Drag the region to the track where you want to play it (**Figure 19.2**).

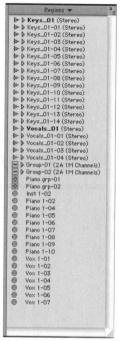

Figure 19.1 MIDI regions appear in the Regions list along with audio regions and region groups.

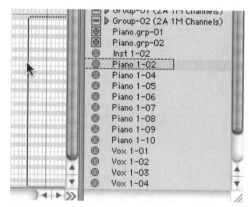

Figure 19.2 Drag a region from the Regions list to a MIDI track.

MIDI REGIONS

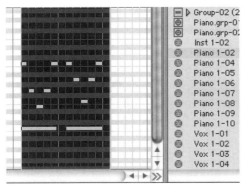

Figure 19.3 The MIDI region after it has been placed on the track.

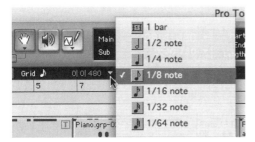

Figure 19.4 Clicking the arrow in the Grid Value field opens a pop-up menu, where you can set the Grid value.

The region is now visible and will play back at this location (**Figure 19.3**).

✔ Tip

- Many MIDI editing processes, including simple ones like moving regions, are most easily done in Grid mode. The Grid value, which determines the meter or time division to which edits will snap, affects how these editing processes behave. The Grid value is displayed at the top of the Edit window (**Figure 19.4**). Most grid-based editing for MIDI is best done in Bars & Beats mode to coincide with the musical performance.

Views for Editing MIDI

Pro Tools gives you many ways to view MIDI data. We'll cover a number of them in this chapter, but two views—the Regions view and the Notes view—merit special attention, since they do much more than just change the way a track looks.

Use the Track View pop-up menu in the Edit window (**Figure 19.5**) to select how you want to view a MIDI track.

Regions view

In Regions view, the MIDI region displays notes on a colored background (**Figure 19.6**). You can't edit single notes in Regions view; instead, regions are moved as a unit. Edits also automatically move MIDI data like MIDI controllers, sysex, and program changes. Use Regions view to move chunks of notes and data, for example, to copy a bar or group of bars to another place in a session.

The starting point of a MIDI note is important in Regions view. If a note starts before the region starts, it will not be included in cut, copy, and paste edits. This is true even if the note extends into the region. If a note starts in a region and extends outside of it, it will be included in cut, copy, and paste edits.

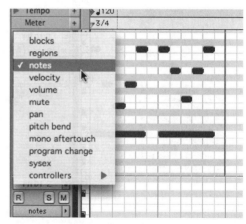

Figure 19.5 The Track View pop-up menu for a MIDI track. The Track view determines what's displayed in a MIDI track in the Edit window.

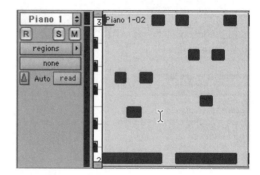

Figure 19.6 A MIDI track in Regions view.

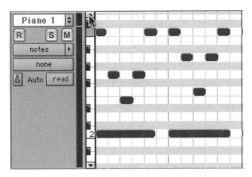

Figure 19.7 The same MIDI track in Notes view.

Notes view

The MIDI track shown in Figure 19.6 looks a bit different in Notes view (**Figure 19.7**). Here, you can add individual notes with the Pencil tool or move them with the Grabber tool. Notes view also lets you edit a group of notes or single notes for duration and timing.

Notes view is best for detailed editing of notes or other MIDI data. Use it to perform tasks like delete a bad note in a performance, copy just the snare part of a track to another measure, or draw a filter cutoff curve for a synthesizer patch.

For more information on MIDI track views, see the *Pro Tools Reference Guide.*

Mirrored MIDI Editing

Pro Tools 7 offers the option to use Mirrored MIDI Editing, which applies edits to all copies of a MIDI region with the same region name. If you are working with looped MIDI regions, you can use this option to edit one region and all other instances of the region in the session will update accordingly. If you are working with copies of a region and want your edits to apply to the current copy only, you should turn off Mirrored MIDI Editing.

To turn on Mirrored MIDI Editing:

◆ Select Options > Mirror MIDI Editing.

or

◆ Click the Mirrored MIDI Editing button in the upper left area of the Edit window (**Figure 19.8**).

When Mirrored MIDI Editing is on, the Mirrored MIDI Editing button flashes when any edit applies to more than one region in the session.

Figure 19.8 The Mirrored MIDI Editing button.

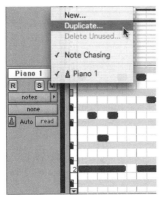

Figure 19.9 Select Duplicate from the Playlist selector pop-up menu.

Figure 19.10 Enter a name for the new MIDI playlist.

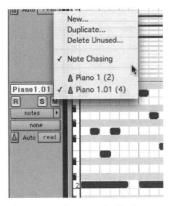

Figure 19.11 The new playlist is automatically chosen in the Playlist selector.

MIDI Playlists

Pro Tools derives a significant part of its audio editing power from the concept of a playlist. Quite sensibly, Pro Tools' MIDI implementation borrows extensively from this tool to manage MIDI parts and session arrangements.

Edits to MIDI data are not permanent until you choose to make them so. Original performances can always be restored until you feel confident that your edits are final. Then the new Flatten Performance command lets you lock the current state of selected MIDI notes.

To work on a copy of a playlist:

1. Click the Playlist selector to open its pop-up menu.

2. From the pop-up menu, select Duplicate (**Figure 19.9**).

   A dialog box opens.

3. Enter a name for the new playlist and click OK (**Figure 19.10**).

   The new playlist is automatically chosen in the track's Playlist selector (**Figure 19.11**).

You can do more with playlists than create copies of MIDI regions. All of the great things that you can do with audio playlists, such as try out different edits and arrangements and automation on a track, can also be done with MIDI playlists.

Pro Tools has a Restore Performance function, which lets you return to an original MIDI-based performance at any time. Working in this non-destructive manner, you can experiment unhindered with the assurance that you can always recover from adjustments made during the course of your project. Of course, if you've settled on changes, the Flatten Performance feature solidifies your edits and gives you a new, permanent basis from which to proceed. Once flattened, a MIDI performance can no longer be restored to its original state.

Entering and Deleting MIDI Notes Manually

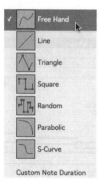

Figure 19.12 The Pencil tool pop-up menu.

Now that you've made a copy of your MIDI data, you can begin editing your MIDI track.

MIDI notes are usually recorded into Pro Tools via an instrument. If you miss or botch a note, however, it's often easier to manually enter the missed note or delete the mistake than it is to replay it on an instrument.

To enter a MIDI note manually:

1. If you're not in Notes view, select Notes from the Track View selector, as previously explained.

2. Click the Pencil tool to display the pop-up menu, and select Free Hand (**Figure 19.12**).

3. If necessary, zoom in to find the location on the track where you want to enter the note.

4. With the Pencil tool, click the location where you want to add a note (**Figure 19.13**).

   Pro Tools adds a new note at that location (**Figure 19.14**).

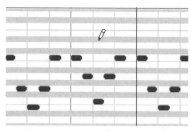

Figure 19.13 Clicking in a track with the Pencil tool adds a note at that location.

✔ Tips

- The Pencil tool allows you to trim MIDI notes and controller data. The Pencil tool has a Custom Note Duration command, which lets you define the note duration for inserting notes manually.

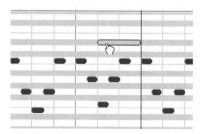

Figure 19.14 The new note is added, and the Pencil tool becomes the Grabber.

- The Grid value determines the location and duration of a manually entered MIDI note. The preceding example uses a Grid value of a quarter note; clicking on the track adds a quarter note at that location. If you set the Grid value to a sixteenth note, the Pencil tool will add a sixteenth note instead (**Figure 19.15**).

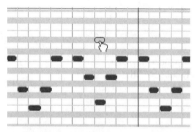

Figure 19.15 Clicking on the same location with the Pencil tool but with a different Grid value will enter a note of a different length.

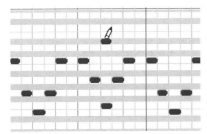

Figure 19.16 Press and hold Option (Macintosh) or Alt (Windows) and click with the Pencil tool to delete a single MIDI note.

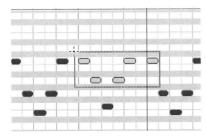

Figure 19.17 The Grabber tool drags over a group of MIDI notes.

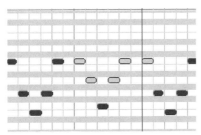

Figure 19.18 The selected notes are highlighted, whereas the unselected notes are still solid.

■ The Pencil tool's various modes enter notes differently. See the *Pro Tools Reference Guide* for more information.

To delete a single MIDI note manually:

1. Be sure you're in Notes view.

2. Select the Pencil tool.

3. Press and hold Option (Macintosh) or Alt (Windows) and position the Pencil tool over the note you want to delete.

   The Pencil turns upside down to indicate that it will erase notes.

4. Click with the upside-down Pencil tool to delete the note (**Figure 19.16**).

To delete a multiple MIDI notes manually:

1. Be sure you're in Notes view.

2. Select the Grabber tool.

3. Drag the Grabber over an area of the track to select all the notes in that area (**Figure 19.17**).

4. The selected notes are highlighted: Instead of appearing as a solid color, they are white with a colored outline (**Figure 19.18**).

5. Press the Delete or Backspace key to remove the selected notes.

Editing MIDI Notes Manually

You can use the Grabber tool to manually move, copy, and transpose MIDI notes. This is an easy way to fix minor timing problems or to copy notes to other parts of a session.

To copy MIDI notes manually:

1. If you're not in Notes view, select Notes from the Track View selector.

2. Using the Grabber tool, drag over an area of the track to select the notes to be copied.

3. Position the Grabber tool over any of the selected notes (**Figure 19.19**).

4. While pressing Shift-Option (Macintosh) or Shift-Ctrl (Windows), drag the MIDI notes to the new location.

   The Shift key keeps MIDI notes from changing pitch when you move them (more on this soon). The Option or Ctrl key copies the notes.

   The notes are copied and selected (**Figure 19.20**).

✔ Tips

- The preceding example was done in Slip mode. If the example was done in Grid mode with a half-note Grid value, the copied notes would snap to the nearest half note.

- To move notes without transposing them, press Shift while dragging them to the new desired location.

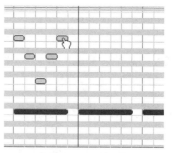

Figure 19.19 The Grabber tool is positioned to copy five notes. Dragging any individual note copies all selected notes.

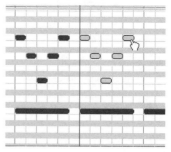

Figure 19.20 The copied notes (right) are selected after the edit is completed.

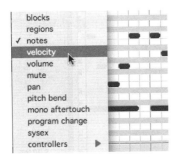

Figure 19.21 Choose velocity from the MIDI Track View selector pop-up menu.

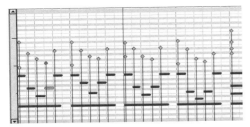

Figure 19.22 Notes and their velocity stalks. Taller stalks mean higher velocity, so the notes with the tallest stalks were struck the hardest.

Figure 19.23 Using the Grabber tool, click the diamond atop the velocity stalk.

Figure 19.24 The same stalk after its velocity has been reduced with the Grabber tool.

Editing MIDI Velocity

MIDI supports a wide variety of performance parameters. In addition to pitch and note duration, MIDI can transmit information like breath control for wind instruments; *aftertouch*, which simulates how much pressure is applied to a key after it's struck; and whether a keyboard's sustain pedal is pressed.

Another common MIDI parameter is *note velocity*. Although velocity can be used to modulate a wide range of parameters in a synthesizer, it's most often used as a volume control for individual notes. Editing velocity is a good example of how MIDI parameters other than pitch and duration work in Pro Tools.

To edit MIDI velocity for a note:

1. Click the Track View selector.

   From its pop-up menu, choose velocity (**Figure 19.21**).

2. Pro Tools displays the velocity of each note as a stalk. A diamond atop each stalk does double duty: It represents the velocity value for that note and acts as a handle that you can drag to edit the value (**Figure 19.22**).

3. Using the Grabber tool, click the diamond atop any of the velocity stalks.

   The stalk is selected and the diamond turns blue (**Figure 19.23**).

4. Drag the stalk to the desired velocity level (**Figure 19.24**).

✔ Tip

■ To edit multiple velocity stalks simultaneously, select a group of MIDI notes with the Grabber tool. All of the notes' velocity stalks will be selected. Dragging any individual stalk will modify all of them.

Editing velocity with the Pencil tool

When working with audio, the Pencil tool lets you perform extremely precise, sample-level edits. The Pencil tool is also useful for performing many types of automated MIDI edits, including velocity edits.

Let's use the Pencil tool to draw velocity for multiple notes—in this case, a volume swell.

To edit MIDI velocity with the Pencil tool:

1. Click the Track View selector.

   Select Velocity for the track you want to edit.

2. Velocity stalks appear for each note.

3. Click and hold the Pencil tool selector to view the pop-up menu.

   Select the Line tool from the pop-up menu (**Figure 19.25**).

4. On the MIDI track showing the velocity stalks, click a low velocity, and then drag to a higher velocity later in the track (**Figure 19.26**).

5. Release the mouse at the location where you want the velocity to reach its highest value.

✔ Tips

- You can use the Trimmer tool to trim MIDI note duration on MIDI tracks set to Velocity view.

- The Pencil Line tool is probably most often used to draw a velocity swell for a sixteenth-note snare fill in a dance tune. You can also use it to fade sounds in and out or to gently modify the volume of part of a drum track.

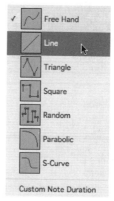

Figure 19.25 Select the Line tool from the Pencil tool pop-up menu.

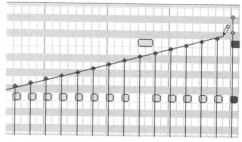

Figure 19.26 Use the Pencil tool in Line mode to draw velocity for multiple notes.

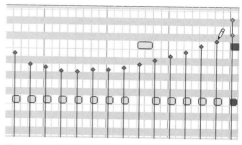

Figure 19.27 The Pencil tool in Free Hand mode lets you draw a softer velocity curve.

- Other tools also work well with velocity. For example, the Pencil tool in Free Hand mode makes it easy to draw the velocity curve in **Figure 19.27**.

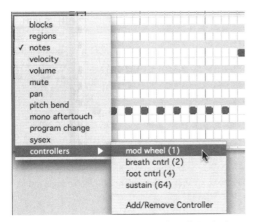

Figure 19.28 Select the Mod Wheel for editing in the Track View selector.

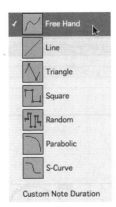

Figure 19.29 Use the Pencil tool in Free Hand mode to custom-draw controller curves.

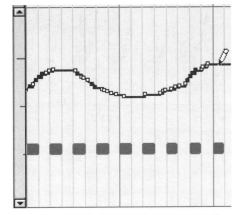

Figure 19.30 Pro Tools creates breakpoints for the curve drawn with the Pencil tool.

Editing MIDI Controller Data

MIDI's designers were smart enough to realize that synthesizers would use more than one kind of data to make sounds. Many parameters were predefined as MIDI Continuous Controllers (CCs), and nearly all devices adhere to the MIDI specification for defining controllers. For example, the Mod Wheel on a keyboard sends CC 1.

Pro Tools records CC information along with MIDI notes. Once CC data is on a MIDI track, you can edit it with the same tools used to edit velocity. In addition, you can enter completely new CC data with the Pencil tool.

In this example, you'll enter a curve for CC 1 on a keyboard part. One use for this would be if CC 1 on the synthesizer were set to change the cutoff point of a filter or the feedback on a delay.

To edit CC data with the Pencil tool:

1. Click the Track View selector, and select Controllers > Mod Wheel (1) (**Figure 19.28**).

2. Click and hold the Pencil tool to open the pop-up menu.

3. Select Free Hand mode (**Figure 19.29**).

4. Click and draw on the track to enter the CC data.

   The closer you draw to the top of the track, the higher the CC value will be.

When you've finished, Pro Tools creates *breakpoints* for the curve that you've just drawn (**Figure 19.30**). Breakpoints mark changes in MIDI data and can be grabbed for further editing.

The Pencil tool's other modes make drawing certain common shapes much easier.

To edit MIDI with other Pencil modes:

1. Click the Track View selector and select CC 1, as explained previously.

2. In the Pencil tool pop-up menu, select a different mode.

   For this example, select the Triangle mode.

3. Click in the track at the point where you want the center of the controller data to be.

4. Drag to horizontally define the number of bars and beats where you want to enter the CC data (**Figure 19.31**).

   In this case, click on the leftmost corner of the track and drag to the right.

5. Drag vertically to increase or decrease the degree of change that the Triangle mode creates (**Figure 19.32**).

6. Release the mouse when the CC data appears as you want it.

   Pro Tools draws the correct breakpoints (**Figure 19.33**).

✔ Tips

- The Grid value is very important for entering CC data with the Pencil tool and its various modes. The Triangle and Square modes, for example, change the density of their shape according to the Grid value.

- Since there's a Square wave and a Sawtooth wave Pencil tool, MIDI geeks may wonder where the Sine Pencil tool is. There isn't one—you'll have to draw carefully in Free Hand mode or enter data with something like the Mod Wheel on a keyboard.

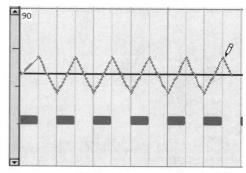

Figure 19.31 Drag with the Pencil tool in Triangle mode.

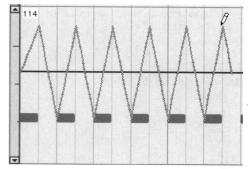

Figure 19.32 Dragging vertically increases the depth of the triangle.

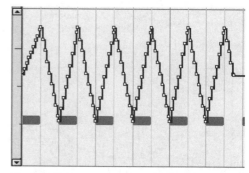

Figure 19.33 Pro Tools draws the breakpoints after you drag in Triangle mode.

- To get more mileage out of your MIDI-aware digital effects box, learn its MIDI parameters and modulate them with CC messages. You can vary sounds from subtle to dramatic by creating controller data with the Pencil tool in Square and Triangle wave mode, and then having that data modulate parameters like delay feedback, filter frequencies, EQ settings, and reverb. In Grid mode, you can even use these tools to automatically create tempo-synchronized modulations.

- These examples only scratch the surface of what you can do with CC editing. See the *Pro Tools Reference Guide* for more information.

Using Pro Tools MIDI Operations

Most of the editing you've done so far has been fairly simple manual additions, deletions, or modifications to MIDI data. Pro Tools can also automatically perform more complex edits on MIDI data via *MIDI operations*. These functions, located in the MIDI Operations window, modify data offline. In other words, after you select a group of MIDI notes (or an entire track), Pro Tools modifies parameters such as timing, note length, and pitch for the entire selection or track. The MIDI Operations window floats over other Pro Tools windows, which helps make MIDI recording and editing faster and more efficient.

Covering all the ways you can use MIDI Operations is beyond the scope of this book, but some basic rules apply. We'll use a common MIDI operation called *quantizing* to show how MIDI operations work in Pro Tools. Quantizing is the process of automatically changing the timing of a group of MIDI notes. You can use it to either tighten up the timing of sloppy playing or to add a certain rhythmic feel to notes that were not played as desired.

To quantize MIDI in Pro Tools:

1. Select the notes that you want to quantize.

   In this example, you'll tighten up the timing of the hi hats in a drum part. By zooming in closely and setting the Grid value to eighth notes, you can see that the hi hats vary quite a bit. Use the Grabber tool to select only the hi hat (**Figure 19.34**).

2. Select Event > MIDI > Grid/Groove Quantize.

   The MIDI Operations dialog box opens; Grid/Groove Quantize is already selected (**Figure 19.35**).

3. For this example, accept most of the default Quantize parameters (**Figure 19.36**):

   Leave Attacks checked, because you want to quantize according to the start of the notes.

   Leave "Preserve note duration" checked. This will keep the note length as is.

   Choose 1/8 note (eighth note) from the pop-up menu to set quantizing on an eighth-note grid.

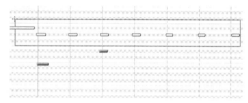

Figure 19.34 The hi hat notes selected on an eighth-note grid. Note that the kick and snare notes are not selected and will not be quantized.

Figure 19.35 The MIDI Operations dialog box with Quantize selected.

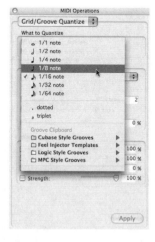

Figure 19.36 Choosing 1/8 note will snap the selected notes to an eighth-note grid.

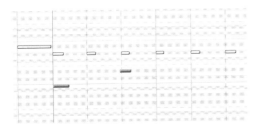

Figure 19.37 The hi hat notes have all been moved to fall exactly on an eighth note, but the kick and snare remain unchanged.

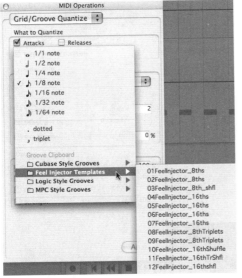

Figure 19.38 Groove Quantize options in the MIDI Operations window.

4. Click the Apply button.

Pro Tools moves the selected notes to the nearest eighth note (**Figure 19.37**).

MIDI Operations use the same methods to transpose, change velocity, shorten or lengthen, split, and select MIDI notes. See the *Pro Tools Reference Guide* for more information about editing with MIDI Operations.

✔ Tips

■ Quantizing affects only the selected notes; other notes on the track remain unchanged. This is helpful for changing the timing on only one part of a drum track.

■ Quantizing can make a part sound extremely exact and robotic. Sometimes this is the desired effect, but if it's not, you can modify both the degree to which a note is quantized and the rules that are used to select notes for quantizing. See the Pro Tools Reference Guide for more information.

■ Pro Tools allows numerous different Groove Quantize models (**Figure 19.38**). This allows any performance to be modeled after rhythm templates that have been created by other programs, such as Logic Audio or Cubase, or after the MPC drum machine patterns.

Another option unique to Pro Tools is Digidesign's Feel Injector templates. These various groove quantizers add feel to shuffle, swing, and straight quantization, making for much less robotic-like quantizations of your performance.

Using MIDI Real-Time Properties

Pro Tools 7 lets you edit certain properties of MIDI data and audition their effects in real time during playback. This feature makes it easy to try out changes while playing through or looping a passage but without committing the edits. You can then choose whether you want to apply the real-time changes to the MIDI data after auditioning them.

These *MIDI Real-Time Properties* can be enabled for editing on an entire track or on individual selections or regions using the Real-Time Properties window. The Real-Time Properties window is another floating window that helps speed up MIDI editing.

We'll show one of the uses of MIDI Real-Time Properties with MIDI Velocity as an example. Other MIDI properties that can be adjusted in real time include quantization, duration, delay, and transposition.

To audition MIDI Real-Time Properties for velocity:

1. Select a MIDI or instrument track whose MIDI velocity you want to adjust in real time.

   or

   Select a region in a MIDI or instrument track where you want to adjust MIDI velocity in real time.

2. Select Event > MIDI Real-Time Properties.

   The Real-Time Properties window appears (**Figure 19.39**).

3. Click the Velocity button to activate Velocity Real-Time Properties.

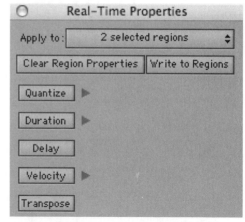

Figure 19.39 The Real-Time Properties window.

USING MIDI REAL-TIME PROPERTIES

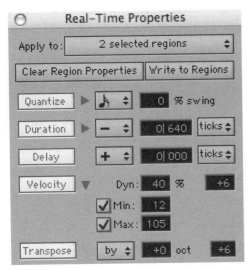

Figure 19.40 Expanded Velocity settings in the Real-Time Properties window.

4. Click the triangle next to Velocity to display the expanded Velocity settings (**Figure 19.40**).

5. Start playback.

6. Enter values in the value fields and press Return (Macintosh) or Enter (Windows) to change MIDI velocity by doing any of these:

   Enter a percentage in the Dynamics field to adjust velocities relative to a median value of 64.

   Enter a value to add or subtract a fixed amount to velocities.

   Enter minimum or maximum value for velocities.

7. Click the Velocity button on and off to audition the effect of the change in Real-Time Properties.

8. When you have arrived at the sound you want, click the Write to Regions or Write to Track button in the Real-Time Properties window.

✔ Tips

■ If you are working with regions in a track, you can enable Loop Playback to audition changes to Real-Time Properties while the selected regions are looping.

■ Before they are applied, changes in MIDI Real-Time Properties are heard during playback, but by default they are not shown in the MIDI data in the Edit window. You can enable the "Display Events As Modified by Real-Time Properties" option in the MIDI Preferences to update the display of MIDI data to reflect real-time changes.

USING MIDI REAL-TIME PROPERTIES

The MIDI Event List

The MIDI Event List displays every last bit of MIDI data for a selected region or track, letting you view and edit nearly any MIDI event in a session. Although it may not be the easiest or most intuitive MIDI feature, it can't be beat for precision and control.

The following example inserts a program change message at a particular point in a song to change the drum loop from mono under the verse to stereo for the chorus. The sampler is set so that patch 10 has a kit mixed to mono, and patch 11 is the same kit mixed to stereo. You can use the Event list to change the patch in the sampler at precisely the right time.

To send a patch change with the MIDI Event List:

1. In the Track View selector for the MIDI track, select Notes view.

2. Find the location in the track where you want to send the patch change.

   For this example, send the change at bar 21, beat 1.

3. With the Grabber tool, select the first note in this bar (**Figure 19.41**).

4. Select Event > MIDI Event List.

   The MIDI Event List window opens. The selected note is highlighted, and an arrow next to the nearest MIDI event indicates the cursor position (**Figure 19.42**).

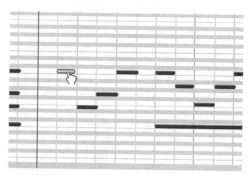

Figure 19.41 With the Grabber tool, select the first note in the bar.

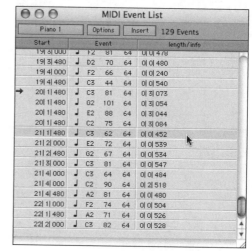

Figure 19.42 The selected note is highlighted in the MIDI Event List; the arrow indicates the cursor's location.

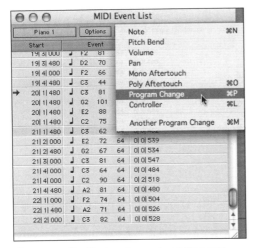

Figure 19.43 Use the Insert menu to create a new program change event.

Figure 19.44 The new MIDI event is at the top of the MIDI Event List window, where you can edit it.

Figure 19.45 Change the timing of the event to 21|1|000.

5. On the Insert menu, select Program Change (**Figure 19.43**).

   This creates the MIDI event at the top of the MIDI Event List, but Pro Tools does not put the event in the list (**Figure 19.44**). You still need to change a few parameters.

6. You want the program change to occur a bit before the first note of the chorus.

   Double-click the last three numbers of the Bars:Beats number and change it to 000 (**Figure 19.45**).

   continues on next page

7. Click on the value under the length/info column, where the value is entered as None.

The Patch window opens.

8. Select patch 11 (**Figure 19.46**).

9. Click Done to close the Patch window.

This changes the event so that at 21|1|000, Pro Tools will send the patch change 11 to the selected device for this track (**Figure 19.47**).

10. Press the Return key (Macintosh) or Enter key (Windows).

The new MIDI event is added to the MIDI Event List (**Figure 19.48**).

You can use the MIDI Event List for much more than program changes. For more information, see the *Pro Tools Reference Guide*.

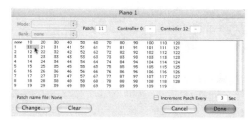

Figure 19.46 Select patch 11 to be sent as the program change.

Figure 19.47 The event is edited for the proper time and patch, and is ready to be entered in the Event List.

Figure 19.48 The new MIDI event is added to the MIDI Event List.

Part VII: Getting the Most from Pro Tools

PRO TOOLS FOR DIGITAL VIDEO

Pro Tools has become the digital audio workstation of choice for most film and television sound editors working today worldwide. Just as Pro Tools has led the way to high-end, low-cost audio production, we've seen an explosive growth of desktop video production.

The field of sound for video draws on all aspects of sound technique. Soundtracks today feature the human voice and naturalistic use of sound effects to create realism, as well as music and theatrical sound designed to underscore character, drama, pacing, and emotion.

In this chapter we'll give you a quick tour of the basics of setting up and using Pro Tools to edit and mix sound for video using a video deck or QuickTime digital video. We hope you'll find the information here helps you get started on your first soundtrack, and that some of the tips save you time and headaches on the way.

Preparing to Edit Sound for Video

Since you'll be working with at least one other piece of technology—the picture editing system—and usually at least one other person—the picture editor—it's critical to coordinate your technical setup and your work approach with them in mind.

The picture editor edits sound along with the visuals, and often will incorporate location dialog recordings, voice over, music, and sound effects. The principal goal in this phase of post production is to tell the story well with final decisions for all the picture edits in the project. These editing decisions made by the picture editor form the basic structure of the soundtrack, but a huge amount of work is left for the sound editor, such as smoothing dialog transitions, tweaking music edits, and selecting sound effects.

The technical process of working on the sound for video begins at the location. Location sound recordists work with a wide range of analog and digital tape and disk recorders. Or they may record the sound directly to the videotape. The technical specifications of the location recordings typically determine the sample rate and bit depth for your work in Pro Tools.

To obtain the best quality sound from your location recordings, you'll want to make a direct digital transfer from DAT (or other digital sources) into Pro Tools. Analog audio should be recorded into Pro Tools at the highest possible sample rate and bit depth. If the picture editor has taken care to digitize the location sound in the best possible way, then getting the audio via the OMF or AAF interchange formats (discussed later in this chapter) is the obvious answer.

Preparing to Edit Sound for Video:
Fundamental Technical Questions

Will you be working with an external videotape player or internal (digital) video?

This basic setup question will determine the type of equipment investment you make.

If you have access to a professional video deck with jog/shuttle wheel, fast and accurate locating, and a separate time-code track, working with a video deck can be a good experience. This approach also requires a time code-to-MIDI time code converter and some form of reference video and digital clock. We discuss the sync to videotape approach in the first section of this chapter after this introduction.

Digitized video in your digital audio workstation (DAW) is the most efficient way to achieve consistent, rapid, and accurate sync between Pro Tools and your picture. Working with digital video files requires a method of obtaining a digitized picture. The random access method of editing to QuickTime picture is discussed in the second section of this chapter.

How will you get the picture editor's sound into Pro Tools?

The third section of this chapter explores some ways you can match the audio in Pro Tools to the audio in the picture editor's video workstation (also known as a non-linear editing system, or NLE).

Use OMF (or AAF) whenever possible to get the sound from your picture editor. This assumes that the picture editor took the time to digitize the audio correctly. You will also need access to DigiTranslator (part of DV Toolkit 2).

If the sound in the NLE is good but OMF/AAF isn't an option, the edited sound from the NLE can be recorded or imported directly into Pro Tools and then further edited and embellished. When this option is used, it is important to maintain the full quality of the audio by using a digital transfer, highest quality analog transfer, or export/import as a full-quality rendered audio file or QuickTime export. There can be as many exported tracks as required.

Picture system sound quality can be compromised, usually by inferior interim stages (analog video) between the audio master and the picture editing system, or by bad analog transfer between the audio master and the NLE. When this happens, it is best to re-digitize and re-sync all the audio from the original recordings.

When going back to the original production sound, you can re-sync the audio by hand or by region by region, or you can use a third-party Edit Decision List (EDL) auto-conform program. In order to use an auto-conforming program, you'll need to get the time code from the recording into Pro Tools while you digitize the audio. So you'll need a third-party time code-to-MIDI time code converter. You'll also need an EDL from the picture editor, which may be hard to provide if the use of an EDL wasn't planned from the beginning of the post.

continues on next page

Preparing to Edit Sound for Video: Fundamental Technical Questions

(continued)

Remember, the results of manually re-syncing are at least as good as the other methods, and may be required in some cases. While it is extremely tedious and generally to be avoided, the techniques for accomplishing this are useful even when working with OMF or auto-conforming.

How was the original production sound recorded?

Check the quality of the original audio from the location and compare it to the audio you are given by the picture editor. If there is a perceptible difference, you may need to go back to the original recordings for best results.

Always load the location sound into Pro Tools in the best possible way. For digital recordings this means going into Pro Tools digitally, so you'll want to set your session up to match the settings used by the location recordist. Music and sound effects can be matched, too, or converted to the same specs.

If the recordings are analog, play back on a properly maintained machine, perhaps the same deck used to record on (or an equivalent device). Since you can't choose a bad sample rate or bit depth in Pro Tools, set your session up for compatibility with music and FX.

What are the specifications for the final product (deliverable tracks)?

Will you be delivering mono, stereo, discrete surround, or matrixed Dolby surround? Will the track be broadcast, played in a movie theater, on videotape, or on a DVD? Each of these options has different dynamic range, frequency response, and number of channels. You need to be aware of the delivery requirements of your format.

When multiple delivery options are to be used, work to the highest, most demanding spec, and mix down to the other versions after completing the main mix master.

Choosing a Sample Rate and Bit Depth for Your New Project

You need to select a sample rate and bit depth to work with your production sound. If you are working with OMF, your session's sample rate and bit depth will come from the picture editor's exported production sound.

When you load the digital audio that you recorded on location into Pro Tools, the session sample rate and bit depth must match the sample rate and bit depth of the recording. Recordings that do not match the session's parameters must be converted when imported into Pro Tools. For more information on importing and converting audio, see *Chapter 8: File Management Basics*.

If the location recordings are analog, you can select the session parameters that are most convenient for your project.

For more information on choosing sample rate and bit depth in a new session, see *Chapter 4: Starting a New Session*.

Synchronization Basics: Position and Clock Concepts

There are two basic requirements for separate devices to play in sync and stay in sync indefinitely: they need to start in the same place and run at the same speed.

One device, the master, starts to play and sends out a time code signal with its position. Another device, the slave, listens for time code from the master and locates to the position indicated, catching up to the master, and then playing.

Once the devices are playing, they will stay in sync if they play at exactly the same speed. This can be ensured by using a common clock reference for both devices.

Getting time code and clock from a video or audiotape deck into Pro Tools LE requires some additional equipment, which is described later.

For more information on synchronization concepts, see *the Pro Tools Sync & Surround Concepts Guide (a PDF file that is installed with Pro Tools)*.

Head and tail leaders

Always use head and tail video countdown leaders with sync beeps for easy sync checking. Since you can't add these onto the picture after you receive it you'll need to insist that the picture editor provide them for you. The key thing is that there is a visible and audible one-frame-long synchronous event just before the start of the program and again just after the end of the program.

Any number of sync-related problems can be solved by having these sync marks. Most obviously it allows unambiguous lining up of the head beep to the picture mark to sync up the picture and track. After synching the head, tail sync can be quickly checked. If there is a sync drift problem, measuring the distance between the tail sync mark and the tail beep can give valuable clues as to the cause.

The standard head countdown leader visually counts down for eight seconds. The first frame is labeled 8. The numbers 8 through 2 are visible at each full second mark, and there is a one-frame-long beep at the 2 mark. The last two seconds are black leader. The first frame of picture comes at exactly eight seconds from the start, or two seconds after the sync beep.

The tail leader is effectively the reverse of the head leader. Exactly two seconds after the last frame of picture there is a tail sync mark on the picture and a corresponding one-frame beep on the track.

Film-specific sound and pull down issues

The slight speed variation necessary when transferring between film and video is an annoying and initially a confusing concept for editors to learn. If you don't have to deal with it, you're better off. Here's how to know if you need to know.

If you are working on sound for a film shot at 24 frames per second and then transferred to NTSC video, which runs at 29.97 frames per second (fps), a speed adjustment called a *pull down* was made in the process.

A neat 4 to 5 ratio exists between the 24 film frames in a second and the 30 video frames in just over a second. Sadly, NTSC video runs at 29.97 fps, so to enable the film frames to line up with the video frames, the film must be slowed down by .1% (one tenth of one per cent).

This adds complications for the sound editor since the sound, which was recorded in real time, must be slowed .1% to stay in sync with the film after it's been pulled down for transfer to video. All Pro Tools systems require an external clock source to pull down the audio playback speed. The Session Setup window *does not* change the playback speed of the sound.

DV Toolkit 2 for Pro Tools LE

DV Toolkit 2 is an optional add-on bundle of tools for Pro Tools LE that can help with several video- and film-specific tasks. The following are two crucial capabilities it adds to Pro Tools LE:

◆ DV Toolkit 2 unlocks time code and feet/frames counting capability to the ruler and the other measuring tools of Pro Tools.

◆ Audio and video pull up/down adjustments become available.

Included with these nearly essential functions for sound for video and film are three very useful tools for audio post work:

◆ DigiTranslator is required for reliable and flexible opening of exported OMF or AAF files from Avid, Apple, and most other NLEs. It also allows for OMF/AAF export from Pro Tools to many other systems.

◆ The DINR BNR AudioSuite plug-in is useful for reducing broadband noise and hiss from some location recordings and analog audiotapes. (DINR is an acronym for Digidesign Intelligent Noise Reduction, and BNR stands for Broadband Noise Reduction.)

◆ VocALign is another AudioSuite plug-in. Its unique function is to adjust the sync of one recording to precisely match another. VocALign was designed to quickly match ADR recordings to the original location dialog. It also has other applications in music and sound design.

CHOOSING A SAMPLE RATE AND BIT DEPTH

Using Time Code or Feet.Frames Counter and Ruler (DV Toolkit 2 Only)

Installing DV Toolkit 2 adds two more counter modes and Timebase rulers to Pro Tools LE:

◆ Time Code

◆ Feet.Frames

These counter modes can be used for location indicators, in the Event Edit area, and for grid and nudge increments (**Figure 20.1**).

Like the standard Minutes:Seconds and Samples rulers, both of these new rulers count from the Session Start and share other general ruler properties. For more information on rulers, see *Chapter 10: Editing Basics*.

The Time Code ruler counts from the Session Start time set in the Session Setup window.

The Feet.Frames ruler counts from 0 at the Session Start time.

Since video frames are uniquely identified by a time code value, referring to video requires a time code counter. Time code numbers have four character fields: hours, minutes, seconds, and frames.

Figure 20.1 The top of the Edit Window shows the two post-production-related options unlocked by DV Toolkit 2 for rulers and counters, grids and nudges.

Figure 20.2 To offset the footage counter, Choose Setups > Feet.Frames.

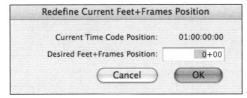

Figure 20.3 Enter a footage (positive only) for the Session Start time.

When working on sound for film, the picture is typically a video transfer from the film. The preferred counter for 35mm film work is feet and frames, with 24 frames per second and 16 frames per foot. Pro Tools lets you display 35mm feet and frames counting from zero. The Session Start time is defined as zero feet and frames plus the offset defined in the Setups > Feet.Frames menu.

To select the Feet.Frames start frame:

1. Press Return (Mac) or Enter (Windows) to locate to the beginning of the session.

2. Choose Setup > Current Feet + Frames Position (**Figure 20.2**).

3. Enter the number you would like to use as the Feet.Frames of the Session Start (**Figure 20.3**).

   Zero is the default. Negative numbers are not permitted.

✔ Tip

■ To perform calculations with the time code or Feet.Frames counters in the location indicator or Event Edit area, select the time field you want to work on, Press + (plus sign) or - (minus sign) on the keyboard, and the time you want add or subtract. Press . (period) to change fields while entering your time. When done entering the number, press Enter to have the result appear in the field. Pressing Enter again will accept the new value. Escape will undo the calculation.

TIME CODE OR FEET.FRAMES COUNTER & RULER

Working with a Video Deck

The following sections introduce concepts and issues to keep in mind when you work with a video deck.

Synchronizing to time code from external videotape (or audiotape) players

Pro Tools LE can be easily slaved to an external time code stream (also known as LTC or Linear or Longitudinal Time Code). The LTC must be converted to MIDI Time Code (or MTC). MTC is transmitted along with other MIDI data into the computer through a MIDI converter, typically into the computer's USB port. Several third-party USB MIDI converters will accept LTC and pass it to the computer.

The source of the LTC could be a videotape deck or a DAT machine or any other LTC (or MTC) source.

LTC to MTC converters

There are several standalone LTC-to-MTC converters and others that are also MIDI interfaces. The Mbox 2, Mbox 2 Pro, and 002/002 Rack have MIDI inputs built in and so can work with a stand-alone LTC-to-MTC converter.

For working to video, there are other converters that accept VITC (Vertical Interval Time Code, often found on videotapes) as well as LTC.

Some clocking options

In order to maintain sync over time, it is necessary to have a common clock for your tape deck and your Pro Tools hardware.

The only way to clock a professional video deck to an external source is with a video sync generator. Home video players cannot be clocked to an external source.

With an Mbox 2 Pro, you can generate Word clock or slave to other Word clock-capable devices with Pro Tools LE.

With an Mbox, Mbox 2, or 002/002 Rack, you can only slave to digital audio word clock on the S/PDIF (or ADAT) input with Pro Tools LE.

The traditional and most stable system for clocking a video and audio system is to have a video sync generator feeding all the devices in the system (**Figure 20.4**). There are several devices that can do this while producing a synchronous Word clock for Pro Tools LE to follow.

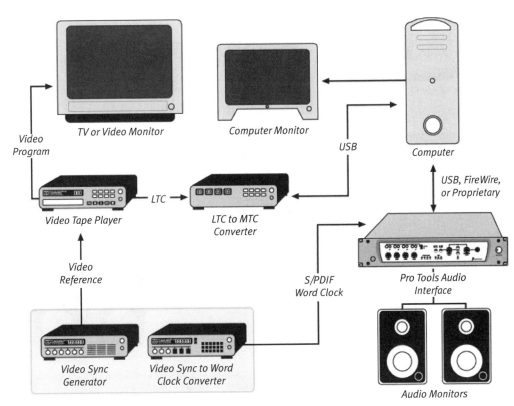

Figure 20.4 A setup for work in sync to a video tape deck with Pro Tools LE. The video sync generator and video sync-to-Word clock generator can be the same device.

If you have a DAT recorder with a video sync input, it can be used to clock Pro Tools LE. Other professional digital tape recorders could be used in this manner, too.

If you have a video sync generator you can clock the video deck and a video sync-to-Word clock generator to create a synchronous word clock for Pro Tools (**Figure 20.5**). This is the most inexpensive and flexible way to sync to any deck.

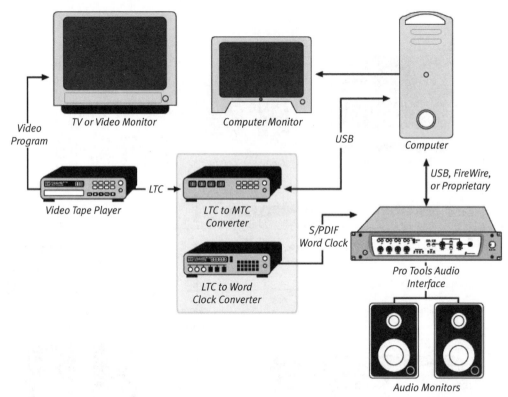

Figure 20.5 The setup for work to sync Pro Tools LE to a video tape deck by deriving word clock from LTC. The LTC-to-MTC converter and the LTC-to-word clock converter can be the same device.

Table 20.1

Time Code Format Uses

Time Code	Uses
NTSC/SMPTE (Non-Drop Frame)	
30	Film sound location recordings Music studio work
29-97	Sync to NTSC video
NTSC/SMPTE (Drop Frame)	
30DF	Broadcast TV uses, rare
29-97DF	Sync to broadcast video
PAL/EBU	
25	All uses in PAL-land
Cinema/SMPTE	
24	Specific cinema uses, rare

Setting up your MTC converter

Follow the instructions supplied by the manufacturer to configure your LTC to MTC converter. You'll need to know the format of the time code on your tape. Configure the computer to receive the MIDI according to the manufacturer's setup instructions. **Table 20.1** lists time code format uses.

Setting up your system clock

The word clock input to Pro Tools needs to be set for the correct sample rate. Bit depth is not relevant for clocking. Set the clock speed to the session's sample rate. Adjusting the clock for pull down (or pull up) can be done at the word clock generator, if you need to pull your audio down or up in Pro Tools. Adjusting the pull factor of your word clock on the word clock generator is the *only* way to actually adjust pull down or up in Pro Tools LE. **Table 20.2** lists scenarios for when to pull up or down.

To set up Pro Tools peripherals synchronization:

1. Choose Setup > Peripherals.

2. Click the Synchronization tab.

3. Select Any from the MTC Reader Port pop-up menu (**Figure 20.6**).

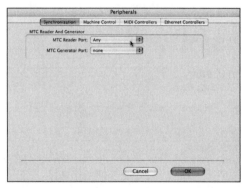

Figure 20.6 A Port selection of Any will work with a USB MIDI interface.

Table 20.2

When to Pull Down or Pull Up	
PULL FACTOR	USES
No pull	Location recordings for film or video
	All sound for picture shot on video
1% pull down	To sync location recordings to film to NTSC video
1% pull up	Some location recordings for Digital Cinema
	NTSC video origination for film release
4% pull up	Sync 24fps location recordings to film transferred to 25fps PAL video
	24fps film for release in 25fps PAL video
4% pull down	25fps PAL video to 24fps film

Figure 20.7a and 20.7b The type of external Clock source available in Pro Tools LE depends on the type of interface you are using.

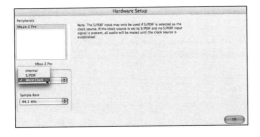

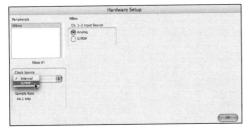

Figure 20.8a and 20.8b The Hardware Setup window is an alternate place to change the Clock Source.

Session Setup for Accurate Synchronizing

There are two ways to select the digital word clock input when you want to clock to an external source. There are also two ways to set the Session Start time.

To set the clock source in the Session Setup window:

1. Choose Setup > Session.

2. If you have an Mbox 2 Pro, select Word clock from the Clock Source pop-up menu. (**Figure 20.7a**)

   or

   If you have an Mbox, Mbox2, or 002/002 Rack, select S/PDIF (or ADAT) from the Clock Source pop-up menu (**Figure 20.7b**).

To set the clock source in the Hardware Setup window:

1. Choose Setup > Hardware.

2. If you have an Mbox 2 Pro, select Word clock from the Clock Source pop-up menu. (**Figure 20.8a**)

   or

   If you have an Mbox, Mbox 2, or 002/002 Rack, select S/PDIF (or ADAT) from the Clock Source pop-up menu (**Figure 20.8b**).

✔ Tip

- While switching between analog and digital inputs for recording, Pro Tools automatically switches the clock source from Internal to the appropriate digital clock and back. However, this feature can work against our desire to clock to the Word clock source while playing and editing. Be careful to leave the clock source to the correct digital input for your word clock source when playing and editing in sync to your tape deck.

To select Session Start time code value:

1. Choose Setup > Session.

2. Enter the appropriate time code value into the Session Start field.

3. If the new Session Start time is earlier than the first region or automation data in any track (whether hidden or not) you will be given the option to maintain time code or maintain relative position. Typically when working with sync sound, you'll want to maintain time code (**Figure 20.9**).

4. If the new Session Start time is later than the first region in any track, you will be given the option to maintain relative position or to cancel the change in Session Start time (**Figure 20.10**).

5. If there are no data in the tracks, the change in Session Start time goes ahead immediately.

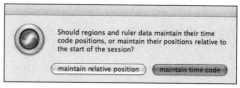

Figure 20.9 Making the Session Start time earlier in a session you've begun working on will require you to make a choice.

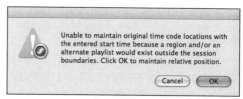

Figure 20.10 Moving the Session Start time later also requires a choice.

Figure 20.11 Choose Setup > Current Time Code Position for an alternate method of changing the Session Start time.

To change Session Start time code value by redefining the current time code position:

1. Select a position in a track that corresponds to a known time code location (such as a sync beep).

2. Choose Setup > Current Time Code Position (**Figure 20.11**).

3. Enter the appropriate time code value into the Desired Time field.

   If the new Session Start time is later than the first region in any track, you will be given the option to maintain relative position or to cancel the change in Session Start time.

4. Otherwise, the change in Session Start time goes ahead immediately.

✔ Tips

- Set the Session Start time to a whole number of hours or minutes. This makes it easier to change and then return to various times, if needed.

- There can be no audio before the Session Start time. This may seem obvious, but it means that any test tones or sync beeps that precede the program must be allowed for when selecting a Session Start time.

- When working in Feet+Frames the Session Start time is equivalent to zero. That means that in Pro Tools your sync beep cannot be before zero feet and frames. The custom in film sound in America is to have the zero feet (and the Session Start time) at an even time code hour, a sync beep at nine feet (or six seconds) and the first frame of action (and sound) at 12 feet (eight seconds).

To check that the time code rate is right for your session:

1. Choose Setup > Session.

2. Select the appropriate time code format and rate from the Time Code Rate pop-up menu (**Figure 20.12**).

    The time code rate should match the time code being received by the MTC converter.

Figure 20.12 Usually, when working to NTSC video, you'll want to select 29.97 fps non-drop, or sometimes drop. For PAL video, select 25 fps. Select 30 fps when working with time code from location recordings in NTSC land. There are exceptions to these general rules.

To set Pull Up/Down for your session (DV Toolkit 2 only):

1. Choose Setup > Session.

2. Click the triangle control to the left of Time Code Settings (in the lower left of the Session Setup window) to reveal the Time Code Settings panel.

3. In the Pull Up/Down section, select the appropriate pull amount from the Audio Rate Pull Up/Down pop-up menu (**Figure 20.13**). Note that this setting does not and cannot actually pull the audio up or down. Only the word clock generator setting can do this. This pop-up menu only adjusts the ruler and counters to reflect the speed varying caused by the word clock settings.

Figure 20.13 You only need to worry about pull down if your video image was originally shot on film. Changing the Pull Up/Down setting in the Session Setup window does not change the pull factor of the audio in the session; it only adjusts the ruler to compensate for clocking to a pulled word clock.

✔ Tips

■ If you need to pull Pro Tools LE up or down, but don't have the DV Toolkit 2 option, remember that the only thing the Audio Rate Pull Up/Down menu actually adjusts is the ruler and counter settings. The audio actually follows the word clock settings, whatever version of Pro Tools you have. Since a typical use of audio pull down is working with film sound to NTSC video picture, a workaround is to set the frame rate to 30, instead of the actual 29.97. This results in the same pulled down ruler you'd get with a setting of 29.97 with pull down.

■ When working with time code, one inevitably encounters dropouts. Having a freewheel in the system helps to play over these hiccups. In the Session Setup window, Time Code Settings, Freewheel section you can choose whether to have Freewheel off or on, how many frames of freewheel, up to forever (Jam Sync). The longer the freewheel, the longer Pro Tools will play on after the incoming time code has stopped. The default eight frames is a good starting point.

SESSION SETUP FOR ACCURATE SYNCHRONIZING

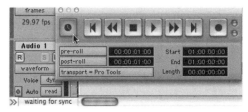

Figure 20.14 The Transport window does not need to show since the status indicator tells you whether Pro Tools is waiting, locking, or locked to external time code. You don't need to take Pro Tools offline to play normally.

Using the video player as the time code master, with Pro Tools as the slave

Having completed all the setups described above, you should now be ready to play your videotape in the deck, with Pro Tools online, have it lock to the incoming time code and play in sync with the video. In this case the video player is the master, and Pro Tools is the slave. Whenever you play the video forward at play speed, Pro Tools will lock on and follow in sync.

To put Pro Tools online with the Transport control:

1. Choose Window > Transport.

2. To toggle the online status of Pro Tools, click the Online (clock) button to put Pro Tools online.

   Pro Tools will play at the incoming time code location for as long as time code is present.

   The status indicator at the bottom left of the Edit window shows that Pro Tools is waiting for time code (**Figure 20.14**).

To put Pro Tools online with the keyboard:

◆ To toggle the online status of Pro Tools, press Command-J (Mac) or Ctrl-J (Windows), or press Option-spacebar (Mac) or Alt-spacebar (Windows).

To put Pro Tools online with a menu selection:

◆ To toggle the online status of Pro Tools, choose Options > Transport Online.

To move the insertion point to the current incoming time code position:

1. Press = (equals sign) on the numeric keypad once to select the Main Time Scale in the location indicator.

2. Press = again to place the incoming time code value into the indicator.

3. Press Enter to move to the new location.

To move the selection to the current incoming time code position:

1. Press the Down Arrow key to move the selection start to the current time code location.

2. Press the Up Arrow key to move the selection end to the current time code location.

3. While Pro Tools is playing online, pressing the down and up keys will create a selection.

Making Pro Tools the Transport Master with MMC

Pro Tools supports MIDI Machine Control which allows Pro Tools to be the transport master, controlling devices which support MMC, or professional Sony 9 Pin (RS-242) video decks via an MMC to RS-242 interface.

Depending on the accuracy of your system, this type of setup comes closest to a professional sound for picture system involving a video deck.

Digitizing Your Guide Track from the Videotape

In order to test the sync accuracy of your setup, and to have a reference guide track for your editing work, it is necessary to digitize the guide track from the videotape. The true test of the sync capability of your system is if it can maintain sync during playback of a guide track recorded online from the video. The process of recording online is explained here.

Online recording from the videotape

All the components of your time code and clock system must be on and correctly configured for online recording to work properly.

The audio outputs from the deck should be plugged into the appropriate inputs of the Pro Tools system. If the video has analog audio outputs and there are level reference tones on the videotape, you should adjust the input gain so the tones are at −20 dBFS (typically).

For more information on recording in Pro Tools, see *Chapter 6: Getting Ready to Record*, and *Chapter 7: Recording and Playing Back Audio*.

What is a Guide Track?

The guide track is the audio that has been edited in sync with the picture, played out to videotape or audiotape, or exported as a QuickTime audio track, or audio bounce from the picture editing system. It is an essential reference for the sound editor(s). It should contain a head and tail sync beep.

When the picture editor produces a guide track for the sound editor it is useful to separate production sound from other, added sounds such as music or sound effects. A common solution is to have production sound split onto the left channel of a stereo pair, and music and effects on the right. This can be prepared by the picture editor for playout to videotape or exporting to QuickTime. Sometimes further splitting is useful for the composer, and sound effects editors, to keep temp music separate from the sound effects, but these splits require more playouts or exports, or require the use of a multitrack tape recorder to keep separation of more than two categories of sound.

To define online record options:

1. Choose Setup > Preferences.

2. Click on the Operation tab.

3. In the Record, Online Options section, select Record Online At Time Code (or ADAT) Lock (**Figure 20.15**).

✔ Tip

■ If you select the Record Online at Insertion/Selection option, Pro Tools will only record from the insertion point onward, or into the selected area. This can be useful when recording specific sounds while locked to picture, such as ADR or Foley from an external source, or layered or processed sounds or sound design from within your session.

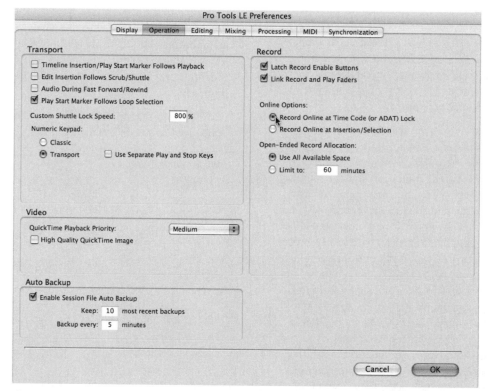

Figure 20.15 For most applications, you want Pro Tools to lock as soon as it sees running time code.

Figure 20.16 You'll need to enable record after each time you roll. Press Option-Command-spacebar (Mac) or Alt-Ctrl-spacebar (Windows) to quickly put Pro Tools back into online record ready mode.

To record online:

1. Cue the videotape to a location several seconds before the first desired sound, which may be the sync beep.

2. Set the tracks to the appropriate inputs for the video deck outputs.

3. Name the tracks so that the recorded files will have meaningful names.

4. Record enable the tracks.

5. To put Pro Tools into online record ready mode, click the Online button in the Transport window, then click the Record button in the Transport window (**Figure 20.16**).

6. Press Play on the video deck.
   Pro Tools should go into record as it locks and stay there until you stop the video deck. After the tail sync beep has gone by, stop the video deck.

7. When the recording is complete, immediately name the recorded sound file.

8. Take the track out of record.

✔ Tips

- To check whether time code is being generated by the deck, plug the LTC out into your monitor somehow. Time code has a distinctive square wave whine.

- Make sure the signal is being seen and sent by the LTC to MTC converter. A front panel indicator will alert you to proper time code being received by the unit.

- Make sure the Pro Tools Clock Source is set to the correct input, and that a word clock signal (or digital audio signal) is actually present at the input.

- If Pro Tools will record, but the results lock up out of sync when played from the middle or end of the program, instead of the beginning, your clock is running at the wrong speed. If you record a bit of the guide track onto another track just at the end of the program (the tail beep, for example), you can calculate the percent of error, which may lead you to the correct setting.

Visible time code

Make sure you have visible time code in your video image for sync setup and checking, and easy spotting and locating while you work. Most professional video decks allow the time code window to be superimposed while playing. If your deck can't do this, get the picture editor to provide a tape with a time code window burn-in. This is the superimposed time code image recorded onto the tape.

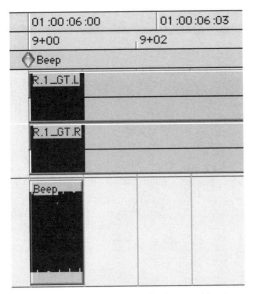

Figure 20.17 It is impossible to check sync without an accurate sync beep at a known frame at both the head and tail of your program.

Checking Sync Accuracy

Once the guide track is recorded, it is useful to compare the recording to the picture and audio tracks on the videotape to ensure they are correctly in sync.

To check sync by eye:

1. First check that the head beep is in sync with the correct time code. Typically this is 01:00:06:00, or 9+00 feet and frames (**Figure 20.17**).

2. Play the video while listening to Pro Tools.

   Is the head beep in sync with the visual mark in the leader?

   Is the dialog in sync with the lips?

   Is the tail beep in sync with the leader?

To check sync by listening for phasing:

◆ Play the video while listening to an equal mix of the recorded guide track and the track coming from the tape.

   The head beep should sound as one, not doubling.

   The dialog and other sounds from the program should be so closely in sync with each other that the higher frequencies cancel out, creating a distinctive phasing sound. The sound should not be drifting in or out of sync at any time, but rather stay in the exact sync relationship indefinitely.

   The tail beeps should also play as one, whether the program has been played from the beginning, or if the beeps are played from nearby.

✔ Tips

■ If there is a clock error, checking sync by playing from the beginning of the program will not reveal it. The clocks in modern video and audio equipment are quite stable, so the same timing errors will be reproduced during playback. A timing error can be revealed most clearly by checking lock and sync late in the program.

■ Because the clocks are so stable, it is often workable to have both the video deck and Pro Tools running on internal clocks. This is possible only when pull down or pull up is not required. This method is not reliable or repeatable enough to be recommended for professional applications.

Editing with the video deck as master

Working with a video deck is only for those who already own the requisite parts. If you don't already own the gear, it is more expensive to purchase, and it is less productive to use to edit to picture. However, it works.

Since there is no direct coupling between a video deck and Pro Tools except at play speed, it is difficult to place sounds at the correct picture hit points without a time code or feet and frames ruler. Thus DV Toolkit 2 becomes an essential part of a system involving an external video deck. Equally important is the visible time code burn in on the videotape.

To sync a sound to picture with a video deck with DV Toolkit 2 involves a several step procedure.

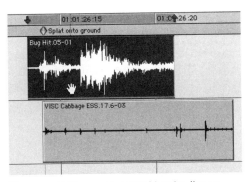

Figure 20.18 After marking your hit point, line up your sounds. Markers allow you to easily return to your hit points.

To put sounds in sync to videotape:

1. Using the jog/shuttle wheel on your video deck, locate a picture hit point.

2. Press = (equals sign) to select the main counter. Press = again to grab the incoming time code to the main counter.

3. Press the Enter key to move the insertion point to the time code location. This usually is close to the current location, but is likely to be several frames off, since LTC can't be read at slow jog speeds.

4. Using the plus (+) and minus (–) keys on the numeric keypad, nudge the insertion point until its time code location matches the visible time code on the video screen.

5. Record this location by pressing the Enter key to create a Marker. Name the marker so you can find the place again quickly.

6. Once the location is marked, it is easy to place a sound in sync with the hit point (**Figure 20.18**).

7. Roll the video deck back and press Play on the video transport.

   Pro Tools will lock to the time code and play across the edited sound. Check the sync relationship, and nudge the sound earlier or later as needed.

✔ Tip

- If you have a VITC (Vertical Interval Time Code) reader, you can grab the time code from the videotape even when it is stopped. The VITC code is embedded in the first few scan lines at the top of the video frame, outside of the viewing area. A VITC reader makes a video deck quite useable.

CHECKING SYNC ACCURACY

Using Digital Video To Sync Pro Tools To Picture

The more elegant way to sync Pro Tools to the picture is by using digital video. Importing a QuickTime digital video track into your Pro Tools session allows accurate and instantaneous sync between the picture and your tracks. There's no question that this is the easiest way to work with sync picture in Pro Tools.

The QuickTime video file can be obtained in many ways. It can originate as an export from Avid (using Apple DV codec), Final Cut Pro, or iMovie. Or you can digitize your file from a DV camera through FireWire, or from a DV to analog video converter. If you digitize your own QuickTime files, you'll need appropriate video digitizing software.

Importing the digital video with sync audio

Pro Tools will import and play any QuickTime movie at any size or frame rate. For sync to video use, QuickTime movies should be digitized at the same frame rate as the NTSC or PAL videotapes they come from. Imported movies play along in sync with the timeline. Pro Tools can also import the sound from the QuickTime movie at the same time. If you have DV Toolkit 2, you can have more than one video track, and each video track can contain more than one QuickTime movie file.

To import a movie:

1. Choose File > Import > Video (**Figure 20.19**).

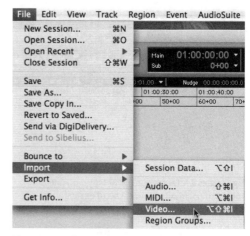

Figure 20.19 Choose File > Import > Video.

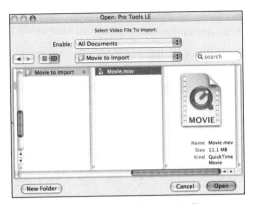

Figure 20.20 Select the QuickTime movie file you want to work with.

Figure 20.21 Place the imported movie in a new video track and set its location in the Video Import Options dialog.

2. Select a QuickTime movie file to import from the Open File dialog and click Open (**Figure 20.20**).

In the Video Import Options dialog, select New Track, set the location for the movie, and select Import Audio from File (**Figure 20.21**).

✔ Tips

■ Spotting the movie to a particular time code location is easiest with visible time code in the picture and with DV Toolkit 2 installed. You can spot the picture to the time code location of the first frame of the file.

■ Without visible time code or DV Toolkit 2 installed you can still sync your 29.97 video to the correct session time code. Make sure your session start time is set to an even hour (zero minutes, seconds or frames). Place a sync mark in the video track at the leading edge of the 2 frame in the countdown leader. Spot the Sync Point of the movie to 0:06.006 (0.1% later than 6 seconds from the start of the session). Even though the Minutes:Seconds time counter will drift slowly out of sync, the time code is correctly handled by Pro Tools. You can see this for yourself by synching to external code, or examining the time stamping of a file recorded in your session.

■ If you zoom in to the Video track in frames mode, with a small track height, so that just a one or two frames are visible with a large gap between them, the left edge of the frame you see on the screen is the leading edge of that frame.

Viewing digital video

Once your movie is in place you should hide the video track since it takes up space in the edit window. Also, if the video track is showing, and its display mode is frames, extra CPU power is consumed drawing the frames in the Edit window. On an LE system, available CPU power is directly related to audio track and plug-in count. For more information on optimizing performance, see *Chapter 21: Optimizing Performance.*

After importing a QuickTime movie, there are several options for viewing it.

◆ View the Video window on single computer monitor along with Pro Tools.

When working with only one computer screen (unless it's huge) you'll find the Video window is always in the way. To temporarily hide the window, use the Command-9 (Mac) or Ctrl-9 (Windows) (on the numeric keypad only) to toggle the visibility of the Video window.

◆ View the Video window on a second monitor.

If you have a second monitor, you can probably find a place for the Video window so it isn't always in the way. The mixer and plug-in windows may also find a good home there (**Figure 20.22**).

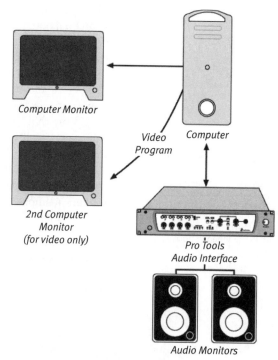

Figure 20.22 Working with your video image on a second computer monitor may be the simplest way to work, but it requires a fast computer.

◆ View the Video window on a second monitor with pixel doubling.

If you have a second computer monitor that you can run in 640 x 480 VGA resolution, you can use pixel doubling to fill the screen with a 320 x 240 QuickTime image. This provides a very workable environment, and many modern computers come with dual monitor capability built in.

◆ Play the Movie out of the FireWire port, convert to analog video, and view on TV or video monitor.

If the Options > Video out FireWire command is selected, the picture will not be shown in the Video window, but rather will be routed out the FireWire port in sync with the timeline, at any speed (**Figure 20.23**).

You need a FireWire-to-analog video converter to pass the signal on to a video monitor or TV. As D-to-A converters take a fraction of a second to do their conversion, you will need to advance the Video track to compensate for this. This can be done with the Setup > Video Sync Offset command. There you can type in the amount of picture delay introduced by the converter in quarter frames.

By offloading the display of the DV data onto a FireWire-to-analog video converter, the computer's CPU is actually required to do much less work, so Pro Tools LE feels zippier, and audio performance is increased.

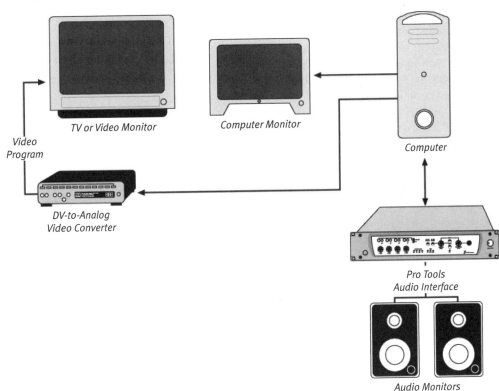

TV or Video Monitor

Computer Monitor

Video Program

Computer

DV-to-Analog Video Converter

Pro Tools Audio Interface

Audio Monitors

Figure 20.23 Using a FireWire DV-to-analog video converter gives excellent picture quality but causes a noticeable delay in the image output, which must be compensated for.

USING DIGITAL VIDEO TO SYNC TO PICTURE

Getting Sync Audio from the Picture Editor

The picture editor can provide the following:

◆ Audio from production sound, sequence information from EDL or Assemble List

◆ Audio from NLE, sequence information from OMF or AAF interchange files

◆ Audio (and sequence) from edited audio tracks from videotape or exported audio track files

Getting audio from the picture editor using OMF or AAF (DV Toolkit 2 only)

Open Media Framework (OMF) and Advanced Authoring Format (AAF) are accepted formats for interchanging files containing edit decisions and other sequence data between editors using systems from different manufacturers. OMF Interchange (OMFI) and AAF files are like an EDL, only they contain descriptions of many more aspects of an editor's work than just cut or dissolve points (**Figure 20.24**). For a sound editor, OMFI and AAF deliver a sample-accurate duplicate of the sound regions from the picture editor, complete with fades and certain types of automation. The OMFI or AAF file can optionally contain embedded media files, or it can refer to sound files you've copied from the picture editor's system onto your hard drive.

sc.73_7.18.03_CUT 2section.omf

Figure 20.24 The same icon is shared by Avid OMF and AAF interchange files. Even though the icon is labeled with the word "Media," the icon shown here is from a composition or sequence file and contains no media.

Guidelines for exporting OMF and AAF

The specific methods of exporting OMF or AAF files from a NLE are beyond the scope of this book. Generally, try to use the most compatible interchange format, referring to files in the most compatible form for your hardware, operating system, NLE, and Pro Tools version.

✔ Tip

■ If the picture is completely finished, an OMFI or AAF file with embedded media is a single file to export/import, and can save some file management hassles.

However, if the picture may be changed and you anticipate needing another export from the video workstation, you should use OMFI or AAF with external file references. Later, when the picture and sound have been updated, instead of requiring a new embedded audio export, your new interchange file will refer to the audio you already have. The extra audio file management work you'll need to do will pay off. Do not consolidate the media at any time in the NLE or in Pro Tools, or this technique will not work.

GETTING SYNC AUDIO FROM THE PICTURE EDITOR

Using DigiTranslator to import an OMF or AAF sequence into Pro Tools (DV Toolkit 2 only)

After installing DV Toolkit 2, DigiTranslator 2 is incorporated directly into Pro Tools LE. Its functions are seamlessly integrated into Pro Tools' normal operations. DigiTranslator allows Pro Tools to import audio, video and edited sequences from other AAF or OMF compatible applications. It also allows Pro Tools to export audio files and audio tracks to other compatible systems.

Whether you use external or embedded media, you'll need to have the files on a valid audio drive. You'll also need the OMF or AAF interchange file with the sequence data in it.

The benefits of OMF and AAF are lost if the sound in the NLE was not recorded in well. If the sound was recorded on DAT or other digital audiotape format, or if it was recorded on a hard disk recorder, the chances are that the sound files in the NLE are identical clones of the original recordings. However, if the sound in the NLE has been degraded due to poor load in procedures, the efficiencies of sequence interchange are offset by permanent sound quality loss if OMF/AAF techniques are used. In this case audio should be reloaded into Pro Tools from the original recordings.

To open an interchange file:

1. Choose File > Open Session.

2. Select your OMF or AAF document and click OK (**Figure 20.25**).

3. Choose a name and a location for the session file that will be created from the interchange document (**Figure 20.26**).

Figure 20.25 Select the OMF or AAF file using the standard File Open dialog.

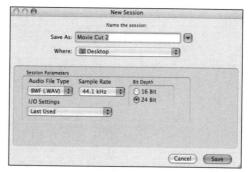

Figure 20.26 Enter a name for your new session file. If you don't change the Session Parameters, the original audio file settings will be used.

The selections in the Session Parameters section of the dialog reflect the settings in the OMFI or AAF document. You may change the Audio File Type, Sample Rate and Bit Depth. If you do change any of these parameters, Pro Tools will convert all the referenced audio files to the newly selected format. This happens as a background task as the session is opened.

4. Set the session parameters and click Save.

5. In the Import Session Data dialog that appears you will see what's in the interchange file. You can adjust many parameters here, but typically you'll want to refer to source media, maintain absolute time code, and convert clip-based gain to automation.

6. Select the tracks you want to import. Shift-click on a track name, and drag through to select all tracks. Option-click (Alt-click in Windows) on a pop-up menu to select Import As New Track for all tracks (**Figure 20.27**).

7. Click the OK button.

continues on next page

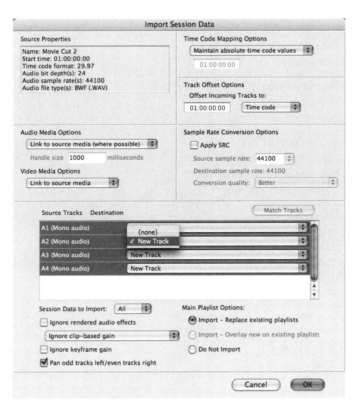

Figure 20.27 Select which tracks you want to import, and many other session parameters in the Import Session Data window.

8. Since the audio files may not be where Pro Tools expects them to be, you may get a Missing Files dialog. Select Automatically Find & Relink and click OK to let Pro Tools try to find the audio for you. This happens as a background task (**Figure 20.28**).

9. When the various background processes are complete, save the session.

Figure 20.28 Pro Tools can quickly and automatically find and relink audio files on any valid audio drive.

Importing Tracks into Pro Tools with DigiTranslator (DV Toolkit 2 only)

Since the extra functionality of DigiTranslator is built right into Pro Tools, many of the standard Pro Tools commands for opening or importing file and tracks work with OMF and AAF files, including the following:

◆ Double-click an AAF or OMF file in the Finder (Mac) or Explorer (Windows) to open it into a new session.

◆ Choose File > Import Session Data and select an interchange file and import tracks from it into an open session.

◆ Double-click an OMF or AAF file in the DigiBase Workspace browser to either open it into a new session, to import tracks from the selected file into the current session.

◆ Drag and drop an interchange file from the DigiBase Browser window onto an open Edit window to import tracks.

Reloading from the original recordings

If the production sound was recorded on DAT or other digital audiotape format, it is an easy setup to get a digital clone of the sound into Pro Tools. Loading directly from the digital output of a DAT machine into the S/PDIF input of Pro Tools will give you an identical copy (clone) of the original recording, and you can't get better quality than that.

In order to proceed with the loading, you'll need a list of all the sound takes required. The key to efficient tape handling is to go through each tape only once, and load the needed takes in the order in which they appear on the tape. Even if the portion of a take used in a sequence is quite small, you should consider loading the entire take. The editing process is much smoother if you don't have to go back into the tapes looking for extra bits of sound.

The recent introduction of location hard disk recorders have made direct copying from the location recorder into Pro Tools possible. If these recordings were available to the picture editor, the audio files exported from the NLE should be perfect. Otherwise you can just import the audio directly from the location recorder's disk(s), bypassing the chore of real time load in from tape.

Recording from DAT with time code sync

The setup required for recording with time code from a digital source is essentially the same as recording the guide track from a videotape, described earlier in this chapter. The only difference is that Pro Tools maintains sync while clocked directly to the digital audio stream itself, rather than needing an external clock for the system.

Getting time code from the audio deck requires an LTC-to-MTC converter and a time code tape player (**Figure 20.29**).

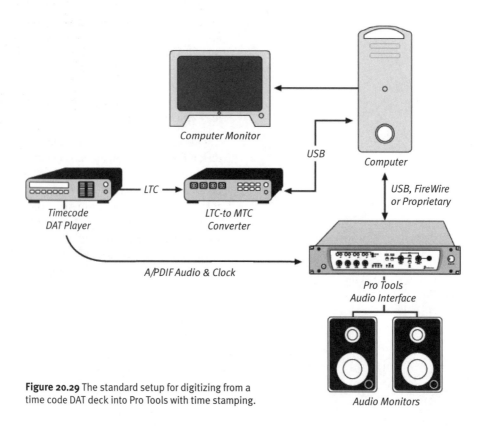

Figure 20.29 The standard setup for digitizing from a time code DAT deck into Pro Tools with time stamping.

Create a new session for loading with Session Parameters that match the format of your production sound. In the Session Setup window, make sure the various parameters are correctly configured (**Figure 20.30**).

◆ Clock Source = S/PDIF

◆ Ch 1-2 Input = Digital

◆ Time code frame rate matches the time code on the DATs

◆ Under Time Code Settings, a few frames of Freewheel is good, but don't use Jam Sync.

Once you have configured your setup, you should be able to cue up your tape to the first take to be loaded. In order to hear the tape as you cue it, the track you will be recording into must be in record ready, and the session should not be playing. It is helpful to retain the voice ID (at the head of most takes) in the portion of the take that you load. This makes finding correct takes (and troubleshooting) easier.

If the take was recorded onto two channels with different sound on each, load it into a stereo track. This allows naming both tracks at the same time, which is faster and more consistent. However, if the take was recorded onto one track, or with one microphone onto two identical tracks, it is easier to edit if you record that one channel only into a mono track. Editing and mixing is much easier if there aren't redundant copies of your audio involved.

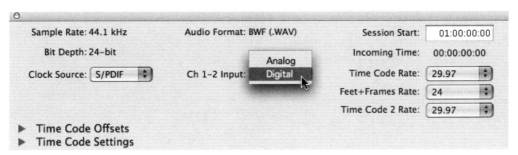

Figure 20.30 Select your digital input, making sure the Input and Clock Source settings are matching.

To record online:

1. Cue the audio tape to a location after the beginning of the take you want to record, but enough before the section where you want the recording to begin to allow Pro Tools to lock to the incoming time code when it begins playing.

2. Set the track to the appropriate S/PDIF inputs.

3. Name the track so that the recorded files will have meaningful names.

4. Record-enable the track.

5. To put Pro Tools into online record ready mode, press Option-Command-spacebar (Mac) or Alt-Ctrl-spacebar (Windows). Or, click the Online button in the Transport window, then click the Record button in the Transport window.

6. Press play on the DAT deck.

   Pro Tools should jump to the location matching the time code from the take, go into record and stay there until you stop the DAT machine, or when there is a break in the time code.

7. When the recording is complete, immediately name the recorded sound file (**Figure 20.31**).

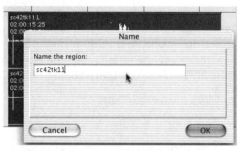

Figure 20.31 Name your digitized files immediately. It's too easy to forget which take is which after you have a few unnamed files to deal with.

Synchronizing takes to the guide track

In order to reconstruct the picture editor's work in Pro Tools from the newly digitized takes, you need to know what portions of which takes have been used to make up each part of the guide track. Guided by an EDL from the picture editor, it is possible to piece together the audio to match the editor's track. This can be done quickly and easily if you have an auto-conforming program, an EDL, and were able to load from a time code DAT player.

Use the sound from the guide track as your source for sound editing

Getting a series of guide tracks or bounced files from the picture editor is a good workaround for having no OMF/AAF. If the picture editor can provide you with exported audio or QuickTime files of the various tracks in the picture system, you will be able to have perfect sync effortlessly. And if the sound was properly loaded into the system, you will have master quality audio as well.

You'll probably want to get the audio tracks twice from the editor. Once as they were cut, and once with each track split out or checkerboarded, and with its handles pulled out as far as possible. The original track becomes the guide, and the second set of tracks has the head and tail extensions you'll need to smooth out the production sound.

Auto-conforming with an EDL

At this writing, Digidesign includes an audio-conforming program, Virtual Katy's VK Conformer, with the purchase of DV Toolkit 2. A detailed discussion of its use is beyond the scope of this chapter. For more information on auto-conforming with VK Conformer, see the Virtual Katy website at www.virtualkaty.com.

GETTING SYNC AUDIO FROM THE PICTURE EDITOR

Editing Dialog (Production Sound)

At the heart of sound editing for video is the cleaning up of the sound from the shoot. This sound often has technical problems that can be repaired in editing or mixing, though some sounds are technically impossible to fix and must be replaced.

The goals of the dialog track

The goals of the dialog track are fairly straightforward, but sometimes difficult to achieve.

- The entire dialog should be clear and intelligible.

- The voices should sound natural and pleasant.

- Separate takes edited together within the same scene should sound smooth and continuous.

- The lines of dialog should play at a consistent level.

- Some sounds will need special treatment, such as reverberation, or editing to sound as though heard through a telephone or public address system.

It's impossible to stress enough the importance of clean location sound recordings. Excess environmental noise, distant or off-axis miking, or distortion caused by poor level control ruin the quality of production recordings. These problems can be modestly improved in editing and mixing, but cannot be eliminated. The old adage, "we'll fix it in post," often is true only if you can afford to replace all the sound with new ADR and Foley recordings, and this is not possible in many situations.

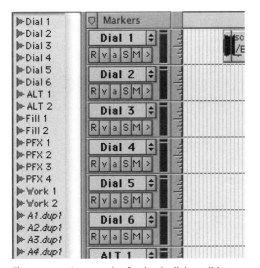

Figure 20.32 An example of a simple dialog editing track layout. Notice the inactive duplicate original OMF tracks: A1.dup1 through A4.dup1.

In dialog editing, all the sounds are put in the right places and smoothly overlapped, and any new sounds are added to fill unwanted gaps in the track. Momentary clicks, pops and bumps are removed. Alternate takes can be searched for cleaner and clearer renditions of lines, words, or even syllables, which can be used to replace poor sections of sync sound.

Laying out the tracks for dialog editing

Before editing begins you have to have obtained the sync sound from the picture editor. Your next task is to duplicate these tracks. Lock all the regions in the duplicate tracks and make the tracks inactive so they are accessible, but don't use any CPU resources. Now hide them. They'll be available to refer to if needed.

Create enough new tracks to do all your dialog editing. You might need eight to sixteen new tracks. Several will be used for splitting the principal dialog. A couple may be used for alternate takes. Two or four tracks may be enough for fill, or air and movement tracks. If preparing for an alternate language version, extra tracks can be created to hold non-language sounds, or production effects. Create a couple of work tracks that will only be used as a temporary work space, but never to hold finished cut material.

Once you've created the tracks, name them according to their use. Appropriate names might be Dial 1 through 6, Alt 1 & 2, Fill 1 through 4, PFX 1 through 4, Work 1 & 2 (**Figure 20.32**).

Basic dialog editing tasks

Once you have all the sounds in sync, the three basic dialog editing tasks are *splitting*, *smoothing* and *filling*. This is the basic requirement for delivery tracks to the mix.

When a source take's qualities are very different from the preceding take, it should be split to another track. This allows the mixer to more easily apply a different set of plug-ins or tools, or different settings to the various tracks and not have to change them at every region boundary, which may be difficult to accomplish on a conventional mixing console, and saves time.

On the other hand, if a take's sound qualities match those of the preceding sound, both should be placed on the same track if possible. The mixer should not have to copy the same settings from one track to another in order to match takes on different tracks.

Splitting tracks is the first step in dialog editing. The next steps can only properly occur after the splitting decisions have been made. After splitting, the tracks are smoothed out to obscure the transitions between takes. This involves trimming out the ends of the takes for as far as possible, and then creating long fades in and out over the length of the head and tail extensions of the takes.

Filling holes is the process of coming up with *air* or *room tone* and movement sounds from the location recordings to fill out a scene that has used picture-only takes.

It is also necessary to fill the track when the sync sound has been eliminated by the picture editor for having the wrong content. There are many reasons for the holes that occur in a dialog track, but the best solution is always to look at the picture for clues and listen to the surrounding sound takes for the most likely candidates for fill.

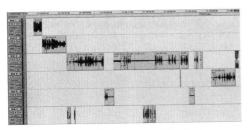

Figure 20.33 After splitting, these dialog tracks are ready to be smoothed out.

To split dialog:

1. Listen carefully to dialog and background qualities while playing along through the conformed production sound.

2. When you play across an edit and the sound qualities seem to match, leave the takes together on the same track, even if the edit itself is bad. If the takes will require the same treatment in the mix, they should remain on the same track. The bad edit can be repaired now, or after the splitting is complete.

3. If the takes do not match qualitatively, they should be split. With the grabber tool, select the region to be split to another track.

4. Hold down the Shift and Option keys together (Shift-Alt in Windows), and press the Return key to select from the currently selected region to the end of the track.

5. In Command Focus mode, press X to cut the audio from the original track.

6. Press P or ; to move up or down to the desired track.

7. Press V to paste the audio, in sync, to the new track. You have now split the track (**Figure 20.33**).

✔ Tip

- If you'd rather, after selecting the audio to split, you can Control-click (Mac) or on the selection and drag it with the Grabber to the desired track.

EDITING DIALOG (PRODUCTION SOUND)

To smooth out transitions between dialog tracks:

1. To smoothly fade into the head of a block of regions, use the trim tool to drag the head out a couple seconds (**Figure 20.34**). (These descriptions work the same way for the tail extension.)

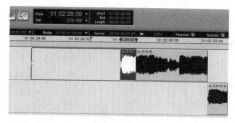

Figure 20.34 Drag the "handle," or end of a region, out a ways to see whether there's any air there.

2. Looking at the waveform, you can usually see at a glance where unusable sounds occur. Common unusable sounds are dialog or distinctive unwanted sounds, such as doors or other effects.

3. Trim the extension back to the apparently useable section of sound (**Figure 20.35**).

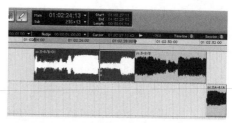

Figure 20.35 Trim the handle back to the beginning of the air. Often these visual approaches works well, but always check your work by listening carefully to the results.

4. Listen carefully to the extension and make sure it's innocent of any offensive material.

5. Create a fade up through the extension to the first frame of the original clip (**Figure 20.36**).

6. Listen to the transition through the fade out from the outgoing region and the fade in to the incoming region.

7. If necessary, adjust the shapes and lengths of the fades to make the transition as smooth as possible. Typically, noisier backgrounds will need to be introduced or withdrawn more gradually and over longer times than quieter backgrounds (**Figure 20.37**).

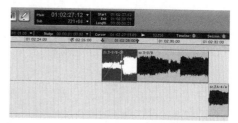

Figure 20.36 Create a fade over the length of the handle. You may need more or less handle than is immediately available. Change the fade shape if needed to make a smooth segue with the adjacent audio. Always use your ears.

✔ Tip

■ You may find that pulling out the end of the region doesn't give you enough of an extension to make a smooth transition. This is a common problem. Look into the filling holes section below for steps to obtain more of the needed sound than is immediately to hand.

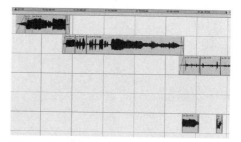

Figure 20.37 These tracks play smoothly now.

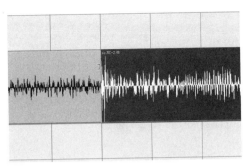

Figure 20.38 The incoming air will bump at the cut, so trim the outgoing air longer to smooth the cut.

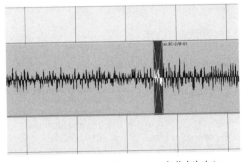

Figure 20.39 The cut has been moved slightly later and a crossfade completes the smoothing of the internal edit.

To smooth cuts from region to region:

1. To smoothly cut from region to region within a block of regions, you can use a combination of two basic techniques: move the edit earlier or later, or cross-fade between the regions.

2. If the offensive sound is at the end of the outgoing region, use the trim tool to drag the head of the incoming region earlier to cover the distracting sound.

3. If the problem is at the start of the incoming sound, drag the tail of the outgoing sound later to cover the problem (**Figure 20.38**).

4. Once the edit point is in the best place, a short crossfade will usually smooth the cut further (**Figure 20.39**).

✔ Tips

■ When cutting from region to region in a track, make sure to listen carefully for subtle sounds which may be interrupted or upcut. Use a high quality, comfortable set of headphones to eliminate room noise. You'll be surprised how much more you'll hear.

■ Putting the edit immediately before an incoming transient will usually mask the cut.

To find air to fill holes:

1. To find air in a take, lay the take out in a work track. Using visual clues, find a quiet passage in the take, starting at the beginning. Listen to confirm the absence of dialog or distracting sounds. Select the useful portion, staying clear of distinctive sounds at the edges of the selection, and cut it.

2. Paste the section into the other work track.

3. Repeat steps one and two, pasting the air at the end of the previously assembled bits until you have found and assembled all the useful air from the take (**Figure 20.40**).

4. Play through the assembled pieces, listening through the mostly bad edits for the best selections. Discard any clips that don't work well with the others.

5. Crossfades may help smooth out the assembled clips.

6. Once you've created a useful assembly of clips it's easier to handle if you consolidate it. Choose Edit > Consolidate (**Figure 20.41**). After the new air file has been rendered, immediately name it with the take name and the word "Fill" or "Air" or "Mvmnt" or similar description. As always, be consistent with your naming.

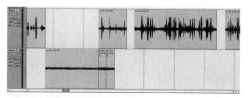

Figure 20.40 Track Work 2 contains the regions of useful air from the take in Work 1.

Figure 20.41 Select the smoothed assemblage of regions of air and Choose Edit > Consolidate to save your work as a convenient file. Remember to name the new file immediately.

✔ Tips

■ If there is an evolving sound, like a long jet by, through the take, it may be impossible to edit pieces from different parts of the take together.

■ A piece of air can be doubled in length by duplicating it and reversing it. This results in one iteration of a "backwards/forwards" loop. Backwards/forwards loops are always smooth since the head and tail always match. However, you can't make an unobtrusive b/f loop from sounds with transients that can't be transparently reversed.

■ You may have to search through any number of nearby takes looking for better candidates for useful air.

■ Often the best air is after sound has rolled, but before "action" is called, or after the action is over, but before "cut" is called.

■ Don't hesitate to use sections of air with light movement in them, but don't repeat short bits of movement or breaths, as the ear picks up the loopiness of it very quickly.

■ You can randomize the order of short clips when repeating them in order to minimize loopiness.

■ You can stretch the chunk of air you've created using the TCE Trim tool to get a longer piece.

■ Look for wild sound recordings of "Room Tone" for the location. When available, this is always the easiest place to look for a long section of clean air. The problem here is that the air is often too "dead." With the camera off, and no movement from the actors, the air may not match the background in the actual takes from the same location.

EDITING DIALOG (PRODUCTION SOUND)

To fill holes with the air:

1. Once you've got a chunk of air in a work track, select and cut it. Paste the air into a work track alongside the area where it is needed (**Figure 20.42**).

2. Select the area you want to fill.

3. Transfer the selection to the work track by pressing P or ; (in Command Focus mode) (**Figure 20.43**).

4. Copy the required amount of the fill.

5. Move the selection back to the track to be filled with P or ; and paste the fill into the selection. This works for a hole of certain length within a take or for a head or tail extension.

6. Crossfading in and out of your fill may smooth out a bumpy cut (**Figure 20.44**).

7. To create a long fill loop to smooth out a rough scene, or to fill for MOS shots, you may need to duplicate the chunk of air many times.

✔ Tips

- You can paste a small fragment of your air into a space, and then trim the end(s) out to fill your hole.

- If you need to fill a series of holes, don't always use the beginning of your piece of air. Use other sections of a longer piece of air to avoid repetition.

- When filling a long section, it is advisable to use more than one fill loop. Use a two or three different fill loops on different fill tracks and let the mixer move the faders up and down to vary the sound.

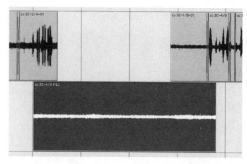

Figure 20.42 A piece of fill standing by below the hole that needs filling.

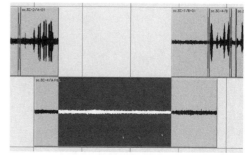

Figure 20.43 The fill is selected and ready to copy.

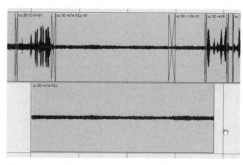

Figure 20.44 The fill has been pasted into the hole and the ends have been crossfaded to smooth the joins.

Dialog microsurgery

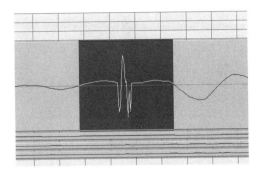

Figure 20.45 Clicks like this extremely short glitch are usually from some sort of digital source. The selected area is ready to delete.

Once the basics of splitting, smoothing and filling have been taken care of, there are the small clicks and bumps to remove. These sounds are often artifacts of the recording process: mic bumps, electrical crackles, digital glitches. Sometimes they are undesirable sounds recorded on set, like the distracting snap of a piece of gravel underfoot during a close-up of a face. Occasionally a click is actually a desired sync sound, so watch the picture to be sure the click you are about to attack is actually a suitable target. Let's divide these sounds into three categories and describe how to remove them.

Clicks are so short they can be removed without creating a dropout. After removing a longer click, which we'll call a pop, you'll need to fill the resulting hole. To remove low frequency bumps without losing the dialog or other important sound, use an AudioSuite EQ plug-in to attenuate the bump.

To remove clicks:

1. Locate the click precisely. Tab to transient will find many, but not all, of the audible clicks you might want to remove. Scrub to find the click if Tab to transient can't find it.

2. Once located, zoom in to the click until you can clearly see the cycles in the waveform.

3. Select the noise impulse. The selection start and end should be at zero crossing points. You may need to zoom in vertically to clearly see the points where the waveform samples cross the zero line (**Figure 20.45**).

continues on next page

EDITING DIALOG (PRODUCTION SOUND)

4. If the selection is less than about 200 samples, it is usually safe to delete it without worrying about needing to fill it. Press the delete key to remove the click.

5. Play across the deletion to be sure that there is no audible drop-out.

✔ Tips

■ This technique is fast, but only works when the click is very short.

■ Create a zoom preset for microsurgery and use it to instantly get to the working view after finding the click.

To remove pops by editing:

1. Locate the pop as above.

2. Select the pop (**Figure 20.46**) and delete it (**Figure 20.47**).

3. Find a small piece of fill from nearby in the take that will match the sound quality surrounding the deletion.

4. Select a portion of the sound that is slightly shorter than the length of the deletion. Copy the selection.

5. Select the start of the deletion and paste the fill from the clipboard (**Figure 20.48**).

6. Now trim the fill out until it fills the hole.

7. Listen to the repair.

8. If necessary, make tiny crossfades to smooth out the in and out of the fill (**Figure 20.49**).

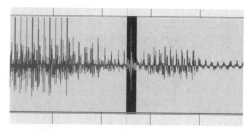

Figure 20.46 The pop is selected.

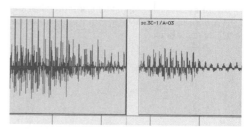

Figure 20.47 The pop is deleted.

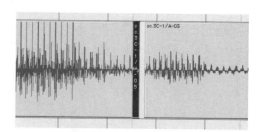

Figure 20.48 A piece of fill shorter than the hole has been pasted at the start of the hole, ready to be trimmed out to fill the hole.

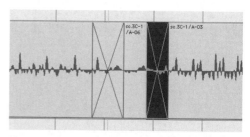

Figure 20.49 Very short crossfades have been made to eliminate the possibility of clicks at the edits.

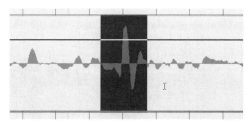

Figure 20.50 This pop is selected and in volume automation mode, ready to be turned down.

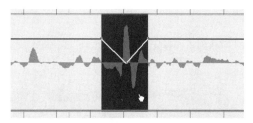

Figure 20.51 The center of the pop has been attenuated. The amount and shape of the attenuation is based on trial and error and listening.

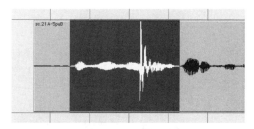

Figure 20.52 A phrase of dialog containing a large low frequency bump is selected.

Figure 20.53 Use an AudioSuite EQ plug-in to roll off the lower frequencies.

To volume graph pops out:

1. Locate the pop as above.

2. Select the pop and switch to volume automation view by pressing the minus (-) key in Command Focus mode (**Figure 20.50**).

3. Pull the volume level down around the pop. Use trial and error to find the correct attenuation. Try different shapes for the volume graph (**Figure 20.51**).

4. Play through the repair. If the pop is not too long, the attenuated pop makes good fill for itself. This works particularly well within words.

To remove bumps with EQ:

1. Locate the bump by listening and looking at the waveform.

2. Select the bump and perhaps as much as half a second on either side of the bump (**Figure 20.52**).

3. Choose AudioSuite > 1-Band EQ III.

4. Select the High Pass EQ Type and set the frequency to something like 100 to 250 Hz (**Figure 20.53**).

continues on next page

5. Process the selection (**Figure 20.54**).

6. Listen to the processed audio, the bump will be attenuated, but the dialog will sound thin.

7. Trim the unprocessed audio back to almost cover the peak of the bump on both sides of the bump (**Figure 20.55**).

8. Create short crossfades into and out of the EQed section (**Figure 20.56**).

9. Listen. Be sure not to go too high with the high pass frequency, or let the EQed section play any longer than necessary. Use trial and error to find the best balance of no bump and full voice.

10. If the higher frequencies remaining in the bump are annoying, use a volume graph to attenuate the bump further (**Figure 20.57**).

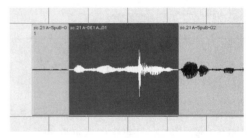

Figure 20.54 After processing, the bump is much reduced, but the surrounding dialog has been affected by the EQ.

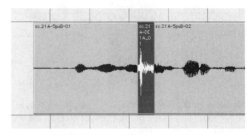

Figure 20.55 Trim the original dialog in towards the bump.

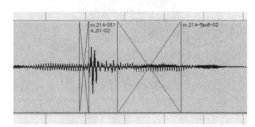

Figure 20.56 Use crossfades to help smooth the EQed section into the take.

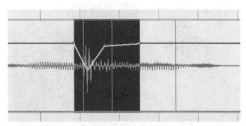

Figure 20.57 The mid- and high-range frequencies are still present in the bump, so a little attenuation helps minimize the flaw. Don't go too far or you'll have a dropout instead of a bump.

Working with Sound Effects

Adding sound effects can bring the world around the action of the video to life. Atmospheric background can create an off-screen world that can help set and tell the story of the video. Background tracks can mask problems in the dialog recordings and help smooth out bumps in the production sound. Specific sound effects that work in sync with the picture can add presence and character to objects and actions on the screen. The attention of the audience can be focused on a particular thing on the screen by placing a sound effect that syncs with the object of interest.

In addition to sound effects recorded on location during the shoot, sound editors often draw on the many excellent commercially available libraries of professionally recorded sound effects. Whenever feasible, however, it is advisable to record your own custom sound effects which are likely to fit the action and character of your video better than canned effects. Recording Foley sound effects in a studio to picture can help fill out the many detailed sync sounds of movements, small and large, which are nearly impossible to record or edit in any other way. Special sound effects and atmospheres are created by sound designers, who use a variety of techniques and equipment to bend sound recordings to the needs of the video. Sound designers create sounds for monsters and space ships, but they also create sounds to use as an almost musical underscore that has a subliminal and evocative effect on the audience.

Editing sound effects

Whatever the source of your sound effects, there are some basic ways they can be cut in to your sound track.

Backgrounds need to be laid out so they start and stop at the picture cuts that define the scene edges. Spot effects need to line up with the action on the screen. Most sound effects benefit from layering. Balancing the levels of sound effects while editing helps judge their impact while editing, and helps during the mix.

Finding sync and editing sounds to picture, as sound effects editors do, is much easier with digital video than with videotape. Working with videotape requires a lot of playing the tape, rewinding and jogging to find a particular frame you need to spot to establish sync. With digital video, wherever you click, there you are. The picture plays along with the session, and the picture will also scrub with the audio. This makes identifying sync points as easy as possible. Essentially, when you are editing sound to video you have to locate the hit point and then make a sync mark in Pro Tools, often by nudging with trial and error, or typing numbers into the Spot Dialog. Because time code numbers are so important when working this way, DV Toolkit 2 is nearly essential for sound effects editing to videotape. Due to space limitations we'll focus on the processes of sound effects synching using digital video, covering the basic principles most succinctly. You will be able to work out the process of synching sound effects to videotape for yourself with these guidelines.

To play and scrub to find a scene boundary (without DV Toolkit 2):

1. To edit backgrounds, you must identify the scene boundaries. Play your video to the scene change point. When you get close, stop.

2. Using the scrubber tool, scrub forward or back as needed to locate the leading edge of the first picture frame in the new scene.

3. Place a marker at this location by pressing the enter key.

4. Select Marker from Time Properties, and name the Marker with a short, meaningful name. An example of a name is "EXT courtyard." Click the OK button.

5. Proceed through the video to the end, placing a named marker at each change in location, time or perspective requiring a change of background.

✔ Tip

■ If you don't have DV Toolkit 2, you can make your own frame line grid of sorts. By careful sample accurate selection between the leading edge of the first two fames, you can then use Edit > Identify Beat to set up a custom bars and beats grid which is aligned to the picture frames. Call the Start Location 1|1|000 and the End Location 1|2|000. Define a 30/32 time signature for NTSC (25/32 for PAL) so that a 32nd note grid will match the rhythm of the frames, and the bar numbers will count seconds of time code from the first defined frame. It is quicker to locate scene boundaries with DV Toolkit 2.

To play and nudge to find scene boundaries (with DV Toolkit 2):

1. Set the ruler to time code.

2. Set the edit mode to grid mode.

3. Set the grid to 1 frame.

4. Play to the beginning of a new scene and stop.

5. Click near where you stopped playing. In grid mode, the insertion point is forced to a frame boundary.

6. Use the plus and minus keys on the numeric keypad to nudge forward or back as many frames as needed to arrive at the very first frame of the scene. This is the leading edge of the frame, and thus the scene.

7. Place a marker at this location and name it, as above.

8. Proceed through the video as above.

✔ Tip

■ If there is a fade to black or fade up from black or a dissolve between scenes, you can mark the start and end of the visual effect as a guide to the fades you should make in your background tracks.

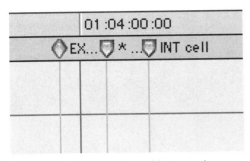

Figure 20.58 Marker text gets hidden; sometimes you can only see the first character of the marker name.

Figure 20.59 Checkerboard backgrounds to give the mixer easier control of the tracks. Marking the scene boundaries makes cutting backgrounds much easier.

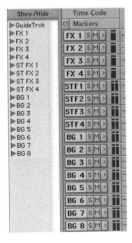

Figure 20.60 Mono and stereo sound effects and background tracks for a typical Pro Tools LE sound effects session.

To play and scrub to find a hit point:

1. To locate a hit point in the action, such as a door close, scrub the picture, or nudge in frame grid mode, until you have identified the leading edge of the moment of impact of the door against the door frame.

2. Once you have identified a hit point, you can use it immediately, or store it by placing a named marker at the point.

✔ Tip

- Adding a distinctive first character to the Marker name, such as an asterisk, helps to quickly see the difference between a hit point and a scene boundary (**Figure 20.58**).

Laying out your effects tracks

Before actually editing sound effects, you'll need to create tracks to hold them. It's best to use mostly stereo backgrounds, and mostly mono effects for video sound tracks. You'll probably want at least two, and maybe three or four, stereo backgrounds for each location. You should checkerboard the sounds from location to location, for the same reasons we split tracks in dialog editing: the mixer needs to be able to adjust levels, EQ and other parameters at each distinct new sound or scene. Checkerboarding is the alternating of track usage, switching the edited sounds for each scene back and forth between two (or more) sets of tracks (**Figure 20.59**). You'll also need several mono and several stereo sound effects tracks. These tracks tend to be sparsely populated for most videos (**Figure 20.60**).

Placing, looping, and trimming backgrounds

Once you've marked up your session to iden-tify where the scene boundaries lie, you can fairly quickly lay up your background tracks. If the sound files are long enough and the sounds have no internal problems, you can quickly lay them over the markers, and trim off the ends. The process is a bit more time consuming if the sounds are not long enough to cover the scenes.

A field recording typically has mic handling, voice slates, starts and stops, and other unwanted interruptions. Internal flaws in the sounds can take a while to fix or remove. It can be helpful for your future work to take care of these fixes early on, and then bounce the fixed regions to a single, new, cleaned-up file.

Once the regions are trimmed, they need to be smoothed. The smoothing step is the most tedious part of the process. Many sound recordings contain low frequency sounds that can click if they cut off abruptly, so the region ends need to be trimmed out and faded. Other sound anomalies can often occur at edit points and result in annoying bumps or "ffftt" sounds. Like all sounds, each region needs to be auditioned in its entirety, paying special attention to the ends. Problems can be corrected quickly.

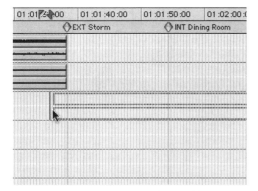

Figure 20.61 Drag the background sound file into a free track so that the head of the file can be cut off at the scene marker.

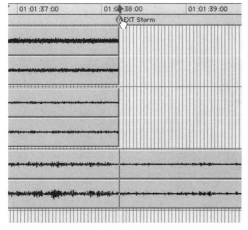

Figure 20.62 Click on the marker to put the insertion point at the scene boundary.

To lay out and trim the background sounds:

1. Grab a background sound file and drag it to the first available BG track, placing it so that it overlaps the markers defining the in and out of the scene (**Figure 20.61**).

2. Click the marker identifying the in time of the scene to move the insertion point to the head of the scene (**Figure 20.62**).

3. Trim the head of the sound by pressing the A key in Command Focus mode.

4. Click the marker identifying the end time of the scene to move the insertion point to the tail of the scene.

5. Trim the tail of the sound by pressing the S key in Command Focus mode.

✔ Tips

- Drag two or more sounds at once from the Region list to lay them up together.

- If you have already cut sounds that come up later in the track you want to place a new untrimmed sound into, you should drag the new sound to a work track and trim it there before dragging it up to the destination track.

To smooth the edges of background sounds:

1. Set the edit mode to grid mode and the grid amount to 1 frame, or 10 milliseconds. This makes it easier to make a consistent small adjustment.

2. Set the tool to Smart Tool for faster operation.

3. Trim the ends of the regions out by a frame (about 40 ms) to give an overlap to fade with. Do this to all the background regions that start or stop at that picture cut (**Figure 20.63**).

4. Apply a one-frame fade into the head of each incoming sound and a one frame fade out to the tail of each outgoing sound (**Figure 20.64**).

✔ Tip

- While you are pulling the background regions in and trimming them to length, you can nudge the insertion point over a frame and trim the sounds so they have an overlap built in from the start. Then they'll be ready to fade.

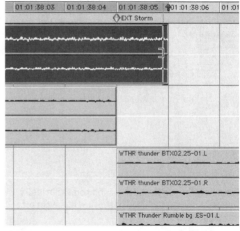

Figure 20.63 Zoom in and trim the background regions out by a frame before fading in or out. If you don't overlap the regions at the boundary, there will be a drop out at the scene change after you apply the fades.

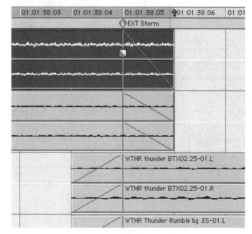

Figure 20.64 The background regions all have a one-frame fade.

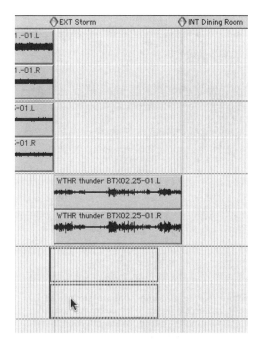

Figure 20.65 The region being dragged from the Region list is shorter than the scene.

To loop background sounds to fill out the scene:

1. When you pull a sound in from the region list, it's likely to be too short to fill the entire scene. Place it so that it covers the start marker for the scene (**Figure 20.65**).

2. We will now loop the sound, so listen to the tail of the region and make sure that it ends while in the midst of the sound. If it doesn't, trim it shorter until it seems like it will be able to be looped.

3. Now find the earliest part of the sound that can be looped with the end of the sound. Select from this point to the end of the region.

4. Choose Edit > Duplicate to duplicate the region and repeat as many times as necessary to fill the scene with the background sound (**Figure 20.66**).

5. Listen to the sound as edited, paying attention to the loop points. If the sound jumps, it may be possible to change the edit points of the start and end to make a smoother loop. Undo and repeat steps 2, 3 and 4 until you get the optimal loop.

continues on next page

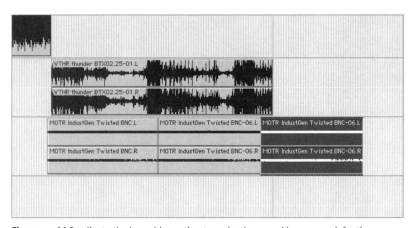

Figure 20.66 Duplicate the loopable section to make the sound long enough for the scene.

6. If the loop point bumps, apply a cross-fade to all the loop points to smooth the joins. Select the entire assembly of regions and choose Edit > Fades > Create Fades.

This will bring up the Batch Fades dialog (**Figure 20.67**).

7. Select the appropriate fade length and shape settings to smooth out your sound. Don't bother with dither. Then select Create new fades and click OK.

8. Your sound is now longer than the scene and you can trim it to length and smooth it out as described earlier.

✔ Tips

■ One of the reasons it is useful to have more than one background track running is that backgrounds frequently need to be looped to get enough length, and different files looping with different lengths sound much less loopy together than alone.

■ Backwards/Forwards loops can work with evolving backgrounds that haven't got any transient sounds within to tip off the audience, such as wind that is steadily getting faster.

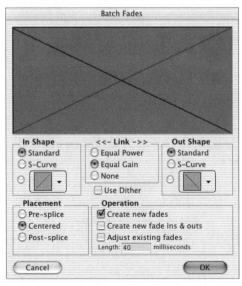

Figure 20.67 Apply a one-frame crossfade to all the edits in a looped region to remove clicks. Longer crossfades may be needed to smooth out a changing background.

To internally clean up sound effects:

1. To remove unwanted interruptions in a background sound file, play through it from the beginning, selecting the problem areas as you go. While playing, hold down the down arrow key. When you hear a problem, release it and start holding down the up arrow key. When you hear the problem area end, release the up arrow. Now the problem area is selected. Adjust the selection if necessary.

2. Press the Delete key.
   The problem is deleted.

3. Hold down Control (Mac) or Start (Windows) and click on the next region of the sound file to snap it to the end of the first region.

4. Now play on in the sound file, as you did in step one, repeating the steps as necessary until you reach the end.

   You should now have a series of regions that may be able to be played together as a single file, or they may need to be used as separate regions, depending on how different the regions are to each other.

✔ Tips

- It is likely that the edits you have made will need to be tweaked and crossfaded to make them work.

- When you have finished, it can be a real time saver to either bounce the new assembly of regions to disk (which preserves automation), or choose Edit > Consolidate Selection to duplicate the regions into one file, which you must rename immediately.

- Spending the time to clean up and organize your sound effects as they enter your library ensure that you'll never have to do the same job again with the same sounds.

A few methods for editing sound effects

Much of the creativity of sound for picture work is in selecting and assembling sound effects to bring an action or an object to life. Starting with a rich library of sounds is helpful, and recording the required sounds for each project you are involved with is the single best way to build this library. Selecting the perfect sound is an art we will leave to the reader to explore.

When pulling together sound effects for a sequence of shots, it's important to try to create a consistency of sound quality. Also, the recordings should be from an appropriate point of view that matches the picture.

Convincing sound effects must have tight sync to picture. If the sound seems to be in perfect sync with the picture, the viewer will be convinced it actually emanates from the picture. Sound effects must also be in sync with the production sound and with each other. When the production sound contains useful sounds, it is easy to sync your sound effects to the waveform of the guide track. Typically this is done to sweeten the PFX, and create a more consistent sound.

Tying sounds from disparate recordings together is a common problem for effects editors. You may have production sound effects, original effects recordings made in the field and library sounds of various sources. The sound qualities of these recordings are bound to vary, and steps must be taken to blend them together. This often involves long crossfades between sounds, as we've seen in dialog editing. Another useful technique is layering of different sonic textures to create a "fatter" sound, which helps tie everything together.

To add depth and variety to your sounds, cut a second or third layer of sound with more detail or complementary sound qualities.

To sync to picture:

1. If you've already marked up your session with the picture hit points, select one. Otherwise, locate a hit point.

2. Hold down Shift-Control (Mac) or Shift-Start (Windows) and drag a sound onto a sound effects track from the Region list. The beginning of the sound will line up with the hit point. (For more information on the other sync modes, see *Chapter 12: Working with Regions*.)

3. Play through the sound to check sync against picture. If the sound is early or late, nudge it into place (**Figure 20.68**).

4. If the sound is too long, trim it to fit.

5. If the sound is too short, build it out by repeating sections as appropriate, or using the TCE trim mode to stretch to fit.

6. Apply fades as necessary (**Figure 20.69**).

✔ Tips

- The steps are simple and familiar. It is the choice of sound, including placement against picture that takes time and much trial and error leading to refinement.

- Sound effects track selection should follow principles similar to dialog tracks. Keep similar sounds on the same tracks, and split different sound qualities to other tracks. Try to keep it consistent to make life easier for the mixer.

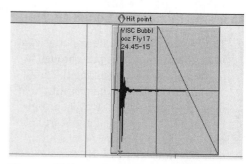

Figure 20.68 Line up the sync mark with the hit point.

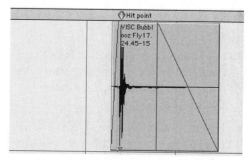

Figure 20.69 Trim the sound and apply fades if necessary to smooth the in and out of the sound.

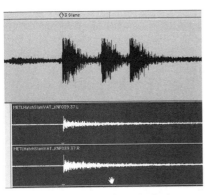

Figure 20.70 Click on the hit point in the guide track and mark it for later, or just hold Control (Mac) or Start (Windows) and drag a sound to sync with the guide track.

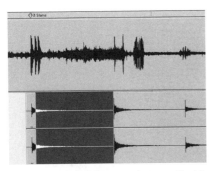

Figure 20.71 Select the space between the hit point in the guide track and the beginning of the desired sound in the uncut sound effect. Delete the space and pull up the later sound to sync with the guide track.

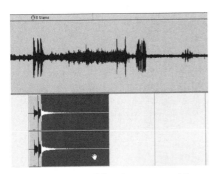

Figure 20.72 Keep tightening up or pushing back the sound effect to sync with the guide track. When you are finished you'll have to fill any holes you made.

To sync to guide track:

1. To find a hit point in the production sound, scrub the guide track and leave the insertion point at the hit point. Often the hit point is easy to spot by looking at the waveform.

2. Place a marker at the hit point.

3. Drag your sound from the Regions list to the appropriate sound effects track.

4. Position the sound's hit point against the track's hit point by dragging the hit point to the marker (**Figure 20.70**).

To maintain ongoing sync with picture or track:

1. Maintain ongoing sync between the sound effect and the picture or guide track by pulling up the sync of the sound repeatedly. Sync the beginning of the sound effect to the first hit point.

2. Play the sound effect and leave the insertion point where it goes out of sync. If the sound is too long, select through to the next wanted sound (**Figure 20.71**).

3. Press the B key in Command Focus mode to separate the region, or the delete key to clear out unwanted sound, and then drag the later region into its new sync position. If you create a hole, you may need to fill.

4. Repeat steps two and three to maintain sync as long as desired (**Figure 20.72**).

WORKING WITH SOUND EFFECTS

To sweeten a sound by adding another simultaneous sound:

1. After cutting a layer of sound effects on a track, go back and add another layer of sound on another track.

2. Drag a "sweetener" from the Regions list and line it up with the first sound.

3. Add contrasting sounds as additional layers, for example, add high cracks to low booms to create more powerful explosions. Line up the sounds so the sync is tight and the sounds blend into each other.

4. Alternatively, the second sound can add missing details to the first sound. In this case line the second sound up so the hit points work around the original sound (**Figure 20.73**).

Assembling sound effects from various sources

To blend sound effects from different sources there is a range of useful techniques:

◆ As in dialog editing, use long overlaps to blend sounds seamlessly.

◆ Hit hard with a new incoming sound, cutting in on a large transient, so that it overwhelms the outgoing sound, distracting the ear.

◆ Cut layers of sound effects, where possible, weaving tracks from the different material, so that none of the sounds ever fully disappears. All the layers don't have to be doing equal work at all times, but can come to the fore as appropriate.

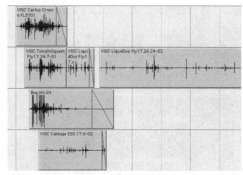

Figure 20.73 Some complementary sound effects layered to create a complex bug squashing sound.

Editing Music for Video

The principles of dialog and sound effects editing also apply when editing music.

Music often enters the project at an early stage, and is used during the picture editing to give a rhythm and tempo to a scene. So the picture is edited to the music.

Just as often, the music is brought to the picture later. In this case the sound editor may be asked to adapt the music to fit the rhythms and hit points of the picture. This is a challenging task, as it calls into play all the tools at the sound editor's disposal, as well as a musical sensibility. Most professional music editors are musicians themselves, which gives them a depth of understanding of musical forms. However, everyone has some musical sensibility and can learn to edit music in effective ways.

Mixing for Video

Film and video have always been mixed in elaborate facilities with expensive audio, projection, and interlock equipment. The field has been the exclusive domain of highly trained engineers and crafts people. Since Pro Tools has become the dominant tool in the industry for post production sound editing, a few forward thinking sound engineers have been adapting the powerful mixing tools in Pro Tools to the mix to picture field.

The details of mixing for video and film are beyond the scope of this introductory chapter, so we will merely touch on some of the major topics of mixing for video here.

The stages of a mix

The three stages of a mix are

◆ Premixing

◆ Final Mixing

◆ Print Mastering and Versions

A premix is where you focus on getting the details of a particular category of sound just right, without regard to the rest of the tracks.

The dialog premix focuses on getting the dialog clear, clean, smooth and balanced. Reverb and other effects are added as needed to place the dialog into the proper setting. ADR is matched in to the production sound.

The effects pre-mix is where you balance the sounds against each other and against the dialog track. EQ, panning and effects are added. Foley is similarly premixed.

Once the premixes are complete, the final mix begins. In the final mix the dialog, ADR, sound effects, Foley, and music are balanced and final adjustments are made to the EQ and other effects. Since the music is making its first appearance, it often gets most of the attention in the final mix.

During the final mix, the sounds are kept separate by category (dialog, ADR, effects, Foley, and music), using *stems*, which ease mix fixes and later re-purposing of your mix. Stems are summed together and monitored during the final mix, but are recorded and stored separately as the ultimate master for the sound track. From the stems any number of different versions of the sound track can be produced.

The print master is a copy of the stems tailored for the particular release format required. Any number of different print masters can be made for different release requirements. Examples of different release formats with differing audio requirements include IMAX, 35mm film, 16mm film, DVD, VHS, broadcast television, broadband Internet, dial-up Internet, and even cell phone!

Simple mixes can be effectively done in an editing room with a mouse and keyboard. More complex mixes require video or film projection, surround sound monitoring, one or more Pro Tools TDM systems and control surface(s).

For more information on mixing in Pro Tools, *see Part V, Mixing Audio.*

OPTIMIZING
PERFORMANCE

In Pro Tools LE, every processing task—from the number of tracks you can record and play back at one time to the performance of RTAS plug-ins—depends on the CPU power of your computer. Thus, using the fastest computer possible is the best way to optimize your system's performance.

But computer speed is not the only factor. The amount of RAM in your computer makes a big difference too, as does the way you allocate your system's CPU power. Allocating CPU resources judiciously allows your system to handle audio processing tasks without interruption. This chapter offers some useful tips for enhancing your computer's performance. We'll show you how to manage CPU power by assigning resources where they're needed. And we'll provide suggestions for running plug-ins efficiently, and for maximizing limited hard drive space.

If your system's performance starts to lag, you may want to try some (or all) of these tricks. In other words, keep this chapter bookmarked.

Managing CPU Power

Managing CPU power in Pro Tools LE is somewhat of a balancing act. Because you're limited by the host computer's processing power, it's sometimes necessary to juggle CPU resources among different functions. and you may occasionally need to shuffle plug-ins around. The good news is Pro Tools has many features that can help you manage CPU power quite effectively.

The System Usage window

The System Usage window (**Figure 21.1**) lets you keep an eye on the overall perform-ance of your Pro Tools system. It displays how much CPU power Pro Tools is using. Keep this window open so you can monitor CPU resource allocation and make adjust-ments, if necessary.

CPU usage limit

The Playback Engine dialog box lets you set the amount of total CPU power dedicated to Pro Tools. Single processor computers run-ning Mbox 2 or Mbox 2 Pro systems let you allocate up to 85 percent. Single processor units running Digi 002 systems let you allo-cate up to 99 percent of your CPU to pro-cessing tasks.

Multiprocessor computers let you use between 90 and 95 percent of each CPU depending on the number of processors selected in the RTAS plug-in for RTAS plug-in processing.

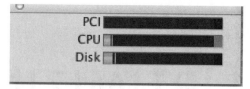

Figure 21.1 The System Usage window helps you track your system's overall performance.

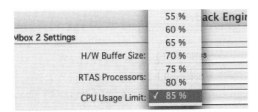

Figure 21.2 The Playback Engine dialog box lets you set the amount of total CPU power dedicated to Pro Tools.

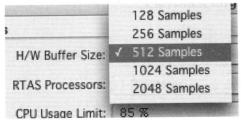

Figure 21.3 The Playback Engine dialog box also lets you set a hardware buffer size.

To set the CPU usage limit:

1. Choose Setup > Playback Engine.
   The Playback Engine dialog box appears.

2. From the CPU Usage Limit pop-up menu, select a percentage of CPU resources to allocate to host processing (**Figure 21.2**).

For more information on the Playback Engine dialog box, see *Chapter 2: Pro Tools Software Basics.*

Hardware buffer size

The Playback Engine dialog box also lets you set a hardware buffer size (**Figure 21.3**). This determines the size of audio data blocks that are sampled and processed at one time by the CPU. Larger buffer sizes let you use more plug-ins but increase latency. Smaller buffer sizes decrease latency but decrease the number of plug-ins that you can use.

During recording, use a smaller buffer size (128 or 256 samples) to keep latency to a minimum. During mixing, when latency is less relevant, increase the buffer size so you can use more tracks and plug-ins.

To set the hardware buffer size:

1. Choose Setup > Playback Engine.
   The Playback Engine dialog box appears.

2. From the H/W Buffer Size pop-up menu, select the audio buffer size (in samples) for host-processing tasks.

For more information on the Playback Engine dialog box, see *Chapter 2: Software Basics.*

MANAGING CPU POWER

DAE playback buffer size

The DAE Playback Buffer Size option controls the amount of RAM that's allocated as a holding area for data coming from your hard drive. The buffer size determines initial time lag that occurs when you initiate playback or recording. The higher the buffer size, the longer the time lag.

Smaller buffer sizes can increase system responsiveness but may make recording and playback on slower hard drives less reliable. Larger buffer sizes can make hard drive performance more reliable but may cause time lags to occur before recording or playback begins.

To set the DAE playback buffer size:

1. Choose Setup > Playback Engine.

   The Playback Engine dialog box appears.

2. From the DAE Playback Buffer pop-up menu, select a buffer size (**Figure 21.4**).

For more information on the DAE Playback Buffer, see *Chapter 2: Software Basics* or the *Pro Tools Reference Guide.*

Reducing levels of undo

Pro Tools lets you undo up to 32 editing operations. These operations are stored in a temporary queue inside your computer's RAM. Reducing your system's levels of undo will free up RAM for other uses.

To reduce levels of undo:

1. Choose Setup > Preferences.

2. Click the Editing tab.

3. In the Levels of Undo field, enter a number from 1 to 32 (**Figure 21.5**).

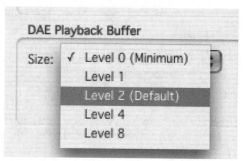

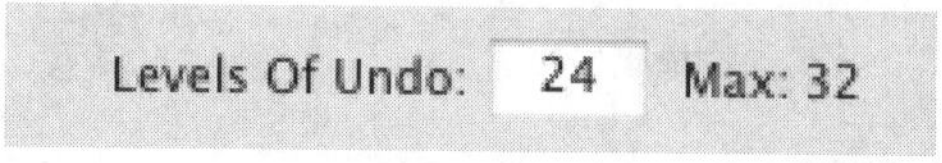

Figure 21.4 The DAE Playback Buffer pop-up menu.

Levels Of Undo: 24   Max: 32

Figure 21.5 Reducing levels of undo can help free up RAM and enhance system performance.

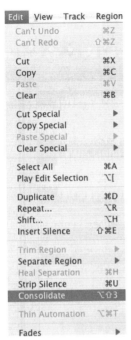

Figure 21.6
Consolidating regions is another way to save CPU power.

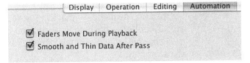

Figure 21.7 Smoothing and thinning automation removes unnecessary breakpoints and makes automation playback less CPU intensive.

Consolidating regions

Consolidating multiple separate regions into a single region reduces the number of edits on a track. This creates fewer edits for Pro Tools to manage, which saves CPU power.

To consolidate regions:

1. Select the regions that you want to consolidate.

2. Choose Edit > Consolidate (**Figure 21.6**).

Smoothing and thinning automation

Pro Tools writes automation data as a series of events called breakpoints. Smoothing and thinning automation removes superfluous breakpoints and makes automation playback less CPU intensive.

To smooth and thin automation data automatically after an automation pass:

1. Choose Setup > Preferences.

2. Click the Automation tab.

3. Select the Smooth and Thin Data After Pass option (**Figure 21.7**).

For more information on thinning automation, see *Chapter 16: Automating a Mix.*

MANAGING CPU POWER

Making tracks inactive

In Pro Tools you can make audio, auxiliary input, and master fader tracks inactive. You can also make individual sends, inserts, plug-ins, bus paths, and track inputs and outputs inactive. When items are made inactive, they release their CPU resources (although their setting configurations are saved).

To make a track inactive:

1. Click the track name to select it.

2. Choose Track > Make Inactive.

   or

   Command-Control-click (Macintosh) or Control-Start-click (Windows) on the track type indicator in the Mix window (**Figure 21.8**).

   The track becomes inactive. Its name is italicized and the track's channel strip turns a monotone shade of gray (**Figure 21.9**).

For more information on making tracks and other items inactive, see *Chapter 4: Starting a New Session* and *Chapter 14: Mixing Basics*, or see the *Pro Tools Reference Guide*.

Figure 21.8 To make a track inactive, in the Mix window, Command-Control-click (Macintosh) or Control-Start-click (Windows) on the track type indicator.

Figure 21.9 The names of inactive tracks (and other items) become italicized and their channel strips become a monotone shade of gray.

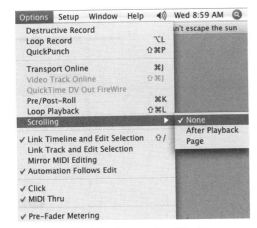

Figure 21.10 Disabling the Page Scroll During Playback setting can help free up processing power.

Disabling page scroll during playback

Disabling the Page Scroll During Playback setting frees your computer's CPU from having to constantly redraw the screen during playback. This can save a lot of processing power that may be better used elsewhere.

To disable page scroll during playback:

◆ Choose Options > Scrolling > None (**Figure 21.10**).

Disabling moving faders

Although being able to display automated moving faders is a nice feature, it can monopolize a fair amount of CPU power, because Pro Tools constantly redraws the screen. Try disabling this setting to recover some of that CPU power.

To disable moving faders:

1. Choose Setup > Preferences.

2. Click the Automation tab.

3. Deselect the Faders Move During Playback option.

Disabling Sends View meters

Sends View meters can also monopolize CPU power. Try turning this option off to regain some processing power.

To disable Sends View meters:

1. Choose Setup > Preferences.

2. Click the Display tab.

3. Deselect Show Meters in Sends View.
   or
   Choose View > Sends A–F or Sends F–J > Assignments.

MANAGING CPU POWER

Using Plug-ins Efficiently

Real-time DSP plug-ins are undoubtedly one of the most useful features in Pro Tools, but they're also one of the most power hungry. Here are a few ways to ease the power crunch.

Allocating RTAS Processors

Pro Tools LE now supports multiprocessor computers. Pro Tools lets you decide how many processors to devote to RTAS plug-ins.

To designate the number of RTAS processors (multiprocessor computers only):

1. Choose Setup > Playback Engine

   The Playback Engine dialog box opens.

2. Open the RTAS Processors pop-up menu and select the number of processors you want to dedicate to RTAS Plug-in processing (**Figure 21.11**).

   The number of processors available in the pop-up menu will depend on how many processors the computer contains.

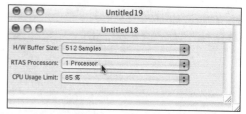

Figure 21.11 Select the number of processors you want to allocate to RTAS plug-in processing (multiprocessor computers only).

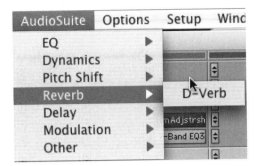

Figure 21.12 Using nonreal-time AudioSuite plug-ins instead RTAS plug-ins is a good power-saving alternative.

Using AudioSuite plug-ins instead of RTAS plug-ins

RTAS plug-ins consume lots of CPU power because they apply effects in real time. If you're hitting the limit on the number of real-time plug-ins you can use, try using a nonreal-time AudioSuite plug-in instead.

Most RTAS plug-ins also come in AudioSuite versions. You can save RTAS plug-in settings and then import them into the AudioSuite version. This lets you find effects in real time, but apply them in non-real time. For example, if you have a favorite EQ setting created with an RTAS EQ plug-in, import the setting into the AudioSuite version and process your audio while Pro Tools is not playing back. This conserves CPU power for other power-intensive RTAS plug-ins such as delays and reverbs.

To switch from an RTAS plug-in to its AudioSuite version:

1. Configure and save the desired RTAS plug-in settings.

2. Remove the RTAS plug-in from the track insert.

3. In the Edit window, select the same track using the Selector or Grabber tool.

4. Choose the desired AudioSuite plug-in from the AudioSuite menu (**Figure 21.12**).

5. Import the saved setting.

6. Click Process.
   The desired effect is applied to the track.

USING PLUG-INS EFFICIENTLY

Using fewer CPU-intensive plug-ins

Some plug-ins are more CPU intensive than others. Generally speaking, RTAS plug-ins consume the following amounts of CPU power:

◆ Delay effects (such as flange, slapback, chorus, and echo) and reverbs tend to consume large amounts of CPU power.

◆ Single-band EQs, gates, compressors, limiters, expanders, and dither require small amounts of CPU power.

Using effects loops

Effects loops let you apply the same effect to multiple channels of audio simultaneously. They work especially well for reverbs and other CPU-intensive plug-ins that are frequently used on more than one track. By making one plug-in available to multiple tracks simultaneously, an effects loop can help you get the most out of power-hungry plug-ins like delays and reverbs.

When you create an effects loop, audio is sent from audio tracks to an auxiliary input, where an inserted effect is applied. The effected signal is then returned to the main mix, where it's combined with the original signal. For more information on effects loops, see *Chapter 15: Adding Effects to a Mix.*

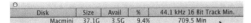

Disk	Size	Avail	%	44.1 kHz 16 Bit Track Min.
Macmini	37.1G	3.5G	9.4%	709.5 Min

Figure 21.13 The Disk Space window lets you keep an eye on how much space remains on each disk.

Using Hard Drives Efficiently

Recording digital media (audio and video) requires significant hard disc space. Fortunately, the relatively low cost and high capacity of hard drives these days make it possible for most users to outfit their systems with adequate hard drive storage space.

If you're storage space is limited, however, or you find yourself running out of storage space in the middle of an project, consider the following methods to get the most out of your hard drive.

The Disk Space window

Similar to the System Usage window, the Disk Space window (**Figure 21.13**) lets you gauge how much space remains on each disk. Keep an eye on this window: You don't want to run out of disk space in the middle of recording.

To view the Disk Space window:

◆ Choose Window > Disk Space.

Using disk allocation

Pro Tools lets you record audio tracks simultaneously to different hard drives. Using disk allocation can help ease the workload on individual hard drives. For more information, see *Chapter 6: Getting Ready to Record*.

Removing unused regions and deleting audio files

Removing unused regions is a great way to keep your sessions organized. And if you're not using the underlying audio files, deleting them from your hard drive can help you recover valuable hard drive real estate.

Figure 21.14 Removing unused regions is a great way to keep your sessions organized.

To remove unused regions or delete audio files:

1. From the Regions List pop-up menu, choose Select > Unused (**Figure 21.14**).

   Currently unused regions are highlighted in the Regions list.

2. Choose Clear from the pop-up menu.

   The Clear Regions dialog box appears (**Figure 21.15**).

3. Click Remove to clear the unused region from the session.

   or

   Click Delete to erase the underlying audio file from the hard disk.

For more information on using the Regions list, see *Chapter 10: Editing Basics.*

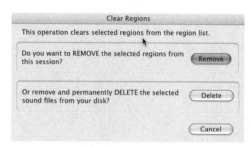

Figure 21.15 The Clear Regions dialog box.

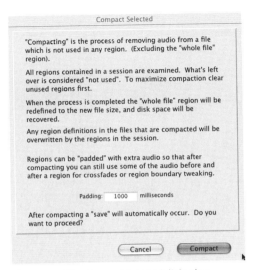

Figure 21.16 The Compact Selected dialog box.

Compacting audio files

Another good way to recover hard drive space is to compact audio files. This process deletes unused portions of an audio file that aren't referenced by a region in the session. If an audio file is referenced in the session, compacting erases the entire audio file *except* the referenced portion.

Be careful when compacting audio—it permanently erases audio data from your disk. In fact, it's a good idea to wait until the session is over and the audio is mixed before you compact any files.

To compact audio files:

1. Select the regions you want to compact in the Regions list.

2. Choose Compact from the Regions List pop-up menu.
   The Compact Selected dialog box appears (**Figure 21.16**).

3. Enter the amount of padding in milliseconds.

4. Click Compact.

For more information on compacting audio files, see *Chapter 8: File Management Basics.*

Creating submixes

When you create a submix, you bounce multiple audio tracks down to a premixed mono or stereo track. Once you've created a submix that you want to keep, you can delete the parent audio files and free up additional disk space.

For more information on submixes, see *Chapter 14: Mixing Basics.*

Using lower bit depths and sample rates

Audio file size is determined by the bit depth and sample rate at which it's recorded. Recording at 16-bit/44.1 kHz (CD quality) consumes about 40 percent less hard drive space than recording at 24-bit/48 kHz. And 16-bit/44.1 kHz audio still sounds quite acceptable.

For more information on hard drive space requirements, see *Chapter 1: Setting Up Your Pro Tools LE System.* For more information on bit depth and sample rate, see *Chapter 4: Starting a New Session.*

USING HARD DRIVES EFFICIENTLY

CONNECTING YOUR STUDIO

Your studio equipment needs will vary depending on which Pro Tools LE system you're running—Digi 002, Digi 002 Rack, Mbox, Mbox 2, or Mbox 2 Pro—and the type of audio source, external hardware, and monitor system you want to connect it to.

If you already have a studio full of great-sounding peripheral hardware, don't worry: You can connect all types of external hardware to Pro Tools LE systems. How many pieces of external hardware you can connect at one time, however, depends upon which Pro Tools LE system you're using.

Connecting Your Studio to the Digi 002, Digi 002 Rack, Mbox, Mbox 2, or Mbox 2 Pro

The minimum studio setup needed to record with Digi 002, Digi 002 Rack, Mbox , Mbox 2, and Mbox 2 Pro is a mic and mic cable (or instrument and instrument cable), and a pair of headphones. **Figures A.1–A.4** show basic studio setups for Digi 002, Digi 002 Rack, Mbox, Mbox 2, and Mbox 2 Pro systems, respectively.

With eight channels of analog I/O (including four balanced mic preamps with individual high pass filters) and 24-bit, 96 kHz A/D input signal conversion, Digi 002 and Digi 002 Rack give you the best audio quality and most input versatility of the LE systems.

Digi 002 and Digi 002 Rack also give you eight channels of optical I/O, two channels of S/PDIF digital I/O, and two alternate analog inputs (RCA plugs) for connecting an external sound source, such as a CD player or tape deck.

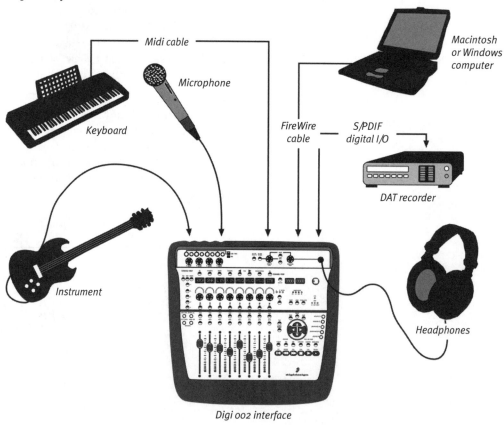

Figure A.1 A basic Digi 002 studio setup.

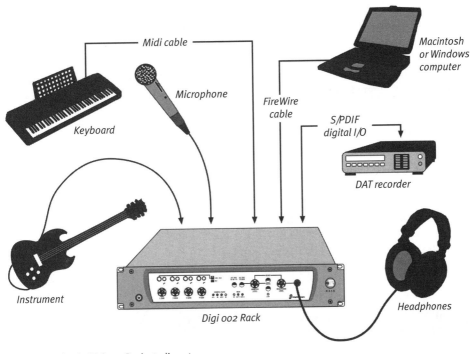

Figure A.2 A basic Digi 002 Rack studio setup.

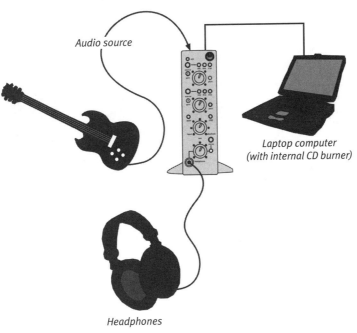

Figure A.3 A basic Mbox studio setup.

The original Mbox has far fewer I/O options than the Digi 002. You can, however, connect external hardware using the system's two channels of analog I/O and two channels of S/PDIF digital I/O. Mbox also provides two 1/4-inch line inserts, which let you add external hardware effects during recording.

Mbox 2 and Mbox 2 Pro offer significantly more I/O options than the original Mbox.

The USB-based Mbox 2 audio interface includes two mic preamps (XLR), two 1/4-inch TRS inputs, and two DI inputs (1/4-inch TS). It also gives you two channels of S/DIF Digital I/O, two channel 1/4 (TRS) monitor outputs, as well as one MIDI In and one MIDI Out port.

The FireWire-based Mbox 2 Pro provides the same I/O features as the Mbox 2, with some key upgrades. The interface includes two built-in mic preamps (XLR-1/4-inch TRS combo jacks), which can record at sample rates up to 96 kHz. In addition, Mbox 2 Pro includes a two-channel auxiliary input section with both 1/4-inch TRS (balanced) and RCA stereo plug (unbalanced) inputs, It has four 1/4-inch TRS analog outputs, two channels of S/PDIF digital I/O, two channel 1/4 (TRS) monitor outputs, one MIDI In and one MIDI Out port, and Word Clock I/O.

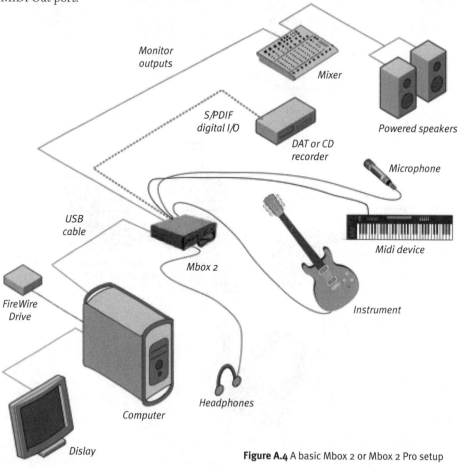

Figure A.4 A basic Mbox 2 or Mbox 2 Pro setup

Connecting Audio Sources to Digi 002 and Digi 002 Rack

The Digi 002 and Digi 002 Rack's eight channels of balanced analog I/O (including four mic preamps) and 24-bit, 96 kHz A/D input signal conversion make them useful for live recording, studio sessions, or any situation requiring multiple high-quality mic or instrument inputs.

The Digi 002 and Digi 002 Rack have identical audio input controls, monitor controls, and status indicators, located on the front panels of their respective hardware interfaces (**Figures A.5** and **A.6**) as follows:

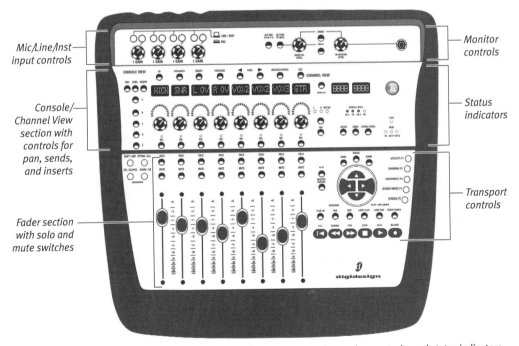

Mic/Line/Inst input controls

Console/ Channel View section with controls for pan, sends, and inserts

Fader section with solo and mute switches

Monitor controls

Status indicators

Transport controls

Figure A.5 The Digi 002's front panel includes Mic/Line/Inst Input controls, monitor controls, and status indicators (top section). The interface also includes transport controls, level faders with solo and mute buttons, and channel strip controls for sends, inserts, and pan (lower and middle sections).

Mic/Line/Inst Input Controls

◆ **Mic/Line/Instrument selectors:**
These selectors let you toggle inputs
between microphone and line-level operating levels. (Note: Toggling to mic position without a XLR mic cable attached
may introduce low-level noise).

◆ **High Pass Filter switch:** This switch
enables a high pass filter (75 Hz, 12 dB/
octave rolloff) on the input. This filter is
useful for reducing low-end rumble from
sources such as air-conditioning units.

◆ **Input Gain control:** This knob lets you
adjust input level of Mic/Line inputs 1–4.

Monitor Controls

◆ **Monitor Level control:** This knob con-
trols the level of the Monitor Outputs.
The Monitor Outputs mirror the Main
Outputs (outputs 1–2).

◆ **Monitor Mute switch:** This switch
mutes the Monitor Outputs only. It has
no effect on the Main Outputs or
Headphone Output.

◆ **Mono Output switch:** This switch combines output signals 1 and 2 in both the
Monitor and Headphone outputs. This is
useful for checking phase relationships of
stereo material. The Mono Output switch
has no effect on the Main Outputs.

◆ **Headphone jack:** This jack accepts a
standard 1/4-inch stereo headphone
connector.

◆ **Headphone Level control:** This knob
lets you control headphone output level.
Headphones let you monitor the Main
Outputs (outputs 1 and 2).

Status Indicators

◆ **Session Sample Rate indicators:**
The Session Sample Rate LEDs indicate
the sample rate of the current Pro Tools
session.

◆ **Pro Tools Connection Status indicator:**
This LED, marked "1394," indicates that
communication has been established
between the hardware interface and
Pro Tools LE software via FireWire.

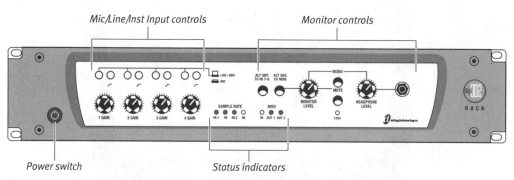

Figure A.6 The Digi 002 Rack's front panel includes Mic/Line/Inst input controls, monitor controls, and status indicators.

The Digi 002 and Digi 002 Rack's respective back panels (**Figure A.7a** and **A7b**) provide the following audio I/O features:

- **Mic Inputs 1–4:** These four balanced XLR mic preamps let you boost the input signals from microphones and other low-level audio sources requiring amplification.

- **Line/Instrument Inputs 1–4:** These four balanced 1/4-inch TRS inputs let you record line-level audio sources from line-level audio sources, such as keyboards, mixers, and preamps.

- **Phantom Power switches:** These switches let you apply 48V phantom power to Mic/Line inputs 1–2 and inputs 3–4, respectively.

- **Analog Inputs 5–8:** Analog inputs 5–8 accept balanced or unbalanced 1/4-inch connectors and are switchable between –10 dBV and +4 dBV line levels.

- **Operating Level switches for Inputs 5–8:** These switches let you switch the nominal line-level of channels 5–8 between –10 dBV and +4 dBV.

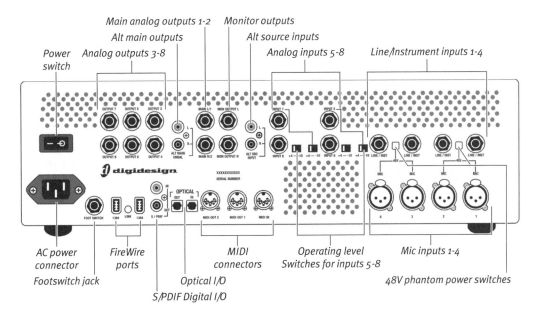

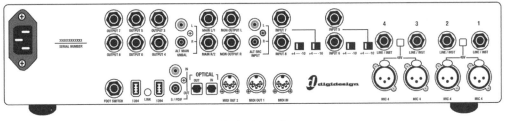

Figure A.7a and A.7b The Digi 002 and Digi 002 Rack's back panels.

- **Footswitch jack:** Lets you connect a standard footswitch to punch in audio or MIDI when recording

- **Alt Source Inputs:** This pair of unbalanced RCA-connectors let you input audio from alternate sources such as a tape deck or CD player.

- **Monitor Outputs:** These balanced 1/4-inch TRS jacks let you monitor stereo output. These outputs play output routed to analog outputs 1 and 2 in Pro Tools.

- **Main Analog Outputs 1–2:** These balanced 1/4-inch TRS jacks output audio routed to analog outputs 1 and 2 in Pro Tools. These outputs are useful for stereo mixdown to an external stereo device (such as a two-track analog tape machine). Output is balanced, +4 dBu line-level.

- **Analog Outputs 3–8:** These balanced 1/4-inch TRS jacks output audio routed to analog outputs 3–8. Outputs are balanced, +4 dBu line-level.

- **S/PDIF Digital I/O:** These unbalanced RCA jacks input and output 24-bit digital data at sample rates up to 96 kHz. (See the sidebar *Making Connections* for more information on S/PDIF.)

- **Optical I/O:** This pair of optical connectors input and output eight channels of ADAT-format or two channels of S/PDIF-format digital audio. ADAT format supports sample rates of 44.1 and 48 kHz, whereas S/PDIF format supports sample rates up to 96 kHz. Both Optical formats support 16-bit, 20-bit, and 24-bit data resolution. (Select the desired Optical format in the Hardware Setup dialog.) Optical I/O uses standard optical "light-pipe" cables.

- **MIDI I/O:** The Digi 002 and Digi 002 Rack's 5-pin MIDI connectors include one MIDI input and two MIDI outputs.

- **Footswitch jack:** Lets you connect a standard footswitch to punch in audio or MIDI when recording

- **IEEE-1394 (FireWire) Ports:** These two ports let you connect to your computer and external storage devices via FireWire. The Link LED (located between the FireWire ports) indicates an active connection is established between the interface and the computer.

To connect an analog audio source to the Digi 002 or Digi 002 Rack:

◆ Connect either an XLR cable from a microphone or 1/4-inch TRS cable from a line-level device or instrument to any of the Mic/Line inputs 1–4 on the interface's back panel. Mic preamps are necessary for microphones and instruments using magnetic pickups (such as electric guitars and other string instruments) that generate lower-level audio signals requiring amplification.

or

◆ Connect a balanced or unbalanced 1/4-inch cable from a line-level audio source (such as a keyboard, preamp, or mixer) to any of the analog inputs 5–8 on the interface's back panel. If necessary, use the adjacent Operating Level switches for inputs 5–8 to switch between –10 dBV and +4 dBV line-level.

To connect a digital audio source to Digi 002 or Digi 002 Rack using optical cables:

1. Connect an optical cable from the optical output of the external digital device to the optical input on the Digi 002 or Digi 002 Rack's back panel.

2. Connect an optical cable from the optical output on the Digi 002 or Digi 002 Rack's back panel to the optical input of the external digital device.

To connect a digital audio source to the Digi 002 using S/PDIF cables:

◆ Connect a S/PDIF cable (75-ohm coaxial cable with RCA plugs) from the S/PDIF output of the external digital device to the S/PDIF input on the Digi 002 or Digi 002 Rack's back panel.

◆ Each S/PDIF input and output carries a stereo signal. The following step is required only if you want to send a digital signal from Pro Tools to a digital device.

◆ Connect aanother S/PDIF cable from the S/PDIF output on the Digi 002 or Digi 002 Rack's back panel to the S/PDIF input on the digital device.

For more information on connecting analog and digital hardware to Digi 002 and Digi 002 Rack, see *Getting Started with Digi 002 and Digi 002 Rack*.

Connecting Audio Sources to Mbox

Mbox provides two combination Mic/Line preamps. These Mic/Line preamp inputs accept either XLR (3-pin) or 1/4-inch TRS cables. Mbox also provides two channels of S/PDIF digital I/O.

The front panel of the Mbox (**Figure A.8**) has the following features:

◆ **48V LED:** When lit, the 48V LED indicates that 48V phantom power is available at the Mic/Line input.

◆ **Source selector:** The Source selectors let you switch between three input level options for the Mbox's Mic/Line inputs: Mic (microphone), Line, and Inst (Instrument).

◆ **Gain controls:** Gain controls let you adjust the input level of the Mic/Line inputs.

◆ **Peak LEDs:** Peak LEDs light up just below analog clipping levels. This warns you that the input signal may be approaching clipping.

◆ **USB LED:** The USB LED indicates that the USB port is active, and audio can pass in or out of the system.

◆ **S/PDIF LED:** The S/PDIF LED indicates that channels 1 and 2 are set to receive digital input (rather than analog).

◆ **Mix (Ratio) control:** The Mix (ratio) control lets you monitor an adjustable blend of live input signal (with zero latency) and audio playback from disk. To hear the input signal only, turn the Mix knob hard left to Input. To hear Pro Tools output only, turn the knob hard right to Playback.

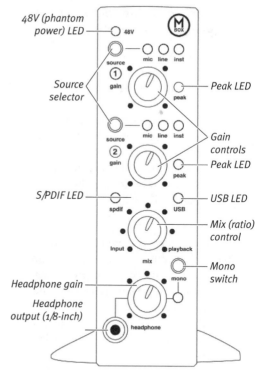

Figure A.8 Mbox front panel.

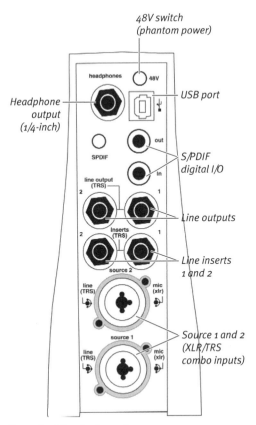

48V switch
(phantom power)

Headphone
output
(1/4-inch)

USB port

S/PDIF
digital I/O

Line outputs

Line inserts
1 and 2

Source 1 and 2
(XLR/TRS
combo inputs)

Figure A.9 Mbox back panel.

◆ **Mono switch:** The Mono switch lets you hear live input signals in mono. You can use this switch to check for stereo phase cancellations. (Typically, out-of-phase tracks sound hollow and lacking in low frequencies.)

◆ **Headphone gain:** Headphone gain controls the output level of the headphones on both the front and back panels.

◆ **Headphone output (front panel):** The front panel headphone output is a 1/8-inch stereo mini connector. (Inserting a 1/4-inch TRS connector into the rear panel headphone disables the 1/8-inch headphone output on the front panel.)

The back panel of the Mbox (**Figure A.9**) has the following features:

◆ **Headphone output (back panel):** The back panel headphone output features a 1/4-inch TRS connector.

◆ **48V switch:** The 48V switch activates phantom power for use by microphones (especially condenser mics).

◆ **USB port:** The USB port lets you connect Mbox to any compatible USB-enabled computer.

◆ **S/PDIF Digital I/O:** S/PDIF digital inputs and outputs use RCA plugs.

◆ **Line outputs:** Line outputs are balanced TRS outputs, which you can connect to a mixer or stereo system to monitor mixes.

◆ **Source 1 and 2:** Combination Mic/Line (balanced/unbalanced) audio inputs. Accepts XLR (3-pin) or 1/4-inch TRS connections.

CONNECTING AUDIO SOURCES TO MBOX

◆ **Inserts 1 and 2:** Inserts 1 and 2 are line inserts, which let you insert an effect into the audio input path of Source 1 and 2 inputs. The inserted effect is added to the analog audio input signal before it's converted into digital audio. These inserts are useful for adding analog effects processors (such as equalizers and compressors) to a track.

To connect an analog audio source to the Mbox:

◆ Connect an XLR or 1/4-inch cable to the Source 1 or Source 2 input on the Mbox's back panel.

◆ Using the Source button on the Mbox's front panel, select the input source type (mic, line, or instrument).

To connect a digital audio source to the Mbox:

1. Connect a S/PDIF cable (75-ohm coaxial cable with RCA plugs) from the digital audio source's S/PDIF output to the S/PDIF input on the Mbox's back panel.

2. Connect another S/PDIF cable from the Mbox's S/PDIF output to the digital audio source's S/PDIF input.

Connecting Audio Sources to Mbox 2 and Mbox 2 Pro

The Mbox 2 and Mbox 2 Pro's pairs of balanced mic preamps offer high-quality 24-bit analog to digital (A/D) audio conversion. And the Mbox 2 Pro's 96 kHz sample rate recording capability place it on a par with many higher-end recording systems.

The Mbox 2 and Mbox 2 Pro audio interface front panels include the following features (**Figures A.10** and **A.11**):

Audio Input 1–2 controls

- **Source selectors and LEDs:** These selectors let you switch between Mic or DI inputs for that channel. The Mic and DI LEDs indicate the currently active input source. In addition, the Mbox 2 Pro's front panel includes 1/4-inch DI input jacks for each channel.

- **Gain controls:** These knobs let you adjust the input gain levels (volume) of the Mic/Line inputs for each channel.

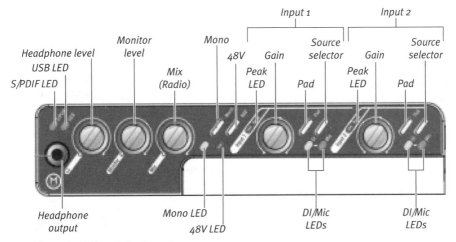

Figure A.10 Mbox 2's front panel

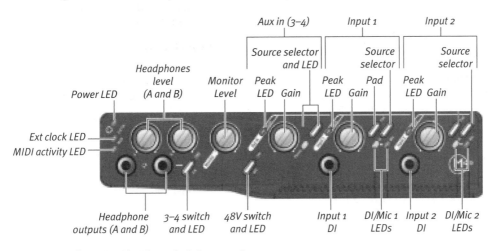

Figure A.11 The Mbox 2 Pro's front panel

◆ **Peak LED:** The Peak LED indicates digital audio signal clipping on the input channel. If you see this light flickering red, reduce the audio input level using the Gain control knob and/or the output level of the external audio source. Also, try engaging the Pad switch to reduce input level.

◆ **Pad:** The Pad switch engages a –20 dB attenuation (reduction in level) on the input channel. If you notice the Peak LED is clipping, try using the Pad switch to cut the input level.

◆ **Aux In 3–4(Line/Phono Inputs) (Mbox 2 Pro only):** The Mbox 2 Pro has an additional pair of inputs with input connections for both balanced 1/4-inch TRS connectors and RCA phono plugs. Controls for the Aux 3–4 inputs on the front panel include a line/phono source selector, Gain controls, and Peak LEDs.

◆ **48V (Phantom Power) switch:** The 48V switch activates phantom power, which is required for the operation of ultrasensitive *condenser* microphones. *Dynamic* microphones (such as the ubiquitous Shure SM57) do not require phantom power to operate. For more information on microphone types, see *Chapter 6: Getting Ready to Record.*

Monitor Controls

◆ **Mix (Ratio):** This knob lets you adjust a monitoring balance between your analog input signal and the output signal from Pro Tools. This feature can help reduce disorienting effects caused by latency (time delays between input and output signals) in host-based recording systems.

◆ **Monitor Level control:** This knob controls the level of the stereo (L/R) monitor outputs. This stereo signal is routed from Pro Tools outputs 1–2.

◆ **Mono Output switch:** This switch combines output signals 1 and 2 in both the monitor and headphone outputs. This is useful for checking phase relationships of stereo material. The Mono Output switch has no effect on the Main outputs.

◆ **Headphone jacks:** These jacks accept a standard 1/4-inch stereo headphone connector. The Mbox 2 Pro provides two headphone outputs (A and B).

◆ **Headphone Level controls:** This knob lets you control headphone output level. The Mbox 2's single headphone lets you monitor the Main outputs 1–2. Mbox 2 Pro provides two separate headphone level controls: Headphone A and B.

◆ **Headphone 3–4 switch and LED:** This switch toggles Headphone B between Main outputs 1–2 and the output of channels 3–4.

Status Indicators

◆ **S/PDIF LED:** This LED indicates that Mbox 2 is using the S/PDIF inputs as the clock source.

◆ **USB LED:** This LED indicates that communication has been established between the hardware interface and Pro Tools LE software via USB.

◆ **Ext Clock LED (Mbox 2 PRO):** This LED indicates that S/PDIF or Word Clock I is the current clock source. When not lit, the clock source is internal.

◆ **MIDI activity LED (Mbox 2 Pro):** This LED indicates that Mbox 2 Pro is sending or receiving MIDI.

◆ **Power LED:** This LED indicates Mbox 2 Pro is powered on.

The Mbox 2 and Mbox 2 Pro respective back panels (**Figures A.12** and **A.13**) provide the following audio I/O features:

- **Inputs 1–2:** Mbox 2 provides two balanced XLR mic inputs, two balanced 1/4-inch line inputs, and two DI inputs. The Mbox 2 Pro provides two balanced XLR-1/4-inch (TRS) combo mic preamps and two DI inputs located on the interface's front panel.

- **Line outputs 1–4 (Mbox 2 Pro):** These four balanced 1/4-inch TRS let you run additional speakers, run multiple effects, or setup additional headphone mixes during recording.

- **Aux In 3–4 (Mbox 2 Pro):** Aux In 3–4 provides jacks for RCA phono plugs and balanced 1/4-inch Line inputs. You can switch between connection types using the Aux IN 3–4 selector switch on the Mbox 2 Pro's front panel.

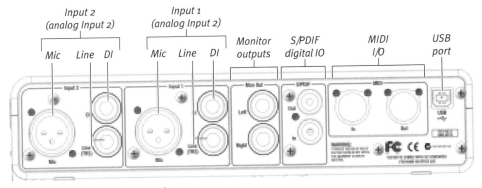

Figure A.12 The Mbox 2's back panel

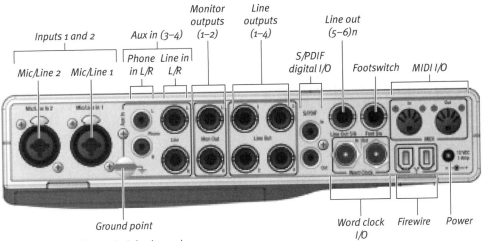

Figure A.13 The Mbox 2 Pro's back panel

◆ **Line outputs 5–6 (Mbox 2 Pro):** These two outputs let you run two channels of unbalanced output to an additional analog device.◆

◆ **Footswitch jack:** Lets you connect a standard footswitch to punch in audio or MIDI when recording

◆ **Monitor Outputs 1–2:** These balanced 1/4-inch TRS jacks output audio routed to analog outputs 1 and 2 in Pro Tools. These outputs are useful for stereo mixdown to an external stereo device (such as a two-track analog tape machine). Output is balanced, +4 dBu line-level.

◆ **Word Clock I/O (Mbox 2 Pro):** Word clock input and output are provided for synchronizing external recording devices with Pro Tools.

To connect an analog audio source to the Mbox 2 or Mbox 2 Pro:

◆ Connect either an XLR cable from a microphone or 1/4-inch TRS cable from a line-level device or instrument to either of the Mic/Line inputs 1–2 on the interface's back panel.

Mic preamps are necessary for microphones and instruments using magnetic pickups (such as electric guitars and other string instruments) that generate lower-level audio signals requiring amplification.

or

◆ Connect a balanced or unbalanced 1/4-inch cable from a line-level audio source (such as a keyboard, preamp, or mixer) to a DI input on the back panel of the Mbox 2 or DI input on the front panel of the Mbox 2 Pro.

To connect a digital audio source to Mbox 2 or Mbox 2 Pro:

1. Connect a S/PDIF digital cable from the output of the external audio source to the S/PDIF input on the Mbox 2 or Mbox 2 Pro.

2. Connect a S/PDIF digital cable from the S/PDIF output on the Mbox 2 or Mbox 2 Pro to the input of the external digital device.

For more information on connecting analog and digital hardware to Mbox 2 or Mbox 2 Pro, see the *Getting Started Guide* that came with your system.

Connecting Audio Monitors

If you're using Digi 002, Digi 002 Rack, Mbox 2, or Mbox 2 Pro, the easiest way to monitor audio is with headphones plugged into the jack on the front of their respective interfaces. Original Mbox users have two headphone options: a 1/8-inch stereo mini connector on the front panel and a 1/4-inch TRS connector on the rear panel. Mbox 2 and Mbox 2 Pro users have to use the 1/4-inch headphone jacks provided.

While monitoring over headphones is useful for hearing accurate stereo mixes, whenever possible, it's best to monitor your audio through a set of speakers as well. Speakers give you a more accurate representation of how most listeners will experience your mixes—in a 3-dimensional space, over an average home stereo system.

Caution: Listening to headphones at even moderate volumes for prolonged periods can cause hearing damage and permanent ringing in the ears, or tinnitus. *Always* make sure your headphone volume is turned down before listening, and then turn the volume up slowly and carefully!

To connect monitor speakers to the Digi 002 or Digi 002 Rack:

1. Connect 1/4-inch TRS cables to the left and right monitor outputs on the back of the Digi 002 or Digi 002 Rack.

2. Connect the 1/4-inch TRS cables to left and right inputs on your power amp, mixer, self-powered speakers, or home stereo.

   Most home stereo systems use RCA connectors and will require an adapter.

CONNECTING AUDIO MONITORS

To connect monitor speakers to the Mbox, Mbox 2, and Mbox 2 Pro:

1. Connect 1/4-inch cables to the left and right monitor (or line) outputs on the back panel of the interface.

2. Connect the 1/4-inch cables to the corresponding left and right inputs on your power amp, mixer, self-powered speakers or home stereo.

   Most home stereo systems use RCA connectors and will require an adapter.

✔ Tip

- During the recording and mixing process, it's useful to listen over as many different sets of speakers as possible. Most studios have small, medium-size, and large monitor speakers (some even have ultra-tiny and extra-large speakers), which can help you gain perspective on the frequency balance and overall sound quality of your mixes.

Connecting MIDI Devices

The Digi 002 and Mbox 2 systems' built-in MIDI ports make it easy to connect MIDI devices (such as MIDI keyboard controllers, MIDI instruments, and sound modules). A MIDI driver for these ports is installed with Pro Tools LE and recognized by Midi Studio Setup (Windows) and Audio MIDI Setup (Macintosh).

Original Mbox users will need a third-party MIDI interface to record MIDI into Pro Tools LE.

For information on recording and editing MIDI in Pro Tools 7 LE, see *Chapter 18: Recording MIDI* and *Chapter 19: Editing MIDI.*

To connect a MIDI device to the Digi 002 or Digi 002 Rack:

1. Connect a standard five-pin MIDI cable from the MIDI Out port on your MIDI device to the MIDI In port on the Digi 002 or Digi 002 Rack's back panel.

2. Connect a standard five-pin MIDI cable from either of the two MIDI Out ports on the Digi 002 or Digi 002 Rack's back panel to the MIDI In port on your MIDI device.

3. Connect the audio outputs of your device to an available audio input on the Digi 002 or Digi 002 Rack's back panel.

To connect a MIDI device to Mbox 2 or Mbox 2 Pro:

1. Connect a standard five-pin MIDI cable from the MIDI output on your MIDI device to the MIDI input on the Mbox 2 or Mbox 2 Pro's back panel.

2. Connect a standard five-pin MIDI cable from the MIDI output on the Mbox 2 or Mbox 2 Pro box to the MIDI input on your MIDI device.

Connecting External Hardware Effects

Pro Tools lets you route both analog and digital audio signals to external hardware effects (such as equalizers, compressors, reverbs, and delays). Using the Digi 002, Digi 002 Rack, Mbox 2, or Mbox 2 Pro's 1/4-inch analog inputs and outputs, or S/PDIF digital inputs and outputs, you can run several external hardware effects with your system.

The original Mbox has two 1/4-inch TRS inserts, which let you place effects into the path of analog audio entering Source 1 and Source 2 Mic/Line inputs. The inserted effect is added to the incoming signal before it's converted into digital audio. These inserts are useful for adding effects such as equalizers and compressors to tracks during recording.

Connecting external analog hardware effects

To connect an external analog hardware effect to the Digi 002 or Digi 002 Rack:

1. Connect a mono (single) or stereo (pair) output from analog outputs 5–8 to the corresponding inputs of the hardware effect.

2. Connect the outputs of the hardware effect to the corresponding analog inputs on the Digi 002 or Digi 002 Rack's back panel.

To insert an external hardware effect on the Mbox's input signal path:

1. You'll need a TRS Y cable (a TRS connector that splits into two unbalanced connectors).

2. Connect the unbalanced connector that corresponds to Tip to the input port of the hardware device.

3. Connect the unbalanced connector that corresponds to Ring to the output port of the hardware device.

4. Insert the TRS connector into the desired insert port on the Mbox.

Connecting external digital hardware effects

To connect an external digital hardware effect to the Digi 002 or Digi 002 Rack:

◆ Connect the S/PDIF (RCA plug) inputs and outputs on the Digi 002 or Digi 002 Rack's back panel to the corresponding inputs and outputs of the external digital hardware effect.

or

◆ If the hardware effect has optical inputs, connect the optical inputs and outputs on the Digi 002 or Digi 002 Rack's back panel to the corresponding optical inputs and outputs of the external digital hardware effect.

To set up an effects loop between an external digital hardware effect and Digi 002 or Digi 002 Rack:

1. Connect the digital inputs and outputs of the external digital hardware effect to the appropriate connectors (S/PDIF RCA connectors or Optical ports) of the Digi 002 or Digi 002 Rack.

2. In Pro Tools, choose Setup > Hardware.

3. Under Digital Input, select one of the following options:

   ▲ If the external effects device is connected to the S/PDIF RCA jacks, select "RCA = S/PDIF."

   ▲ If the external effects device is a S/PDIF device connected to the Optical ports, select "Optical = S/PDIF."

   ▲ If the external effects device is an ADAT Optical device, select "Optical = ADAT."

4. Choose Internal from the Clock Source pop-up menu.

5. Click OK.

For more information on setting up effects loops, see *Chapter 15: Adding Effects to a Mix*.

✔ Tips

■ You can send signals to external hardware effects using the Mbox's S/PDIF digital I/Os and analog I/Os.

■ The I/O Setup dialog box lets you label channel inputs and outputs. This can help you keep track of sends and inserts during a session. For more information on I/O Setup, see *Chapter 4: Starting a New Session*.

■ Most external hardware effects have 1/4-inch connectors. Higher-end units generally include both XLR and 1/4-inch connectors.

CONNECTING EXTERNAL HARDWARE EFFECTS

SETTING PREFERENCES

Figure B.1 The Preferences dialog box's seven tabbed windows.

Figure B.2
Choose Setups >
Preferences.

The Preferences Dialog Box

The Preferences dialog box contains seven tabbed windows (**Figure B.1**), which let you specify settings for many Pro Tools session parameters.

To open the Preferences dialog box:

◆ Choose Setup > Preferences (**Figure B.2**). The Preferences dialog box opens.

Display Preferences

The settings on the Display tab (**Figure B.3**) let you customize many Pro Tools viewing features. Preferences include:

Basics section

Draw Grids In Edit Window: This setting displays grid lines in the Edit window. To define a grid size, enter a value in the Edit window's Grid Value field.

Draw Waveforms Rectified: This setting shows waveforms summed together in a single positive direction starting at the bottom of the track. This lets you see more waveform detail in reduced track height views. It's especially useful when you're editing volume-level automation data.

Recompute Invalid Overviews: This setting prompts Pro Tools to re-create overviews of missing or corrupted waveform display data.

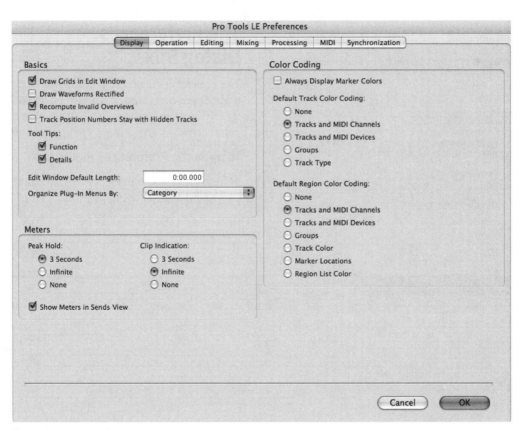

Figure B.3 Display preferences.

Track Position Numbers Stay With Hidden Tracks: When this setting is selected, hidden tracks keep their track numbers. When not enable, only visible tracks retain their track numbers.

Tool Tips display options

Function: Displays an item's basic function.

Details: Displays information about an item, such as name, parameter values, and input and output assignments.

Edit Window Default Length: This lets you set a default recording length for the Edit window in hours, minutes, seconds, and frames. The maximum session length is 13 hours at 48 kHz.

Organize Plug-In Menus By options:

Pro Tools provides the following options for displaying and organizing plug-ins in the plug-in pop-up menu.

Flat List: Displays all plug-ins in one long list.

Category: Organizes and displays plug-ins by effects type. For example, all EQ plug-in effects are under the EQ category.

Category and Manufacturer: This option orders plug-ins first under the effects type. The secondary menu lists the plug-ins' parent company.

Meters section

Peak Hold options

These options determine how long the peak indicators on the track meters stay lit after a peak is detected.

- ◆ **3-Second:** Displays last peak level for three seconds.

- ◆ **Infinite:** Displays last peak level until you clear it by clicking the level indicator.

- ◆ **None:** No hold; meter moves freely.

Clip Indication options

These options determine how long clip indicators on plug-in, send, and track level meters remain lit after a signal has clipped.

- ◆ **3-Second:** Displays last clip detected for three seconds.

- ◆ **Infinite:** Displays last clip detected until you clear it by clicking the level indicator.

- ◆ **None:** No hold; meter moves freely.

- ◆ **Show Meters In Sends View:** This setting displays the level meters of individual send controls in the Sends view. The Show Meters preference can tax CPU power, so disable it if you have a slow computer.

Color Coding section

Always Display Marker Colors: This setting lets you view Marker colors in the Markers ruler, even if you turn off settings for Marker Locations in the Default Region Color Coding section.

Default Track Color Coding

These options determine the default color assignments for tracks in the Edit and Mix windows.

- ◆ **None:** Turns off color assignments to tracks.

- ◆ **Tracks and MIDI Channels:** Assigns colors to waveforms according to the track number and MIDI channel assignment.

- ◆ **Tracks and MIDI Devices:** Assigns colors to waveforms according to the track number and MIDI device type.

- ◆ **Groups:** Assigns colors to waveforms according to group ID.

- ◆ **Track Type:** Assigns a color to each track according to its type (audio, MIDI, instrument, aux. input, or master fader).

DISPLAY PREFERENCES

Default Region Color Coding

These options determine the default color assignments for regions in the track playlist.

◆ **None:** Turns off color assignments for regions. Regions appear black in track playlist.

◆ **Tracks and MIDI Channels:** Assigns colors to each region in the Edit window according to the track number and MIDI channel assignment.

◆ **Tracks And MIDI Devices:** Assigns colors to each region in the Edit window according to the track number and MIDI device type.

◆ **Groups:** Assigns colors to waveforms according to group ID.

◆ **Track Color:** Assigns colors to regions based on the color of the track.

◆ **Marker Locations** Assigns a color to data across all tracks based on the nearest preceding maker.

◆ **Region List Color:** Assigns colors to each region based on its color in the Regions list.

Operation Preferences

The settings on the Operation tab (**Figure B.4**) determine the function of various Pro Tools recording and playback features. Preferences include:

Transport section

Timeline Insertion/Play Start Marker Follows Playback: When this setting is selected, the cursor automatically updates to the track location where playback stops.

Edit Insertion Follows Scrub/Shuttle: When this setting is selected, the cursor automatically updates to the track location where scrubbing stops.

Audio During Fast Forward/Rewind: This setting makes audio audible during fast-forward and rewind.

Play Start Marker Follows Loop Selection: When this option is selected, the Play Start Marker snaps to the Timeline Selection Start Marker when you change the Timeline Selection. When deselected, the Play Start Marker doesn't move with the Timeline selection.

Custom Shuttle Lock Speed:

This option lets you set the highest fast-forward Shuttle Lock speed when in Shuttle Lock mode, with available settings from 50–800%.

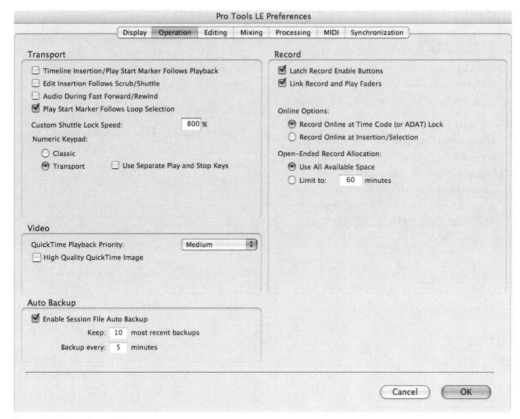

Figure B.4 Operation preferences.

OPERATION PREFERENCES

Numeric Keypad Mode: This setting lets you determine the function of the numeric keypad (options include Classic and Transport). For more information on the Numeric Keypad Mode, see the *Pro Tools Reference Guide*.

Record section

Latch Record Enable Buttons: This setting lets you record-enable multiple tracks simultaneously.

Link Record And Play Faders: This option prevents volume faders from inadvertently changing positions when switching between record and playback modes.

Online Options: This setting lets you determine how recording is initiated when Pro Tools is set to receive time code from an external source.

◆ **Record Online At Time Code (or ADAT) Lock:** Online recording begins as soon as Pro Tools receives and locks to incoming time code or ADAT signal.

◆ **Record Online At Insertion/Selection:** Online recording begins at a chosen insertion point in a track. Recording continues until Pro Tools stops receiving time code. If you make a selection, Pro Tools records online for the length of the selection.

Open Ended Record Allocation: This setting lets you determine how much hard drive space is dedicated for recording.

◆ **Use All Available Space:** Allocates the hard drive's entire available space. This can slow down performance on some hard drives.

◆ **Limit To:** Sets the maximum allowable recording duration (in minutes). This can improve performance on some hard drives.

Video section

QuickTime Playback Priority options

This option lets you set the priority of movie playback relative to screen updates in the Pro Tools windows.

High Quality QuickTime Image

This option sets QuickTime movies to play back at the highest resolution. Deselect this option if you experience performance issues while playing back a session with video.

Auto Backup section

Enable Session File Auto Backup: This setting lets you enable the AutoSave feature and select the frequency and quantity of saves.

Editing Preferences

The settings on the Editing tab (**Figure B.5**) determine the function of various Pro Tools editing features. Preferences include:

Regions section

Region List Selection Follows Edit Selection: When this preference is chosen, selecting a region in a track also selects it in the Regions list.

Edit Selection Follows Region List Selection: When selected, selecting a region in the Regions list causes Pro Tools to highlight that region in a track.

Auto-Name Separated Regions: This setting automatically names newly separated regions by appending a number to each region's name.

"Matching Start Time" Takes List: Command-clicking (Macintosh) or Control-clicking (Windows) in a track displays a list of regions whose start times match the current cursor location. The following preferences determine which takes appear in this list:

◆ **Includes Take Region Name(s)That Match Track Names:** Only regions that share names with the track/playlist appear in the Takes List pop-up menu.

◆ **Includes Take Region Lengths That Match:** Only regions that match the length of the current selection appear in the Takes List pop-up menu.

◆ **"Separate Region" Operates On All Related Takes:** Editing a region with the Separate Region command affects all other related takes with the same user time stamp. This helps you compare different sections from a group of related takes.

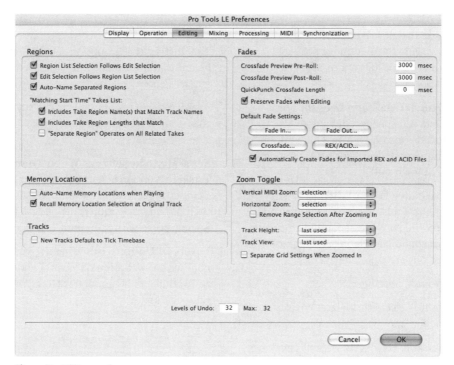

Figure B.5 Editing preferences.

Memory Locations section

Auto-Name Memory Locations When Playing: When this preference is selected, Pro Tools gives default names to new memory locations based on their time locations.

Recall Memory Location Selection at Original Track: When selected, memory locations that recall a selection also recall the track in which the selection was made.

Tracks section

New Tracks Default to Tick Timebase: When this option is selected, all newly created audio tracks are automatically tick-based. When deselected, newly created audio tracks are sample-based.

Fades section

Crossfade Preview Pre-Roll: This setting lets you specify the amount of pre-roll added when you audition crossfades in the Fades dialog box.

Crossfade Preview Post-Roll: This setting lets you specify the amount of post-roll added when you audition crossfades in the Fades dialog box.

QuickPunch Crossfade Length: This setting lets you specify a default length for crossfades created during QuickPunch recording. Crossfades occur before punch-in and after punch-out.

Preserve Fades When Editing: When selected, Pro Tools preserves fade-ins and fade outs, and converts separated crossfades into corresponding fade-ins and fade-outs when regions are edited in tracks.

Default Fade Settings:

- ◆ **Fade In:** Selects the default envelope shape for fade-ins.

- ◆ **Crossfade:** Selects the default envelope shape for crossfades.

- ◆ **Fade Out:** Selects the default envelope shape for fade-outs.

- ◆ **REX/ACID:** Selects the default envelope shape for crossfades between regions in REX or ACID files.

Automatically Create Fades for Imported REX and ACID files: When selected, this option automatically applies crossfades between regions when you import REX or ACID files.

Zoom Toggle section

Vertical MIDI Zoom: This option sets the vertical zoom for MIDI tracks when you use Zoom Toggle.

Horizontal Zoom: This option sets the horizontal zoom that is automatically displayed when you use Zoom Toggle.

Remove Range Selection After Zooming In: When this option is selected, the current Edit selection changes to an Edit cursor when you use Zoom Toggle.

Track Height: This option sets the track height that is automatically displayed when you use Zoom Toggle.

Track View: This option sets the track view that is automatically displayed when you use Zoom Toggle.

Separate Grid Settings When Zoomed In: When this option is selected, the current Grid setting is retained when Zoom Toggle is used. When this option is deselected, the grid setting stored with the Zoom Toggle is used.

Levels Of Undo: This setting lets you choose the maximum number of actions (up to 16) that can be undone with the multiple undo feature.

EDITING PREFERENCES

Mixing Preferences

The settings on the Mixing tab (**Figure B.6**) determine the function of various Pro Tools mixing and automation features. Preferences include:

Setup section

Sends Default To "–INF": This sets the initial fader level of newly created sends to minus infinity (no audible signal level).

Send Pans Default to Follow Main Pan: When this option is selected, pan controls on newly created sends are set to follow the pan controls of the track.

Link Mix/Edit Group Enables: This setting links the enabling and disabling of Mix and Edit groups. For example, enabling Group A in the Edit window automatically enables Group A in the Mix window.

Default EQ: This setting lets you choose any EQ plug-in as a default, making it available for quick assignment at the top of the plug-in menu,

Default Dynamics: This setting lets you choose any Dynamics plug-in as a default, making it available for quick assignment at the top of the plug-in menu,

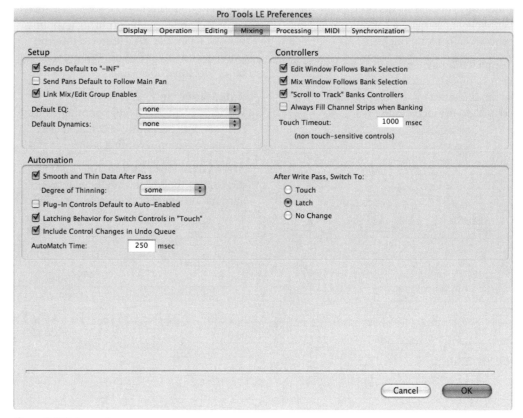

Figure B.6 Mixing preferences.

Controllers section

Edit Window Follows Bank Selection: This setting automatically updates the view of tracks in the Edit window whenever you switch banks on an external MIDI controller.

Mix Window Follows Bank Selection: This setting automatically updates the view of tracks in the Mix window whenever you switch banks on an external MIDI controller.

"Scroll To Track" Banks Controllers: This option lets you bank faders of a control surface to a numbered track when using the Scroll to Track command (Track > Scroll to Track).

Always Fill Channel Strips when Banking: This setting maximizes the number of channels that appear on control surfaces when banking tracks.

Touch Timeout: This setting lets you specify how quickly automation recording stops or times out after you stop moving a MIDI controller in Touch mode.

Automation section

Smooth and Thin Data After Pass: When this preference is selected, automation is smoothed and thinned by the amount specified by the Degree Of Thinning option.

Plug-In Controls Default to Auto-Enabled: When selected, all controls of newly inserted plug-ins are automatically enabled for automation.

Latching Behavior for Switch Controls in "Touch": When this option is selected, automatable switched controls (such as mute) that are in Touch mode will latch in their current state after they are touched.

Include Control Changes in Undo Queue: When this option is selected, mixer control changes, such as moving a volume fader or a pan slider, are entered into the Undo queue, and are undone along with other Pro Tools operations.

AutoMatch Time: This setting lets you specify how quickly a fader or other control returns to its previously automated level after automation recording stops.

After Write Pass, Switch To: This option directs Pro Tools to switch to an appropriate automation mode after writing a pass of automation. Choose from Touch, Latch, or No Change.

Processing Preferences

The settings on the Processing tab (**Figure B.7**) determine the function of many Pro Tools DSP (digital signal processing) features. Preferences include:

AudioSuite section

Buffer Size: This setting lets you set a memory buffer size for audio processing and for previewing AudioSuite plug-ins. Smaller buffers are recommended for previewing plug-ins; larger buffers for processing files.

AudioSuite Dither: Dither is randomized noise added to a digital audio signal to help reduce distortion. For more information on dither, see *Chapter 15: Adding Effects to a Mix*. Pro Tools lets you customize the following AudioSuite dither functions:

◆ **Use AudioSuite Dither:** When this preference is selected, dither is applied to specific audio processing tasks.

◆ **Dither Plug-In:** This setting lets you specify the plug-in used for dither processing when the Use AudioSuite Dither option is selected.

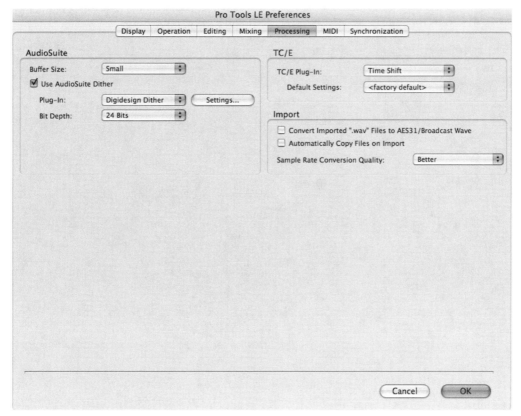

Figure B.7 Processing preferences.

◆ **Edit Settings:** This setting lets you apply either normal or noise-shaped dither to Digidesign's dither plug-in.

◆ **Bit Depth:** This setting lets you select a bit depth for dithered audio.

TC/E section

TC/E Plug-In: This setting lets you choose the Time Compression/Expansion plug-in used when you perform edits with the TC/E Trim tool.

Default Settings: This lets you choose a Plug-In Settings file for the TC/E Plug-In when it is invoked by the TC/E Trim tool.

Import section

Convert imported ".wav" files to AES31/BroadcastWave: When selected, imported WAV files are automatically converted to AES31/EBU Broadcast standard format.

Automatically Copy Files on Import: When selected, Pro Tools automatically copies all imported audio files to the session's Audio Files folder regardless of sample rate, bit-depth, or conversion requirements.

Sample Rate Conversion Quality: This setting lets you select the sample rate conversion quality for several Pro Tools conversion features including importing, bouncing, and saving audio.

MIDI Preferences

The settings on the MIDI tab (**Figure B.8**) include:

Basics section

Play MIDI Notes when Editing: When this preference is selected, MIDI notes will sound when you insert them with the Pencil tool or drag them with the Grabber tool into a MIDI track.

Use MIDI to Tap Tempo: When this option is selected, you can tap a key on a MIDI keyboard to enter a tempo into Pro Tools.

Display Events as Modified by Real-Time Properties: When this option is selected, the effects of Real-Time Properties on MIDI notes are displayed in the Edit window and the MIDI Event List.

Use F11 Key for Wait For Note: This setting lets you use the F11 key to put MIDI recording in Wait for Note mode.

Automatically Create Click Track in New Sessions: When this option is selected, Pro Tools automatically adds a click track when you create a new session.

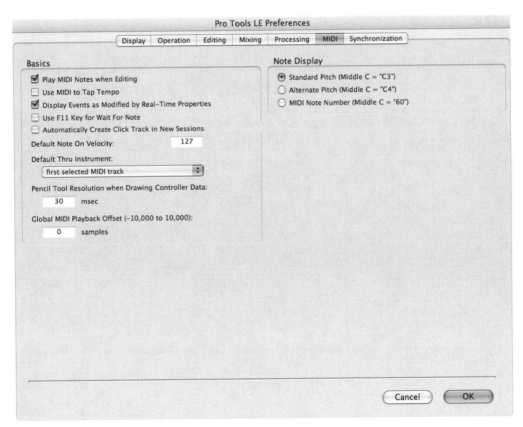

Figure B.8 MIDI preferences.

Default Note On Velocity: This setting lets you specify the default Note On Velocity for MIDI notes inserted in the Edit window and MIDI Event list.

Default Thru Instrument: This setting lets you choose a default instrument where Pro Tools will route all incoming MIDI data. This saves you the trouble of creating a MIDI track to hear a particular MIDI device and channel.

Pencil Tool Resolution when Drawing Controller Data: This setting lets you specify a default resolution for MIDI controller data created with the Pencil tool. Lower resolutions help avoid creating unnecessarily dense controller data. The value range is 1 to 100 milliseconds.

Global MIDI Playback Offset: This setting lets you specify an offset in samples to compensate for MIDI latency.

MIDI Note Display: This setting determines how pitches for MIDI notes are displayed in the Edit window and the MIDI Event list.

Synchronization Preferences

The settings on the Synchronization tab include:

Machine Control section

These settings let you determine how the transport of a connected MIDI Machine Control device responds to Pro Tools.

◆ **Machine Chases Memory Location:** The connected transport chases to a selected memory location.

◆ **Machine Follows Edit Insertion/Scrub:** The connected transport follows to a new insertion point or chases to a location where scrubbing begins.

Synchronization section

Minimum Sync Delay: This option lets you specify the amount of time external devices need to achieve synchronization lock when using Machine Control.

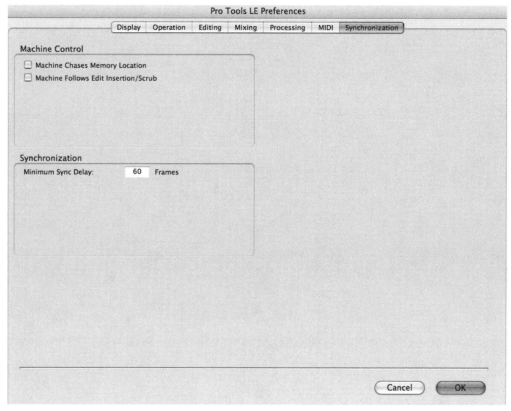

Figure B.9 Synchronization preferences.

GLOSSARY

A

AES/EBU: Audio Engineering Society/
European Broadcast Union. A professional
transmission protocol that specifies two
channels of data through an XLR cable as
the standard for digital audio.

Audio region: A visual representation of a
Pro Tools audio file. Regions can be whole
audio files or segments of audio files and are
usually displayed during editing as audio
waveforms.

Audio signal flow: The path that audio
takes through a mixer. In Pro Tools, this
path is generally fixed, moving from top to
bottom through audio track, auxiliary input,
and master fader channel strips.

Audio track: In Pro Tools, a channel that
holds and controls recorded or imported
audio files.

AudioSuite plug-ins: Digidesign's nonreal-
time plug-ins. They process audio directly to
disk, creating a new audio file that includes
the effected signal.

Automation pass: In Pro Tools, automation
recorded during the playback of a session.

Automation playlist: In Pro Tools, a visual
representation of a track's automation
parameters (such as volume, mute, and pan).
Pro Tools creates a separate automation
playlist for each parameter that you write.

Auxiliary input: In Pro Tools, an input
that lets you add mono or stereo effects to
bussed signals. It's also useful for submixes
and other audio-routing tasks.

B

Balanced line: A cable with two conduc-
tors and a ground connection surrounded
by a shield. Balanced lines are less prone to
interference than unbalanced lines; thus,
they help keep recordings free of noise.

Binaural auditory system: The two-ear
auditory system that lets us locate sounds
in space.

Bit depth: The number of bits used to
describe each sample taken during recording. For example, if you're recording at 24-bit
resolution and a sample rate of 44.1 kHz,
there will be 44,100 individual 24-bit representations of the sound recorded each second. Also known as bit resolution.

BNC/word clock: The coaxial cable (resem-
bling video cable) that connects devices that
run in sync.

Breakpoints: Breakpoints indicate changes in the value of an automation parameter. They're displayed along a graphic curve, which you can grab and move when performing edits.

Bus: An audio bus carries audio signals from different tracks and delivers them to other destinations within a mixer. In Pro Tools, busses are used mainly to send audio signals from one or more audio tracks to a single auxiliary input, where a DSP effect is added.

C

Cardioid mic: A heart-shaped mic pick-up pattern that accepts sounds from the front (on-axis) and attenuates signals that are 180 degrees off-axis.

Channel: The physical inputs and outputs of the Pro Tools system.

Channel strip: Each track in a Pro Tools session is displayed in the Mix window as a channel strip. Channel strips let you control the mix functions of a track, such as level, mute, pan, and sends. The five types of channel strips are audio tracks, auxiliary inputs, instrument tracks, master faders, and MIDI tracks.

Click track: An absolute time reference that can help you produce takes with a steadier feel. It can also help you properly align tracks when you're overdubbing, editing, and mixing.

Clipping: Digital distortion that occurs when you record a signal at levels that overload your system's inputs. When a signal clips, it distorts, and the peaks of its waveform are literally clipped off.

Condenser mic: More sensitive, accurate, and expensive than dynamic mics, condenser mics are used frequently in recording studios.

Conductor ruler: In Pro Tools, a ruler that indicates important track locations within a session.

Controller: Any device that's used to send MIDI without necessarily making a sound on its own.

Crossfade: An overlapping fade-out and fade-in placed between two adjoining audio regions. Crossfades let you smooth transitions between separate audio regions on a track.

D

Delay time: The length of time it takes for a sound to return to its source. The delay time tells you how big a space is.

Destructive editing: Editing functions in Pro Tools that permanently alter the parent audio file on disk.

Dither: A form of randomly generated noise that helps smooth out fade-ins or fade-outs from silence. Dither can also help smooth crossfades between low-level audio regions.

DSP: Digital signal processing. In Pro Tools, DSP refers to the manipulation or processing of digital audio. In Pro Tools LE systems, all DSP tasks are handled by the host computer's CPU. The system's total DSP power thus depends on the processing power of the host computer.

DSP plug-in: Software that lets you add effects such as reverb, compression, and EQ to audio signals within the Pro Tools environment.

Dynamic effects: Dynamic effects act upon an audio signal's volume level. Examples of dynamic effects are compressors, limiters, expanders, and gates. Each of these effects alters the volume level of an audio signal above or below a specified volume threshold.

Dynamic mic: The least expensive type of mic. It can handle lots of volume and is durable enough to survive most live settings. It tends to accentuate mid-range and can sometimes make tracks sound boxy.

Dynamic range: The difference between the softest and the loudest volume produced by a sound source.

E

Edit playlist: In Pro Tools, a visual representation of a track's current arrangement of regions. An edit playlist can contain a single region or multiple regions.

Edit selection: In Pro Tools, the actual audio region and/or track space that's highlighted when you make a selection. Edit selections can include a single region or multiple regions and can include the space before, after, and in between regions.

Effects loop: An effects loop lets you add an effect to multiple tracks simultaneously. Also known as a send-and-return submix.

EQ: Equalization. The process of cutting or boosting the volume level of specific frequencies of an audio signal. EQ is used to open up frequency ranges and thus enhance the clarity, spaciousness, and blending of sounds in a mix.

F

Fade: A volume curve that controls the rate of increase (fade-in) or decrease (fade-out) of a region's volume. Fades let you smooth the entrance and exit of audio during a mix. Fade-ins are placed at the start of regions; fade-outs are placed at the end.

Feedback loop: Created when an active microphone picks up its own signal from a loudspeaker and amplifies that signal again in a self-perpetuating cycle.

Figure-8 mic: A figure-8 mic picks up sound from both the front and back. Also known as a bidirectional mic.

G

Gain stage: Any point in an audio signal path where the audio signal is amplified (boosted) or attenuated (cut). The volume knob on your stereo, for instance, is a gain stage. Likewise, every amp, pre-amp, fader, and effect in your Pro Tools system is a gain stage.

Gain staging: The process of setting all gain stages in a system to their optimal values.

H

Handle value: In Pro Tools, a preserved segment of the original audio file before and after each region. It can be useful for fine-tuning the boundaries of a region.

I

Input selectors: Controls that let you assign audio input from external sources (via the Pro Tools interface) or from internal busses.

Inserts: Controls that let you add effects on channel strips. You can assign internal software effects and external hardware effects to inserts.

Interleaved stereo files: Single-file stereo files.

I/O: Input/output. The direction of an audio signal with respect to an audio device. Input is where audio signal enters the device; output is where audio signal leaves the device.

K

Keyboard workstation: A keyboard that includes an onboard synthesizer, sequencer, effects, and often, a sampler. Originally conceived as "one-stop shopping" for full audio production, keyboard workstations are more often used today as hot-rod controllers and for onstage performance.

L

Latency: The lag time between audio entering and leaving your recording system. Pro Tools LE systems are susceptible to latency because of the heavy processing load placed on the host computer's CPU.

Line insert: In Pro Tools, a line insert applies its effect only to the track on which it's inserted.

Line-level: A nominal preamplified signal between +4 dB (pro) and +10 dBV (consumer) that's used to connect certain studio hardware devices such as keyboards, preamps, and mixers.

M

Main paths: In Pro Tools, logical groupings of inputs, outputs, inserts, or busses, such as a stereo (two-channel) output.

Master controller: A device, usually a keyboard or synthesizer, that's used to play back all of the other MIDI equipment in the studio.

Master fader: In Pro Tools, a master fader controls the level of a session's main outputs. Master fader inserts let you add effects post-fader to the main mix.

Mastering: The process of preparing mixes for duplication. It involves optimizing dynamics and tonal balance, matching the volume levels of all of the songs, and sequencing tracks.

Memory locations: Settings in Pro Tools that store information about specific edit points and selected track ranges.

Metadata: Metadata refers to general data that describes the attributes of a file, such as file name, creation date, file size, and so on. DigiBase collects metadata about audio files and other Pro Tools session-related files during the indexing process and stores this information in an associated database file.

MIDI: Musical Instrument Digital Interface. A communication protocol originally designed to allow synthesizers created by different manufacturers to communicate with each other.

MIDI cable: A cable that uses a five-pin connection standard to transmit MIDI information between MIDI devices such as sequencers, controllers, sound modules, keyboards, and effects.

MIDI interface: A hardware device that connects to a computer to send and receive MIDI.

MIDI keyboard: A device with piano- or organ-style keys that sends MIDI information when played.

MIDI region: A visual representation of a segment of MIDI data. MIDI Regions can be arranged in tracks in the same way as audio regions.

MIDI track: In Pro Tools, a channel that holds and controls MIDI note, instrument, and controller data.

Mixdown: The process of combining all tracks, edits, effects, and automation events into a final two-track master.

Modulation: A parameter of many delay effects that lets you adjust changes in delay time over time. Effects such as phase shifting, flanging, and chorus use short delay times with modulation.

N

Non-destructive editing: In Pro Tools, editing functions that let you change audio regions without altering their parent audio files.

The Nyquest Theorem: A basic rule of digital audio. It states that the sample rate must be twice the value of a sound's highest frequency for that sound to be accurately reproduced. For example, CD audio is sampled at 44.1 kHz, whereas the human hearing range extends to only 20 kHz.

O

Omni-directional mic: A mic that captures sounds from all directions.

Optical connectors: Fiber-optic cables that transmit digital audio signals. They were originally developed to link Alesis ADATs to compatible gear. Also known as lightpipe.

Output selectors: Controls that let you route audio output to internal busses or external destinations (via the Pro Tools interface).

P

Parametric EQ: A tonal control (equalizer) that lets you target specific frequency ranges.

Performance volume: A performance volume is a storage volume that has been designated as suitable for recording and/or playback of media in a Pro Tools session.

Phantom power: A low-level electric current sent from the mic preamp to a condenser mic.

Phase cancellation: A type of audio interference that occurs when sound waves overlap and cancel each other out. This can cause frequencies to lose clarity or drop out.

Playlist: In Pro Tools, an arrangement of regions on an audio , MIDI or instrument track. A playlist can include a single region or multiple regions.

Precedence effect: The process by which humans locate sounds in a three-dimensional space: The ear that first hears a sound perceives it as significantly louder than the other ear does. Our two-ear auditory system uses this difference in perceived loudness to automatically triangulate the location of the sound source.

Punch recording: In Pro Tools, pressing (punching) the Record button in or out of Record mode at precise track locations. Used frequently during recording to redo unsatisfactory vocal or instrumental segments.

Q

Q: An adjustable parameter that determines the range of frequencies selected by a parametric EQ. The Q represents the number of octaves that the applied EQ affects.

Quantization distortion: Noise that occurs as a result of errors introduced when low-level audio signals are sampled or when digital audio is converted from higher to lower bit depths (such as when converting 24-bit audio to 16-bit for CD mastering).

Quantizing: The process of automatically changing the timing of a group of MIDI notes.

R

RCA plug: Unbalanced connectors used in most home stereo and video equipment. The tip is audio signal and the surrounding shield is ground. Also called phono plug.

Region: In Pro Tools, a visual representation —usually a waveform—of a parent audio file stored on disk. A region can be any length—from an entire audio file to a single verse, hook, bar, or note.

Region groups: Pro Tools lets you select multiple regions and place them together in a single region group. Region groups can help you keep your regions organized and speed up editing tasks.

Regions list: A list found in the Edit window that lets you manage the flow of audio and MIDI regions in and out of a Pro Tools session. When you record, import, or create a new region, it appears in the Regions list.

Reverb: A natural property of any enclosed room that occurs when sound waves bounce off walls, ceilings, and floors. Its three basic sound components are direct sound, early reflections, and reverberations.

Ribbon mic: An expensive and fragile mic that can produce a unique silky tone—the result of a slight roll-off that tends to occur in the high end. Ribbon mics were popular from the 1930s to the 1960s, but were pretty much replaced in the studio by condenser mics.

RTAS plug-ins: Digidesign's Real-Time AudioSuite plug-ins use your computer's CPU to process audio non-destructively in real time. They don't change the original audio file saved on disk; effects are applied only during playback or when bouncing to disk.

S

Sample rate: The number of times per second that sound wave information is gathered, or sampled, during the digital audio recording process. Measured in kilohertz (kHz). Sample rate determines a recording's frequency range and thus, its accuracy. Higher sample rates generally produce more accurate audio recordings.

Sampler: A sound generator that plays back individual sounds, or samples, when triggered by a MIDI note.

Scrub: A term borrowed from analog recording, scrubbing refers to running the tape manually back and forth over the playback head. It's useful for locating edit points that might be difficult to find visually.

Sends: Channel strip controls that let you route audio to an internal bus or external output for effects processing or submixing.

Separation: The technique of using left/right panning to spread tracks out across the stereo image. Separation lets you hear tracks with more clarity and introduces the perception of width in the stereo image.

Sequencer: Hardware devices or computer programs that are used to record, edit, and play back MIDI data. Sequencers can work with not only MIDI notes, but controller and sysex data as well.

Session: A Pro Tools session is analogous to a session in a real-world recording studio: It contains all the elements you need to record, edit, process, mix, master, and store audio recordings.

Session file: When you start a new Pro Tools project, you create a new session file. A session file maps all the elements in a session, including audio files, MIDI data, edits, and mix information.

Side-chain processing: Audio signal routing that involves an effect on a track being triggered by audio from a different track.

Signal path: The way that audio is routed in, out, and through a Pro Tools session.

Sound module: A MIDI synthesizer without a keyboard.

S/PDIF: Sony/Phillips Digital Interface. A transmission format for digital audio devices. It's commonly used in consumer devices. S/PDIF inputs and outputs generally have unbalanced RCA connectors.

Splice point: In Pro Tools, the location where two cross-faded regions join.

Stereo image: A simulation or image of a three-dimensional acoustic space that's constructed during the creation of a stereo mix. Techniques such as left/right panning, spatial effects (reverb, delay, chorus, and flange), and EQ shaping help trick our two-ear auditory system into perceiving sound in the three dimensions of width, depth, and height.

GLOSSARY

Sub-paths: In Pro Tools, these are signal paths within the main path. For example, a main path stereo output has two mono sub-paths.

Submix: Created by merging multiple tracks of audio into a single track.

Synthesizer: An electronic instrument used to make sounds. There are many different kinds of synthesizers and different methods for synthesizing sounds, including analog, sample playback, wavetable, granular, physical modeling, and virtual analog synthesis.

Sysex data: System-exclusive data. Specialized MIDI data that manufacturers can use to define MIDI events and messages that work only with their MIDI devices.

T

Timeline ruler: In Pro Tools, a ruler that provides a timing reference for track material.

Timeline selection: In Pro Tools, a selection of a range of time in a Timebase ruler. Timeline selections automatically apply across all tracks in a session.

Track: A designated space in a recording system that's assigned to carry a single audio signal. In Pro Tools, tracks let you direct the flow of audio into your system, through DSP effects, and then back out to your ears and/or mixdown machine.

Transfer volume: Transfer volumes are storage volumes that cannot be used by Pro Tools for recording or playback, such as a CD-ROM or network storage volume.

Transient: A sound that occurs for a brief time period, such as a drum hit, a piano note, or a guitar strum.

Transient peak: The instance of strongest attack in a transient. For example, a snare drum hit consists of a strong initial attack—a transient peak—followed by a period of decay.

TRS: Tip-ring-sleeve. A 1/4-inch stereo (two-channel) connector commonly found on headphones. The tip is left channel, the ring is right channel, and the sleeve is ground. TRS connectors can be used for balanced inputs and outputs. Sometimes called phone plugs.

TS: Tip-sleeve. A 1/4-inch unbalanced mono connector. The tip is audio signal and the sleeve is ground. It's commonly used for electric guitars, keyboards, and other unbalanced line-level connections.

U

Unbalanced line: A cable with one conductor and a surrounding shield at ground potential. Unbalanced lines are more prone to pick up interference. As a result, they can add noise to a recording.

W

Waveform: A graph of an audio signal's sound pressure level (in decibels) versus time.

X

XLR: A three-pin connection usually found on balanced microphone cables. It's used for analog and digital (AES/EBU standard) audio signals. Also called a Canon connector.

Z

Zero crossing: In Pro Tools, the point at which a waveform crosses its center line, and the waveform's amplitude is zero.

GLOSSARY

INDEX

INDEX

INDEX